Building
STRONG
Congregations

May this token of
thanks bless your
ministry as you
have blessed mine!

To order additional copies of
Building Strong Congregations,
by Bruce Wrenn, Philip Kotler, and Norman Shawchuck,
call **1-800-765-6955**.

Visit us at
www.AutumnHousePublishing.com
for information on other Autumn House® products.

Building
STRONG
Congregations

Attracting, Serving, and Developing
YOUR MEMBERSHIP

Autumn
House® Publishing
www.autumnhousepublishing.com
A Division of **REVIEW AND HERALD**® PUBLISHING
Since 1861

Published by Autumn House® Publishing, a division of Review and Herald® Publishing, Hagerstown, MD 21741-1119

Autumn House® titles may be purchased in bulk for educational, business, fund-raising, or sales promotional use. For information, please e-mail SpecialMarkets@reviewandherald.com.

Autumn House® Publishing publishes biblically based materials for spiritual, physical, and mental growth and Christian discipleship.

The author assumes full responsibility for the accuracy of all facts and quotations as cited in this book.

Scripture quotations identified CEV are from the Contemporary English Version. Copyright © American Bible Society 1991, 1995. Used by permission.

Texts credited to Message are from *The Message*. Copyright © 1993, 1994, 1995, 1996, 2000, 2001, 2002. Used by permission of NavPress Publishing Group.

Texts credited to NIV are from the *Holy Bible, New International Version*. Copyright © 1973, 1978, 1984, International Bible Society. Used by permission of Zondervan Bible Publishers.

Scripture quotations marked NLT are taken from the *Holy Bible,* New Living Translation, copyright © 1996. Used by permission of Tyndale House Publishers, Inc., Wheaton, Illinois 60189. All rights reserved.

Bible texts credited to NRSV are from the New Revised Standard Version of the Bible, copyright © 1989 by the Division of Christian Education of the National Council of the Churches of Christ in the U.S.A. Used by permission.

This book was
Edited by Jeannette R. Johnson
Copyedited by James Cavil
Designed by Trent Truman
Cover photo by © istockphoto.com/timsa
Interior designed by Heather Rogers
Typeset: Bembo 12/14

PRINTED IN U.S.A.

13   12   11   10   09   5   4   3   2   1

Library of Congress Cataloging-in-Publication Data
Wrenn, Bruce.
  Building strong congregations: attracting, serving, and developing your membership/ Bruce Wrenn, Philip Kotler, and Norman Shawchuck.
    p. cm.
1. Church marketing. I. Kotler, Philip. II. Shawchuck, Norman, 1935- III. Title.
  BV652.23.W74 2009
  254'.5—dc22

                                        2008049325

ISBN 978-0-8127-0490-7

The business of religion and the running of a house of worship is a huge challenge in our world today. Seminaries educate clergy, but the practical knowledge and valuable tools to help effectively run our religious institutions are often overlooked. This valuable book provides practical tools to clergy and lay leaders alike to help build stronger and more advanced institutions and organizations. Through relevant examples, interesting tools, and carefully crafted worksheets, we are able to reflect on our sacred work and to build up our communities to be stronger and more vibrant. We no longer need to be "winking in the dark."

—Rabbi Steven Stark Lowenstein
Congregation Am Shalom
Glencoe, Illinois
Kellogg Jewish Leaders Class of 2008

Contents

List of Exhibits

Preface

The cover of the January 2009 issue of *Christianity Today* read: "Marketing Jesus: How to Evangelize Without Turning God Into a Brand." The author's thesis was that marketing fosters a consumerist soteriology that is totally inappropriate for the evangelistic message of "knowing Christ."[1]

In the 17 years that have passed since we published *Marketing for Congregations*, two parallel trends have occurred in the literature. The religious press has largely followed the line of the *Christianity Today* article and condemned the use of marketing by religious organizations. Meanwhile, the business press has continued to crank out how-to books with helpful advice on putting church marketing into practice. Such books make a de facto (if not de jure) assertion that marketing can and should be used by churches when and wherever possible. Thus, both camps take an absolutist perspective on the role of marketing by religious institutions. How did we get to such an impasse?

The Road to Alienation

Religious institutions may well mark the first instance in which the irresistible march of marketing thinking's adoption in other domains has been checked. Previously, initial resistance to adopting a marketing philosophy and marketing practice by skeptics in such areas as the arts, professions (e.g., legal, accounting, etc.), health care, and others was based on a general distaste for the idea that what was seen as crassly commercial methods needed to be resorted to in order to be successful. Increased competition, declining demand, and a greater understanding of what is really marketing (i.e., separating its sometimes crude practice from authentic marketing theory) were usually sufficient to overcome that resistance. With many in the religious world, however, resistance is not based on a vague sense of distaste for the idea of needing to do marketing, or the belief that circumstances are not dire enough to necessitate its adoption, or that marketing may not be efficient or affordable, or fear that it might be ineffective in such a novel application. The basis for their opposition is that the marketing doctrine is antithetical to the foundational identity of the religious institution and its divinely mandated mission.

Indeed, some in the religious community see the use of marketing as akin to "dining with the devil."[2] Marketing, both the philosophy and the process, is seen by such critics as the embodiment of postmodernism[3] and its therapeutic interests (i.e., person-centeredness and focus on felt needs and their satisfaction) and principles of market rationality (i.e., pragmatism, efficiency, and quantifiable measures of success), which are inimical to religious tradition and its focus on submission and selflessness. An appeal to these critics on marketing's record of success in achieving exchange objectives in all types of organizations demonstrates a total lack of understanding of the genesis of the complaint. In fact, these critics concede that marketing is fully capable of achieving success as marketers define it; they just do not believe those measures to be relevant:

"The marketing of the church, then, may well be attended by considerable success. Indeed, I believe it will be. But, unlike its advocates, I do not believe that this validates the effort."[4]

For such traditionalists, religion resists adaptation as a means of self-preservation.

For their part, marketing proponents have persistently and persuasively argued that marketing is more than an organic set of activities and functions that facilitate exchange processes. They have insisted that the "marketing philosophy" embodied in the marketing concept (aka marketing orientation or market orientation—the philosophy that "products should be created in response to the latent or expressed desires/interests of their consuming publics")[5] become the mantra of everyone in the organization. Such diffused and integrated marketing thought is considered a prerequisite to effective modern marketing practice.

Framing challenges faced by ecclesiastical leaders as problems that marketing can aid in solving is a common theme in books on church marketing. Marketing works to solve such challenges by making peoples' needs, including latent needs, more salient to them, motivating them to seek satisfaction of those needs, identifying the means by which satisfaction can occur, and providing satisfaction of needs via exchange processes. Marketing is successful when its use consummates information, communication, and exchange. That success is based upon an appeal to the felt needs of the exchange partner and the offering of a "product" (goods, service, idea, organization, information, person, place) that has value because of its ability to satisfy those needs. Thus, it is ironic that the most ardent opponents as well as proponents of the use of marketing by religious organizations point to the same defense for their position—marketing "works."

The Road to Reconciliation

Many, if not most, religious organizations profess missions that, like the Ten Commandments, reflect concern with both spiritual and social matters. Such organizations seek to serve both God and humankind, and have mission statements that detail how they intend to fulfill these dual purposes. One well-known example of a multi-faceted mission is described in Rick Warren's *Purpose Driven Church,*[6] which specifies five purposes, or mission components, of churches: worship, discipleship, evangelism, fellowship, and ministry. The first three purposes on this list have been the subject of much discussion by theologians. Both theologians and social commentators have addressed the last two purposes.

Discussing social capital, i.e., the connections among individuals that produce norms of trust and reciprocity in society, Putnam reports that faith communities are "the single most important repository of [such] in America."[7] He argues that churches play important societal roles by offering bonding activities, such as providing social support and identity creation, and by encouraging bridging activities, such as engendering civic engagement and philanthropy and providing social services. Putnam contends that decreasing religious involvement is one reason for the country's precipitous decline in social capital.

Harold Kushner, well-known rabbi and author, has identified in

Who Needs God?[8] the following social roles of religious institutions in society:

(1) bringing structure and meaning to the lives of members

(2) promulgating a sense of community

(3) fostering a sense of mutual obligation for each other's welfare

(4) being an antidote for loneliness

(5) giving hope and peace to those who seek for them

These all reflect a strong sense that religious institutions should inculcate a sense of concern among members for the welfare of others, a feeling of being morally obligated to tend to the needs of others. A succinct expression of this is found in the New Testament writings of Paul:

> "Each of you should look not only to your own interests, but also to the interests of others" (Philippians 2:4, NIV).

Other Old and New Testament writings also emphasize the importance in understanding and meeting the needs of others:

> "If there is a poor man among your brothers in any of the towns of the land that the Lord your God is giving you, do not be hardhearted or tightfisted toward the poor brother. Rather be openhanded and freely lend him whatever he needs" Deuteronomy 15:7, 8, NIV).

> "Suppose a brother or sister is without clothes and daily food. If one of you says to him, "Go, I wish you well; keep warm and well fed," but does nothing about his physical needs, what good is it?" (James 2:15, 16, NIV).

> "If anyone has material possessions and sees his brother in need but has no pity on him, how can the love of God be in him?" (1 John 3:17, NIV).

> "Our people must learn to devote themselves to doing what is good, in order that they may provide for daily necessities and not live unproductive lives" (Titus 3:14, NIV).

There are likewise many verses in Scripture that emphasize the desirability of adopting a service posture when relating to others. This "service mentality" is present in some form in the "fellowship" and "ministry" purposes of a church's existence. Marketing thought, as exemplified by the marketing concept, is also focused on such a service mentality. All marketers have been admonished to think of what they offer as providing a service to address a need, rather than as an object to sell. It is, in fact, this service mentality, or concern with addressing the needs of others, that provides the common ground upon which marketing thought and religious institutions stand. Marketers who adopt the marketing concept as a guiding philosophy are vitally interested in understanding the needs of those people the marketer is focused on serving.

It is our belief that a church that achieves the last two purposes without succeeding at the first three has failed. Flawlessly implementing every good idea in this book cannot save a church that has failed in its spiritual calling. But a church that achieves all five purposes has come closer to being that "city on a hill" whose light "cannot be hidden" than one that does not. As you'll discover in reading *Building Strong Congregations*, we restrict our discussion of the use of marketing to purposes consistent with the fourth and fifth components of Warren's list. It might come as a surprise to readers that we share the conviction of some critics that religion (i.e., the first three of Warren's purposes) should not—indeed, cannot—be marketed. However, we sincerely believe that marketing at its best (and here we mean more than effectiveness, we also mean adopters having an authentic service mentality implicit in the last two purposes) can be a powerful force for the good within religious institutions.

The Road to Success

Restricting the use of marketing to the purposes of fellowship and ministry in no way unnecessarily limits the ability of marketing to make meaningful and essential contributions to a religious organization. Rather, it concentrates the use of marketing where it can, and we believe should, be used to help the organization achieve its goals. We have no doubt that some will find our conceptualization of marketing to represent a departure from a conventional understanding of the discipline's application in this setting. But this re-thinking of what marketing is and how it works in this setting is essential if you are to reap the rewards from its implementation. We harbor no illusions that this book can convert an ardent marketing critic into a supporter of its use by religious organizations. Our hope is more modest—that supporters will realize marketing's true potential for their institution.

Does attracting believers without a congregational home to become members of your church, or offering fellowship programs to your membership, such as grief recovery and small group cells (both of which we discuss in this book as "marketable" ministries), or providing social service ministries to external groups have a place in a twenty-first-century church trying to be true to its interpretation of Scripture? If this type of question is answered in the affirmative, marketing can, and perhaps should, at least from our perspective, be used to better serve the needs of others through an exchange process. For the thesis of this book is that marketers should not go where they don't belong, but that they are duty-bound to serve the interests of others where they can. That was our motivation in writing this book, and what we hope the reader will achieve from its reading.

---

[1] Tyler Wigg-Stevenson, "Jesus Is Not a Brand," *Christianity Today,* January 2009, pp. 20-26.

[2] Os Guinness, *Dining With the Devil* (Grand Rapids: Baker Book House, 1993).

[3] See, for example, Philip Sampson, Vinay Samuel, and Chris Sugden, *Faith and Modernity* (Oxford, Eng.: Regnum Books International, 1994).

[4] David F. Wells, *God in the Wasteland* (Grand Rapids: William B. Eerdmans Pub. Co., 1994), p. 86.

[5] Phillip Kotler, "A Generic Concept of Marketing," *Journal of Marketing* 36 (April 1972): 46-54.

[6] Rick Warren, *The Purpose Driven Church* (Grand Rapids: Zondervan Pub. House, 1995).

[7] R. D. Putnam, *Bowling Alone* (New York: Touchstone: Simon & Schuster, Inc., 2000), p. 66.

[8] Harold Kushner, *Who Needs God?* (New York: Summit Books, 1989).

Introduction

The fact that you have bought this book and are now reading this sentence likely means that you don't need reminding of just how dramatically different the environment surrounding religious organizations is in this century versus the one just past. Indeed, the twenty-first century is markedly different in many ways for both religious institutions and for marketers as well. It stands to reason, therefore, that when you combine these two to get religious institutional marketers you are looking at a sea change for those with such responsibilities. Such dramatic change necessitates a new approach to discussing the subject. The book is divided into six parts.

Part 1 provides an overview of the challenges facing contemporary congregational marketers, including a rethinking of the problem set where marketing and religion intersect. In part 1 we also describe how the use of marketing actually enhances the ability of religious institutions to fulfill their calling. At the end of part 1 we introduce the effective marketing process (EMP) model, whose steps define the other five parts of the book.

In **part 2** we discuss the first step of the EMP model, adopting a philosophy. We indicate what a highly responsive, marketing-oriented organization looks like in describing this stage of the process.

The next step of the EMP (understanding) is described in **part 3.** This involves both *how* to understand (marketing research) as well as *what* to understand (the factors influencing our decisions and behavior).

Part 4, developing a marketing plan, describes the third step of the model. Here we detail what it means to think like a marketing decision-maker, and how to segment a market, choose segments as targets, and then position your offerings to those targeted segments. The final act in this step is the planning process itself, with the output being a strategic marketing plan for your organization.

In **part 5** we continue our discussion of the EMP model by describing its fourth step, "doing" marketing (designing and implementing marketing tactics), by focusing on the "marketing mix"—the mix of product (ministries or programs), price (what target audiences must give up in terms of time, money, and psychological or social costs), place (the location or means of delivering the ministry), and promotion (the message and media by which we communicate the product's benefits). These four tactical tools are the means of carrying out the position we plan to occupy in the minds of the targeted segment. The reward for having successfully completed the effective marketing process is to make a connection with the other party to the exchange process. By "connection" we mean establishing a long-term mutually beneficial exchange relationship. This was our goal from the beginning. We were not seeking to only make an exchange—we wanted something more lasting, more meaningful, and more consonant with the mission of our institution. We sought to make a positive impact on the lives of those we serve within the compass of our mission, and when we successfully achieve that goal we make a connection with them. Consequently, at each step of the process we did not lose sight of our ultimate goal of connecting with our exchange partner.

In **part 6** we focus on nurturing the relationship, and evaluating the effectiveness of the process that led to this conclusion. Here we describe the means by which we can forge stronger bonds with our members and encourage an active engagement with our organization. We also provide a description of an assessment program by which we can evaluate our effectiveness in generating these connections. Continuous improvement in our processes is insurance in maintaining these hard-won connections.

It was our goal in writing this book to provide you with cutting-edge marketing thought for religious organizations while increasing the practical application value of the material. Consequently, at the end of each chapter we have included worksheets that walk you through a step-by-step application of the chapter material for your organization. By the time you arrive at the end of the book you should be well on your way to having a solid plan for *building strong congregations* by *attracting, serving, and developing your membership.* Please turn the page to begin our new journey together.

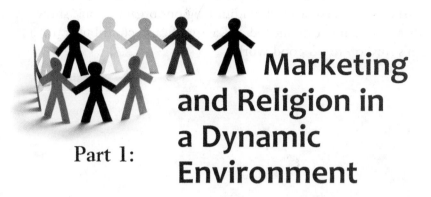

Marketing and Religion in a Dynamic Environment

Part 1:

S aying that churches currently exist in a "dynamic" environment is an obvious understatement. As this is written in the spring of 2009, the world is struggling with a global economic crisis unsurpassed since the great depression of the 1930s. Churches are facing reduced funding, declining membership, and competition from sources that did not exist just a few years ago. Faced with critical decisions about how to meet these challenges, congregational leaders are realizing that they cannot afford to "learn from their mistakes"— they must make the right decision the first time. Leaders must combine abiding faith with proven methods for tackling intractable problems.

In this first part of the book we describe the environmental threats and opportunities facing congregational leaders that can be successfully addressed through the use of marketing tools and processes. We are careful not to overreach when delineating where marketing can contribute to the success of the organization. Some might say we are being *too* restrictive in indicating where marketing thought should be proscribed. We use chapter 1 to explain our position on what can and cannot be marketed within religious organizations. Chapter 2 then lays out a process by which organizations, adopting marketing practices, can best gain the benefits that derive from that implementation. A supplement to chapter 2 demonstrates the marketing process at work within religious organizations, showing that marketing can indeed be a significant contributor to a church's mission to do good works.

CHAPTER 1:

The Intersection of Marketing and Religion

"For we are not peddlers of God's word like so many" (2 CORINTHIANS 2:17, NRSV).

In this chapter we will address the following questions:

1. What challenges do religious institutions face today that marketing can help address?

2. How have leaders of some religious institutions applied marketing activities in their congregations?

3. What have been some of the arguments for and against the marketing of religion?

4. What is our position on what about religion and religious institutions can and cannot be marketed?

When John Roh, a Korean-American living near Chicago, graduated from the University of Chicago seminary, he did what many newly minted seminarians do—he waited for "the call." It never came. Roh came to the conclusion that God wanted him to step out in faith and start a church that would serve the Korean immigrant community around Chicago. But where should such a church be located, and how would he get the word out in the community? What should be its ministry focus, or even its name? Where should he turn to get answers to these questions?[1]

The church board at the Springs Community Church was in a quandary. The 700-member nondenominational congregation was outgrowing the church building they had occupied since the mid-1950s, and now they learned they had an infestation of termites, requiring extensive and expensive repairs. Members of the board saw this latest development as a sign that the time was ripe to improve and enlarge the church facility. The problem now was how to finance such a massive building effort—only three faithful families whose membership went back decades had supported the church building fund. No one on the church board had had any experience in fund-raising, but they would need to become good at it, and soon. The termites had had a say in that!

The St. Elizabeth's Episcopal Church in Allentown, Pennsylvania, faced the most important decision in its 100-year history. The church's membership had been steadily declining, and now the remnant of 40 or so people, the majority of whom were over 50 years old, had just lost their 60-year-old rector to a brain aneurysm. The part-time interim vicar sent by the Diocese in Bethlehem confronted them with the cold hard facts: "You can't just go along and keep doing what you are doing and expect to survive. You have to take a serious look at yourself and your neighborhood, and then decide who you are and what you are going to do." The choices were: (1) stay and keep doing what they were doing (and continue to decline); (2) hire a part-time priest and hope the older members could come up with a ministry that would cause an influx of new members; (3) close and let members choose to join other Episcopal churches in surrounding towns; (4) form a joint congregation with a local Lutheran church; or (5) change locations and attract new members from that new community with ministries suited to that location. What to do?[2]

The worldwide economic crisis, caused in part by sub-prime mortgage lending practices, has had a devastating impact on some churches in the U.S. Mark Holbrook, president and CEO of the Evangelical Christian Credit Union of Brea, California, which specializes in lending to churches, says, "We are seeing more [financial] stress in churches than we have in modern history." His organization foreclosed on five churches in late 2008, and expected to foreclose on five more in early 2009. Until now, it had foreclosed on only two churches in its 45-year history. "There have been too many churches with a build-it-and-they-will-come attitude," says N. Michael Tangen, executive vice president at American Investors Group in Minnetonka, Minnesota. "They had glory in their eyes that wasn't backed up with adequate business plans and cash flow."[3] The current economic climate causing these troubles is expected to last at least through 2010.

Religious organizations of all persuasions and sizes are facing challenges that many leaders feel unprepared to meet. The current environment bears little resemblance to that of just a few decades past. Kirbyjon Calswell, senior pastor at Windsor Village United Methodist Church in Houston, describes how religious practices have changed in his lifetime this way:

"When I was growing up, you could make the argument that Christian faith had a monopoly on society. It wasn't just on Sunday. When someone talked about the Lord on Monday, you knew which Lord, which God, they were talking about. Now that's not the case. We're no longer a monopoly. Christianity is now a competitive situation. But for any local church the real competition today is television, the Internet, shopping malls, and other social options. The culture offers so many alternatives. Culture— not the 'church across town'— is the local church's primary competitor.

> *"Our churches have to adapt, not necessarily who we are, but what we do. We must intentionally identify, predict, and meet the needs of people—or else decline. It's a basic business and spiritual principle: when you don't adjust your methodology and strategy, you will lose market share—for pastors, that means members."*[4]

Bill Hybels, a founding and senior pastor of Willow Creek Community Church in South Barrington, Illinois, provides this insight into why church attendance looks the way it does:

> *"Less church attendance doesn't necessarily mean that people are less dedicated to knowing Christ or loving their families. To me, these are pace-of-life issues. The number of schedule activities has bled way over into Sunday. We have people at Willow Creek who 15 years ago would be in church 50 weeks a year, simply because their lives allowed that kind of schedule. Now, baseball and soccer games are on Sunday mornings, and a lot of student activities happen over weekends. Less church attendance is an American culture issue."*[5]

John Throop described some key shifts in American society that are presenting challenges for many congregations:

1. *Secularization has created a new kind of person: a seeker.* Younger seekers look for relevance and benefits in their purchases, and their lack of religious ties causes them to consider religious organizations from the same perspective.

2. *The "megachurch" is more appealing than the denomination.* Many baby boomers have grown up with a distrust of large institutions. Denominations, to them, represent institutional bureaucratic religious relics. Independent, unaffiliated "megachurches" appear to be free from religious traditions that they find constrain the worship experience.

3. *An increasingly affluent culture that values personal freedom wants more choices.* The consumer accustomed to a wide variety of options in media, goods, and services brings that expectation to the religious organization with them. They desire a wide range of choices for their family with respect to the religious organization as well.

4. *Open immigration policies have brought a flood of new cultures, lan-*

guages and activities, especially to urban centers. Virtually every medium-to large-size metro area has a diverse and growing ethnic population. Such language and cultural diversity is presenting significant challenges to religious organizations that seek to retain a corporate identity.

5. *The Internet is beginning to replace the local with the virtual church.* Increasingly, religious organizational leaders seek to reach and remain relevant to groups who choose to interact online, requiring new competencies not gained during their ministerial training.[6]

In response to these challenges facing their congregations, some church leaders, such as John Wimberly, have turned to church marketing consultants for help:

> "His church, Western Presbyterian in the District, had its membership decline over the years, once nearly closing its doors. Then, in 1994, its leaders decided to move from their aging building near the World Bank to a residential area of Foggy Bottom. Wimberly worried that the relocation might scatter his flock.
>
> "So he turned to the Alban Institute, a church consulting firm based in Herndon. Armed with demographic reports and professional advice on how to appeal to a neighborhood full of families with young children, Wimberly adjusted his sermons and created new ministries.
>
> "In the past decade, Sunday attendance has doubled to about 220. More important, he said, the place is brimming with energy. 'It was a great investment,' Wimberly said of hiring a consultant. 'It was clearly a turning point. We were either going to go in one direction or the other.'"[7]

Such willingness to experiment with new approaches to meeting contemporary challenges is not restricted to Christian denominations either. Witness what a group of New York area Jewish congregations have been doing to reverse the decline in their congregations' populations:

> "A hipster synagogue grows in SoHo, drawing large crowds with its 'Torah cocktail parties' in fancy loft apartments and user-

friendly prayer services designed especially for the uninitiated. . . .

"Congregations . . . refashion their synagogues into religious multiplexes on the Sabbath, featuring programs like 'Shabbat yoga' and comedy alongside traditional worship.

"Several synagogues on Long Island . . . station volunteers in supermarket aisles as part of a national program that started several years ago to reach out to Jews who are buying matzos for Passover but do not belong to a house of worship. . . .

"Jewish leaders are revamping worship in their synagogues to make the experience more lively and participatory; they are re-configuring their sanctuaries to make them less intimidating; they are rethinking how to welcome newcomers; and they are getting increasingly creative about getting people in the door. . . .

"The Manhattan Jewish Experience, an Orthodox outreach organization for young Jewish professionals on the Upper West Side, offers slickly advertised social events, including a regular 'Monday Night Lounge' that features music and lecture on topics ranging from dating to kabbalah. . . ."

"The Society for the Advancement of Judaism, a Reconstructionist and Conservative synagogue on the Upper West Side of Manhattan, . . . has organized Sabbath programs around tai chi and nature walks. Others have tried yoga classes and stand-up comedy as a means of Sabbath observance."[8]

In recent years there have been many inspirational stories published describing how congregations have overcome severe challenges by adapting to their changed environment. However, controversy has accompanied some of this success.

According to the *Wall Street Journal*, the country's more than 50 million evangelicals are deeply divided over the use of "Madison Avenue" techniques supposedly advocated by Rick Warren's "Purpose Driven Church" church growth movement. Built around Warren's five "fundamental purposes" of a church—worship, fellowship, discipleship, ministry, and evangelism—the movement is felt by its opponents to use modern management techniques such as market research, mission statements, and strategic planning methods inappropriate for religious organizations. Angered by the adoption of these approaches to evangelism, some older members of congregations have left their churches after longtime memberships. Advocates of the purpose-driven movement claim it energizes the congregation and leads to significant gains in new members. More than 400,000 pastors worldwide have received training in the purpose-driven methods of church growth. Such attempts at modernizing the worship experience have come under harsh criticism by some. According to Rev. Bob De Waay, author of a book critical of this approach, "the Bible's theme is about redemption and atonement, not finding meaning and solving problems." In response, a Warren spokesperson says the Bible addresses human problems as well as sin and redemption. The *WSJ* article cites several examples of churches whose membership has declined as a result of radical new worship service innovations such as adding a second worship service with Christian pop songs, guitars, and elaborate sound systems, while other congregations have doubled in size after-making changes.[9]

In San Francisco, the largest mosque in the Bay Area took the controversial step of removing the eight-foot wall that separated male and female worshippers. The mosque is now the only one in San Francisco that has removed the barrier, and the action has divided both male and female members. Some females find it liberating, while others feel it disturbs the privacy needed for prayer. Some men believe the wall should have been removed because walls did not separate men from women during Muhammad's time (walls were a cultural artifact introduced during the eighth century). Other men believe the visible presence of women in the mosque is provocative and invites "temptation." Ingrid Mattson, a professor of Islamic Studies at Hartford Seminary, says that such controversies can threaten the "unchanging pillar" that religion is for many adherents. Some members of both genders have left the mosque and attend the area mosques that retain the partition between men and women.[10]

In the time that has passed since we first wrote *Marketing for Congregations* the use of marketing practices by religious organizations has increased dramatically, but with a corresponding increase in opposition by critics. Despite these objections, many leaders of religious organizations faced with declining memberships, severely strained budgets, and loss of congregational vitality have turned to marketing experts for help. The changing landscape of religion in America presents both problems and opportunities for congregations seeking to remain a vital force in contemporary society. Congregations struggle to resolve such growing issues as divorce, childless couples, homosexuality and gay marriages, multilanguage and multicultural congregations, population shifts, increasingly scarce financial resources, and the intrusion of cultural secular values among younger congregants.

As the link between an organization and its environment, marketing can play a significant role in helping religious organizations conquer their problems and take advantage of their opportunities. Let's consider the current state of religion in America, to see some of these problems/opportunities.

Religion in America

Do religious organizations in America really need marketing? By some accounts, religion could be described as a "growth business" in the U.S.:

• A 44-nation survey by the Pew Global Attitudes Project in 2002 found 59 percent of those polled in the U.S. said religion was very important to them, and 86 percent said it was very or somewhat important to them. In comparison, 30 percent in Canada, 33 percent in Great Britain, and only 11 percent in France reported that religion was very important in their lives.

• A 2006 Baylor University study revealed that only 11 percent of those polled indicated no religious affiliation whatsoever. Interestingly, 14 percent checked "none" when asked their religion, but almost one out of five of these respondents later listed a place of worship, leading researchers to conclude that many people might not have a denomination, but do have a congregation.

• Research by the Barna Group indicates the incidence of Bible reading among adults has increased from 2000 to 2006, with almost half the adults polled reporting themselves as Bible readers.

• More than 80 percent of Americans say they believe in God.

However, other reports paint a somewhat different picture:

• A 2006 Harris poll indicated that only 36 percent of United States adults claim to attend a religious service once a month or more, approximately the same percentage as in 2003. Other estimates have put the percentage as low as 18 percent.

• Double- and triple-digit growth has been occurring in the less-traditional U.S. religions, while the more traditional United States faiths are losing religious market share.

• Approximately 85 percent of churches in the United States report attendance that is stagnant or in decline.

• While more than 80 percent of people polled in a 2001 study answered the question "What is your religion, if any?" by identifying a specific religion, only 54 percent said they reside in a household where they themselves (or someone else) actually are members of a religious group. Hence, there appears to be a wide gap between "identification" with a religion, and "membership" in a religious institution.

• Research by Barna supports a general trend toward the "privatization of faith." For example the study found that roughly 10 million adults who consider themselves "born again" do no attend any type of church or worship service.

• More than 33 million American adults report changing their religious preference or identification, and by some estimates, up to a third of adults will change their religious affiliation at least once in their lifetime.

• A literature is growing that attacks the belief in a God. Richard Dawkins and others are making a case for atheism that is generating controversy. They are engaged in marketing a competing worldview.[11]

The conclusion one might draw from these two lists is that while religious *sentiments* might be characterized as healthy and growing in the U.S., religious *institutions* are not always the beneficiaries of those sentiments. We believe that religious institutions can, and should, close that gap with the appropriate use of marketing practices. However, this opinion is not universally held.

A short history lesson on the use of marketing by religious institutions will provide some needed perspective on how we arrived at the current controversial status of marketing's use by religious organizations.

Marketing and Religion: A Brief History

The origin of religious marketing practice is open to debate. One author makes the claim that "the Bible is one of the world's great marketing texts."[12]

We don't subscribe to this point of view, but it does suggest that the intersection of marketing and religion is not a recent phenomenon.

In America, historians have maintained that preachers used "marketing" practices at least as far back as Colonial times. Stout described George Whitefield, a famous evangelist during the Great Awakening of the 1730s-1740s, as presenting religion as "a product that could be marketed."[13] When did we begin to see writers discuss the use of marketing for religious institutions? We'll look at the earliest literature before examining more contemporary writings on the subject.

Early Literature

The earliest example of "marketing-like" thought applied to religion in the literature might be Jay Benson Hamilton's book *Empty Churches and How to Fill Them*, published in 1879. Beginning in the early part of the twentieth century books began to appear that described how to promote the church, such as:

Principles of Successfull [sic] Church Advertising (1908)
Advertising the Church (1913)
Church Publicity: The Modern Way to Compel Them to Come In (1913)
How to Fill the Pews (1917)
Church Advertising: Its Why and How (1917)
How to Advertise a Church (1920)
Handbook of Church Advertising (1921)
Church and Sunday School Publicity (1922)

It was around the beginning of the twentieth century that advertising in general saw its earliest writings. So one of its first applications was for religious institutions. This example of the immediate application of marketing thought to religious organizations illustrates the fervor with which some religious leaders seek out effective means for "spreading the word." John Wesley embodied this philosophy when he declared that "I would observe every punctilio of order, except where the salvation of souls is at stake. There I prefer the end before the means."[14] As we'll see, there is a sharp division of opinion between the "whatever works" school and those who find no redeeming qualities of marketing's application by religious institutions. However, early application of marketing tools to religious organizations leaned more toward adoption of the "whatever works" school of thought.

Contemporary Literature

The early literature, as can be seen above, concentrated on the use of marketing tools, primarily promotion, for religious organizations. In the latter half of the twentieth century we see the term *marketing,* rather than *promotion* or *publicity,* gain currency in its application to religion. This change in terminology reflects the ascendancy of the marketing concept as a core construct for marketing theory. The marketing concept's focus on customer needs and consumer sovereignty will become a major focal point of the opponents of marketing in religious circles. It is this clash of philosophies (the marketing concept is often referred to as a philosophy) between marketers and theologians that necessitates separating the marketing and religious literature devoted to the subject.

Marketing Literature

The first article written in support of the use of marketing by religious organizations was entitled "A Marketing Analysis of Religion,"[15] written in 1959 by James Culliton, dean of the College of Commerce at the University of Notre Dame. A review of the marketing literature by Cutler[16] revealed that in the next 30 years only 35 articles were written on the application of marketing for religious institutions. Most of these articles appeared in conference proceedings, casebooks, or *Marketing News,* the newsletter of the American Marketing Association. Nearly 80 percent of the articles were published in the 1980s. The 1990s saw increased interest in the topic by marketing scholars, and the birth of a journal, the *Journal of Ministry*

The First Book on Church Marketing?

In 1879 Jay Benson Hamilton wrote what may well be the first book on how to market the church, entitled *Empty Churches and How to Fill Them* (New York: Philips and Hunt, 1879). Below are listed a sampling of quotes that reflect church marketing thought, although the use of that term to describe these ideas would not gain credence for another 80 years.

Page 6: "An old recipe for cooking a hare is 'To cook a hare, first catch it.' The motto of the modern minister should be "To save men, first reach them.' "

Page 7: "Not more than one in five of our Protestant population are regular attendants upon religious worship."

Pages 9, 10: "[Locate a church in a place with lots of churchgoers.] Fishermen say, 'If you want to catch fish, set your nets where the fish run.' "

Page 54: "Every church ought to have an organization connected to it whose sole aim is to invite persons to attend divine worship."

Page 54-55: "By dividing [the large town or small city] into districts, and systematically visiting, street by street, and house by house, those who have no church home . . . hundreds would be induced to go [to church] who never think of it. . . . By reporting to the visiting committee the names and residences of those they have invited, the work can be followed up by others and cannot fail."

Page 58: "Why is trying to do business without advertising like winking at someone in the dark? You know what you are doing, but nobody else does."

Page 59: "The column of the secular as well as the religious press should be utilized wherever possible to attract attention to divine worship."

Page 62: "Newspaper advertising is not enough. . . . Posters, circulars, and cards fill an important place [in promoting the church]."

Page 63: "The salvation of souls should be a business and not mere sentiment."

Marketing and Management, provided increased coverage of religious marketing scholarship.

The stance taken by these marketing writers has been, as might be expected, almost entirely supportive of the use of marketing by religious organizations, cautionary notes being infrequently voiced.

Empirical studies by marketers have indicated that the clergy, who indicate they make use of many marketing tools, also see marketing positively.[17] Marketing literature, therefore, has generally been unrestrained in its enthusiastic pursuit of broadening marketing thought into the religious realm.

Religious Literature

Attitudes toward marketing in religious literature have been more mixed. An interesting phenomenon occurred: the pro-marketing books written by marketers in the late 1980s and early 1990s were followed by a "backlash" of anti-marketing books written by religious authors in the mid- to late 1990s. While there are still many leaders of religious organizations who continue to believe in the Wesleyan "whatever works" school of thought, and adopt marketing when it helps them achieve their goals, the anti-marketing group is philosophically opposed to the use of marketing. As we'll see, this opposition centers on their perception of the nature of marketing and the marketer's worldview, and their belief that these are fundamentally at odds with the nature of religion and religious institutions.

The Intersection of Religion and Marketing—
Where Do the Twain Meet?

The ongoing controversy over if and where marketing should be used by religious organizations continues to rage. In an attempt to add some light to the heat, we present Exhibit 1 below, which maps out the four components of many religious organizations' mission.

We identify two "directions" of relationships fostered by an institution's mission and two types of audiences served by the mission:

Direction of Desired Relationship:

Vertical: Seeking to foster a spiritual connection between humankind and God.

Horizontal: Seeking to foster a service mentality and cohesiveness among people.

Focus of Relationship:

Internal/Intimate: Relationships that involve interactions between two or more entities within the body of believers.

External/Mass: Relationships between the institution and its publics.

These four components of mission combine to produce four missional relationship objectives (shown along with their Greek terms) common to most churches.

Exhibit 1	**Relational Objectives as Components of Religious Organizational Mission**	
Direction of	**Focus of Relationship**	
Desired Relationship	**Internal/Intimate**	**External/Mass**
Vertical (Spiritual)	Worship *Latreuo* and *Mathêteuô* **1**	Evangelize *Euaggelizo* **2**
Horizontal (Social)	**3** Create Community *Ekklēsia* and *Koinonia*	**4** Offer Social Services *Diakoneo*

Definitions:

latreuo: to worship, to render homage.

mathêteuô: to make a disciple, instruct, teach

euaggelizo: to bring good news or glad tidings of the coming kingdom of God

ekklēsia: gathering of the called out ones

koinonia: to have fellowship

diakoneo: to serve, to minister to

Marketing has been proposed by some writers as appropriate for activities in all four cells of the table. Others maintain there is no cell where marketing should be used. We will refer to cells 1 and 2 as the "marketing of religion" controversy, and cells 3 and 4 as the "marketing of religious organizations" controversy.

Should "Religion" be Marketed?

From a theological perspective, the central objection to the application of marketing to religion is that such practice mixes the profane with the sacred. Marketing is anthropocentric, embodying the world (Greek, *kosmos*) in the sense of the ways of fallen humanity, while religion is theocentric—life is to be understood from "the perspective that God himself has provided for its understanding."[18] It is not just that religion doesn't need marketing; it is also that it is inappropriate for an anthropocentric method to tell a theocentric story—using the ways of fallen humanity to reveal the truths about a transcendent God. God's supernatural nature, His transcendence, is lost when "theocentric faith (i.e., faith centered on God as an objective reality)" becomes "anthropocentric faith (i.e., faith centered on the therapeutic interest in the self)."[19] Because marketing's focus on exchange is an appeal to self-perceived value, its use in trying to consummate religious "exchanges" limits God's ability to reveal Himself to us in His own way. A knowledge of God requires us to abandon self as an epistemological filter and use theocentric methods (e.g., study of Scripture, meditation) as the means for God's character to be revealed to us. Marketing should not be used as a channel for a theocentric method of knowing God. To do so is to profane the sacred.

From a marketing theoretical perspective, we must determine if an exchange of values is possible with respect to religion. Marketing scholars have generally conceded exchange as the central concept for the disciple.

Five conditions are considered necessary for exchange to occur:[20]
1. There are at least two parties.
2. Each party has something that might be of value to the other party.
3. Each party is capable of communication and delivery.
4. Each party is free to accept or reject the exchange offer.

5. Each party believes it is appropriate or desirable to deal with the other party.

Four axioms of marketing have been proposed, the first of which is: "Marketing involves two or more social units, each consisting of one or more human actors."[21] Other conceptualizations of marketing as exchange also refer to the exchange parties as social actors, or marketing as occurring within a social system. The American Marketing Association definition of marketing states that marketing is performed to "create exchanges that satisfy individual and organizational goals."[22] Even in broadly defined terms, it is not possible to stretch the exchange paradigm outlined above to include religion as it has been conceived here with the premise of a divine being. While exchange is a decidedly human, worldly endeavor, religious beliefs involve an "other worldliness" that cannot be explained using exchange concepts. Indeed, religion and some of its core beliefs (e.g., divine grace) have been referred to as "blocked exchanges,"[23] that is, things which can't be formalized as exchanges since they involve that which cannot be owned: "The reason one cannot sell divine grace is that one does not own it to begin with."[24] Thus, there are compelling reasons to argue that the activities contained in cell 1 (*latreuo*, meaning to worship, and *mathêteuô* meaning to make a disciple), where we see the intimate relationship between the divine and humankind, and cell 2 (*euaggelizo*, meaning to evangelize), where spiritual messages are shared with those external to the body of believers, neither can or should be "marketed" (i.e., a marketing orientation [chapter 2] has not been used in the development of the message).

Not everyone, it should be stated, finds our reasoning compelling. Much has been written in support of "marketing religion," and some who seek new converts to their religion are avid readers and aspiring practitioners of modern marketing theory. We, however, do find the arguments against the marketing of religion to be difficult to refute.

What, then, is the purpose of this book, if not to provide guidance on how to "market religion" more successfully? This is a simple question with a complex answer that involves a look at cell 3 and cell 4 components.

Can Religious Institutions Be Marketed?

When we say that we are marketing a religious institution, what exactly is being marketed? While we will be expanding at greater length on the what and how of religious organizational marketing throughout this text, at this point we will consider three forms of religious institutional marketing. In cell 3 of Exhibit 1 we consider two forms of "community" marketing: ecclesiastical or adherent marketing (i.e., marketing to the believers to join the congregation), and fellowship marketing (i.e., marketing within the local congregation). In cell 4 we look at social service marketing (i.e., marketing the local congregation's services to the larger society).

Adherent Marketing

In this type of marketing, a congregation is marketing itself to those who belong to the universe of believers. This gathering of people is called *qahal* or *edah* within Judaism, *ummah* in Islam, and *ekklesia* within Christianity. Most books dedicated to describing how churches could apply marketing identify the "problem" churches have that marketing can assist in solving:

> Churches and ministries face a number of problems that would be treated as marketing problems if they were found in the business sector. Churches and ministries are having difficulty attracting and maintaining active members/supporters; they are having difficulty determining if they are meeting these people's needs; and they are unable to explain why members and supporters leave or stop supporting their organizations.[25]

> The church is not making inroads into the lives and hearts of people. My contention, based on careful study of data and the activities of American churches, is that the major problem plaguing the church, is its failure to embrace a marketing orientation in what has become a marketing-driven environment.[26]

For all religious organizations, a marketing perspective can provide rich insights into more effectively conducting a number of major activities, including:

1. Starting a new congregation.
2. Targeting prospective members.

3. Attracting first-time visitors.
4. Building membership involvement and commitment.
5. Attracting and managing volunteers.
6. Keeping members.
7. Involving members in measuring the importance and performance of the organization's ministries and services.
8. Attracting funds and other resources.[27]

Framing current challenges faced by religious organizational leaders as problems that marketing can aid in solving is a common theme in these books. The prevailing justification for proposing the use of marketing by religious organizations is that it works—marketing can generate quantifiable gains in the areas listed above, and its use can lead to improvements in member satisfaction measures.

Religious writers can be roughly categorized as being receptive, cautious, or hostile to the idea of using marketing to achieve religious organizational objectives. The following examples are typical comments of these three categories:

Receptive: "The question isn't marketing versus calling; we must see the connection between marketing and mission, and thereby regain our perspective and initiative in a selling world as we market a biblical and fulfilling gospel that is neither legalistic nor simplistic."[28]

Cautious: "Is 'marketing' the new *contextualization*, enabling the church to reach our world for Christ? Or is it merely *capitulation* to our culture?"[29]

Hostile: "The problem, however, as this essay has attempted to suggest, is that when marketing models, marketing values, marketing language, and marketing strategies and tactics are allowed to structure the life of a Christian congregation, much that has been previously understood to be central to the Christian faith, and perhaps to the church itself, likewise becomes superfluous."[30]

Interestingly, the most scathing opposition to the use of marketing by these institutions is the same reason offered by its proponents—marketing "works" (i.e., marketing makes people's needs, including latent needs, more salient to them, motivates them to seek satisfaction of those needs, helps identify the means by which satisfaction can occur, and provides satisfaction of needs via exchange processes). Opponents of marketing don't believe that churches should be in the exchange business, even with those who belong to the body of believers but who do not belong to a local congregation. We respectfully disagree with these critics, and believe that religious institutions can more effectively achieve this component of their mission when they adopt and appropriately implement marketing practices.

Fellowship Marketing

The objective of sponsoring a sense of community or fellowship among members is common to many congregations. To "market fellowship" would imply promotion of a sense of concern with the common welfare of the faith community. It would also mean encouraging participation by members in the mission of the institution.

Is it possible to market a sense of community, mutual concern, or "brotherhood"? Can you market such values as kindness, generosity, and nurturing? Very little has been written on this topic in the field of marketing, but the customer service literature has devoted some attention to instilling a sense of generosity and social profit among customer service personnel. Berry maintains that one of the characteristics of service organizations notable for their sustained success is that they have values-driven leadership, that is, certain values are sought in new hires, taught, and rewarded in the company. One of these values is "social profit," or doing good works for the benefits that derive to the recipients of the works rather than the doers. One example of a company that illustrates this philosophy:

The Container Store values giving, not just getting; it believes in enriching—economically or otherwise—all of its stakeholders. . . . Although businesses commonly are involved in charitable activities and community support programs, the centrality of social profit creation to the sample company's "reason for being" is highly unusual. Creating social profit is part of the company's mission; it is a core value that guides and motivates behavior in the daily life of the organizations.[31]

Berry observes that one of the roles of values-driven leaders of these excellent service organizations is that they "encourage the heart"—the values they promote "bring a sense of achievement, collaboration, civility, purpose, and contribution to the employee." Finally, Berry describes the basic thesis of the book in terms consistent with the proposition that fellowship can be marketed: "The book is about the overriding importance of humane values in building a lasting service business. Great service companies build a *humane* community (the organization and its partners) that *humanely* serves customers and the broader communities in which they live."[32]

Marketing such values among members is referred to as "internal marketing" in our book, and includes the use of marketing to gain the participation of members (i.e., recruiting volunteers) in carrying out the institution's mission. Internal marketing also involves educating them in an understanding that their interactions with each other should be thought of as Moments of Truth,[33] an interaction that can result in the reinforcement of a positive value consistent with preserving a sense of fellowship (kindness, inclusiveness, generosity, etc.), or can be a failed moment of truth, leading to a dissolution of the sense of community.

Internal marketing can also serve to support theological principles governing the way people relate to one another within the church. A market orientation within the church is consistent with Martin Buber's I-Thou treatise, which distinguishes between treating others as objects (I-It) (in which we see them in terms of what functions they serve for us) and as subjects (I-Thou) (in which we realize they have feelings about the interaction even as we do).

Social Services Marketing

Religious organizations have long been at the forefront of providing charitable services in America. These services include such diverse activities as:

food banks and pantries
home delivery of meals to invalids
donations of clothing to needy individuals
adoption services
disaster relief
blood banks
summer camps
legal assistance
safe houses for victims of domestic violence
home building and repair for those who are disadvantaged
drug addiction rehabilitation
job training and welfare-to-work programs
family and marital counseling
HIV/AIDs counseling
day-care services
jail inmate visitation

Articles in marketing literature on social marketing began appearing in the early 1970s. Marketing's role in operation of social service organizations is now indisputable: "The question is no longer whether social sector institutions should adopt marketing, but how to implement marketing strategy."[34]

There is little doubt then that social services and social causes can be, and are, marketed.

The fact that we wrote the first edition of this book and that more than 10,000 of you bought it and used it is eloquent testimony to support the claim that many of us do believe that marketing can and should be responsibly used by religious institutions. As mentioned earlier, most clergy are in agreement that marketing can and should play a legitimate role in helping their congregations achieve specific missional objectives. While "religion" cannot be marketed, religious organizations have shown they can apply modern marketing techniques to conduct *Adherent, Fellowship,* and *Social Services* marketing while remaining true to their calling. We hope this revised edition of our book will continue in that tradition. Chapter 2 will describe the model that we believe can be followed to help religious organizations achieve marketing objectives.

---

[1] Adapted from "The Business of Faith," Percept Web site: http://www. link2lead.com/MyWorld/QuikStory/v1n10/QS_v1n10.aspx.

[2] Adapted from "O Little Town of Schnecksville," Percept Web site: http://www. link2lead.com/MyWorld/FullStory/F_v1n7.aspx.

[3] Suzanne Sataline, "In Hard Times, Houses of God Turn to Chapter 11 in Book of Bankruptcy," *Wall Street Journal,* Dec. 23, 2008, pp. A1, A7.

[4] Rebecca Barnes and Lindy Lowry, "Special Report: The American Church in Crisis," *Outreach,* May/June 2006, p. 2.

[5] *Ibid.,* p. 11.

[6] John Throop, "The Church Goes to Market," *Your Church,* May/June 2003, p. 61.

[7] David Cho, "The Business of Filling Pews: Congregations Employ Marketing Consultants to Step Up Appeal," Washington *Post,* Mar. 6, 2005, p. C01.

[8] Michael Luo, "With Yoga, Comedy and Parties, Synagogues Entice Newcomers," New York *Times,* Apr. 4, 2006.

[9] "A Popular Strategy for Church Growth Splits Congregants," *Wall Street Journal,* Sept. 5, 2006, pp. A1, A10.

[10] "San Francisco Mosque Drops Gender Barrier—Worshippers Are Still Adjusting," San Francisco *Chronicle,* June 6, 2006, p. A-1.

[11] Richard Dawkins, *The God Delusion* (Boston: Houghton-Mifflin, 2006).

[12] George Barna, *Marketing the Church* (Colorado Springs, Colo.: NavPress, 1988).

[13] Harry S. Stout, *The Divine Dramatist* (Grand Rapids: William B. Eerdmans Pub. Co., 1991), p. 35.

[14] Frances Gerald Ensley, *John Wesley: Evangelist* (Nashville: Tidings, 1958).

[15] James W. Culliton, "A Marketing Analysis of Religion," *Business Horizons* 2 (Spring 1959): 85-92.

[16] Bob D. Cutler, "Religion and Marketing: Important Research Area or a Footnote in the Literature?" *Journal of Professional Services Marketing* 8, no. 1 (1991): 153-164.

[17] Stephen McDaniel, "Church Advertising: Views of the Clergy and General Public," *Journal of Advertising* 15, no. 1 (1986): 24-29.

[18] D. F. Wells, *God in the Wasteland* (Grand Rapids: William B. Eerdmans Pub. Co., 1994), p. 45.

[19] *Ibid.,* p. 122.

[20] P. Kotler, "A Generic Concept of Marketing," *Journal of Marketing* 36 (April 1972): 46-54.

[21] *Ibid.*

[22] Peter D. Bennett, *Dictionary of Marketing Terms* (Chicago: American Marketing Association, 1988), p. 115.

[23] Judith Andre, "Blocked Exchanges: A Taxonomy," *Ethics* 103 (October 1992): 29-47.

[24] *Ibid.,* p. 33.

[25] Robert E. Stevens and David L. Loudon, *Marketing for Churches and Ministries* (New York: Haworth Press, 1992).

[26] Barna, p. 23.

[27] Norman Shawchuck, Philip Kotler, Bruce Wrenn, and Gustave Rath, *Marketing for Congregations* (Nashville: Abingdon Press, 1992).

[28] Carnegie Samuel Calian, "Marketing the Church's Ministry," *The Christian Ministry* 14, no. 3 (1983): 22-23.

[29] Craig Parro, "Church Growth's Two Faces," *Christianity Today* 35, no. 7 (June 24, 1991): 19.

[30] Philip D. Kenneson, "Selling [Out] the Church in the Marketplace of Desire," *Modern Theology* 9 (Oct. 1993): 326-349.

[31] Leonard L. Berry, *Discovering the Soul of Service* (New York: Free Press, 1999).

[32] *Ibid.*

[33] Jan Carlzon, *Moments of Truth* (Cambridge, Mass.: Ballinger, 1987).

[34] Seymour H. Fine, *Social Marketing* (Boston: Allyn and Bacon, 1990).

WORKSHEETS: CHAPTER 1

Meeting the Objections to the Use of Marketing

1. Identify any concerns among the leadership team over the use of marketing by your organization.

_____

_____

_____

2. List the statements from the chapter that you believe best address these concerns.

_____

_____

_____

3. In which cells in Exhibit 1 will your organization be engaged in conducting marketing activities?

_____

_____

_____

We suggest that all church decision-makers involved in programs that fall within these cells read chapter 1 and discuss any concerns over the use of marketing with the leadership team.

4. Identify the specific programs, ministries, etc., that you desire to market:

Adherent Marketing

_____

_____

_____

Fellowship Marketing

_____

_____

_____

Social Services Marketing

_____

_____

_____

CHAPTER 2:

The Heart of Twenty-first-Century Marketing

"Each of you should look not only to your own interests, but also to the interests of others" (PHILIPPIANS 2:4, NIV).

In this chapter we will address the following questions:

1. In what ways have marketing practices changed in the past decade?

2. What are the steps of the effective marketing process?

3. How is a marketing philosophy consistent with the mission of religious institutions?

4. How can congregational marketers match their methods with their markets?

A s was made clear in chapter 1, the debate over making changes to religious organizations to enhance the member's experience is far from just a philosophical disagreement between marketing academicians and theologians. The implementation of such change to achieve marketing goals is roiling congregations nationwide. The question is: Is marketing by its very nature inimical to the practice of religious traditions, or is genuine marketing philosophy actually consistent with those traditions? We will attempt to answer these questions in this chapter by exploring what we believe to be the heart of twenty-first-century marketing.

Effective Marketing in the Twenty-first Century

There has been a sea change in the way marketing is practiced by for-profit (and many not-for-profit) enterprises in the past decade. In the commercial arena mass advertising is not nearly as effective as it was. Marketers are exploring new forms of communication, such as experiential, entertainment, and viral marketing. Firms now sell goods and services through a variety of direct and indirect channels. The Internet has multiplied the number of ways that consumers buy and companies sell, and has increased customer price sensitivity. Cellular phones have enabled people to exchange messages and buy and sell on the go. Consumers are increasingly reporting to other consumers what they think of specific companies and products, using digital media to do so. Company messages are becoming a smaller fraction of the total "conversation" about products and services.

Customers are increasingly telling companies what types of products or services they want and when, where, and how they want to buy them. They tell companies what communications they will tolerate, what incentives they expect, and what prices they will pay.

In response, companies have shifted gears from managing product portfolios to managing *customer* portfolios, compiling databases on individual customers so they can understand them better, and constructing individualized offerings and messages. They are doing less product and service standardization and more niching and customization. They are replacing monologues with customer dialogues, using Web 2.0 technology to do so. The focus today is on customer relationship management (CRM). Companies emphasize keeping and growing customers instead of being totally fixed on finding new ones. They are improving their methods of measuring customer profitability and customer lifetime value. They are intent on measuring the return on their marketing investment and its impact on shareholder value. They are also concerned with the ethical and social implications of their marketing decisions.

As corporations change, so have their marketing organization. Marketing is no longer a company department charged with a limited number of tasks—it is a company-wide undertaking. It drives the company's vision, mission, and strategic planning. Marketing includes decisions like who the company wants as its customers; which needs to satisfy; what products and services to offer; what prices to set; what communications to send and receive; what channels of distribution to use; and what partnerships to develop. Marketing in for-profit organizations succeeds only when all departments work together to achieve goals: when engineering designs the right products, finance furnishes the required funds, purchasing buys quality materials, production makes quality products on time, and accounting measures the profitability of different customers, products, and areas.

Not all of these changes that have occurred in the for-profit realm have parallels in religious organizations. However, some of the same forces acting on for-profits (advancing technology, societal value changes, pubic access to information, increasingly demanding "customers," household composition, etc.) have had a significant impact on religious institutions as well. We contend that the basic "meta-model" for effective application of marketing practice is the same for all organizations. We present this model below, and then describe the relevance of its respective parts for religious institutions.

Exhibit 2.1 **The Effective Marketing Process**

Adopt a Marketing Philosophy
↓
Develop an Understanding
↓
Plan the Marketing Strategy
↓
Design and Implement the Marketing Tactics
↓
Connect With Exchange Partners

Step 1: Adopt a Guiding Philosophy

Leaders of religious institutions, perhaps more than any other leaders, understand the importance of adopting a set of precepts, principles, or a guiding philosophy that can be used to direct their path through the decisions they face. Lacking such a guiding philosophy, leaders can be beguiled by the latest management approaches, following a "flavor of the month" approach to organizational administration. A clearly articulated management philosophy provides a benchmark for determining whether new techniques are "better" techniques for implementing the philosophy. It is particularly important that marketers, whether in the corporate or religious arenas, consciously adopt a philosophy to guide their exchange practices. This is because a changing environment most directly impacts marketers, among all organizational administrators. Facing such environmental turbulence, some organizations have made radical changes in their approach to "doing business," to disastrous effect. Others have been able to adapt to the new environment by changing their way of implementing a timeless philosophy. By "philosophy" we mean the way an organization's members think about the organization and its relationship to its "products," its exchange partners, and its publics. Some of the more common philosophies that marketers have adopted over time are shown in Exhibit 2.2.

The term *dominant* in the table identifies the core objective that gives the orientation its name. *Present* means that the orientation includes that objective but does not use it as the centrally controlling goal in orienting the leader's philosophy. *Not pertinent* means that characteristic has no relevance, pertinence, or connection with the orientation described. Several conclusions can be drawn from this table:

• The first three philosophies or orientations (production, product, selling) are entirely focused on issues *internal* to the organization: how it "produces" its "product," the quality of the offering, and its exchange goals being achieved by generating interest in its product by its exchange partners.

• Only the last two philosophies are dominated by a focus on those things that are *external* to the organization: exchange partners

Exhibit 2.2   Organizational Orientations

Characteristic	Production Orientation	Product Orientation	Selling Orientation	Marketing Orientation	Societal Marketing Orientation
Desire to capitalize on production efficiencies	dominant	present	present	present	present
Attention to designing and production of a quality "product"	not pertinent	dominant	present	present	present
Dedicated resources to stimulating interest and desire for product acquisition	not pertinent	not pertinent	dominant	present	present
Focus on identifying and satisfying needs and wants of exchange partners	not pertinent	not pertinent	not pertinent	dominant	present
Consideration of the short- and long-term effects of actions on exchange partners and on publics	not pertinent	not pertinent	not pertinent	not pertinent	dominant

and publics, and the needs and wants of these parties as they are affected by their environments.

• Those who adopt the most advanced of these philosophies—the societal marketing orientation—are concerned with achieving efficiencies of operation (i.e., production concerns), designing an offering that meets high standards of quality (i.e., product concerns), effectively communicating how the offering delivers value to the exchange partner (i.e., selling concerns), and focusing on identifying and satisfying the needs and wants of exchange partners (i.e., marketing concerns). All of these concerns are present in the mind of a societal marketing oriented administrator. What distinguishes this philosophy from the others is that the individual who adopts such an orientation is concerned with addressing the long-term as well as the immediate needs, the contribution the organization makes to the social welfare of the exchange partner and society, and also with the collateral effects of the exchange process on the organization's other publics.

The reader might correctly conclude that the authors are proponents of the societal marketing orientation (SMO) as a guiding philosophy for twenty-first-century organizations, including religious organizations, when it comes to marketing decisions. In fact, we might go so far as to state that such an orientation is *particularly* well suited to religious organizations with the SMO's emphasis on efficiency (e.g., being admonished to practice faithful stewardship), quality (e.g., doing what you do with all your might), effective communication (e.g., not putting your light under a basket), and service (e.g., serving one another in love). However, we think you have every right to remain skeptical at this point about the appropriateness of adopting a marketing philosophy, even one with the qualities of the SMO, as an operating philosophy for the leadership team of your organization. Now we would like to try and address that skepticism.

Is a Societal Marketing Orientation Consistent With a Religious Organization's Mission?

What are the "marketable" aspects (i.e., components of cells 3 and 4 of Exhibit 1) of an institution's mission? That is, what is the role of the institution in addressing "horizontal" social relationships beyond the "vertical" spiritual reasons for the institution's existence? Discussing social capital, i.e., the connections among individuals that produce norms of trust and reciprocity in society, Putnam reports that faith communities are "the single most important repository of [such] in America."[1] He argues that churches play important societal roles by offering bonding activities, such as providing social support and identity creation, and by encouraging bridging activities, such as engendering civic engagement, philanthropy, and providing social services. Putnam contends that decreasing religious involvement is one reason for the country's precipitous decline in social capital. Harold Kushner, well-known rabbi and author, has identified the following social (horizontal in our table) roles of religious institutions in society:

1. Bringing structure and meaning to the lives of members.
2. Promulgating a sense of community.
3. Fostering a sense of mutual obligation for each other's welfare.
4. Being an antidote for loneliness.
5. Giving hope and peace to those who seek for them.[2]

These all reflect a strong sense that religious institutions should inculcate a sense of concern among members for the welfare of others, to feel morally obligated in tending to the needs of others. This precept of how we should relate to or treat others is reflected in the traditions of all major world religions:

1. Christianity: "Do unto others as you would have them do unto you."
2. Judaism: "What doth the Lord require of thee: only to do justly, and to love mercy, and to walk humbly with thy God."
3. Islam: "Islam's man gives his substance to kinsmen and orphans, the needy, the traveler, and beggars."
4. Buddhism: "A boundless heart toward all human beings."
5. Hinduism: "The highest yogi judges pleasure or pain everywhere by looking on his neighbor as himself."
6. Confucianism: "Do not do to others what you would not want others to do to you."

Clearly, infusing all these dictums is a sense that members of any faith community should be concerned with serving, at some level, the needs of others. A succinct expression of this is found in the New Testament writings of Paul:

"Each of you should look not only to your own interests, but also to the interests of others" (Philippians 2:4, NIV).

This "service mentality" is present in some form in all three horizontal missional components of religious institutions in cells 3 (create community) and 4 (offer social services) of Exhibit 1. Modern marketing thought, as exemplified by the societal marketing orientation, is also focused on such a "service mentality." As previously mentioned, the societal marketing orientation is fundamentally different from the first three orientations in its external focus—first looking at the needs of others to determine the institution's response. All marketers have been admonished to think of what they offer as providing a service to address a need, rather than as an object to sell.

It is, in fact, this service mentality, or concern with addressing the needs of others, that provides the common ground upon which modern marketing thought and religious institutions stand. Marketers who adopt the societal marketing orientation are vitally interested in understanding the needs of those people the marketer is focused on serving. In fact, it has been said that the entire purpose of marketing is to "find a need and fill it." There is a close affinity between this conceptualization of the goal of marketing and a goal of religious institutions to "find others in need and help them." The difference between these two goals is that marketing is intended to effectuate satisfaction of needs through *mutually beneficial exchange* processes, while religious institutions do not always ostensibly require an exchange of something of value to occur between the person in need and the institution. The institution may engage in a transfer of value to the recipient without expecting something of value in return. However, a close examination of the adherent, fellowship, and social services missional components of religious institutions (i.e., cells 3 and 4 of Exhibit 1) reveals numerous instances where exchanges are the goal of religious institutions:

Exhibit 2.3	Examples of Exchange for a Religious Organization	
Religious Institution Desires:	**◄Exchange►**	**Exchange Partner Desires:**
Membership commitment	Adherent Exchange	One or more of items on Kushner's list
Volunteers for the institution's activities	Fellowshipper Exchange	A sense of contribution to something significant
A contribution to improving someone's quality of life/a Change of someone's behavior	Social Service Exchange	A service performed/a product received

We want to reiterate what we stated in chapter 1: Not all of the interactions between a religious institution and its various publics constitute exchange. Opponents will argue that even those interactions that do involve exchange should not be managed by marketing principles. However, we would argue that an authentic societal marketing orientation is compatible with the charge of religious institutions to be concerned with the needs of others, and to, in some instances, engage others in an exchange of values to address those needs. Those who feel likewise will benefit from acquiring a better understanding of marketing as they seek to serve others more effectively and efficiently. Not only will they be more successful in achieving their exchange goals—they will also foster a greater sense of external focus and a service mentality among all their members.

Step 2: Understand Exchange Partner Needs

A fundamental requirement for those adopting a societal marketing orientation is that they develop an understanding of:

- their exchange partner's needs and wants.
- exchange partner characteristics (geographics, demographics, psychographics, behavioral patterns).
- their exchange partner's sense of value.
- barriers to the exchange.
- "costs" incurred in acquiring the institution's offering.
- what constitutes competition to the institution in the eyes of

exchange partners.

- environmental forces influencing exchange.
- other publics that play a role in influencing the exchange.
- number of potential exchange partners (i.e., "size of market").

Acquiring this understanding does not necessarily involve a major commitment in financial resources, but it does necessitate a commitment to *desire to understand* before acting. As Francis of Assisi said: "O divine Master, grant that I may not so much seek . . . to be understood as to understand." Solomon's wish was also that God would grant him an understanding mind: "Give your servant therefore an understanding mind to govern your people" (1 Kings 3:9, NRSV). We demonstrate our genuine concern for others when we take the time to understand them before we act.

Stephen Covey, in his book *The Seven Habits of Highly Effective People*, describes a personal experience when he failed to first seek understanding before he acted:

"I remember a mini-paradigm shift I experienced one Sunday morning on a subway in New York. People were sitting quietly—some reading newspapers, some lost in thought, some resting with their eyes closed. It was a calm, peaceful scene.

"Then suddenly, a man and his children entered the subway car. The children were so loud and rambunctious that instantly the whole climate changed.

"The man sat down next to me and closed his eyes, apparently oblivious to the situation. The children were yelling back and forth, throwing things, even grabbing people's papers. It was very disturbing. And yet, the man sitting next to me did nothing.

"It was difficult not to feel irritated. I could not believe that he could be so insensitive as to let his children run wild like that and do nothing about it, taking no responsibility at all. It was easy to see that everyone else on the subway felt irritated too. So finally, with what I felt was unusual patience and restraint, I turned to him and said, 'Sir, your children are really disturbing a lot of people. I wonder if you couldn't control them a little more?'

"The man lifted his gaze as if to come to a consciousness of the situation for the first time and said softly, 'Oh, you're right. I guess I should so something about it. We just came from the hospital where their mother died about an hour ago. I don't know what to think, and I guess they don't know how to handle it either.' "

"Can you imagine what I felt at that moment? My paradigm shifted. Suddenly I *saw* things differently, and because I *saw* differently, I *thought* differently, I *felt* differently. I *behaved* differently. My irritation vanished. I didn't have to worry about controlling my attitude or my behavior; my heart was filled with the man's pain. Feelings of sympathy and compassion flowed freely. 'Your wife just died? Oh, I'm so sorry! Can you tell me about it? What can I do to help?' Everything changed in an instant."[3]

One of Covey's seven habits is "Seek First to Understand, Then to Be Understood." It is important to realize that we are not talking about understanding your exchange partners so you can manipulate them to do what you want them to do. That is not the spirit of the societal marketing orientation. *We are seeking to understand because we are committed to serving their needs through mutually beneficial exchange.* They engage in a voluntary exchange of value with us because we have listened to them and made sure that what we offer in exchange with them has real value from their perspective. Failure to acquire such an understanding reveals a lack of concern for their needs, and betrays a philosophy founded on self-interest alone. In other words, we must now "walk the talk"—actually carry out the principles of the societal marketing orientation to be externally focused.

This is the point of the effective marketing process at which it will become clear whether the members of the institution (and we mean *everyone*, not just the leaders) are truly committed to the philosophy espoused by the societal marketing orientation. We have found many (in the for-profit and not-for-profit sectors) who say they are committed to the orientation's axioms will, when push comes to shove, act in ways consistent with a production, product, or selling orientation. It is our goal to educate the readers of this book as to how they can avoid such hypocrisy and actually act according to their convictions to serve the needs of others.

What should be emphasized at this point is that it is very important that the orientation that led to step 2 is the operating philosophy for all members of the organization. The decision rule of "understanding before acting" may be intuitively attractive, but it has been our experience that many who find it intellectually appealing lack the discipline to carry through with its demands. In part 3 of the book we will be sharing with you some cost-effective means for acquiring such an understanding.

Step 3: Plan Marketing Program Strategy

In this step we develop plans based on our understanding of relevant information obtained in step 2. If we have followed "best practice" procedures in developing the understanding we sought in step 2, we have faith in using that understanding to develop our plans. Effective plans are effective precisely because they are based on "if-then" reasoning. "*If* this is what they need, *then* we will offer a ministry with these attributes to satisfy that need." Plans are direct translations of "understanding" into response. However, sometimes (most times?) the "understanding" is subject to multiple interpretations, and it will be up to the leader of the religious organization to help the others on the planning teams to "think like marketers" when performing this translation. A story helps to illustrate what we mean by this.

The story is told about a Hong Kong shoe manufacturer who wonders whether a market exists for his shoes on a remote South Pacific island. He sends an *order taker* to the island, who, upon a cursory examination, wires back: "The people here don't wear shoes. There is no market." Not convinced, the Hong Kong shoe manufacturer sends a *salesman* to the island. This salesman wires back: "The people here don't wear shoes. There is a tremendous market." Afraid that this salesman is being carried away by the sight of so many shoeless feet, the Hong Kong manufacturer sends a third person, this time a *marketer*. This marketing professional interviews the tribal chief and several of the natives, and finally wires back:

> The people here don't wear shoes. However, they have bad feet. I have shown the chief how shoes would help his people avoid foot problems. He is enthusiastic. He estimates that 70 percent of his people will buy the shoes

at the price of $10 a pair. We probably can sell 5,000 pairs of shoes in the first year. Our cost of bringing the shoes to the island and setting up distribution would amount to $6 a pair. We will clear $20,000 in the first year, which, given our investment, will give us a rate of return on our investment (ROI) of 20 percent, which exceeds our normal ROI of 15 percent. This is not to mention the high value of our future earnings by entering this market. I recommend that we go ahead.

Different people can examine the same "facts" and arrive at very different conclusions about their meaning to the organization. The leader must help others to think like marketers as they examine the results of the previous step's development of an understanding, and decide on a plan of action.

Someone said, "If you fail to plan, you are planning to fail." Granted, marketing planning is not much fun. It takes time away from doing. Yet plan we must. The process of planning may be more important than the plans that emerge. The planning occasion requires leaders to schedule "thinking time." Planners must think about what might happen. Planners must set goals and get agreement. The goals must be communicated to everyone. Progress toward the goals must be measured. Corrective actions must be taken when the goals are not being achieved. Thus planning turns out to be an intrinsic part of good administration. We believe religious organizations will benefit from developing marketing plans, and we discuss how they can develop effective marketing plans in part 4 of the book. We are not saying, however, that unless you become an expert marketing planner, you cannot succeed in your goal to achieve mutually beneficial exchanges with your exchange partners. But we do believe that if we can help you to be a better planner, you will definitely reap the benefits from that improvement. Incremental improvements in this task can result in disproportionately large rewards.

Step 4: Design and Implement Marketing Tactics

Several years ago *Harvard Business Review* published an article entitled "Hustle as Strategy," making the point that an organization gains more from having a good plan with great implementation than from a great plan with good implementation. Whether this is empirically true or not is beside the point—good planning must be followed by successful implementation if we are to capitalize on that good plan. If we use the term *strategy* to describe the plan, then *tactics* are the ways we put the plan into action. Frequently religious organizations must rely on the work of volunteers to implement tactical activities specified in the plan. We address issues related to tactical goals in part 5 of the book.

Step 5: Connect With Exchange Partners

If the previous four steps in this process have been successfully completed, the organization will make a "connection" with its exchange partner. This connection might consist of attracting a new member to your church, getting a lapsed member to reestablish involvement with the organization, increasing interest in fellowship activities by current members, getting members to volunteer for delivery of social services to the community, attracting and serving people in need of those services, an increase in resources coming from your exchange partner, and so on. We will examine connecting in greater depth in part 6 of the book.

Step 5 in fact brings us full circle in the process: we began with a *philosophy* (societal marketing orientation) that espoused a commitment to serving others. Our goal was to have a positive impact on the lives of people (our exchange partners), and we made it our goal to *understand* their needs so we could best serve them. We developed, based on that understanding, *plans* for how we could effectively and efficiently accomplish that end, and put those plans into *action*. Our *connection* with them was the culmination of this process. In other words, we lived out our philosophy; we were faithful to our calling. We didn't need to know about marketing to make a positive difference in the lives of others, but knowing about marketing contributed to our accomplishing that goal more effectively and efficiently. That made us better stewards of the resources we'd been given, and increased the scope of our service—both worthy goals.

The EMP model can be used to guide in the development of marketing plans for adherent, fellowship, or social services programs.

Beginning with chapter 3 and continuing through chapter 13, you are able to use the end of chapter worksheets to construct the strategy and tactics that make it possible to achieve your goals for attracting new members to your congregation, engaging current members more fully in congregational ministries, and serving external publics through delivery of social services. The accompanying resource guide provides an extensive list of resources for those desiring to learn more about any aspect of the EMP covered in these chapters.

Before we begin our chapter by chapter walk through the steps of the effective marketing process, we want to elaborate a bit more on how we think you should approach the use of marketing for your organization.

Matching Methods to Markets

As we elaborated upon in chapter 1, we believe it is important that the leaders of religious organizations institute practices appropriate for the Exhibit 1 cell in which they are operating. We've indicated that two groups of people occupy cell 3 (create community) that would be appropriate for the kind of twenty-first-century marketing that we've proposed in this chapter—Adherent and Fellowship marketing. To reiterate, adherents are those who belong to the larger community of faith (i.e., Judaism's *qahal* or *edah,* Islam's *ummah,* and Christianity's *ekklesia*), while fellowshippers are those who belong to the local congregation. Exhibit 2.4 portrays how these might be envisioned:

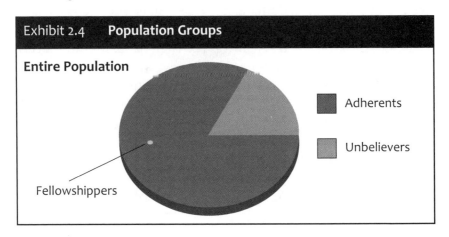

Exhibit 2.4   **Population Groups**

Entire Population

Adherents

Unbelievers

Fellowshippers

We have made it clear that we believe that any religious organization that, as part of their mission, seeks to target unbelievers (18 percent of the population in Exhibit 2.4) for conversion (i.e., achieve missional goals related to cell 2's evangelism) should not see that goal as a task for marketing to achieve. Certainly those organizations that seek those ends will want to use effective communication methods and harness technology to help accomplish their goals, but that does not mean that they are "doing marketing." Authentic marketing means you have implemented a true marketing or societal marketing orientation as a means of achieving mutually beneficial exchange. This means you have been willing to adjust what you are offering to fit your understanding of your exchange partner's needs, and that approach is incompatible with cell 1's worship and cell 2's evangelism activities (e.g., you don't alter your doctrine to fit your audience's needs). So if marketing is not helpful in guiding efforts expended in cells 1 and 2, is there enough "market potential" in cells 3 (create community) and 4 (offer social services) to make it worth your while to learn how to put the effective marketing process model into practice?

There are many religious organizations that would flourish if they did nothing but improve customer retention, what we call fellowship marketing, getting current members to become more active in the organization. Others could grow strong through adherent marketing—getting people who belong to the larger community of faith to join your specific organization.

Focusing on just the adherent and fellowship groups for the moment, there appears to be a huge opportunity for congregations to benefit from the use of marketing with these groups. See Exhibit 2.5 for some statistics, mentioned in chapter 1, indicating the "size of the market" for adherent marketing.

A Pew Forum survey of 35,000 adult Americans released in February 2008 contributed further insight into the status of religion in America. Among the findings:

• Of the 16.1 percent polled who say they are not affiliated with any faith, only 4 percent are self-described atheists or agnostics. The remaining 12 percent are equally divided between "secular unaffili-

Exhibit 2.5	Religious Practice Among Americans	
		Percentage of Adults
Those who believe in God		82[1]
Those who identify with a religious group		81[2]
Those who say religion is very or somewhat important in their daily life		86[3]
Those who say religion is extremely or very important in their daily life		59[4]
Those who live in a household in which one or more people belong to a house of worship (church, synagogue, etc.)		54[2]
Those who attend religious service at least once a month or more		36[5]
Those who attend religious services "regularly"		18[6]

---

[1] Harris interactive poll (http://www.harrisinteractive.com/harris_poll/index.asp?PID=618).

[2] American religious identification survey (http://www.gc.cuny.edu/faculty/research_briefs/aris/key_findings.htm).

[3] AP_IPsos poll, June 5, 2005 (http://www.ipsos-na.com/news/pressrelease.cfm?id=2694).

[4] PollingReport.com (pollingreport.com/religion.html).

[5] Harris interactive poll (http://www.harrisinteractive.com/harris_poll/index.asp?PID= 408).

[6] "Special Report: The American Church in Crisis," *Outreach*, May/June 2006, p. 2.

ated" (religion isn't important to them) and the "religious unaffiliated" (religion is at least somewhat important to them).

• Catholics are the religious group with the greatest loss of adherents (23 million have left the Catholic Church). A total of 28 percent of Americans have left the faith of their childhood for another faith, or have not joined another faith. Including changes from one form of Protestantism to another, 44 percent of Americans have changed their faith or dropped their connection to a faith.

• While 62 percent of Americans older than 70 are Protestant, only 43 percent of those aged 18-29 are. Protestants currently comprise 51 percent of the total U.S. adult population.

• Thirty-seven percent of marriages involve couples with different religious affiliation.[4]

Research published in March 2008 by the Barna Group has identified five groups of people participating in faith communities:

• Unattached—people who had attended neither a conventional church nor an organic faith community (home church, etc.) during the past year: 23 percent.

• Intermittents—adults who are "underchurched," people who have participated in either conventional or organic church in the past year but not during the past month: 15 percent.

• Homebodies—people who in the past month attended a home church but not a conventional church: 3 percent.

• Blenders—people who have attended both a conventional and home church in the past month: 3 percent.

• Conventionals—people who attended a conventional church but not a home church in the past month: 56 percent.[5]

Based strictly on the size of the "market opportunity," it is obvious that there is a larger market of people who already belong to the larger community (i.e., the adherent and fellowship categories in cell 3) than who don't believe in God or who don't think of religion as important in their life. In marketing parlance there is considerable market demand, but only a modest amount of brand-specific demand, and considerable brand switching among those who are adherents. The opportunity to engage in exchange with these groups is also obvious when one considers the much lower incidence of *active participation* of adherents in attending religious services (the 18 to 36 percent numbers in Exhibit 2.5). Clergy confirm the accuracy of these numbers when they maintain that only 40-60 percent of their members are "active" (and we're sure that some readers will be saying, "I'd *love* to have that level of participation by members on our books!"). The point is made—adherent and fellowship market opportunities are real and significant.

It is our belief that successful implementation of the Effective Marketing Process (EMP) model can be of help to those religious organizations seeking to capitalize on these "market opportunities."

But the model is about more than just achieving growth goals; it is about connecting in meaningful ways with all exchange partners. Fellowship marketing goals include energizing current congregants to become more engaged in the life of the organization. As demonstrated in this chapter, we believe that "marketing oriented" congregations will evidence a heightened service mentality and concern for others' needs.

The supplement to chapter 2 provides an example of how the effective marketing process model could be implemented to better serve the needs of congregants. Then in chapter 3 we extend the discussion of step 1 of the model (adopting a philosophy) by discussing how religious organizations can increase their "responsiveness" to their fellow congregants' needs.

---

[1] R. D. Putnam, *Bowling Alone* (New York: Touchstone: Simon & Schuster, Inc., 2000), p. 66.

[2] Harold Kushner, *Who Needs God?* (New York: Summit Books, 1989).

[3] Stephen Covey, *The Seven Habits of Highly Effective People* (New York: Fireside, 1989), pp. 30-33.

[4] http://pewforum.org/news/rss.php?NewsID=15041.

[5] http://www.barna.org/FlexPage.aspx?Page=BarnaUpdateNarrowPreview&BarnaUpdateID=293.

WORKSHEETS: CHAPTER 2

What Type of Approach Does Your Organization Have?

1. Which of the following approaches does your organization take to its ministry?

Product/Production Approach

Do you: Yes   No

1. Believe that the ministry's environment has not changed over the years?   _____ _____

2. Continue to "produce" the ministry year after year with no changes?   _____ _____

3. Have more devotion to the ministry "product" itself than in achieving the desired results of the ministry's "consumption" by its intended "market"?   _____ _____

Selling Approach

Do you: Yes   No

1. Focus primarily on your objectives for a ministry instead of the "market's" needs?   _____ _____

2. Stress the need to be "persuasive" in getting your ministry's target audience to do what you want them to?   _____ _____

3. Believe your objectives have been achieved solely based on your success in getting the desired number of people to "consume" your ministry?   _____ _____

Marketing Approach/Societal Marketing Approach

Do you: Yes   No

1. Believe that ministries sometimes must be adjusted to fit a changing environment?   _____   _____

2. Make an effort to understand the needs and desires of your target audience?   _____   _____

3. Take those needs and desires into consideration when developing the ministry and its implementation plan?   _____   _____

Your approach currently consists of the one with the most Yes checks. If you have Yes checks spread across more than one approach, don't be concerned. Many commercial businesses don't have a pure approach either. However, in the for-profit sector of the economy it has been a consistent finding of research studies that a thoroughgoing marketing orientation leads to greater success than the other two approaches. It is our intent in the remainder of this book to help you learn how to put into practice as much of a marketing orientation approach to your ministry(ies) as you are comfortable in adopting.

2. List those beliefs, church mission statement passages, or objectives for those programs/ministries you described in number 4 of the chapter 1 Worksheet that are compatible with the societal marketing orientation's principles.

Adherent Marketing

_____

_____

_____

Fellowship Marketing

_____

_____

_____

Social Services Marketing

_____

_____

_____

In the chapters that follow we will describe how you can use the effective Marketing Process to market successfully the programs/ministries whose objectives are compatible with the SMO.

An Application of the Effective Marketing Process Model:
STARTING A GRIEF MINISTRY

Background

The wife of one of the authors (we'll call her Kate, not her real name) is a licensed social worker who worked in family counseling for years before becoming a member of the social work department faculty at a small private college. She is an active member of a congregation of 3,000 in the Midwest. In 2006 she began discussions with leaders of the congregation regarding the initiation of a grief counseling ministry for congregants in need of that service. What follows is how the effective marketing process might be used to guide the development of this ministry.

Step 1: Adopt a Philosophy

Adopting a societal marketing orientation (and becoming fully responsive, as we'll see in chapter 3) means that you are vitally concerned with achieving organizational goals by serving the needs of your targeted exchange partners (i.e., consummating mutually beneficial exchange). Sometimes the impetus for development of an offering capable of satisfying those needs comes as requests from the market, and sometimes it is initiated by the organization as an idea for a new offering. In either case, the orientation dictates that the organization's philosophy is to meet needs, rather than to try to persuade the market to "buy" something the organization wanted to "produce." If there is market justification for the organization's offering, then certainly the organization will want to be efficient in the production of the offering, make sure the offering is of appropriate quality, and appropriately stimulate interest in the offering by effectively communicating the offering's benefits (see Exhibit 2.2), but the dominant philosophy is to let marketplace needs have a voice in determining the characteristics of the offering.

This congregation's corporate mission statement reads "Forward on Our Knees: Readying Our Lives, Reflecting His Love, Reaching Our World"—a statement that professes concern for those in need. In the grief ministry case, there had been numerous requests by friends of bereaved members for counseling help. Also, Kate teaches a course in grief counseling in the social work department, so she was sensitive to the fact that some grieving people would not make an overt request for development of the ministry, but would take advantage of such a service if offered. So a societal marketing orientation (SMO), on the part of church leaders as expressed in the mission, is a natural companion to a social worker's ethic to be concerned with serving the needs of others, and talks began on the formation of the ministry.

Step 2: Develop an Understanding

It is totally inconsistent to claim you have a SMO, but then give no thought to your exchange partners when developing offerings intended to address their needs. This does not mean that you have to expend a large amount of organizational resources on expensive and extensive market research studies intended to study the market. Nor will it always be the case that the exchange partners will be able or willing to articulate their needs. In fact, the needs might be latent, and therefore not easily identifiable. People weren't sending e-mails to Steve Jobs saying, "When are you going to invent the iPod, Steve?" before Apple came out with that product, yet it has definitely addressed a real market need. Developing an understanding of your market can be an elusive goal, but the failure rate for new products in the commercial field bears eloquent testimony of its value to product success.

In our grief ministry situation, Kate could draw on her own understanding of the well-documented needs of those grieving loss, coupled with some exploratory research to determine how the ministry could best meet the needs of the congregation. Unscripted (i.e., "in-depth"; see chapter 4) interviews with the pastors who primarily call on recently bereaved members, members who experienced a past loss who could provide insights on how they might have been best served by such a ministry, and leaders of those sister congregations that have successfully instituted grief ministry programs, would help provide the kind of *understanding* desired in this case. After drafting the outlines of this program based on these inputs, it would be possible to get more specific reactions to program content, location, and timing of counseling sessions, desire for individual versus group meetings, etc., by surveying members via a short online questionnaire sent from the church office to the Listserv of church members. The net result of these efforts to *understand* is a much better feel for how the program can be formulated to address the needs of the congregation. Chapter 5's discussion of why people behave as they do helps us to know what we need to *understand* about our exchange partners.

Step 3: Plan Marketing Strategy

At this point you are now ready to put the understanding you gained in the previous step to good use in developing your marketing program. We will take three chapters (chapters 6, 7, and 8) to discuss what goes into marketing planning, but for now the heart of a plan is a strategy (where do you want to go?). In the grief ministry case, step 2's research should provide the information needed to know the parameters of the program's strategy: Do we need separate sessions for both adults and children? If so, how does the program content vary for those groups? Is there a need for special groups grieving the loss of pets? other losses, such as job loss, friendship, etc.? By what means to we become aware of and invite people to use the service? Do we need to train people to be grief counselors, or can Kate do all the counseling herself? A strategy should be formulated to indicate exactly who the exchange partners are and how the service will be able to deliver satisfaction of their needs as we've come to understand them from Step 2.

Step 4: Design and Implement Tactics

Tactics (How do we get there?) specified in the plan must be implemented. These are commonly referred to as the marketing mix, or the four P's of marketing: product, place, price, and promotion. Chapters 9, 10, and 11 are dedicated to these and other Implementation topics.

Product issues would include how the grief recovery sessions will be structured, how long each session will last, how many sessions will be in a series, what materials will be used, follow-up after the series are completed, etc. *Place* decisions are concerned with the location of the sessions, use of electronic methods (e-mail, Web sites, blogs, etc.), and other issues related to contact between Kate and the participants. *Price* concerns what participants must give up to obtain the help they are seeking. As we'll cover in chapter 6, these "costs" may include giving up resources (economic, time, energy), preconceived ideas, and/or previous patterns of behavior.

With regard to promotion, it would be important to design attractive, descriptive material to inform people of the new program. The print material should be placed with the other literature the church uses to describe the ministries that serve the needs of the congregation. The design of the materials should conform to an overall design theme that communicates the message that everything with this graphic design is a program intended to serve some need of members. Effective use of graphics, color, format, etc., should convey the intended message that serving the mental, physical, emotional, and spiritual health of the congregation is a high priority. The logo, words, graphics, and design of this material should reflect the depth of understanding of the target audience that was gained from the research conducted in step 2. Refinements to the various tactical components of the marketing mix would be made as the grief ministry gets up and running. The church's Web site would be designed with easy navigation to provide links to the grief ministry site as well as to the other ministry sites of the church.

Step 5: Connect With Exchange Partners

If the previous four steps of the effective marketing process have been successfully implemented, there will be a true connection with the target audience of the grief ministry program—the people who were hurting will have been ministered to. There will be no doubt that the program was designed with their needs as the focal point of all the caregivers. But Kate will not take it for granted that the program has achieved the goals set for it. She will determine the effectiveness of the ministry by collecting evaluative feedback. Both qualitative and quantitative feedback will be collected and analyzed to determine where and how to improve delivery of the ministry. Kate will be sure to join online discussion groups with people at other organizations involved in providing grief counseling. She will constantly be on the alert for ways to connect better with the people who she serves, because she is genuinely committed to the orientation that began (step 1) the process resulting in grieving people being helped. Chapters 12 and 13 discuss *connecting* related topics.

Extending the Ministry to Cell 4: Social Services Marketing

The grief ministry story described here might not end with connecting to congregation members. Kate might pursue opportunities to "reach our world" by assessing the interest of other local religious congregations in serving their members through this ministry. Holding grief groups at their sites or public facilities would be a natural extension of taking this cell 3 *Fellowship* activity into a cell 4 *Create Social Services*. Partnering with other public or private like-minded groups, or training others to serve as grief counselors, might be ways to synergistically extend connections with other grieving populations. The effective marketing process could be used to guide these cell 4 efforts.[1]

In the chapters that follow we will systematically examine how marketing thought and practice can provide the leaders of religious organizations with the means to connect with their exchange partners. Each chapter will also end with a set of worksheets to guide in carrying out the marketing tasks described in the chapter. Marketing resources for religious marketers are provided in the resource guide. Let's get started!

---

[1] For more information on the marketing of social services, see Philip Kotler and Nancy Lee, *Social marketing: Influencing Behaviors for Good* (Thousand Oaks, Calif.: Sage Publications, 2006).

Adopt a Marketing Philosophy

Part 2:

THE EFFECTIVE MARKETING PROCESS

Adopting a Marketing Philosophy
CHAPTER 3 *Serving People Effectively: The Responsive Congregation*

↓

Develop an Understanding

↓

Plan the Marketing Strategy

↓

Design and Implement the Marketing Tactics

↓

Connect With Exchange Partners

If this were the first page someone were to read in this book, they very well might take umbrage at the idea that we are trying to foist a "marketing philosophy" in a place where it "didn't belong." Of course, we are hoping this is not true of you, dear reader, because you have read chapters 1 and 2, and continue to at least be intrigued enough to continue reading at this point. We also hope that if, perchance, you have not yet been fully persuaded that a "marketing philosophy" has merit as a mind-set to adopt when managing exchanges, at least you continue to be open to this idea.

In chapter 3 we expand on the idea introduced in chapter 2, that adopting a societal marketing organization will naturally lead you toward the goal of becoming a "fully responsive congregation," and, as Martha Stewart would say, that is "a good thing."

In the for-profit world there is clear and convincing evidence that the more marketing oriented an organization, the greater its sales, profits and market share.* More important for the readers of this book, there also is a significant correlation with being marketing-oriented and:

- having employees who are more committed to their organization,
- having increased "team spirit,"
- having a customer orientation,
- having higher job satisfaction, and
- having reduced role conflict.

So being marketing-oriented leads to better organizational performance and to more satisfied, highly committed employees, with fewer conflicts over their roles in the organization.

More important for the readers of this book, there is some empirical evidence that having a market orientation is "correlated with improved church performance" with respect to increased numbers of visitors to church services. Apparently, adopting the marketing orientation's "service mentality" has positive consequences for one's sense of well-being—being nice to people and serving their needs makes you feel better about yourself and your organization, and the organization thrives. Serving others is not only a high calling for your organization—it is also a powerful strategy! Of course, these results are for for-profit businesses, but they are grounded in how we as humans (e.g., customers and employees in these studies) positively react to being responsive to the needs of others. It isn't too much of a stretch to believe that this phenomenon holds true for your organization, too; maybe even more so. Let's see how all these "good things" can come to pass.

---

* Ahmet H. Kirca, Setish Jayachandran and William O. Bearden, "Marketing Orientation: A Meta-Analytic Review and Assessment of Its Antecedents and Impact on Performance," *Journal of Marketing,* April 2005, pp. 24-41.

CHAPTER 3:

Serving People Effectively:
THE RESPONSIVE CONGREGATION

"Show mercy and compassion to one another"
(ZECHARIAH 7:9, NIV).

In this chapter we will address the following questions:

1. What characterizes the unresponsive congregation?

2. What characterizes the casually responsive congregation?

3. What characterizes the highly responsive congregation?

4. What characterizes the fully responsive congregation?

The cover story of the March 5, 2007, issue of *Business Week* was entitled "Customer Service Champs."[1] On the cover was a ranking of the four best customer service organizations. Number 4, JetBlue, was "scratched through" and replaced with a new number 4, Nordstrom. Herein lies an object lesson of value to your organization. First, some words of wisdom from the article.

With cheap and powerful technology available to corporations of all sizes, organizations are turning to their people to provide a competitive advantage through responsive customer service. Here are some of the "best practice ideas" from the article that illustrate how people are the real difference makers for these organizations:

1. Emphasize loyalty to workers. The customer service leaders realize that if you expect employees to go to heroic lengths to serve the organization's customers, the employees must believe that they work for an organization that cares about the employees' welfare and values them as persons. *Do your workers and members feel valued and appreciated? How do you know? What can you do to make them feel so?*

2. Establish customer empathy. The best service firms find ways to help their employees "feel" what it is like to be a customer. For example, *Business Week's* number-one customer service firm, USAA insurance agency, serving military families, makes sure its employees can relate to its customers:

"It was Stevie Salinas' second day of new-hire orientation when retired Lt. Col. David Sheets appeared in the doorway. 'Atten-hut!' he commanded, bringing the room of 50 new employees to their feet. Surprised, the 23-year-old single mom watched as Sheets handed out manila envelopes. Inside was a deployment letter identical to that received by the military. 'Report to the personnel processing facility,' the letter began, demanding recipients depart the next day. . . . Earlier the same day, the five-foot-tall Salinas had strapped on a . . . backpack and flak vest. She'd eaten a 'meal ready to eat,' or MRE, the grub soldiers eat in the field. She had even read real letters from troops in Iraq. Hers was from a soldier who later died in the war and was addressed to his mother. 'We were in tears,' says Salinas.

"Many companies give lip service to listening to the 'voice of the customer.' At USAA that voice is transformed into what it calls 'surround sound'—a comprehensive approach to training its employees to empathize with its customers' unique needs. 'We try to develop empathy, not only for our members but also for the family side,'" says Elizabeth Conklyn, executive vice president for people services.[2]

How can you help your congregants feel what it is like for someone to come to your worship service or to your facility for the first time to receive a social service you offer to the community?

3. Adopt tools to your needs. Corporations are warned against adopting off-the-shelf customer service methods and tools without adapting them to fit their personnel and unique circumstances.

How can you adapt the tools discussed in this chapter to fit your particular needs? Who in your organization is best suited to helping you make that adaptation?

4. Assign someone to oversee the operation. As was stated in *Business Week*: "Putting customers first requires collaboration in everything from marketing to operations to human resources and may require someone whose day-to-day job is to coordinate the effort."

While this idea is a bit much to expect of your organization, the idea of asking someone with a thoroughgoing service mentality to oversee your efforts to become a more responsive institution is worth considering. Can you identify such a person in your congregation?

5. Involve at the very top. All the best customer service organizations have the complete and enthusiastic commitment of top management to delivering excellent customer service.

What do you need to do to have your key leadership team become committed to your becoming a fully responsive organization?

Now, back to our object lesson. On Valentine's Day 2007 a devastating ice storm hit New York's JFK airport, home base for JetBlue, the corporation that pledged to "bring humanity back to air travel." Passengers were stuck on planes that sat on the runway for up to 10.5 hours, thousands of flights were canceled over the next six days, and operations had a nearly complete "meltdown." During the weeks following, CEO David Neeleman made numerous appearances on national TV making *mea culpas* and vowing to institute contingency planning and other changes to information systems that track crew locations, improve JetBlue's Web site to permit online rebookings, and train nonoperations personnel how to help out in a crisis. JetBlue has also created a "customer bill of rights" with a service guarantee to try to assuage the host of angry passengers—all commendable recovery measures. However, as *Business Week* stated, "What matters most is execution—doing the deep, hard, organizational work to ensure the crisis never happens again. While JetBlue recognizes that fact, it still has plenty to prove."[3] It is entirely possible that JetBlue will regain its place among the outstanding customer service firms on *Business Week*'s list. (In the March 2, 2009, issue of *Business Week*, JetBlue ranked nineteenth on the list of customer service champs.) In the meantime, what we can all learn from their experience is that a commitment to responsiveness cannot be merely empty platitudes. You must be willing to do the hard work to make the organization really perform in ways consistent with that philosophy.

Businesses provide good customer service to gain a competitive advantage—"killing [competitors] with kindness [to customers]," so to speak. You care about being responsive because you realize that, as chapter 2 described, kind service is in your spiritual DNA ("serve one another in love" [Gal. 5:13, NIV]. We know you want to do it (you can't help being true to your calling), but you need some help in knowing how to institutionalize a natural trait.

We begin our discussion of how to become a more responsive organization—an organization embodying the precepts of the societal marketing orientation—by first providing an example of what that type of organization looks like.

There is a congregation in Brooklyn, New York, that is a sterling example of a responsive congregation whose responsiveness led the founders to a very different approach from that used by many congregations under similar circumstances.

First-generation Norwegian immigrants to this nation's eastern shores founded the church. All services were conducted in the Norwegian language. The congregation flourished, and a beautiful church building was constructed to house the congregation. However, by the second and third generation many of the children could no longer speak Norwegian. The older members were now confronted with a tough decision—whether to force their children and grandchildren to attend Norwegian worship services and classes and to risk losing them altogether, or to discontinue Norwegian services and thereby constrict the older generations to English services in a language they could not understand.

Their response was to build another edifice identical to the first and to connect the two by a common entrance and foyer. In the old building Norwegian would remain the spoken language. The new building would house English-speaking services and programs. Thus, everyone would enter the church through a common entry, but once inside, one would have a choice of language.

Time passed, and with it the older Norwegian-speaking congregation. Changes were also coming to the community. Now, instead of being an entirely English-speaking populace, there were a great many residents whose native language was Spanish.

The English-speaking congregation decided to launch a Hispanic congregation in the building that had previously served the Norwegian-speaking congregation. The Hispanic congregation flourished. Later persons from India moved into the area and were welcomed to use the facilities.

Today Hispanics, Anglos, and Indians enter by the same door and, once inside, have their choice of services. By this means the congregation has continued to renew itself in response to the needs and interests of its community.

Perhaps none of the founders of the Norwegian congregation ever took a course or read a book on marketing. However, they were market-oriented in the best sense of the word. They were responsive to environmental shifts, and were willing to translate their ministry through the new opportunities that the changes in their community offered.

The people who encounter these responsive congregations report high personal satisfaction. "This is the best church I ever belonged to." "This synagogue really cares about people." "This church enriches the spiritual life of all its members." These recipients (consumers) of the congregation's ministry become the best advertisement for that church or synagogue. Their goodwill and the favorable word-of-mouth recommendations reach other ears and make it easy for the congregation to attract and serve more people. The congregation is effective because it is responsive.

A responsive congregation makes every effort to sense, serve, and satisfy the needs and interests of the groups it has targeted to serve within the constraints of the congregation's resources.

There is an ambiance surrounding a responsive congregation that is unmistakable. These congregations have managed to imbue their paid and volunteer workers with a spirit of service to members and strangers alike. Ushers, custodians, and secretaries go out of their way to answer questions, smile, and be helpful. The ministry teams and lay boards continuously ask persons what they think of worship services, church school, music, outside and indoor signs, bulletins, attitude of custodians, office staff, etc. Based on the responses they receive, the leaders constantly work to improve the overall experience that members and strangers feel when they are in contact with the congregation, its buildings, staff, and ministries.

Levels of Congregational Responsiveness

Congregations fall into one of four levels of responsiveness: the unresponsive, the casually responsive, the highly responsive, and the fully responsive congregation, as shown in Exhibit 3 below.

Exhibit 3	Four Levels of Consumer-Response Organizations			
	Unresponsive	Casually Responsive	Highly Responsive	Fully Responsive
Complaint system	no	yes	yes	yes
Surveys of satisfaction	no	yes	yes	yes
Surveys of needs and preferences	no	no	yes	yes
"Customer-oriented"				
Empowered members	no	no	no	yes

The Unresponsive Congregation

An unresponsive congregation is at one extreme. Its main characteristics are: (1) it does not encourage inquiries, complaints, suggestions, or opinions from its members or participants; (2) it does not measure current member or participant satisfaction or needs; (3) it does not train its staff to be member- or participant-minded.

The unresponsive organization typically characterizes a bureaucratic mentality. Bureaucracy is the tendency of organizations to make their operations routine, to replace personal judgment with impersonal policies, to specialize the job of every employee, to create a rigid hierarchy of command, and to convert the organization into an efficient machine.[4]

Bureaucrats are not concerned with innovation; they are not concerned with problems outside their specific authority, nor do they care about human responses and needs. They will serve people as long as the people's problems fall within their jurisdiction. Those problems are defined in terms of how the bureaucratic organization is already set up; bureaucrats don't structure the organization to respond to people's problems. Questions of structure dominate questions of substance, and means dominate ends.

Congregations Intentionally Acting Unresponsive. The extreme types of unresponsive congregations are those that intentionally decide to become unresponsive to the publics they claim to want to serve. Here is an example:

A congregation in a community of about 100,000 people had a membership of 1,700 in 1964. By 1984 the membership had declined to slightly more than 1,000. The congregation is located in the downtown area, which for a short time was the scene of racial unrest in the 1960s. No racial disturbances have occurred since that time. Relationships between the White and Black communities are quite satisfactory.

At the time of the racial unrest in the 1960s, electronic locks were installed on all the church doors, and mirrors were placed so that anyone standing at the only door providing access during weekday office hours could be observed by the office staff before a buzzer in the office unlocked the door. During this time the entire residential area surrounding the church migrated from White to Black.

By the 1980s myths and fears had grown around the dangers of admitting a Black person into the building. Yet the congregation declared that a part of its missional understanding was to reach the community surrounding the downtown area. Members would at times lament the unresponsiveness of the Black community to its programs.

The Connected Congregation

African-Americans with Internet access are much more likely than Caucasians to seek religious information online (www.pewinternet.org).

85

Unresponsive congregations tend to be unresponsive in all their relations. Selective unresponsiveness is hardly possible. Along the way, the church decided not only to be unresponsive to its community, but also to ignore the members of the congregation.

The once-beautiful chapel, adjacent to the sanctuary, was now combination storage and meeting room. Upon entering the office, the visitor was confronted with a four-foot-high Plexiglas window, which separated the visitor from the workers cloistered behind it. Anyone entering the office had to lean over the barrier to converse with a secretary. The wall paneling on the office walls hung loose; there was no chair to sit in while waiting to see a pastor or office worker. A visitor could sit in the church parlor, but it was not heated throughout the winter months.

The offset printer was located in the office area and when it was running, conversation was nearly impossible. The printer sputtered, so that ink besmeared the office carpet. The worship bulletins and monthly newspaper coming off the aged press looked like the office floor, and the curtains in the Sunday school rooms were rotting.

The ushers sat in the parlor drinking coffee during worship services, or stood in the back of the sanctuary, visiting so loudly that people sitting near them complained that they were distracted from the worship experience.

The congregation employed a financial secretary; nonetheless, the members' quarterly statements of giving were often late and consistently inaccurate.

The outdoor signage, lawns and garden were unattended, and there were no interior signs pointing the way to the church offices or rest rooms.

This example demonstrates that when a congregation is unresponsive, it tends to be unresponsive all over. Unresponsiveness is migratory—it creeps into every nook and cranny of the organization. Malcolm Gladwell, in his book *The Tipping Point,*[5] observed that this kind of creeping neglect characterizes neighborhoods that can quickly reach a "tipping point" in a deteriorating slide of decay. The same is true of organizational unresponsiveness. By being unresponsive to the outside community, the leaders set in motion attitudes that move the entire organization toward being unresponsive to the needs and interests of its own members. Whether to be responsive is among the most crucial missional decisions a religious organization will ever make.

An unresponsive organization assumes that it knows what its publics need, or that their needs do not matter. It sees no reason it should consult with those it is attempting to serve. Unfortunately, many congregations fit this description. The leaders assume they know what the members and participants need—or they don't care.

Such an unresponsive congregation brings about a host of undesirable consequences. The programs and ministries are usually poorly done or irrelevant. Members and participants grow frustrated and dissatisfied. Their dissatisfaction leads to conflict, withdrawal, apathy, and decline, and may ultimately doom the congregation to ruin.

There are varying degrees of unresponsiveness within congregations. The example above portrays the most extreme. Unresponsive organizations are grouped into two types: those preferring to concentrate on other things, and those lacking the resources to be responsive.

Congregations Preferring to Concentrate on Other Things.

One type of an unresponsive congregation prefers to concentrate on things rather than on member or nonmember satisfaction.

In a Midwest congregation of about 1,500 members all weddings and social functions are scheduled with the custodian (weddings at least six months in advance) before being scheduled with the pastor or church office. In the church the pastor and members were to bend their schedules to fit the custodian's calendar. Once the custodian had scheduled a wedding, the pastor was to do whatever necessary to accommodate that schedule, since the custodian, having once set a date for the wedding, would refuse to offer another.

This church was unresponsive to its staff, its members, and others who wished to make use of the church's services. No decision was ever made to become responsive. Rather, wanting peace at all costs, the congregation drifted into a situation in which the janitor ran the show, and no one challenged his demands.

The Connected Congregation

A search on Google in 2009 using the key words "church" and "web-sites" received 16 million hits, including the following services available for congregations:

How to design a church Web site

Effective church Web pages

Church Web site hosting

Church Web site templates

A search using "synagogue" and "websites" generated 1.21 million hits.

Congregations Lacking the Will or the Resources to Be Responsive

Another type of an unresponsive congregation is one that would like to be more responsive, but lacks the will or the resources to motivate paid and volunteer staff to higher standards of responsiveness. Alternatively, they see so much human need and opportunities that they become paralyzed. They do not know where to begin, or they lack the resources to meet all the human needs they see surrounding them. We visited with the pastor of a congregation located in one of America's largest cities. The church building is strategically located and unique.

The pastor sees much opportunity, but meanwhile the congregation is declining. During our visit he said, "To the east of us is a large area of expensive high-rise condominiums with about 15,000 affluent executive-type people living there. To the north is a growing community of more than 30,000 yuppies. West of us is a complex of about 15,000 lower-income workers; and south of us, there are thousands of poor and affluent people mixed together."

We asked the pastor whether he had any plans to alleviate the situation. With worry etched into his brow, he said, "I think I'll start a ministry for the homeless." This was a successful ministry for him in a former parish. When we asked how a homeless ministry might be an apt response to the opportunities that were overwhelming him, it became apparent that he could think only of retreating to the comfort zone of a former successful ministry that he thought he could do again.

When resources are meager or opportunities are overwhelming, the responsive church must segment its possibilities, and target the groups to whom it will seek to minister. No matter how meager the resources, any congregation can serve the needs of at least one outside group, while also meeting its own member needs.

The Casually Responsive Congregation

The casually responsive congregation differs from unresponsive congregations in two ways: (1) it encourages members and others to submit inquiries, complaints, suggestions, and opinions; (2) it undertakes periodic studies of members' and participants' satisfaction.

Often, but not always, casually responsive congregations are unresponsive to "the handwriting on the wall." Other casually responsive congregations simply reflect the results of a former highly responsive institution that is now drifting into indifference.

As many seminaries began to experience a decline in student applications, they began to pay more attention to their students and publics. Administrators who once were oriented toward problems of hiring faculty, scheduling classes, and running efficient administrative services—the earmarks of the bureaucratic mentality—now began to listen more to the students. They left their doors open, made occasional surprise appearances in the student lounge, encouraged suggestions from students, created student life committees, and began to elect a student or two to the board of trustees. These steps moved the seminaries toward being casually responsive. The result was to create a greater sense of satisfaction among the students (and, sometimes, among faculty and donors).

This is a first step in building a partnership between the served and the serving. Whether the increased sense of satisfaction continues depends upon whether a seminary merely makes a show of listening or actually undertakes to do something about what it hears. It may merely offer a semblance of openness and interest without intending to use the results in any way. If so, eventually it will become apparent to the students that this is a public relations ploy. This leads to an even greater strain than previously existed. The students now have higher expectations than when the seminary was completely unresponsive. If their voices are ignored, the students resent the school and its leaders—and may very well try to force the school into greater responsiveness.

What has been said regarding seminaries can also be said about many religious organizations.

The Highly Responsive Congregation

A highly responsive congregation differs from a casually responsive congregation in two different ways:

1. It not only surveys the current members for participant satisfaction; it also assesses their unmet needs and preferences, to discover ways to improve its services to the congregation and the community at large.

2. The highly responsive congregation selects and trains its paid and volunteer workers to view the members, participants, and strangers as the raison d'être of their work.

Many religious organizations fall short of being highly responsive. Churches and synagogues rarely take formal surveys of their members and participants' real needs and desires, nor do they sensitize and train their paid and volunteer workers to be member- or participant-minded.

Recently a small liberal arts college recognized this failing and developed a philosophy to guide its faculty and staff. The philosophy states that the students are:

• The most important people on the campus; without them there would be no need for the institution.

• Not cold enrollment statistics, but flesh-and-blood human beings with feelings and emotions like our own.

• Not dependent on us; rather, we are dependent on them.

• Not an interruption of our work, but the purpose of it; we are not doing them a favor by serving them—they are doing us a favor by giving us the opportunity to do so.

If this attitude could be successfully implanted in the paid and volunteer staffs, and in the volunteer administrative committees of a congregation, it would move a long way toward being highly responsive.

Earlier we gave an example of an unresponsive congregation. Happily, the story of this church does not end here.

In 1984 the congregation decided to become responsive to its community. The locks, buzzers, and mirrors were removed to allow its members and visitors ready access to the building during office hours, and during the hours of public services.

Within a few months an African-American congregation requested space in which to conduct its worship services and Sunday school program. The request was granted.

A short while later a predominantly Black Girl Scout troop was invited to utilize the congregation's facilities for its meetings. Three years later the congregation received an African-American pastor onto its ministry team.

Within a few weeks of the congregation's decision to become more responsive to its neighbors, the members began to notice how totally uninviting the main office was, whereupon two members approached the trustees with a blank check to pay for remodeling the area. Even as the remodeling was proceeding, another member asked the trustees to restore the chapel area to its original condition. This request was accompanied by a blank check for the costs of the restoration. Less than two years later the congregation launched a restoration of the entire building, with specific instructions to the trustees and architect to pay attention to the needs of those with physical disabilities who might enter upon the church grounds and use the church's facilities.

Even as unresponsiveness tends to permeate an entire institution, so does the decision to become a responsive entity. The first step toward responsiveness attracts attention, and inspires many people to sense the need for change in other areas of the organization. "Tipping points" can occur in positive ways too; it just requires a group of people committed to making a positive difference.

The Fully Responsive Congregation

The highly responsive congregation is free to accept or reject complaints and suggestions from its members and participants based upon what it thinks is important and what it is willing to do. A fully responsive congregation, however, moves beyond being highly responsive to overcome any sense of the "we-they" mentality that lingers in the highly responsive congregation. The fully responsive church or synagogue blurs the "we-they" distinction by accepting whomever it serves as equals with its members.

Among examples of fully responsive organizations, at least in principle, are local town democracies, democratic nation-states, and rapidly growing churches. The organization was seen as existing to serve the interests of the citizen members. However, there is no question about the organization's going on its own course to pursue goals not in the interest of its members. The organization shows an extreme interest in measuring the will of the members and responding to their wishes and needs.

When these principles are followed, the expectation is that the citizen members will become highly involved, enthusiastic, and satisfied. A Canadian university was searching for strategies to build a more active alumni association. Merely sending out newsletters about the school no longer sustained alumni pride or interest; it decided to confer membership status on its alumni, with privileges and voting rights on major issues. Suddenly the alumni became alive with interest in the school. This gesture proved very meaningful to the alumni, who had previously felt that the university was simply using them for their money.

The characteristics of a fully responsive congregation are:

1. It encourages all who share in its ministries and programs to participate actively in the affairs of the congregation.

2. It responds to the wishes of its members and participants as expressed through the ballot box or other means of less-formal communication.

First United Methodist Church, Marietta, Georgia, is an example of a fully responsive congregation. The church has about 4,500 members and is constantly growing. We visited the church several times to observe it in action.

In a late-night conversation with Pastor Charles Sineath we

asked about the attention paid to the exterior gardens, lawns, and parking lot. He said, "We believe every blade of grass is an evangelist. People see the lawn before they see the sanctuary. The first contact a person has with the church is when he/she turns off the street onto our grounds. Friendship begins in the parking lot. We train our parking lot attendants to be responsive to every question and to spot people who need help before they ask for it."

When we asked a lay staff member about her views of the church's success, her first response was "This church is what it is because we have so many people who really care."

We asked for an example. She said, "We have a custodian here who takes his job as a true ministry. A few weeks ago we had a wedding at which the wedding director did not show up. As soon as the custodian heard about it, he took over. There he was at the back of the sanctuary, sending the wedding party in at the correct times. He fixed the pillow for the rings and helped the bride get over her nervousness. The wedding came off without a hitch."

We asked whether the custodian was trained for this work. She said he had not, "but every worker in the church is trained to put people above their work assignments. Whenever the custodian sees anyone in trouble in the building, he goes immediately to his or her assistance."

This full-time ministry team is composed of clergy and laypersons, but one cannot know who is which by simply observing them in staff meetings or by watching their work. Virtually there is no distinction made between the members on the staff. To an amazing degree, this is true also of the senior pastor. The ministry team was introduced to us during a staff meeting. We could not distinguish between the senior pastor and the other members of the team. Finally we had to ask.

The distinctions between unresponsive, casually responsive, highly responsive and fully responsive congregations are real. Any religious organization fits somewhere on this continuum. Your degree of responsiveness can be determined by interviewing the members and participants, and by observing the responses of the leadership and ministry units to specific situations or persons.

93

"Get Thee Behind Us"
Different Perceptions of a Move Toward Responsiveness

An article in the December 18, 2008, online edition of *Christianity Today*, entitled "Get Thee Behind Us: The Devil's Latest Marketing Guise," provided a different perspective from this chapter's on the use of marketing to improve congregational responsiveness. Here are some selected quotes from the article:

"'Church Check, a division of parent company, Guest Check, Inc., announced today the immediate availability of a new service offering, widely differing in scope from its current client base within the hospitality industry.'

"Thus begins a news release we received at the *Christianity Today* offices this week. The name 'Church Check' naturally caught our attention, as did the offer of the new service. So we read on:

"After years of success focusing only in hospitality, Guest Check was approached by a single church congregation over two years ago and was asked to consider providing inspection services. Their primary goal was to assess the Sunday morning experience of a non-biased third party visitor. . . . The church leadership wanted to get an unbiased and anonymous review of the 'guest' experience."

"It's hard to know where to begin. This is a near-perfect example of what happens when we let marketing experts into the church building. . . .

"All in all, marketing resources like Church Check only exacerbate the fundamental and tragic lie that infects the hearts and minds of so many churches and 'guests' today—that church is about us and our experience.

"In most instances, I try to be open and charitable about any service that can help a church be the church. But more and more, I'm thinking that a tool whose veins run with the blood of marketing is the exception that proves the rule. No, flee from the devil, and run fastest when he comes disguised as an angel of light."

The author of the article decries the use of marketing methods such as Church Check as a means of trying to make congregations more responsive to the needs of visitors. In his words: "Should churches really make it a goal to 'boost your retention rate and make your church grow'? Is that not a product of other things, such as faithful worship, meaningful biblical teaching, and sacrificial love for one another and the neighbor? What has happened to a church that makes 'boosting your retention rate' a focus instead of these other things?"

We also believe in "faithful worship, meaningful biblical teaching, and sacrificial love for one another and the neighbor" as part of the congregational worship experience. But we differ from the article's author in his view that trying to see your worship service through the eyes of a visitor represents the work of the devil. One of your authors posted a response on the blog that accompanied this article and noted that sometimes marketing is defined as the attempt to remove barriers to the exchange process. Going on to say that a service such as Church Check could help to do that by providing a fresh look at something we are so close to that we are unable to see the obstacles that have been put in the way of exchange. We have already gone part way to achieving this goal when we put in wheel-chair ramps and have signing of the speaker's message for the disabled congregants. Perhaps there are less obvious barriers to exchange whose removal would make us more responsive and more successful in reaching our audience. Another blogger saw merit in this response, saying:

"[The book's author] puts forth a great counter-balance to this article. There is some value in improving your first impression. The goal of first impression is to get a second visit. The goal of the second visit is a third. The goal of hospitality and welcome is not evangelism. This is where I think the two are confused. The goal of evangelism is conversion; the method is proclamation. The goal of hospitality is welcome, and the method is removing barriers to hearing the proclamation. Too many churches have substituted one for the other. While hiring a marketing service may not be the most cost-effective, or

Continued on next page

Continued from previous page

even the best way, the idea of having an unconnected visitor make a visit and learning from it is still a good goal. Hospitality doesn't happen on its own."

The reader will make his/her own judgment of whether the use of such a service (or using their own resources to accomplish the same ends) has value in creating a more responsive climate in your congregation. We are of the opinion that being responsive and being faithful to your calling are not mutually exclusive goals. In fact, as we have attempted to propose in the first three chapters, we believe being responsive to needs is one element of your calling.

Source: Mark Gali, "Get Thee Behind Us: The Devil's Latest Marketing Guise," at http://www.christianitytoday.com/ct/2008/ decemberweb-only/151-42.0.html .

The understanding and application of these basic concepts of marketing will almost certainly make any ministry more responsive, effective, and satisfying—both for the ministers and for those who receive the ministry.

Summary

Religious organizations that are aware of their constituents' needs and of the ever-changing social environments are characterized by the high degree of personal satisfaction felt by the people who meet with these organizations. However, being a highly responsive organization does not come naturally to most congregations.

Being a fully responsive congregation requires that the leaders of the congregation measure the will of the members, and respond to their wishes and needs. This means encouraging all who share in its ministries and programs, and inviting leaders and members alike to participate actively in the affairs of the congregation. However, this does not mean that you must abandon your calling to run after the latest social fashion.

The first three chapters of this book have attempted to argue the case that the leaders of congregations can become fully responsive to the needs of their members by adopting a societal marketing orientation without compromising their calling, or abandoning the mission of their institution. Indeed, we believe that the role of marketing is to determine effectively and efficiently that the mission of the church is fulfilled.

In the next two chapters we will discuss the how and what of acquiring an understanding—the second step of the effective marketing process. In this step you begin to put the societal marketing process into practice by learning about the groups you want to engage in exchange.

---

[1] Jena McGregor, "Customer Service Champs," *Business Week*, Mar. 5, 2007.

[2] Jena McGregor, "Soldiering On in Insurance," *Business Week,* Mar. 5, 2007.

[3] Jena McGregor, "An Extraordinary Stumble at JetBlue," *Business Week,* Mar. 5, 2007.

[4] See Anthony Downs, *Inside Bureaucracy* (Boston: Little, Brown, 1967).

[5] Malcolm Gladwell, *The Tipping Point: How Little Things Can Make a Big Difference* (Boston: Little Brown, 2000).

WORKSHEETS: CHAPTER 3

How Responsive Is Your Organization?

Do you have (conduct):	Yes	No
1. A complaint system	_____	_____
2. Satisfaction surveys	_____	_____
3. Needs and preference surveys	_____	_____
4. Customer-oriented personnel	_____	_____
5. Empowered customers	_____	_____

Scoring (1 point for each yes, 0 points for each no):
Score = 0   You are unresponsive
Score = 1-2 You are casually responsive
Score = 3-4 You are highly responsive
Score = 5   You are fully responsive

If your score is less than 5 and you feel compelled to be more responsive, the following chapters will help you learn how to improve your responsiveness. If you are already at a fully responsive level, the following chapters will provide some ideas for sharpening the efficiency and effectiveness of your efforts to remain fully responsive.

Here are some "best practices" ideas of the *Business Week's* "Customer Service Champs":

1. Do your workers and members feel valued and appreciated? How do you know? What can you do to make them feel so?

_____

_____

_____

2. How can you help your congregants feel what it is like for someone to come to your worship service or to your facility for the first time to receive a social service you offer to the community?

_____

_____

_____

3. How can you adapt the tools discussed in this chapter to fit your particular needs? Who in your organization is best suited to helping you make that adaptation?

_____

_____

_____

4. The idea of asking someone with a thoroughgoing service mentality to oversee your efforts to become a more responsive institution is worth considering. Can you identify such a person in your congregation?

_____

_____

_____

5. What do you need to do to have your key leadership team become committed to your becoming a fully responsive organization?

_____

_____

_____

Develop an Understanding

Part 3:

THE EFFECTIVE MARKETING PROCESS

Adopting a Marketing Philosophy

↓

Develop an Understanding
CHAPTER 4 How *to Understand: Marketing Research*
CHAPTER 5 What *to Understand: Factors Influencing Behavior*

↓

Plan the Marketing Strategy

↓

Design and Implement Marketing Tactics

↓

Connect With Exchange Partners

The societal marketing orientation that was described in part 2 of the book provided a philosophical perspective on how to think about your organization, its ministries, and its "markets" when doing Adherent, Fellowship, and Social Services marketing. That philosophy stressed the ethic of considering the needs of others whom you wish to engage in exchange relationships. Adopting such an orientation naturally requires that you would seek to *Understand* (e.g., step 2 of the EMP) the needs, wants, values, etc., of the groups you seek to serve before you set about designing ministries intended to address those needs, wants, values, etc. Hence, the need to cover this step before moving on to the EMP steps of developing and implementing marketing plans. We begin this two-chapter sequence on understanding by describing the marketing research process used to acquire the understanding, and then moving on to a discussion of the behavioral factors that we are seeking to understand about those people and groups that we desire as exchange partners.

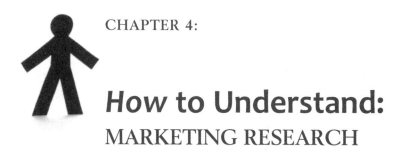

CHAPTER 4:

How to Understand:
MARKETING RESEARCH

"Seek, and you will find" (MATTHEW 7:7, NIV).

In this chapter we will address the following questions:

1. What kind of marketing decisions benefit from marketing research?

2. What are the characteristics of good marketing research?

3. What are the steps in a marketing research project?

4. What are some online research Web sites?

Child Evangelism Fellowship (CEF) is an interdenominational organization operating in 85 countries. It has enjoyed a long record of fruitful ministries spanning its more than 50-year history, but found that two of its ministries—Good News Club, a children's Bible class meeting during the school year; and Five-Day Club, a Bible class for children meeting during the summer—had membership declines between 12 percent and 58 percent. The declines were particularly precipitous in Chile. When the CEF administration realized this, it turned to marketing research for help to determine the cause of the declines and to suggest marketing strategies that might turn the organization around.

The administrators of the CEF program conducted in-depth interviews with 30 pastors, 10 in each of the three major social classes.

From their research CEF discovered that respondents suggested service should be offered that CEF did not currently provide.

Armed with this information, CEF set about to introduce major changes in the Good News Club and Five-Day Club programs: for the first time classes were offered that were aimed toward teaching and training adults to teach the Bible to the children that were enrolled in the CEF clubs. Formerly a teacher was required to study in the CEF teacher training classes on a yearly basis, without any hope of graduating.

Based on these research findings, the training classes are now taught in four levels, with graduation upon completion at each level.

The distribution of the club services changed from central locations to the local churches. This resulted in greater numbers of teachers who were willing to participate and assume more "ownership."

As a result of these changes a differential price structure was instituted, allowing each local CEF area in Chile to decide how much it should charge for the services it provided. This alteration made it possible for CEF to install pricing structures in keeping with the economic situations in different parts of the country.

Finally, CEF expanded its promotional efforts through personal contacts, public speaking, posters, direct mail, exhibitions in conferences, and Christian newspaper advertising where research indicated the best media placement for reaching the target audience.

From these efforts, the two basic ministries grew by 2,500 percent in 6 years, and total income increased by 349 percent during the same period.

The Chilean national director of CEF put the role of marketing research into perspective:

"Why does an evangelical organization need marketing research? Our organization, like many others, is up against a lot of competition. We are competing for the precious time of children and house-wives, whom we train to teach the Bible to children in the Good News Clubs. We need to study the segments of women and children so we can better help them and attract their attention. Regular marketing research needs to take place to review our services and determine whether to change them."[1]

As this example illustrates, having knowledge of how well your program is satisfying the needs of its target audience allows you to make the changes that will keep a program vital and effective. In this first chapter devoted to *developing an understanding*, we will concentrate on the *how* of developing that understanding. In the following chapter we will focus on the *what* of that understanding. The *how* is by use of marketing research. In a nutshell, *marketing research produces the information you need to make your marketing decisions.* What kind of marketing decisions might you be faced with that would benefit from marketing research? Here are some examples.

Knowing Your Customer

• Which groups represent the best target audience for my programs, ministries, etc.?

• How large is the existing and potential market for these programs? What is its rate of growth?

• What unfulfilled needs exist for my programs? How are people currently fulfilling those needs?

• Under what circumstances would people desire the program? What benefits are people seeking to gain in these circumstances?

• Where would people expect to access the program? What decision process do they go through when choosing to utilize the program?

• Who makes the choice decision for this type of program? How do others influence the decisions?

• What is the value people place on having their needs fulfilled by this type of program?

Knowing the Environment

• How are people made aware of this type of program? What

opportunities exist to increase efficiency and effectiveness in promoting the program?

- What technological developments are likely to occur that could affect our ability to deliver this program to the target audience?

- What cultural/social environmental trends could impact our programs? How?

- What economic and demographic trends are occurring in our community that could affect the level of interest in our program? How?

These are merely a few examples of the kinds of questions that marketing research may help you find answers to that reduce the uncertainty of your decision-making.

It is important to reiterate that a study of marketing research should begin with this understanding: marketing research is not focused on the use of surveys or experiments or observations (i.e., techniques). Marketing research is about finding solutions to your problems and helping you make better decisions. When it is obvious that the best method of finding a solution to a problem is to conduct a survey (or interview select people, or use observational methods, etc.), then it is important to use such techniques appropriately, so that we have faith that the findings contain as much "truth" as we can afford.

We would be remiss, however, if we did not follow up that admonition with this caveat: we are not suggesting an "anything goes" approach to research. We must always ensure that we pursue research that is related to both the marketing problem and its related decisional issues, *and* must make certain that our methods are scientific and represent the most efficient means of seeking answers to our questions. Figure 4.1 helps to show the possible combinations of these variables.

Exhibit 4.1		**Outcomes of Research**		
		Is Research Relevant to a Real Problem/Opportunity?		
		Yes	**No**	
Does the research follow scientific methods?	**Yes**	1. Results are relevant and believable.	2. Results are believable but not relevant.	
	No	3. Results are relevant but not believable.	4. Results are neither relevant nor believable.	

Better decision-making by using research results comes only from research that falls into cell number 1, the Yes/Yes cell. However, you can creatively apply scientific methodology that goes against "convention," and still end up in cell number 1. The point being that when we set out to do our research we do not set out to write a questionnaire, or to conduct in-depth interviews, or run an experiment, etc. We set out to solve a problem, to evaluate an opportunity, to test hypotheses, etc., so that we can reduce uncertainty and improve our decision-making. So we need to understand that it is possible to be both scientific *and* unconventional, and we must be open to using whatever method represents the most efficient and effective means of generating relevant and believable results. Exhibit 4.2 lists some characteristics of good marketing research.

Doing Marketing Research

When you are faced with developing the understanding you desire so that you can effectively plan, you will want to develop a budget and then go about collecting the necessary information. First, some thoughts on developing the budget.

Budget

Since you probably perform research on an ad hoc basis, the cost

106

Exhibit 4.2	**Characteristics of Good Marketing Research**
1. Scientific method	Effective marketing research uses the principles of the scientific method: careful observation, formulation of hypotheses, prediction, and testing.
2. Research creativity	At its best, marketing research develops innovative ways to solve a problem, blending research technology with an understanding of the behavioral patterns of respondents to imaginatively gain insights.
3. Multiple methods	Marketing researchers shy away from overreliance on any one method. They also recognize the value of using two or three methods to increase confidence in the results.
4. Value and cost of information	Marketing researchers show concern for estimating the value of information against its cost. Costs are typically easy to determine, but the value of research is harder to quantify. It depends on the reliability and validity of the findings and the administrator's willingness to accept and act on those findings.
5. Healthy skepticism	Marketing researchers maintain a healthy skepticism toward the findings from research. They do not come to a conclusion regarding the findings of the research until all the data are in, and apply logic and common sense to interpreting the findings.
6. Ethical practice	Good research adheres to the ethical standards established to guide research practice, including respect for client and respondent rights.

of each research project must be calculated and the money found to pay for the costs.

Funds must be allocated from an existing account or raised from its members for the purpose of the research study. It is important that all the costs of the research are anticipated so that appropriate funding will be available. One inexpensive (sometimes free) source of help is the marketing teacher at the local college, whose marketing research class may take on the organization's research problem as a project. Also, a member of your congregation might have research training, or know someone who does, and be willing to volunteer time to doing the research study, saving the cost of getting professional researchers involved.

Steps in a Research Project

Exhibit 4.3 describes the five basic steps in good marketing research.

Exhibit 4.3	The Marketing Research Process

Problem Definition and Research Questions
↓
Research Design
↓
Design Data Collection Methods
↓
Fieldwork
↓
Data Analysis and Report Presentation

Problem Definition and Research Objectives

The starting point of a research project should be an attempt by both the user and the provider of information to define the problem clearly. A *problem* exists whenever there is a difference between the desired state and the actual state (e.g., church operating expense offerings have been declining, and are falling short of what is needed to meet operating expenses). An *opportunity* exists whenever you can offer something new that is desired by your target audience (e.g., offering to the community a six-week coronary health program that stresses healthy diet and lifestyle). The first step in successful marketing research is to reach an agreement among those who will be making decisions to solve the problem or take advantage of the opportunity, and those who will be collecting the information, as to the *real* problem/opportunity to be evaluated.

Definition of Problem/Opportunity

One way to seek agreement regarding the reason for the research is to ask all those involved in the decision-making or research to write down the answer to this question: "If you had one wish to improve this situation, what would you wish for?" The intent is to get people to focus on the real problem or opportunity instead of a problem's symptom or only a part of the opportunity.

An example:

Situation: You desire to begin a small group ministry

Bad definition of problem/opportunity: "How do we promote the small group concept to the congregation?"

Good definition: "I would wish for 90 percent of our congregants over the age of 20 to become members of a small group in our church."

An example from the business world helps illustrate the importance of focusing on the real problem/opportunity.

The Compton Company was a capital equipment manufacturer with a market share larger than its next two competitors combined. All companies in this business sold through independent distributors who typically carried the lines of several manufacturers. Compton had for several years been suffering a loss of market share. In an effort to regain share, they fired their ad agency. The new agency conducted a study of end-use customers and discovered that the fired ad agency had done an outstanding job of creating awareness and interest in the Compton line. The study also revealed that these end-users were buying competitors' equipment from the distributors. The switch from interest in Compton to the competition was not a failure of the advertising, but rather the result of distributors' motivation to sell the products of manufacturers' running sales contests, offering cash bonuses, and supplying technical sales assistance.[2]

Had Compton correctly defined the problem as "decline in market share" instead of "bad advertising" they would have used research to determine why the problem existed instead of making a decision that failed to improve the situation. If someone had said "I wish our market share could be better" as an answer to "What would you wish for?" they would have been on their way toward using research to help make better decisions to solve their problem. Avoid becoming a "Compton."

The next step in the research process is to use the statement of problem/opportunity to define the research purpose.

Research Purpose

Decision Alternatives. What actions might we take to solve the problem or exploit the opportunity if the research reveals those actions are warranted (e.g., train people to become leaders of small groups if people feel incapable of leading groups; starting a young couples Sunday school class if there is sufficient interest, etc.)?

Decisional Criteria. The information we need to learn from the environment that helps us choose among the decision alternatives (e.g., if we discovered the reasons for the resistance to becoming a small groups leader we'll better know what training to offer; if we know the number of young couples who say they would "definitely" join a Sunday school class for young couples we'll know whether to begin such a class).

A good way to think of the relationship between the decision alternatives and the decisional criteria is as follows:

"If I knew [*decisional criteria*], then I'd know whether/how to [*decision alternative*].

For example:

"If I knew *the levels of awareness and knowledge of the program*, I'd know whether/how to *change the way we promote the program to our teens*.

Research Purpose. A declarative statement that indicates how the research will contribute to solving the problem or evaluating the opportunity (e.g., "To determine the cause[s] of our decline in church offerings and the possible actions to reverse the decline").

We now need to identify the specific research questions that need to be answered in order to achieve the research purpose.

Research Questions

The specific questions that must be answered by the research in order to provide all the decisional criteria information needed. In other words, what exactly does the research need to discover that will help us know what we should do to ultimately solve our problem or exploit our opportunity?

We'll need numerous questions answered before we are fully ready to choose among our decision alternatives. Here's how this process might look:

Problem:

The attendance at the planned program for our teenage church members is consistently disappointing.

Research Purpose:

Decision alternatives:

1. Change the time the program is offered.
2. Change the content of the program.
3. Involve the teens more in the program planning.
4. Change the way we promote the program to the teens.
5. Change the location of the program.
6. Offer different programs for young teens, middle teens, and older teens.

Decisional Criteria:

1. Number of teenage church members by age group (13-14, 15-16, 17-19).
2. Attendance record of teen members (e.g., percentage never attending, attend once, etc.).
3. Levels of awareness and knowledge of program.

4. Levels of satisfaction of program content by attendees.
5. Interest in new program content.
6. Opinion leadership patterns for teens.

Research Purpose:
Discover the reasons for poor attendance and what, if anything, can be done to improve it.

Research Questions:

1. What has been the pattern of attendance for our planned programs? Do the same few young people attend each one? Do different youth attend each program (but only come to a few before dropping out)?
2. What is common among those attending and those not attending (age, gender, social class, home location, personality, etc.)?
3. Why do those who attend come?
4. Why do some teenagers no longer attend?
5. Why have some never attended any programs at all?
6. Were the young people informed of the programs before they were conducted? Was the advertising/communication prepared and delivered in a manner that would interest young people?
7. What programs do nonattendees say they would attend if offered?
8. How satisfied have attendees been with the offered programs?
9. What roles do parents and peers play in encouraging or discouraging attendance?

Notice that all the research questions require you to go out and collect information. That is the role of a research question: to "nag" you by asking: "Do you have the information yet that answers me? If not, keep looking!" A bad wording for a research question would look like this: "How many days a month should we run programs for the teens?" While you might want to know the answer to that question, the way it is worded requires an answer in the form of *a decision (e.g., "two" or "one")*, not with information. Answers to such research questions as "How frequently do teens say they want programs to be run?" and "How often are the adult program directors available to supervise the programs during the month?" are research questions that contribute to making the decision of how frequently to run the program. Be sure you word research questions that are answered by doing research, rather than by making a decision as the way of answering the research question.

If necessary, someone who has experience in defining marketing problems (college marketing research professor, volunteer retired marketing person, consultant, etc.) can help guide the discussion of the problem and framing the research questions. A simple, inexpensive, but carefully conducted study that explores issues of direct relevance to the decision-maker will go a long way toward helping you solve the problem or know how to capitalize on your opportunity. The researcher is advised to spend all the time necessary and to involve all relevant parties in the development of the research statement before beginning to conduct any research.

Research Design

The next step after stating the problem/opportunity, research purpose, and research questions is to formulate a research design. The starting point for the research design is, in fact, the research questions you have so carefully developed. The research design is a plan of action indicating the specific steps that are necessary to provide answers to those questions and thereby achieve the research purpose that helps you choose among the decision alternatives to solve the management problem or capitalize on the market opportunity.

A research design is much like a road map—you can see where you are currently and where you want to be at the completion of your journey, and can determine the best (most efficient and effective) route to take to get to your destination. We may have to take unforeseen detours along the way, but by keeping our ultimate objective constantly in mind and following our map, we will arrive at our destination. Our research purpose and objectives suggest which route (design) might be best to get us where we want to go, but there is more than one way to "get there from here." Choice of research design is not like solving a problem in algebra to which there is only one correct answer and an infinite number of wrong ones. Choice of research design is more like selecting a cheesecake recipe—some are better than others, but there is no one recipe that is universally accepted as "best." Successfully completing a research project consists of making those choices that will fulfill the research purpose and obtain answers to the research questions in an efficient and effective manner.

Choice of research design will depend upon the fundamental objective implied by the research question:

• To conduct a general *exploration* of the issue, gain some broad insights into the phenomenon, and achieve a better "feel" for the subject under investigation (e.g., "What obstacles exist in the minds of members who are reluctant to join a small group?"). Exploratory research is in some ways akin to detective work—there is a search for "clues" to reveal what happened or is currently taking place, a variety of sources might be used to provide insights and information, and the researcher/detective "follows where his or her nose leads" in the search for ideas, insights, and clarification. Researchers doing exploratory research must adopt a very flexible attitude toward collecting information in this type of research and be constantly asking themselves what lies beneath the surface of what they are learning and/or seeing. An insatiable curiosity is a valuable trait for exploratory researchers.

• To *describe* a population, event, or phenomenon in a precise manner in which we can attach numbers to represent the extent to which something occurs or determine the degree two or more variables co-vary (e.g., determine the relationship between age and degree of interest in a program's content). Descriptive research is highly structured and rigid in its approach to data collection compared to exploratory research's unstructured and flexible approach. As such, descriptive research presupposes much prior knowledge

114

on the part of the researcher regarding *who* will be targeted as a respondent, *what* issues are of highest priority to be addressed in the study, *how* the questions are to be phrased to reflect the vocabulary and experience of the respondents, *when* to ask the questions, *where* to find the respondents, and *why* these particular questions need to be answered in order to make decisions. Thus, exploratory research may often be needed to allow descriptive research requirements to be met.

• To attribute *cause-and-effect* relationships among two or more variables so that we can better understand and predict the outcome of one variable when varying another. While descriptive research is effective in identifying a correlation between variables (e.g., attendance to a program varies by the day of week it is run) it cannot truly indicate causality (e.g., ad message A creates more interest than message B). When we are in need of determining if two or more variables are causally related, we must turn to causal–research procedures (experiments).

Design Data Collection Methods

A research design provides the overall plan indicating how the researcher will obtain answers to the research questions. The researcher must also identify the specific methods that will be used to collect the information. These decisions include determining the extent to which the questions can be answered using secondary data (data that have already been collected for purposes other than the research under investigation) or must be answered by the use of primary data (which are collected explicitly for the research study at hand).

Secondary Data

Secondary data are data previously gathered for some other purpose. The first tenet of data gathering among researchers is to exhaust all sources of secondary data before engaging in a search for primary data. Many research questions can be answered more quickly and with less expense through the proper use of secondary information. The extensive use of secondary data reduces the possibility of "reinventing the wheel" by gathering primary data that someone else has already collected.

A type of secondary data frequently of interest is learning about the people in your local area you will serve as part of your mission (e.g., doing adherent or social service marketing). We will describe some secondary sources you might want to use when seeking such information.

Census Data

The source of secondary information that immediately comes to mind is the United States Census. While many subsites of interest at the U.S. Census Web site might be profitably explored, we suggest the American FactFinder site at http://factfinder.census.gov/home/ saff/main.html?_lang=en as the best place to obtain basic census data about a city, town, county, or zip code. Click on "population finder" to access the latest profile for the area of interest to you.

Numerous commercial organizations have purchased packaged census data and make it conveniently available for a price. Here are some of the major suppliers:

Applied Geographic Solutions: http://www.appliedgeographic.com.

ESRI: http://www.esri.com/data.

MapInfo: http://www.mapinfo.com.

Claritas: http://www.claritas.com.

Many of these are used primarily by for-profit organizations seeking to analyze a geographic trade area. One organization that is dedicated to supplying secondary data for use by religious organizations is Percept: http://www.perceptgroup.com.

Percept offers several demographic profiling products that might be useful to a local congregation. A few include:

First View: a six-page graphical demographic report on a zip code area.

Ministry Area Profile: a full demographic information package on any size and shape geographic area (e.g., a 5-mile radius circle with your local congregation at the center).

See the resource guide CD bound into the back cover of this book for an extensive list of other secondary data sources that could be of value to you.

The Connected Congregation

The Hartford Seminary's Institute for Religion Research (http://hirr.hartsem.edu) lists links to more than 200 denominational home pages, as well as reviews of congregational Web sites.

A sampling of unusual/special features on some congregational Web sites:

hurricane tracking service

free gun locks available to the public

school closings during bad weather

information on Jewish life in the city

a "random encouragement generator" with brief messages of encouragement

sending cyber cards to visitors to encourage return visits

virtual tours of the church

story of the week to encourage frequent visits to site

question-and-answer page for children

a cyber hymnal

(http://www.pewinternet.org)

Primary Data

If primary data are to be collected, decisions must be made with regard to the use of communication and/or observation approaches to generating the data. The specific instruments (forms) that will be used to collect the information of interest are designed during this step. This would involve the design of the exploratory interview form, observation form, questionnaire, or experiment. These forms should coincide with the decisions made with respect to what you are trying to do (e.g., *explore*, *describe*, or determine a *cause-and-effect* relationship).

Constructing a data-collection form is both art and science. You are focusing on the decisions that you are faced with making that will solve your problem or help you take advantage of the opportunity. Thus the data collection instrument must accomplish more than merely generating information—it must provide the insights you need that lead to better decision-making.

Designing the Data Collection Instrument

If we are going to do primary research, we must develop the instrument(s) with which we will collect the information. For exploratory research we would design focus group moderator guides, interview guides, or observation forms. For descriptive research we use a data-collection method. Either way, we are seeking information in a form that allows us to get answers to our research questions.

Fieldwork

We are now ready to actually go to "the field" to collect the information we seek. This means conducting the exploratory research (interviews with key people, moderating group discussions, searching the literature, or doing the observations), descriptive research (selecting a sample of people and getting them to complete

---

Example of Exploratory Research: Starting a Small Group Ministry

Doing research to develop an *understanding* of some issue does not have to be expensive or time-consuming, or require specialized expertise. The following is a document one of the authors provided to members of a task force to which he belonged, who were trying to set up a small group ministry in their church. The only changes to this document have been the removal of the church name.

Research Purpose 1: Determine the obstacles that keep some people from joining a small group in [our church].
Respondents: Any adult that has resisted joining a small group at [the church] (i.e., had the opportunity, but chose not to join). This

---

would not include someone who wants to join but has *not* yet done so.

Discussion Topics: Introduction: Inform them that you are a member of a small group (SG) leadership task force looking into enhancing the SG experience at [our church]. The purpose of the interview is to better understand people's perceptions of small groups as a way of enriching the spiritual lives of members while achieving the church's mission. Make sure they know that the purpose of the interview is to understand, not recruit or persuade. Their identity is confidential between you and her/him, although you will be sharing insights from the interview with the rest of the taskforce.

Topic 1: What comes into their mind when you say "small group"? What do they anticipate that experience would be like?

Topic 2: Have they ever been in a small group before? If so, what was that experience like? If not, have they been asked and declined? Why did they decline?

Topic 3: Probe to discover the degree to which their lack of participation in SGs has been based upon perceptions of the purpose of the groups (ulterior motives by church or group leader?), composition of group ("I'm too liberal [or conservative] to be comfortable with other group members", etc.), logistical difficulties (work schedule conflicts, no access to transportation, etc.), or other obstacles. Try to understand what is not being said as well as what is being said. Is there anything from responses to Topics 1 or 2 that should be explored here?

Topic 4: What would be the possibility of their joining an SG if the Topic 3 obstacles were removed? Here we are trying to see if clearing up misperceptions, structuring a group that they would be comfortable with, or overcoming logistical barriers would get them interested in joining an SG. Is it a "lost cause" with this person (and if so, why?), or something that education and/or planning could result in their joining a group?

Research Purpose 2: Determine the "best practices" that have made SGs so rewarding for those who have had that experience.

Respondents: Anyone who found their SG experience highly re-

Continued on next page

Continued from previous page

warding, exceeded their expectations, highly recommend friends join an SG, look forward to replicating their SG experience, etc. We want to discover what were the contributors to these very positive feelings from SG members, i.e., the "best practices" of SGs. The SG need not have been while a member of [our church]. In fact, learning other churches' best practices would be very helpful, where possible.

Discussion Topics: Introduction: Inform them that you are a member of a SG leadership task force looking into enhancing the SG experience at [our church]. The purpose of the interview is to better understand people's perceptions of small groups as a way of enriching the spiritual lives of members while achieving the church's mission. Make sure they know that the purpose of the interview is to understand, not recruit or persuade. Their identity is confidential between you and her/him, although you will be sharing insights from the interview with the rest of the task force.

Topic 1: Get them to provide some background on the SG that they found so rewarding: when was it run (is it continuing?), how was it formed, how often did they meet as a small group, how long were the meetings, etc. We want to see if there are some structural characteristics common to these positive SG experiences.

Topic 2: Was the group experience as they thought it would be, or did they find it was in some ways very different from their expectations? How so?

Topic 3: To what do they attribute the group's success? Probe to see if it was a compatibility issue, and if so, what were the dimensions along which group members were compatible, or was it because of personal needs that were met, and if so what needs were satisfied, etc.

Topic 4: What would they say is the "formula for success" for SGs? How could their positive experience be replicated for others? For example, what would they say is the key to being a good group leader? How do great groups get formed? What should people who are new to the SG experience understand about SGs before they join that would increase the chances for having a rewarding experience?

a survey questionnaire), and/or causal research (conducting the experiments).

This is merely an example of how to prepare church members for conducting exploratory research to *understand* before you *plan,* then *implement,* a program or ministry. Someone who teaches marketing research at a local college would be a great resource in helping you to set up a research study for issues of interest to you.

Data Analysis and Report Presentation

The basic purpose of the research report is to communicate the results, conclusions, and recommendations of the research project. The key word in the preceding statement of purpose is *communicate.* The report must be an effective tool of communication not only to present the findings and conclusions accurately, but also to stimulate the reader to some action. The research project was predicated on the need for information to aid in the decision-making process. Now the cycle has been completed and the report must address that decision and recommend a course of action in view of the research findings. We will now illustrate the steps of the process with an example project.

Example of a Research Project

Camp Star (name disguised) is an overnight summer camp operated by the Jewish Federation of a major United States city. Camp Star was confronted with serious enrollment declines in the camping programs, ranging as high as 70 percent. The camp director was not certain whether this decline was the result of to a general atrophy in overnight camping, or if it was specific to Camp Star (a shrinkage in the camp's market share). Not knowing the causes, the camp director was not sure about what marketing actions, if any, could halt the enrollment decline. He recognized the need to do some marketing research, although his budget would not permit a large-scale study. He decided to hire a small marketing research firm that was recommended to him. Arthur Sterngold, the proprietor of the firm, agreed to design and implement a low-cost study that would yield useful findings and recommendations.

Problem Definition

Problem Definition: Decline in enrollment of campers.

Decision Alternatives:
1. Change the camp activities to fit the desires of potential campers better.
2. Offer different camping schedules for specific audiences (family camp, couples camp, kids camp, etc.).
3. Change the way camp services are priced.
4. Change the way Camp Star is promoted.
5. Institute "day camp" instead of all overnight camp programs.
6. Close the camp and use the facility for other purposes.

Decisional Criteria:
1. How people make decisions regarding choice of camping and camp facilities.
2. People's perceptions of the "camping experience."
3. Level of competition for camping activities.
4. Number of people expressing a desire to attend a camp.
5. Expressed desires for camp activities.
6. Awareness and knowledge of Camp Star and its advertising.
7. Satisfaction of previous campers with the Camp Star experience.

Research Purpose:
To determine the main factors affecting the decisions to attend camp, and the potential for increasing enrollment.

Research Questions:
1. What is the decision-making process a person goes through in selecting an overnight camp?
2. In general, what are people's images of overnight camps, and of Camp Star in particular?
3. What are the alternative activities that people consider in making summer plans?
4. What are people's motives for selecting overnight camps?
5. What do people look for in an overnight camp?

6. What are the important consumer characteristics and divisions among groups of consumers (market segmentation)?
7. How effective have the promotional materials been in creating awareness and interest in Camp Star?
8. How satisfied have those who have used Camp Star in the past been with its services and the overall camping experience at the camp?
9. Would an expensive, four-color Camp Star brochure sent to prospective campers produce at least twice as many inquiries as the normal one-color brochure?
10. Would Camp Star attract more parent interest if it emphasized the educational or the recreational aspects of summer camping?
11. What impact would a 20 percent increase in tuition costs have on next summer's enrollments?

Research Design

Exploratory Research

This step calls for carrying out preliminary research to learn more about the market before launching any formal research survey. The major procedures at this stage include collecting secondary data, doing observational research, and carrying out informal interviews with individuals and groups.

Descriptive Research

After defining the problem and doing exploratory research, the researchers may wish to carry out a more formal research to measure magnitudes or test hypotheses.

Suppose the Camp Star researchers found that some of the past campers had reported dissatisfaction with their camping experience at Camp Star. The researchers, however, were not sure how extensive the dissatisfaction had been and the relative importance of different factors. In addition, they learned that some camp prospects had little or no knowledge of Camp Star and, among those who did, several had a negative image of the camp. The researchers, however, were not sure how extensive this was. The camp director agreed that it would be desirable to quantify these factors.

Causal Research

It is possible that Camp Star would have some questions that could not be answered by exploratory or descriptive research designs. Research questions 9-11 could best be described as causal hypotheses, requiring experiments to determine if the cause-and-effect relationships stated in these questions are supported by the evidence from the causal research.

Design Data Collection Methods
Exploratory Research Methods

Secondary Data Research: In seeking information, a researcher should initially gather and review secondary data, if any exists. *Secondary data* are relevant data that already exist somewhere, having been collected for other purposes.

Secondary data are normally quicker and less expensive to obtain, and will give the researcher a start on the problem. Afterward, the researcher can gather *primary data*—namely, original data to meet the problem at hand.

In looking for secondary data, the Camp Star researchers can consult the following major sources of secondary data.

1. *Internal records.* The researchers should check Camp Star files for past figures on enrollment, dropouts, complaints, competitive advertising, and other data that might be relevant.

2. *Government.* The Camp Star researchers can use local census data to determine what is happening to the number of children aged 8-11 who are normal prospects for overnight camps.

3. *Trade, professional,* and *business associations.* Camp Star is a member of the American Camp Association, which provides information on camp enrollment and capacity by state, year, and type of camp. The researchers can ascertain whether Camp Star's enrollment decline is in line with a normal decline in its area, or whether it is exceptional.

4. *Competitors and other private organizations.* The researchers could

see whether any useful secondary data can be obtained directly from other camps in the area.

5. *Marketing firms.* Marketing research firms, advertising agencies, and media firms may possess some useful past studies of the overnight camp market.

6. *Universities, research organizations, and foundations.* These organizations may have conducted studies of the camping industry.

7. *Published sources.* Researchers should examine published material in libraries on the subject of camping. A key word search in several databases, such as ABI/Inform, Lexis/Nexis, or Ebscohost, might reveal articles of interest on camping in general.

These secondary data are likely to provide useful ideas and findings. However, the researchers must be careful in making inferences, because the secondary data were collected for a variety of purposes and under a variety of conditions that might limit their usefulness.

Marketing researchers should check these data for relevance, impartiality, validity, and reliability. The researchers are also likely to find that the secondary data leave many questions unanswered, for which they will have to collect primary data through observation or interviewing.

Primary Research: Observation research. A major means for collecting primary data is to carry out personal observations in various situations. The researchers could visit the camp during the season and observe the campers' reactions to the food, facilities, and various activities. Off-season the researchers could observe how the camp staff handles telephone inquiries and personal visits of prospects. The researchers could also examine the camp's brochures and mailings for possible deficiencies. The purpose of the observational method is to discover factors that affect enrollment, the importance of which can be measured later.

Exploratory Interviewing: In addition to gathering data through observation, the researchers need to conduct some interviewing during the exploratory stage of a marketing research project. The purpose of the interviews is to gain further insight into the factors playing a role in the marketing problem that is being investigated.

In the exploratory stage the interviewing should be qualitatively rather than quantitatively oriented. Qualitative interviewing is largely open-ended. People are asked questions requiring extended (not yes or no) answers as a means of stimulating them to share their thoughts and feelings regarding overnight camps or other relevant topics. The distinct uses of qualitative research are to:

1. Probe deeply into consumers' underlying needs, perceptions, preferences, and satisfaction.

2. Gain greater familiarity and understanding of marketing problems of causes not known.

3. Develop ideas that can be further investigated through quantitative research.

On the other hand, quantitative research seeks to generate statistically reliable estimates of particular market or consumer characteristics. Quantitative research entails sampling a much larger number of people than qualitative research, and it assumes one knows in advance what specific questions to ask.

Qualitative research is not only a desirable first step—it is sometimes the only step permitted by the budgets of many religious organizations. For the Camp Star project, the researchers decided to interview new prospects for the camp as well as people associated with Camp Star in the past. The new prospects included parents and their children. The Camp Star group included past campers, counselors, and parents of returnees and nonreturnees. In addition, the researchers interviewed staff members about their attitudes toward the camp. Two methods were used: individual interviewing and group interviewing.

Individual interviewing consists of interviewing one person at a time either in person, via the telephone, or by mail. The Camp Star researchers conducted about 50 individual interviews, half in person and half over the phone.

Focus group interviewing consists of inviting from eight to 12 persons to meet with a trained moderator to discuss a product, service, organization, or other marketing entity. The moderator needs good qualifications, objectivity, knowledge of the subject matter, and some understanding of group dynamics and consumer behavior.

The participants sometimes are paid a small sum for their efforts.

The meeting is held typically in pleasant surroundings (a home, for example), and refreshments are served to increase the informality.

The group moderator starts with a broad question, such as "How would you like to see your children spend their summer vacation?"

The questions would then move to the subject of summer camps, to overnight camps and then to Camp Star versus other camps. The moderator encourages free discussions among the participants, hoping that the group dynamic will bring out real feelings and thoughts. At the same time, the moderator "focuses" the discussion, and hence the name *focus group* interviewing. The comments are recorded through notetaking or, preferably, tape or video recording, and are subsequently studied to understand the consumers' decision process.

The Camp Star researchers conducted two focus group discussions, one with the parents and another with the children, and learned a great deal from this form of interviewing. Focus group interviewing has been one of the major marketing research tools for gaining insight into consumer thoughts and feelings.[3]

Projective Techniques

Researchers might be exploring a topic in which respondents are either unwilling or unable to directly answer questions about why they think or act as they do. Highly sensitive topics involving their private lives are obviously in this category, but more mundane behaviors may also hide deep psychological motivations. For example, researchers made an interesting discovery while investigating the reason some women persisted in preferring a messy, expensive roach spray to a more efficient trap that the women acknowledged had more benefits than their sprays. They found that the women transferred hostilities for the men who had left them to the roaches, and wanted to see the roaches squirm and die. The method used to uncover these hidden motives is one of the so-called projective techniques, so named because respondents project their deep psychological motivations through a variety of communication and observable methods. These methods typically include:

    1. *Word association.* Respondents are given a series of words, and

respond by saying the first word that comes to mind. The response, the frequency of the response, and the time it takes to make the response are keys to understanding the underlying motives toward the subject. If no response is given it is interpreted to mean that emotional involvement is so high as to block the response.

2. *Sentence completion.* Similar to word association, sentence completion requires the respondent to enter words or phrases to complete a given sentence, such as: "People who frequently go camping are _____ ." Responses are then analyzed for content.

3. *Storytelling.* Here respondents are given a cartoon, photograph, drawing, or are asked to draw a scene related to the subject under investigation, and tell what is happening in the scene. In theory, the respondent will reveal inner thoughts by using the visual aid as a stimulus to elicit these deep motivations. Therefore, if the picture is of two people sitting around a campfire at night, the story that is told about the people will reveal how the respondent feels about overnight camping.

4. *Third-person technique/role-playing.* This technique is a reflection of what Oscar Wilde meant when he said, "A man is least himself when he talks in his own person; when he is given a mask he will tell the truth." Respondents are told to explain why a third person (a coworker, neighbor, etc.) might act in a certain way. For example, a stimulus might appear as: We are trying to better understand what features people might consider when choosing a camp for family camping. Please think about people you know and tell us what features would be important to them for such a campground. Role-playing requires the respondent to play the role of another party in a staged scenario, such as asking a camp counselor to play the role of a child camper's first night at teen camp.

5. *Collages.* This technique involves asking the respondent to cut pictures out of magazines and arrange them on poster board to depict some issue of interest to the researcher. For example, respondents might be asked to choose pictures that tell a story of how they decided to go to summer camp, or to choose religious camp over other camp experiences.

6. *Music association.* Here the researcher plays a variety of music se-

lections and asks the respondent to associate the music with one of the brands being evaluated. The objective is to determine a brand's emotional content for the respondent, e.g., associating one campground with hard rock music and another campground with cool jazz.

7. *Anthropomorphicizing.* In this approach the respondent is asked to describe what the product or service being researched would look like if it were a person—age, gender, attractiveness, how would he or she would be dressed, what would his or her occupation would be, what kind of car he or she drives, health status, etc. A variation of this is asking what famous person the product or service would be.

As can be seen from the description of these techniques, one must be skilled not only in structuring these approaches but also must have some experience in interpreting the results. They have been shown to provide intriguing new insights into behavior, but you might want to get the help of a psychologist (congregational member or teacher at local college) when designing and interpreting this type of exploratory research.

Ethnography

Companies are increasingly adapting the ethnographic research methodologies of cultural anthropologists to study consumers. Typically, marketing ethnography involves a marketer experiencing life events along with their consumers—asking questions, observing, and recording their own feelings as they share the experience. Procter & Gamble conducts ongoing ethnographic studies to keep abreast of consumption practices. The company routinely sends scores of researchers, armed with video cameras, into consumer households around the world to tape daily routines and procedures of consumers in all their boring glory. Typically, the ethnographer-filmmakers arrive at the home of the participant when the alarm clock goes off, and stay until bedtime, usually for a four-day stretch. Sometimes the camera is left on with no attendant in a room while family members go about their daily tasks. Taping a mother feeding a child in the consumer's own home can reveal many actions that would go unreported in a focus group session on that subject. Observing multitasking behaviors occurring

Becoming "Doers"
Constituent Surveys

Before conducting a strategic plan for your organization, consider conducting a constituent survey of staff, members, and supporters to gain insight into the needs and desires of the people who support your need to put the plan into action. Constituent surveys perform two purposes: it identifies potential planning-related problem areas in existing operations for targeted improvements; and where attitudes exist, it identifies "attitude gaps" between the planners' and the constituents' perceptions toward planning. Conducting constituent surveys consist of three phases, with substeps within each phase:

Phase 1: Design

Step 1—Initial briefing of ministry staff on the purposes of the survey.

Step 2—Preliminary interviews of constituents using focus groups to begin exploring the nature of constituent knowledge, perceptions, and planning issues.

Step 3—Selecting topics for inclusion in the survey based upon focus group findings.

Step 4—Formulating questions for inclusion in surveys addressing the selected topics.

Step 5—Reviewing questions to weed out inappropriate, misleading, or vague questions.

Step 6—Conducting a pilot test of the survey to ensure its capability to generate the desired information from the constituents.

Step 7—Finalizing questions based on the pilot test.

Phase 2: Administration

Step 1—Determine sample size.

Step 2—Inform constituents of the survey and the importance of their participation.

Step 3—Completing the survey via phone, mail, Internet, or personal interviews.

Phase 3: Interpretation

Use the services of someone familiar with research analysis (college professor, member of congregation, etc.) to determine the findings of the survey. Then the results are factored into the strategic planning process.

Adapted from Roy. J. Clinton, Stan Williamson, and Robert E. Stevens, "Constituent Surveys as an Input in the Strategic Planning Process for Churches and Ministries: Part 1," *Journal of Ministry Marketing and Management* 1, no. 2 (1995): 43-55.

during such sessions could inspire packaging and product designs that could provide a competitive advantage when they reach the market.[4] Every year sees more companies pursing such ethnographic studies to supplement other exploratory research methods. This method may increasingly find its way into research done by religious organizations as well.

Descriptive Research Methods
Descriptive Survey

Many managers take an overly simplistic view of survey work. They think that it consists of writing a few obvious questions and finding an adequate number of people in the target market to answer them. Designing a reliable survey is the job of an experienced marketing researcher. Here we will describe the main things that users of marketing research should know about developing the research instrument, the sampling plan, and the fieldwork.

Questionnaire Design. The questionnaire is the main survey research instrument. The construction of good questionnaires calls for considerable skill. Every questionnaire should be pretested on a pilot sample of persons before using on a large scale. An experienced marketing researcher can usually spot several errors in a casually prepared questionnaire (see Exhibit 4.4).

Exhibit 4.4   A "Questionable" Questionnaire

Suppose the following questionnaire was prepared by a summer camp director for interviewing parents of prospective campers. How do you feel about each question?

1. What is your income to the nearest hundred dollars?

People do not necessarily know their income to the nearest hundred dollars, nor do they want to reveal their income that closely; furthermore, a questionnaire should never open with such a personal question.

2. Are you a strong, or weak, supporter of overnight summer camping for your children?

What do "strong" and "weak" mean?

3. Do your children behave themselves well in a summer camp?

"Behave" is a relative term. Will people want to answer this? Is "yes" and "no" the best way to allow a response to the question? Why is the question asked in the first place?

4. How many camps mailed literature to you last April, or this past April?

Who can remember this?

5. What are the most salient and determinant attributes in your evaluation of summer camps?

What is "salience" and "determinant attributes"? The results of such questions are usually "Don't use your big words on me."

6. Do you think it is right to deprive your child of the opportunity to grow into a mature person through the experience of summer camping?

Loaded question: How can anyone answer yes, given the bias?

There is a common type of error that occurs in the types of questions asked: the inclusion of questions that cannot be answered, or will not be answered, or need not be answered, while omitting the other questions that should be asked.

Each question should be checked to determine whether the

question is necessary in terms of the research objectives. There is a difference between asking for "interesting" information and "essential" information. Questions that are interesting but not essential should be eliminated because they lengthen the required time, anger the respondent, and cause unnecessary work in analyzing the data.

The form of questions can make a substantial difference to the responses. *An open-end question* is one in which the respondent is free to answer in his or her own words. For example, "What is your opinion of Camp Star?"

A *closed-end question* is one in which the possible answers are supplied. The closed-end question can take several forms.

Dichotomous question: Have you heard of Camp Star? Yes ( ) No ( ).

Multiple-choice question: Camp Star is run by (a) the YMCA, (b) the Jewish Federation, (c) the Black Panthers, (d) another group.

Itemized-response question: Camp Star is (a) a very large camp, (b) a large camp, (c) neither large nor small, (d) a small camp, or (e) a very small camp.

Likert scale question: Camp Star plans to turn itself into a music camp. How do you feel about this? (a) strongly approve, (b) approve, (c) undecided, (d) disapprove, (e) strongly disapprove.

The choice of words also calls for considerable care. The researcher should strive for simple, direct, unambiguous, and unbiased wording. Other "do's" and "don'ts" arise in connection with the *sequencing of questions* in the questionnaire. The lead questions should create interest, if possible. Open questions are usually better here. Introduce difficult or personal questions toward the end of the interview in order not to create an emotional reaction that may affect subsequent answers, or cause the respondent to break off the interview. The questions should be asked in logical order to avoid confusing the respondent. Classificatory data on the respondent are usually asked last, because they tend to be less interesting and are on the personal side.

Sampling Plan. The other element of descriptive research is the sampling plan. The sampling plan calls for five decisions:

1. *Sampling unit.* This answers the question: "Who should be surveyed?" The proper sampling unit is not always obvious from the

nature of the information that is being sought. In the Camp Star survey of camping decision behaviors, should the sampling unit be the father, mother, child, or all three? Who is the usual initiator, influencer, decider, user, and/or purchaser?

2. *Sampling frame.* This answers the question "From what list do we draw the sample?" A sampling frame is nothing more than a listing of sampling units that can be used to select a sample. A phone book, for example, can be considered a sampling frame for a survey of local voter opinions on some issues. However, caution must be taken to choose an unbiased sampling frame. If the phone book were used to sample opinions of voting-age citizens, there might be an under representation of lower social classes without phones, or upper social classes with unlisted numbers, or people who use only a cell phone and do not have a land line phone.

In the Camp Star situation a sampling frame consisting of a list of families who had enrolled children in the camp might be biased in omitting the opinions of those who had chosen not to send their children to the camp because of some real or imagined problem with the camp, or those who had not heard of the camp. If the director is to make marketing plans intended to stimulate demand for the camp's services, obviously these two groups, as well as others, need to be surveyed for their opinions.

Perhaps a membership list of Jewish congregations in the area serviced by the camp would be a good sampling frame. A "perfect" sampling frame consisting of every member of the target population and only those members might not be available. Researchers must make those trade-offs necessary to acquire a sampling frame with few and noncritical biases.

3. *Sample size.* This answers the question "How many people should be surveyed?" Large samples obviously give more reliable results than do small samples. However, it is not necessary to sample the entire target market or even a substantial part of it to achieve satisfactory precision. Often samples amounting to less than a fraction of 1 percent of a population can provide good reliability, given a credible sampling procedure.[5]

4. *Sampling procedure.* This answers the question "How should

the respondents be chosen?" To draw statistically valid and reliable inferences about the target market, a random sample of the population should be drawn. Random sampling allows the calculation of confidence limits for sampling error.

However, random sampling is more costly than nonrandom sampling. Some marketing researchers suggest that the extra expenditure for probability sampling can be put to better use. Specifically, the money of a fixed research budget can be spent in designing better questionnaires and hiring better interviewers to reduce response and nonsampling errors that can be just as fatal as sampling errors.

This is a problem that marketing researchers and decision makers must carefully weigh. A standard marketing research text can help in making decisions regarding sampling procedures. (See the resource guide for a list of marketing research texts.)

5. *Means of contact.* This answers the question "How should the subjects be contacted?" The choices are telephone, mail, personal interview, fax machine, or Internet. *Telephone interviewing* stands out as the best method for gathering information quickly. It also permits the interviewer to clarify questions. The two main drawbacks of telephone interviewing are that only people with telephones are interviewed, and the interview must be kept short and not too personal.

The *mailed questionnaire* may be the best way to reach people who will not give personal interviews, or who are biased against the interviewers. On the other hand, mailed questionnaires require simple and clearly worded questions, and the return rate is usually low and/or slow.

Personal interviewing is the most versatile of the methods. The personal interviewer can ask more questions and can supplement the interview with personal observations. However, personal interviewing is the most expensive method and requires more technical and administrative planning and supervision.

Using *facsimile machines* to distribute questionnaires is sometimes acceptable when a high percentage of respondents can access a fax (usually true for contacting businesses), but may not be the best means to reach people in their homes. Also, fax questionnaires should be confined to only a few pages.

The Connected Congregation
Should You Use Internet Surveys?

Advantages

Online research is inexpensive. The cost of gathering survey information electronically is much less expensive than by traditional means. A typical e-mail survey costs about half what a conventional survey costs, and return rates can be as high as 50 percent.

Online research is faster. Online surveys are faster to complete, since the survey can automatically direct respondents to applicable questions and can be sent electronically to you, or the research supplier you use, once finished. One estimate is that 75 to 80 percent of a survey's targeted response can be generated in 48 hours using online methods, as compared to a telephone survey, which can take 70 days to obtain 150 completed interviews.

People tend to be more honest online than they are in personal or telephone interviews. Research has shown that people may be open about their opinions when they can respond to a survey privately and not to another person they feel might be judging them, especially on sensitive subjects, as might be true for religious topics.

Online research is more versatile. The multimedia applications of online research are especially advantageous. For instance, virtual reality software lets visitors inspect 360-degree views of sanctuaries or community centers. Even at the most basic level, online surveys make answering a questionnaire easier and more fun than paper-and-pencil versions.

Disadvantages

Samples can be small and skewed. Perhaps the largest criticism leveled against online research is that not everyone is online. Research subjects who respond to online surveys are more likely to be tech-savvy middle-class males. Some households are without Internet access in the United States. These people are most likely to differ in socioeconomic and education levels from those online. It is important for online marketing researchers to find creative ways to reach certain population segments that are less likely to be online, such as older Americans or Hispanics. One option is to combine offline sources with online findings, or use laptops in personal interviews to keep data in the same database.

Online market research is prone to technological problems and inconsistencies. Because online research is a relatively new method, many market researchers have not gotten survey designs right. A common error occurs in transferring a written survey to the screen. Others overuse technology, concentrating on the bells and whistles and graphics, while ignoring basic survey design guidelines. Problems also arise because browser software varies. The Web designer's final product may be seen very differently depending upon the research subjects' screen and operating system.

Sources: Catherine Arnold, "Not Done Yet: New Opportunities Still Exist in Online Research," *Marketing News*, Apr. 1, 2004, p. 17; Nima M. Ray and Sharon W. Tabor, "Contributing Factors: Several Issues Affect e-Research Validity," *Marketing News*, Sept. 15, 2003, p. 50; Louella Miles, "Online, On Tap," *Marketing*, June 16, 2004, pp. 39, 40; Joe Dysart, "Cutting Market Research Costs with On-Site Surveys," *The Secured Lender*, March/April 2004, pp. 64-67; Suzy Bashford, "The Opinion Formers," *Revolution*, May 2004, pp. 42-46; Bob Lamons, "Eureka! Future of B-to-B Research is Online," *Marketing News*, Sept. 24, 2001, pp. 9, 10.

Internet surveys are becoming more common, and have distinct advantages and disadvantages (see The Connected Congregation exhibit above). If you choose to use this method, you'll obviously want to be sure that there is no inherent bias in the population from which you draw your sample (i.e., those who have an e-mail address versus those who don't), and will need to have a good sampling frame to use in drawing the sample.

More information on Online Research

Some companies specialize in, or at least provide support for, conducting research online. Some of the better-known suppliers are listed below along with their areas of specialization. (See the resource guide for a more complete list of suppliers with Web sites provided.)

Full service Internet research: Greenfield Online

Designing questionnaires: Websurveyor; Insight Express; SurveyMonkey: Zoomerang; SurveyMethods; QuestionPro

Distributing questionnaires online and processing data: Harris Interactive; Knowledge Networks; Socratic Technologies

Obtaining samples for online research: Survey Sampling International

Analyzing data and distributing results: SPSS

Reporting results and additional interactive analysis: ConsumerMetrics, Inc.; Burke Digital Dashboard

Online panels: Lightspeed Research; Greenfield Online

Book

A good book to help you in constructing an Internet survey is Don A. Dillman, *Mail and Internet Surveys: The Tailored Design Method (2007 Update With New Internet, Visual, and Mixed-Mode Guide)* (Hoboken,N.J.: John Wiley & Sons, 2007).

Causal Research Methods

We have talked about formal research in its most common form, that of designing a survey. An increasing number of marketing researchers are eager to go beyond measuring the perceptions, preferences, and intentions of a target market to measuring actual cause-and-effect relationships. For example, the Camp Star researchers want to know the answers to these research questions:

• Would an expensive, four-color Camp Star brochure sent to prospective campers produce at least twice as many inquiries as the normal one-color brochure?

• Would Camp Star attract more parent interest if it emphasized the educational or recreational aspects of summer camping?

• What impact would a 20 percent increase in tuition costs have on next summer's enrollments?

Each of these questions can be answered by the survey method asking people to state their reactions. However, they may not give their true opinions or carry them out. Experimental research is more rigorous. Situations are created when the actual behavior of the target market can be observed and its causes identified. In applying the experimental method to the first question, the Camp Star director would need to design an expensive four-color brochure, as well as a traditional brochure. The researcher might select a subsample that comprises 100 families from the mailing list. Half of these families would receive an expensive brochure, and half would receive a traditional brochure. As inquiries come in, the director checks whether the family received the first or second brochure. The inquiry rate would be calculated from the two groups to learn whether the more expensive brochure stimulated at least twice as many inquiries to cover its higher cost.

If it did stimulate inquiries, and the camp director could think of no other factors that would explain the differences in the inquiry rates, he/she would mail only the expensive brochure to the remainder of the families on the mailing list.

The experimental method in marketing[6] is increasingly recognized as the most rigorous and conclusive, if the proper controls are exercised and the cost affordable. This method requires selecting matched groups of subjects, giving them different treatments, controlling extraneous variables from making a difference, and checking on whether observed differences are statistically significant. To the extent that the design and execution of the experiment eliminates alternative hypotheses that might explain the same results, the researchers and decision-makers have confidence in the conclusions.

One early example of experimentation is found in the Scriptures:

"Then Daniel asked the guard whom the palace master had appointed over Daniel, Hananiah, Mishael, Azariah: 'Please test your servants for ten days. Let us be given vegetables to eat and water to drink. You can then compare our appearance with that of the young men who eat the royal rations, and deal with your servants according to what you observe. So he agreed to this proposal and tested them for ten days. At the end of ten days it was observed that they appeared better and fatter than all the young men who had been eating the royal rations. So the guard continued to withdraw their royal rations and the wine they were to drink, and gave them vegetables'" (Daniel 1:11-16, NRSV).

Fieldwork

The fieldwork phase of survey or experimental research follows after the research design has been finished and pretested. Some organizations use volunteer interviewers. Other organizations hire professional interviewers. Marketing research works to select and train interviewers who can be trusted, who are personable and are able to do their work in a reasonably short time. The fieldwork phase could be the most expensive and the most liable to error. Three major problems need to be dealt with in this phase:

1. *Not present.* When randomly selected respondents are not reached on the first call, the interviewer must call back later or substitute another respondent; otherwise, a nonresponse bias may be introduced.

2. *Refusal to cooperate.* After reaching the subjects, the interviewer must interest them in cooperating; otherwise, a nonresponse bias may be introduced.

3. Respondent interview bias can also be a problem at this stage of the research.

Data Analysis and Report Presentation

The final step in the marketing research process is to develop meaningful information to present to the decision-maker. The researcher will tabulate the data and develop one- and two-way frequency distributions. The averages and measures of dispersion will be computed for the major variables. The researcher might attempt to apply some advanced statistical techniques and decision models in the hope of discovering additional findings. The researcher's purpose is not to overwhelm decision-makers with numbers and fancy statistical procedures. The researcher's purpose is to present major findings that will help the decision-maker make better marketing decisions.

---

[1] See Curtis Young, "Two Ministries Were Saved With Help From Research," *Marketing News,* Jan. 3, 1986, p. 25; and Curtis Young, "Marketing in the Nonprofit Religious Sector," *Journal of Professional Services Marketing* 3, no. 1/2 (1987): 119-126.

[2] Adapted from Irving D. Canton, "Do You Know Who Your Customer Is?" *Journal of Marketing,* April 1976, p. 83.

[3] For more information on how to design, recruit, moderate, and analyze the results of focus groups see Jean Bystedt, Siri Lynn, and Deborah Potts, *Moderating to the Max: A Full-Tilt Guide to Creative Insightful Focus Groups and Depth Interviews* (Ithaca, N.Y.: Paramount Market Publishing, 2003), or David W. Stewart, Prim Shamdassani, and Dennis Rook, *Focus Groups: Theory and Practice* (Thousand Oaks, Calif.: Sage Publications, 2007).

[4] Emily Nelson, "P&G Checks Out Real Life," *Wall Street Journal,* May 17, 2001, p. B1ff.

[5] For a "common sense" discussion of sampling see Bruce Wrenn, Robert E. Stevens, and David L. Loudon, *Marketing Research: Text and Cases,* 2nd ed. (New York: Routledge, 2007).

[6] For more on designing marketing research experiments see Gilbert Churchill and Dawn Iacobucci, *Marketing Research: Methodological Foundations* (Fort Worth: Dryden Press, 2009).

WORKSHEETS: CHAPTER 4

Marketing Research

Problem/Opportunity

For research to lead to better decisions, it must begin with a clear statement of the problem you seek to solve or the opportunity you need to evaluate. Describe the problem or opportunity below (e.g., what do you wish were different from the current situation?):

Problem:

_____

_____

_____

Opportunity:

_____

_____

_____

Research Purpose

List the decisions you are faced with making that, if the research provided evidence supporting it, would be made to solve the problem or exploit the opportunity:

Decision Alternatives:

1. _____

_____

_____

2. _____

_____

_____

3. _____
   _____
   _____

4. _____
   _____
   _____

5. _____
   _____
   _____

6. _____
   _____
   _____

Indicate the decisional criteria that you would use to choose among the decision alternatives (i.e., the information from the research that you need to know before you can make the decisions you are faced with):

Decisional Criteria:

1. _____
   _____
   _____

2. _____
   _____
   _____

3. _____
   _____
   _____

4. _____

_____

_____

5. _____

_____

_____

6. _____

_____

_____

State the Research Purpose:

_____

_____

_____

Research Questions

Identify the research objectives (questions) that you need to get answers to in order to fulfill the criteria so that you can make the decisions that will solve the problem/capitalize on the opportunity.

Research Questions:

1. _____

_____

_____

2. _____

_____

_____

3. _____

_____

_____

4. _____
   _____
   _____

5. _____
   _____
   _____

6. _____
   _____
   _____

Research Design

Indicate the research design you will need to use to get answers to your research questions:

Exploratory   _____
Descriptive   _____
Causal   _____

Data Collection Methods

Exploratory Research. Describe the exploratory research methods you need to employ to begin to get answers to these questions. Be specific and detailed in your description of what you need to do (e.g., identify the specific sources and types of secondary data you will obtain and analyze):

Secondary Data:

_____
_____
_____

Observation Research:

_____
_____
_____

Qualitative Interviewing (interview screener, interview or focus group guide, plan for conducting the interviews or focus groups):

_____

_____

_____

Based on your exploratory findings, what are the revised and continuing research objectives that require descriptive or causal research?

Revised Research Objectives:

_____

_____

_____

Descriptive Research:

Describe the descriptive research methods you need to employ to begin to get answers to these questions. Be specific and detailed in your description of what you need to do.

Which survey method will you use?
Telephone _____
Personal _____
Mail _____
Facsimile _____
Internet _____

Questionnaire or Observation Form

Design the specific questions you will use to get the information that achieves your research objectives:

_____

_____

_____

Sampling Plan

Identify each of the following elements of your sampling plan:

Sampling Unit

_____
_____
_____

Sampling Frame

_____
_____
_____

Sample Size

_____
_____
_____

Sampling Procedure

_____
_____
_____

Causal Research

Design the experiments need to test any cause-and-effect hypotheses that are part of the research questions:

Experimental Design:

_____
_____
_____

Fieldwork

Indicate the specific plans to collect the data using the data collection methods:

_____

_____

_____

Data Analysis and Report Writing

Summarize the findings and write the report

_____

_____

_____

CHAPTER 5:

What to Understand:
FACTORS INFLUENCING BEHAVIOR

"Someone's thoughts may be as deep as the ocean, but if you are smart, you will discover them" (PROVERBS 20:5, CEV).

In this chapter we will address the following questions:

1. What are some intrapersonal factors influencing human behavior?

2. What are some interpersonal factors influencing human behavior?

3. What are the stages of the decision-making choice process?

4. What are some marketing implications for understanding these factors and process?

Why do people behave as they do? Certainly the answer to this question is of considerable interest to all types of marketers. In for-profit marketing, this question is studied in the field of consumer behavior. Most marketing majors in collegiate schools of business are required to take a course in consumer behavior, and the field has entire books and journals devoted to publishing scholarship on the topic. Obviously we cannot do justice to such a comprehensive topic in a single chapter. We will confine our discussion to a few topics that will be of prime interest to congregational marketers. Topics are grouped under three headings: Intrapersonal Factors, Interpersonal Factors, and Decision-making Process aspects of behavior.[1]

Intrapersonal Factors Influencing Human Behavior
Needs, Motives, and Goals

Marketing managers who adopt the effective marketing management process (see chapter 2) as a guiding model naturally begin their study of individuals by seeking to understand their needs. Needs are at the core of the marketing orientation philosophy, and failure to understand those needs and develop need satisfying offerings has doomed many an organization that has not followed a thoroughgoing marketing orientation. We define needs as a state of felt deprivation by the individual.[2]

Marketers have been accused of creating needs, but it is more accurate to say that marketers can, in certain instances, make people more acutely aware of their latent needs than to claim that marketers have created those needs.

Within the for-profit setting it is the marketer's job to so well understand people's needs that they can create need-satisfying products when people are unable to articulate their latent needs when questioned. This brings us to a discussion of the relationship between needs, motives, goals, and wants.

People are motivated, or feel an inner drive, to satisfy a *need* by achieving the *goal* of acquiring something they *want*. For example, when you experience thirst (a need), you are motivated to slake your thirst (a goal) by buying a bottle of spring water (a generic want).[3] The brand you buy (e.g., Poland Springs) represents the *specific want* you have to satisfy your need.

The implication of this way of thinking about needs, motives, goals, and wants is that it is not sufficient merely to have a good product that is capable of satisfying a need. You must also become the specific want of the individual. This is why product-oriented organizations frequently succumb to marketing-oriented organizations—having a high-quality product is a necessary, but not sufficient, condition for long-term success. Marketing-oriented organizations study every aspect of human behavior to develop marketing appeals capable of connecting with people at many levels, not just high-quality-need-satisfying product performance.

While the reader might justifiably argue that these concepts do not translate in exactly this manner for people seeking a congregational home, we would suggest that needs, wants, motives, and goals do remain relevant concepts.

Needs Hierarchy. The concept of a hierarchy underlies many schemes offered to explain the structuring of needs or motives. The most influential motive is seen as enjoying the most dominant position in the hierarchy; the second-most influential holds the second-

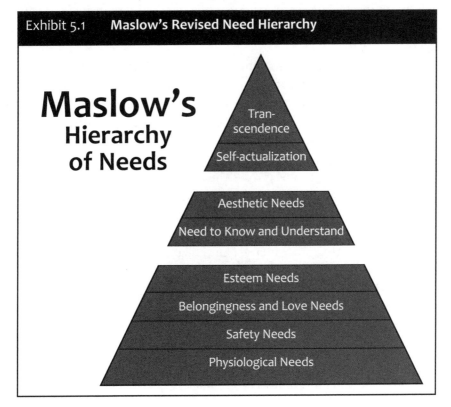

Exhibit 5.1   Maslow's Revised Need Hierarchy

Maslow's Hierarchy of Needs

Transcendence
Self-actualization
Aesthetic Needs
Need to Know and Understand
Esteem Needs
Belongingness and Love Needs
Safety Needs
Physiological Needs

most dominant position, and so on through the entire list. To be useful, however, the hierarchy concept must also help explain what factors influence the relative ordering of motives.

Maslow's Hierarchy. A. H. Maslow proposed perhaps the most widely known hierarchy. His scheme classified motives into groupings and suggested the degree to which each would influence behavior.[4] While the hierarchy originally consisted of five levels, Maslow revised it years later to include eight levels (see Exhibit 5.1).[5]

The lower set of four needs is what Maslow referred to as "deficiency needs," or needs that result from the lack of something innate or primary. The next group of two is called "growth needs," signifying those needs that people are seeking to satisfy when wanting to experience personal mental and emotional growth. The top two needs refer to those desires we have to achieve our highest potential, with self-transcendence consisting of needs relating to achieving the ultimate purpose of human life. These have been referred to by some commentators on Maslow as including "spiritual needs."

It is not difficult to imagine groups of people who might seek from a religious institution satisfaction of needs at each of the levels in the hierarchy. Most congregations have established means of delivering satisfaction for each level, or at least within each grouping, but see their mission as getting people to both experience and gain satisfaction of spiritual needs through affiliation with the institution. However, according to Maslow's theory, people do not "move up" to seek satisfaction of the next-higher order of needs until they have achieved satisfaction of the lowest-level needs. This is acknowledged as an operative model by congregations who believe you must first minister to someone's primary needs (e.g., soup kitchens or food banks) before talking with them about higher-order needs (e.g., Bible study).

From a marketing perspective, the principle is to learn what needs are motivating people in their exchange with the religious institution, group people together with similar needs (see chapter 7 on segmentation), develop marketing plans for stimulating exchange with each group, and then develop plans for demonstrating how the institution can continue to be a source for addressing people's needs as they move up the hierarchy. Marketers should become skilled at probing to learn those needs that are motivating someone's interest in the institution (see chapter 4 on Marketing Research).

Involvement

Consider a person named Jane facing two different choice situations. The first involves purchasing a new pair of running shoes. Because Jane runs an average of 50 miles per week, she is really into the sport and quite interested in her footwear.

In the second situation Jane decides that because five years have passed since she purchased her house, it was time to restain the deck. She wants to spend as little time as possible making a choice of brands, believing that differences between the brands won't be significant.

These two choice situations differ considerably in terms of the energy devoted to choice decisions. Unfortunately, many congregational marketers typically assume that people seeking a new place of worship are always involved to the extent described in the first example (i.e., highly involved). Although this may describe many people, it appears lacking for a wide variety of other religious marketing cases that resemble our second example—people who have little personal concern about their exchange activities and adopt a rather detached, reactive stance to stimuli (such as your attempts to get donations or volunteers for "worthy causes"?). Therefore, a major concern in this relatively new area of inquiry is how the level of involvement affects the amount of effort people devote to learning about your "products" and deciding when to engage in exchange with you.

Research has indicated that high involvement generates rather intense efforts on the part of the person for actively searching out sources of information. Conversely, low involvement is said to result in a passive person who engages in little if any active search for information. Here, exposure to products occurs mainly through advertisements and other information that the individual happens to encounter as a result of engaging in other activities (such as watching TV). Also, because of this lack of interest, little attention will be devoted to these sources. Consequently, only modest amounts of information may be acquired about a specific "brand" (i.e., church, ministry, program, etc.), even after repeated exposure to advertisements for it. In addition, the awareness level for brands may be low.[6] After acquiring information, people will process it to determine its meaning.

The *elaboration likelihood model*[7] describes how people make evaluations in both low- and high-involvement circumstances. There are two means of persuasion in the model: the central route, where attitude formation or change involves much thought and is based on diligent, rational consideration of the most important "product" information; and the peripheral route, where attitude formation or change involves comparatively much less thought and is a consequence of the association of a brand with either positive or negative peripheral cues. Examples of peripheral cues include evocative visual images, use of credible sources, or any other object that engenders positive feelings.

People follow the central route only if they possess sufficient *motivation, ability,* and *opportunity.* In other words, people may want to evaluate a ministry, program, etc., in detail, must have the necessary knowledge of it in memory, and must be given sufficient time and the proper setting to actually process the evaluation. If any one of the three factors (motivation, ability, opportunity) is lacking, people will tend to follow the peripheral route and consider less central, more extrinsic factors in their decisions.

Marketers who believe they have an important "story to tell" about their product, who have devoted considerable energies to designing products with significant need-satisfying ability for targeted groups, want the people they are trying to engage in a long-term relationship to be as highly involved as the marketer. This describes the vast majority of our readers for the vast majority of their exchanges with their publics. The reason marketers such as this want highly involved people is that only highly involved people will pay attention to your "story"—low-involved individuals won't take the time or make the effort to hear the long version of what you have to say. As we've indicated, they have to be reached with low-involvement peripheral communication message strategies.

So is it possible to convert low involvers into high involvers? The answer is maybe, and marketing strategists have used several approaches to try to achieve that goal. First, you can link the product to some involving issue, such as when houses of worship were sought out after the terrorist attacks on September 11, 2001. Second, you can link the product to some personally involving situation, such as divorce, the death of a loved one, job termination, etc. Third, you might design advertising to trigger strong emotions related to personal values or ego defense, such as rearing a child within a faith community or pursuing a social environment with strong moral values. Fourth, you might add an important feature—for example, day care or elementary education. These strategies at best raise involvement from a low to a moderate level; they do not necessarily propel the person into a highly involved relationship with your institution. The transformation of someone with a low involvement with a religious institution usually has to occur within the individual, unless some catastrophic event precipitates the conversion into a high involvement relationship.

Perception

A motivated person is ready to act. How the motivated person actually acts is influenced by his or her view or perception of the situation. *Perception* is the process by which an individual selects, organizes, and interprets information inputs to create a meaningful picture of the world.[8] Perception depends not only on the physical stimuli but also on the stimuli's relation to the surrounding field and on conditions within the individual. The key point is that perceptions can vary widely among individuals who are exposed to the same reality. In marketing, perceptions trump reality, as it is perceptions that will affect people's actual behavior. People can emerge with different perceptions of the same object because of three perceptual processes: selective attention, selective distortion, and selective retention.

Selective Attention. A research study conducted some time ago found that the average American adult is aware of seeing less than 100 major media advertisements per day.[9] However, the daily advertising exposure rate for a typical person has been estimated to range as high as 3,000. This suggests that although exposure and sensory processes both selectively filter stimuli for information processing, additional points of selectivity must also exist. One such filtering mechanism is *attention*, which can be viewed as the allocation of processing capacity to stimuli. That is, attention regulates the amount of additional processing that a stimulus will receive. Generally, the more processing capacity that is devoted to a stimulus, the greater will be the individual's awareness and comprehension of it. Here are some findings that indicate the type of stimuli that people will notice:

1. People are more likely to notice stimuli that relate to a current need. A person who is motivated to join a grief recovery group will notice an announcement in the worship bulletin about a scheduled group meeting. He/she might not see the notice about the blood drive being held during the coming week.

2. People are more likely to notice stimuli that they anticipate. You are more likely to attend to religious literature rather than self-help literature offered on a church's Web site because you do not expect the Web site to offer self-help literature.

3. People are more likely to notice stimuli whose deviations are large in relation to the normal size of the stimuli. You are more likely to notice a message offering $100 off a $595 seminar for early registration than one offering $25 off.

Selective Distortion. Even noticed stimuli do not always come across in the way the senders intended. *Selective distortion* is the tendency to interpret information in a way that will fit our preconceptions. People will often distort information to be consistent with prior beliefs about the product or brand.[10] Selective distortion can work to the advantage of marketers with strong brands when people distort neutral or ambiguous brand information to make it more positive. For example, one study found that people were equally split in their preference for Diet Coke versus Diet Pepsi when tasting both on a "blind" basis.[11] When tasting the branded versions, however, people preferred Diet Coke by 65 percent and Diet Pepsi by only 23 percent (with the remainder seeing no difference).

Selective Retention. People will fail to record much information to which they are exposed in memory, but they will tend to retain information that supports their attitudes and beliefs. Because of selective retention, we are likely to remember *the* good points of a product we like and forget good points about competing products. Selective retention again works to the advantage of strong brands. It also explains why marketers need to use repetition in sending messages to their target market—to make sure their message is not overlooked. Supplying messages to members that reinforces positive feelings about the institution will likely be most effective with those who are already positively inclined toward the institution.

Learning

Learning is an important component of people's behavior. Learning certainly occurs intentionally, as when a problem is recognized and information about products that might solve the problem is acquired. However, learning also can occur unintentionally, and this type of learning can strongly influence the behavior of people. People learn in several basic ways. However, four elements seem to be fundamental to the vast majority of situations: motive, cue, response, and reinforcement.[12] The exact nature and strength of these components influences what will be learned, how well it will be learned, and the rate at which learning will occur.

Motive. As noted above, motives arouse individuals, thereby increasing their readiness to respond. This arousal function is essential, since it activates the energy needed to engage in learning activity. In addition, any success at achieving the motivating goal, or avoiding some unpleasant situation, tends to reduce arousal. Because this is reinforcing, such activity will have a greater tendency to occur again in similar situations. Thus, religious marketers should strive to have their institution's name available when relevant motives are aroused because it is expected that people will learn a connection between the institution and the motive (e.g., Church XYZ is a refuge for the lonely).

Cues. A cue may be viewed as a weak stimulus that is not strong enough to arouse individuals, but capable of providing *direction* to motivated activity. That is, it influences the manner in which people respond to a motive. For example, when we are hungry we are guided by certain cues, such as restaurant signs and the aroma of food cooking, because we have learned that these stimuli are associated with food preparation and consumption. Smiling greeters at the sanctuary door are cues that you are welcomed and that it is a friendly congregation.

Response. A response may be viewed as a mental or physical activity the person makes in reaction to a stimulus situation. Responses appropriate to a particular situation are learned over time through experience in facing that situation. As we have noted, the occurrence of a response is not always observable. Therefore, it must again be emphasized that our inability to observe responses does not necessarily mean that learning is not taking place.

Reinforcement. Perhaps the most widely acceptable view of reinforcement is anything that follows a response and increases the tendency for the response to reoccur in a similar situation.[13] Because reinforced behavior tends to be repeated, individuals can learn to develop successful means of responding to their needs or changing conditions.

Various theories have been developed to explain different aspects of learning.[14] These theories, however, can be grouped into several major categories for the focus of our present discussion. The first major division is between the behavioral and cognitive schools of thought. While *cognitive* interpretations place emphasis on the discovery of patterns and insight, *behaviorists* argue that what humans learn are connections or associations between stimuli and responses. The behavioral school may be further subdivided on the basis of the type of conditioning employed. Each of these subdivisions will be discussed in turn.

Behavioral Theories. Some learning theorists maintain that learning involves the development of connections between a stimulus and a response to it. That is, the association of a response and a stimulus is the connection that is learned. Reinforcement is employed in conjunction with two fundamentally different methods of learning connections: classical and instrumental conditioning.

Classical Conditioning. Essentially, classical conditioning (sometimes called respondent conditioning) pairs one stimulus with another that already elicits a given response. Over repeated trials, the new stimulus will also begin to elicit the same or a very similar response.

To appreciate the process involved, it is useful to review an experiment conducted by Ivan Pavlov, who pioneered the study of classical conditioning.[15] Pavlov reasoned that because food already caused his dog to salivate, it might be possible to link a previously neutral stimulus to the food so that it too would be able to make the dog salivate. This would demonstrate that the dog had learned to associate the neutral stimulus with the food. Pavlov used a bell as the neutral stimulus.

Instrumental Conditioning. The behavioral theory of instrumental conditioning (sometimes called operant conditioning)[16] also involves developing connections between stimuli and responses. It is not necessary to reinforce every "correct" response in order for learning to occur.

Instrumental conditioning differs from classical conditioning in several important respects. Although classical conditioning relies on an already-established stimulus-response connection, instrumental conditioning requires the learner to discover an appropriate, or "correct," response—one that will be reinforced. For this reason, instrumental conditioning involves the learner at a more conscious and purposeful level than does classical conditioning.[17]

A second distinction between these two methods concerns the *outcome* of the learning situation. In classical conditioning the outcome is not dependent on the learner's actions, but with instrumental conditioning a particular response can change the learner's situation or environment. The response then is actually *instrumental* in producing reinforcement or making something happen in the environment, hence the name for this type of conditioning. Experiencing a worship service that someone finds inspirational reinforces the behavior of attending the service again instead of just hearing a message via Web casting. A hearty "Amen" during a sermon reinforces a pastor's choice of sermon topics, and so on.

Because of these differences, each conditioning method is suited to explaining different types of learning. Learning to adapt and control one's environment is better explained by instrumental conditioning because it requires that the learner discover the response that leads to reinforcement. Alternatively, classical conditioning is often more useful in explaining how people learn "brand" names (see chapter 9 for more on branding for religious institutions) and acquire or change their opinion, tastes, and goals. That is, the material to be learned in such cases is associated with stimuli that already elicit favorable or unfavorable experiences. We will now examine an alternative to the behavioral learning theories—cognitive learning theory.

Cognitive Learning Theory, Instead of viewing learning as the development of connections between stimuli and responses, cognitive theorists stress the importance of perception, problem solving, and insight. This viewpoint contends that much learning occurs not as a result of trial and error or practice, but through discovering meaningful patterns that enable us to solve problems. A key component in cognitive learning theory is the role of memory in affecting learning and subsequent behavior. Several views regarding the structure of memory and its operation exist.[18] One, termed the *multiple store* approach, views memory as being composed of three distinct storage registers (sensory, short-term, and long-term) that differ in capacity, storage duration, and functioning.

Information is first received by *sensory memory*. Input is in the form of sensations produced by the sensory receptors. Information is stored for only a fraction of a second and will be lost through decay (fading away) unless sufficient attention is allocated to it so that it can be analyzed and transferred to short-term memory for further processing. Advertisers concentrate a great deal of effort on designing stimuli in their ads to be vivid and easily recognized in order to draw attention and to provide strong sensory impressions for individuals.

To a large extent, *short-term memory* can be viewed as the workspace for information processing. That is, it is a portion of memory activated to store and process information temporarily in order to interpret it and comprehend its meaning. This is accomplished by combining incoming information with other information (past experiences, knowledge, and the like) stored in long-term memory.

Although the duration of this memory register is considerably longer than that of sensory memory, it still is very brief, lasting less than one minute. In addition, the capacity of short-term memory is quite limited.

The *long-term memory* system can be thought of as a relatively permanent storehouse for information that has undergone sufficient processing. Material can be maintained in long-term memory for as little as a few minutes to as long as many years. In addition, this system has the capacity to store an almost unlimited amount of information.

A predominant key to coding material for storage in long-term memory is *meaningfulness*, the personal understanding an individual can derive from the information. That is, through elaborative rehearsal the individual uses existing knowledge to interpret incoming information and code it in a way that is consistent with existing cognitive structure (knowledge base). The degree of success in accomplishing this will affect how well the new information can be retained and made available for future use.[19]

Retrieval is the process of accessing information in long-term memory and activating it into consciousness. The retrieved data may then be combined with other material available in short-term memory, elaborated on, and formed into a coherent package of meaningful information. Therefore, retrieval may be viewed as the means of transferring information from long-term memory into the activated workspace of short-term memory so that it can be processed further.

Cognitive learning theories have considerable implications for advertising strategies and tactics. The following are some examples of this theory's application to the advertising function:

1. *Advertising messages with unique aspects have a greater potential for being remembered.* This occurs because material with unusual aspects is least affected by forgetting. This is one factor that motivates advertisers to seek novel approaches and themes for their messages. Another potential benefit is that products characterized by ads as somewhat unique may actually lead to a more favorable evaluation by individuals.[20]

2. *The order in which material is presented seems to influence how well it will be retained, with the middle portion being the most easily forgotten.* This occurs apparently because the beginning and ending of messages stand out the most and interfere with remembering material in-between (retroactive and proactive inhibition). The implication is that the most important parts of advertising messages should be placed at the beginning or end, or both. Conversely, some direct-mail advertisers bury the price of their merchandise in the middle of a long letter so as to minimize its negative impact on an exchange decision.

3. *Messages that encourage immediate rehearsal of material stimulate its retention.* Maintenance rehearsal keeps material in short-term memory. Elaborate rehearsal will encourage the transfer of material to long-term memory. This is why some radio and television advertisers encourage listeners to repeat a telephone number or address several times, and also attempt to develop some meaningful pattern to the numbers.

4. *More information can be processed and retained if it is chunked.* Because the capacity of short-term memory is approximately seven items, chunking—grouping material into sets that can more easily be remembered, such as listing phone numbers as (123) 456-7890—can be viewed as a way to package a greater amount of information efficiently. This suggests that advertisers should attempt to find appropriate methods of chunking information for individuals so that they can deliver a greater amount of message content in the limited time or space at their disposal.

5. *The amount of information that can be transferred to long-term memory is a function of the time available for processing.* When recall of a message will be required, approximately five to 10 seconds is required to transfer one chunk of information to long-term memory through memorization. The amount of information that an advertiser presents should therefore be tailored to the amount of time available for processing and the way the information can be packaged.[21]

6. *Memory is cue-dependent, and presentation of relevant cues will stimulate recall.* Apparently, certain cues present during the learning context become associated with the material in memory. Their presentation at a later date facilitates recall of the learned material.[22] In a similar fashion, a narrative or song can sometimes be devised to

promote retention of other information. This process can be very effectively employed by designing packages and point-of-purchase displays to contain the same cues used in advertisements for the product. For example, a picture of a babbling mountain brook reminds some people of Coors beer, and just the word "blimp" reminds others of Goodyear.

7. *Material retained in long-term memory might be quite different from the information presented in a learning situation.* This is so because some information will be lost from short-term memory, the person may generate inferences and cognitive responses, and material will also be drawn from long-term memory. It is important for advertisers to understand these activities and their potential in any specific situation for influencing the meaning that individuals derive from promotional messages.

8. *Material that is meaningful to the individual is learned more quickly and therefore has a greater chance of being retained than does nonmeaningful material.* Apparently meaningful material actively involves the individual's mental capacities, and this leads to its greater retention. Therefore, the recommendation is to design advertisements that stimulate peoples' mental involvement, thereby making messages meaningful to them. However, the marketer should develop the specific meaning desired for the message rather than relying on chance for individuals to determine what meaning they will derive from it themselves. Some methods of accomplishing this are listed below. Of course, the specific situation will dictate the degree to which they are appropriate.

   a. *Visual material.* Information presented as visual content is frequently more memorable than verbal content. This suggests that, where possible, advertisers find ways to "say it with pictures" rather than conveying information with advertising copy.[23]

   b. *Interactive imagery.* Use of pictures, symbols, and other visual devices that depict how two concepts or properties relate to each other can be a highly effective aid to people's memory. Such imagery can be used to link a specific brand to particular needs or to a general product group. An example is using the image of the sun kissing an orange for the Sunkist brand of oranges.

   c. *Showing mistakes.* During demonstration of mechanical

skills, performance, or decision-making, it is often useful to show how things should not be done, as well as how they should be done. The Midas muffler commercial that depicts a car owner's trauma when attempting to get his muffler replaced at service stations is such an example. An additional technique, which also heightens involvement, is to simulate situations as if the viewer were actually experiencing them.

  d. *Incomplete messages.* Leaving some messages open-ended so that people must become involved to complete them has been found to increase retention.[24] Incomplete messages have also been found to influence brand attitudes, purchase intentions, and brand choice positively for highly involved individuals but not for individuals having low involvement.[25] This may be done simply by not completing the entire message, or it may be more subtly accomplished by having the announcer ask a question or pose a decision problem for the viewer to answer.

  e. *Mnemonic techniques.* The art of mnemonics involves the development of a pattern for a series of seemingly unrelated facts so that they can be more easily remembered.[26] Therefore, any technique that allows people to "see" some pattern for associating otherwise-meaningless facts will usually be helpful. When possible, you should provide word associations for telephone numbers.

Attribution

  Attribution theory attempts to explain how people arrive at conclusions of cause and effect for the behavior of themselves or others.[27] It is seeking to understand the answer to the question "Why?": "Why did he invite me to go to church with him?" "Why did I lie about that?" People typically make internal or external attributions about their own behavior. For example, let's say someone uses a new graphics program to design the cover of the worship bulletin and receives compliments on the design. If the person thinks to himself or herself, *I have a real natural talent for graphic design,* this would be an example of an internal attribution. If, on the other hand, he or she would think, *That was strictly luck—the software just somehow turned that out; I couldn't do that again,* that would be an external attribution.

Social psychologists have used internal and external attributions to explain the "foot-in-the-door" phenomenon.[28] Here a person's compliance with a small request (the "foot-in-the-door") affects compliance with a larger subsequent request. This is because the individual looks at his or her prior behavior (i.e., compliance with the small request) and concludes he or she is the kind of person who says yes to such requests, (i.e., the person makes an internal attribution). This phenomenon also helps explain why people who make a small donation are more likely to follow up with a larger donation when asked, compared with the person who is first asked for a large donation.

Marketers have been interested in understanding how incentives offered to initiate trial behavior affect subsequent exchange behavior. Too large an incentive, for example, might cause someone to make an external attribution ("I tried this because it was free") instead of the more desirable internal attribution ("I used this brand because I like it"). So contrary to conventional wisdom, it is not the largest incentive that is most likely to result in positive attitude change. Attribution theory might be used to explain, and inform strategies for, numerous marketing-related interactions with current and prospective members.

Interpersonal Factors Influencing Human Behavior
Reference Groups

A person's reference groups consist of all the groups that have a direct (face-to-face) or indirect influence on his/her attitudes or behavior. Groups having a direct influence on a person are called membership groups. Some membership groups are primary groups, such as family, friends, neighbors, and coworkers, those with whom the person interacts fairly continuously and informally. People also belong to secondary groups, such as religious, professional, and trade union groups, which tend to be more formal and require less continuous interaction. However, in some circumstances a person's groups formed around their community of faith can be a more influential reference group than even some primary groups, including one's own family.

Reference groups influence people in several ways. Reference groups expose an individual to new behaviors and lifestyles, influence attitudes and self-concept, and create pressures for conformity that may affect decision-making. People are also influenced by groups to which they do not belong. Aspirational groups are those a person hopes to join; dissociative groups are those whose values or behavior an individual rejects.

Where group influence is strong, marketers must determine how to reach and influence opinion leaders in these reference groups. An opinion leader is the person in informal, product-related communications who offers advice or information about a specific product or product-category, such as which synagogue has the best religious day school or what is the best book of daily devotions to buy. Marketers try to reach opinion leaders by identifying demographic and psychographic characteristics associated with opinion leadership, identifying the media used by opinion leaders, and directing messages at opinion leaders. The use of expert spokespersons with high credibility is an attempt to portray a reference group whose behavior the target market desires to emulate. Conversely, suggesting that your product is disapproved of by a negative reference group (i.e., a group that the target-market members do not want to emulate) is another way to use reference groups in developing marketing strategy. See Exhibit 5.2 for an example of the latter approach.

Exhibit 5.2   Using a Dissociative Reference Group in an Ad

Social Class

Social class, or "social stratification," is the general term whereby people in a society are ranked by other members of a society into higher and lower social positions, which produces a hierarchy of respect or prestige.[29] Social classes are multidimensional, being based on numerous components. While income, education, and occupation are among the more common variables used in defining someone's social class, other variables have been used as well. It is important for the marketer to realize that some of these variables are more reliable "proxies" (substitutes) than others. Income is often misleading as an indicator of social-class position. Yet money, far more than anything else, is what Americans associate with the idea of social class.[30]

On the other hand, occupation generally provides a fairly good clue to one's social class; in fact, some believe it is the best single indicator available, because certain occupations are held in higher esteem than others by Americans. Educational attainment is also closely associated with social class. In fact, these three variables—income, occupation, and education—are the basis for the government's socioeconomic status score, often used as a measure of social class. Housing is another key social-class ingredient, according to most theories.

Most marketers believe that "birds of a feather flock together" and thus "you are where you live." Consequently, some marketers use geodemographic data to segment markets on the basis of lifestyles or social class. As will be discussed in chapter 7, the Claritas organization characterizes those at the top of the social class ladder as "the upper crust," followed in descending order by "blue-blood estates" and "movers and shakers," and further down the scale to "kids and cul-de-sacs" and "white picket fences," to "shotguns and pickups" and "low-rise living," the lowest of the 66 social class segments.

Social class may frequently serve as an aspirational reference group, with people behaving in ways that follow the behavioral patterns of the social class to which they aspire. Joining organizations whose members belong to the aspirational social class is one means people use to achieve their need to "belong." Media usage varies by social class, and advertisers trying to reach people in a particular social class must not only use the media preferred by that class but also must design message strategies that speak to those in the targeted class.

Culture and Subculture

Culture may be defined as *that complex whole that includes knowledge, belief, art, morals, law, customs, and any other capabilities and habits acquired by man as a member of society.*[31]

The importance of having an understanding of culture to marketers is reflected in this observation: *People both view themselves in the context of this culture and react to their environment based upon the cultural framework that they bring to that experience. Each individual perceives the world through his own cultural lens.*[32]

Thus, an understanding of culture enables the marketer to interpret the reaction of people to alternative marketing strategies.

Chapter 1's observations on the status of religion in America were statements identifying the role that religion plays in our culture. While those statistics reflect some change in the role that organized religion plays in the lives of some individuals, we remain a culture that places a great deal of value on religious institutions. Many of the most vigorously debated social issues are related to religion (e.g., separation of church and state, rights of the unborn, same-sex marriages, etc.), and are likely to continue to dominate our social discourse in the future.

Not all segments of a society have the same cultural patterns. The marketer can distinguish more homogeneous subgroups within the heterogeneous national society. We refer to these groups as subcultures because they have values, customs, traditions, and other ways of behaving that are peculiar to a particular group within a culture. Individuals may be members of more than one subculture at the same time. Thus, it is imperative that religious marketers understand who constitutes the most relevant subculture for their particular product. By knowing the characteristics and behavioral patterns of the segment they are trying to reach, they are in a better position to refine the marketing mix required to satisfy that target segment properly.

Decision-making Process

The intrapersonal and interpersonal factors influencing a person's behavior exert that influence during a decision-making process. Marketers have typically seen this process, for high-involvement decisions consisting of five stages:

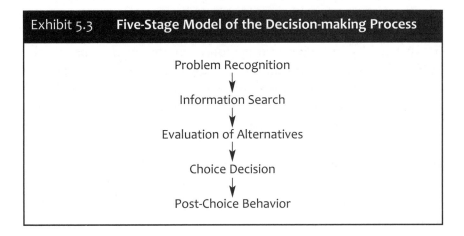

Exhibit 5.3	**Five-Stage Model of the Decision-making Process**

Problem Recognition
↓
Information Search
↓
Evaluation of Alternatives
↓
Choice Decision
↓
Post-Choice Behavior

Problem Recognition

Problem recognition results when a person recognizes a difference of sufficient magnitude between what is perceived as the desired state of affairs and what is the actual state of affairs. It must be enough to arouse and activate the decision process.[33]

This process integrates many of the concepts previously discussed in this chapter. For example, information processing and the motivation process are highly relevant here. Individuals must become aware of the problem or need through processing of information arising internally or externally. They then become motivated. Thus, the process of problem recognition means that the person becomes aroused and activated to engage in some purposeful exchange-decision activity.

This motivation to resolve a particular problem, however, depends on two factors: the magnitude of the discrepancy between the desired and actual states, and the importance of the problem.[34]

A person who runs out of milk or bread has a clear definition of the problem. Other situations exist, however, in which the individual may not have a clear definition of the problem, even though problem recognition has occurred. For example, the matter of self-image may lead to such an occurrence, such as when the person feels that the expression of a desired image is not quite right and yet is unable to define exactly what is wrong. In such cases, information search may be engaged in to identify the problem more clearly.

Marketers need to identify the circumstances that trigger a particular need by gathering information from a number of people the marketer is trying to engage in exchange. They can then develop marketing strategies that trigger their interest. This is particularly important for religious organizational marketers dealing with highly involved, emotionally charged decisions.

Information Search

Of key interest to the marketer are the major information sources to which the individual will turn and the relative influence that each will have on the subsequent choice decision. These information sources fall into four groups:

1. *Personal.* Family, friends, neighbors, acquaintances, e-mail.
2. *Institutional.* Advertising, Web sites, displays.
3. *Public.* Broadcast media, Internet postings, periodicals, blogs.
4. *Experiential.* Interaction with the institution and its members.

The relative amount and influence of these sources vary with the choice under consideration and the decider's characteristics. Institutional sources normally perform an information function, whereas personal sources perform a legitimizing or evaluation function. Again, it is important that you acquire an understanding of the ways in which the people access and use sources of information when making decisions about your institution.

Evaluation of Alternatives

A person evaluates an object (e.g., an institution, ministry, program) on the basis of a number of choice criteria. They define the preferred features that a person seeks in an exchange and may be either objective or subjective in nature.[35] No matter how many criteria are evaluated by the individual, they are likely to differ in their importance, usually with one or two criteria being more important than others. Thus, while several evaluative criteria are *salient* (important) to the individual, some are *determinant* (they are most important and are also perceived to differ among the alternatives).

Choice Decision

When making their choice decision, people might use one of several different *choice heuristics*.

Noncompensatory Decision Rules. Decision rules are said to be noncompensatory when good performance on one evaluative criterion does not offset or compensate for poor performance on another evaluative criterion of the object.

Compensatory Decision Rule. People using a compensatory decision rule will allow perceived favorable ratings of evaluative criteria to offset unfavorable evaluations. That is, an object's strengths can compensate for its weaknesses. This decision rule evaluates each object along all attributes. The object performing the best for the collective sum of the attributes would be the object selected by the person.

It should be emphasized that while it is rare for someone to actually calculate scores for objects, they do (1) determine the objects to be considered, (2) define their needs and order them, (3) determine the degree to which each object meets their needs, and (4) select the object that will best meet their most important needs, as they perceive them.[36]

Intervening Factors. Two general factors can intervene between the choice intention and the choice decision.[37] The first factor is the attitudes of others. The extent to which another person's attitude reduces the preference for an alternative depends upon two things: (1) the intensity of the other person's negative attitude toward the decision-maker's preferred alternative and (2) the individual's motivation to comply with the other person's wishes.[38] The more intense the other person's negativism and the closer the other person is to the decision-maker, the more the decision-maker will adjust his or her choice intention. The converse is also true: A decision-maker's preference for a choice object will increase if someone he or she respects favors the same object strongly.

The second factor is *unanticipated situational factors* that may erupt to change the choice intention. Changes in the person's personal life (job transfers, change in marital status, birth of child, etc.), or environmental changes (closing or opening of alternative houses of worship, changing of pastoral staff, etc.) may intervene to change preference or choice.

Choice Based on "How Do I Feel About It?" Marketers have begun to devote more attention to individual choice based on feelings, or affective choice, in contrast to the rational choice models of exchange decisions.[39] Emotion-based choice is more wholistic in nature, centering on the individual's overall sense of how they feel about the exchange, instead of breaking the decision into an evaluation of the individual attributes and combining the results (e.g., the compensatory and noncompensatory decision rules). In emotion-, or affective-, based decision-making, people have a mental image of having or using the product, and get a sense for how that would make them feel.[40] For example, a female student might imagine dinner with a boyfriend at a club, or at an intimate café and make a choice on where she would feel was the best place for dinner. Marketers whose individuals are making choices based more on emotion than logic should strive to produce products capable of delivering emotional satisfaction,[41] and help people to imagine the consequences of consuming the product.[42]

Post-Choice Behavior

Because the person is uncertain of the wisdom of his/her decision, he/she rethinks this decision in the post-choice stage. There are several functions that this stage serves. First, it serves to broaden the individual's set of experiences stored in memory. Second, it provides a check on how well the individual is doing as a person in selecting products. Third, the feedback that the person receives from this stage helps to make adjustments in future choice decisions.

Satisfaction/Dissatisfaction. Satisfaction is an important element in the evaluation stage. *Satisfaction* refers to the buyer's state of being adequately rewarded in an exchange situation for the sacrifice he/she has made. People form certain expectations prior to an exchange. These expectations may be about (1) the nature and performance of the object (that is, the anticipated benefits to be derived directly from the object), (2) the costs and efforts to be expended before obtaining the object's benefits, and (3) the social benefits or costs accruing to the person as a result of the exchange (that is, the anticipated impact of the exchange on significant others).[43] Advertising may often be an important factor influencing these expectations. People may have a variety of product performance expectations, including what the individual hopes will be ideal level of performance, what would be fair and equitable given the individual's expenditure of time and money in obtaining and using the product, and what the person expects to actually occur.

Once people exchange for a product, they may then become either satisfied or dissatisfied. Research has uncovered several determinants that appear to influence satisfaction, including demographic variables, personality variables, expectations, and other factors. For example, older individuals tend to have lower expectations and to be more easily satisfied. Higher education tends to be associated with lower satisfaction. Men tend to be more satisfied than women. The more confidence one has in exchange decision-making and the more competence in a given product area, the greater one's satisfaction tends to be. There is also greater satisfaction when relevant others are perceived to be more satisfied.[44] Persons who are more satisfied with their lives as a whole also indicate higher levels of satisfaction.[45]

Satisfaction with an exchange results in more-favorable post-choice attitudes, higher intentions to repeat the exchange, and greater brand loyalty. On the other hand, if people are dissatisfied, they are likely to exhibit less-favorable post-choice attitudes, lower or nonexistent repeat exchange intentions, brand switching, complaining behavior, and negative word-of-mouth.

What happens when people experience dissatisfaction? There are several negative outcomes possible.[46] First, individuals may exhibit unfavorable word-of-mouth communication; that is, they tell others about their problem. In fact, studies show that customers tell twice as many people about bad experiences as good ones. Second, people may not continue to exchange for the object. Those who are not fully satisfied with an object are less likely to desire it again than are satisfied decision-makers. A third action for the individual is to complain. Several generalizations exist from research on complaining:[47]

- Complainers tend to be members of more upscale socioeconomic groups than noncomplainers.
- The severity of the dissatisfaction or problems is positively related to complaint behavior.
- Complaining is more likely when there is a more positive perception of responsiveness to customer complaints.

It is important for marketers to realize that complaints are actually opportunities.[48] Simply listening to complaints boosts brand loyalty tremendously. The key is getting people to complain to the organization rather than telling the typical nine or 10 people about their problem. But for everyone who complains, there are 26 others who feel the same way but did not voice a complaint. See chapter 12 for more on how to deal with dissatisfied exchange partners.

Post-Choice Dissonance

Cognitive dissonance occurs as a result of a discrepancy between a person's decision and the person's prior evaluation. Dissonance theory was derived from two basic principles: (1) dissonance is uncomfortable and will motivate the person to reduce it, and (2) individuals experiencing dissonance will avoid situations that produce more dissonance.

Dissonance Reduction. There are several major ways in which the individual may strive to reduce dissonance: (1) change his or her evaluation of the chosen object, (2) seek new information to support his or her choice, or (3) change his or her attitudes.

1. Changing Object Evaluations. One of the ways individuals seek to reduce dissonance is to reevaluate product alternatives. This is accomplished by the individuals' enhancing the attributes of the products selected while decreasing the importance of the unselected products' attributes. That is, people seek to polarize alternatives in order to reduce their dissonance.[49] In addition, selective retention may operate to allow the person to forget positive features of the unselected alternative and negative features of the chosen product while remembering negative attributes of the unchosen item along with favorable features of the chosen alternative.

2. Seeking New Information. A second way that people may reduce dissonance is by seeking additional information in order to confirm the wisdom of their product choice.

3. Changing Attitudes. As a result of dissonance, individuals may change their attitudes to make them consonant with their behavior. For example, when the marketer secures trial among target customers who initially have an unfavorable attitude toward the item (let's say they engaged in exchange because of some offered incentive), this situation is likely to produce dissonance. That is, unfavorable attitudes toward the product are inconsistent with the behavior of product trial. Motivation to achieve consonance will likely take the form of attitude change, because that is easier than renouncing the choice. Reevaluating the product and adopting a positive attitude toward it allows attitudes and behavior to become consistent, and consonance is achieved.

Marketing Implications for the Decision-making Process

Problem Recognition. Promotion is an important vehicle used by marketers to cause problem recognition to occur among potential customers. Activities may be focused on the individual's *desired state* and/or perceptions of the *actual state*, such that a difference of sufficient magnitude occurs between them. People may also need to become aware of problem situations they have simply become accustomed to and have therefore ignored. Many organizations' ads attempt to bring such problems out in the open for peoples' consideration by making potential exchange partners aware of a problem before it becomes critical.

Information Search. In order for marketers to influence the process of search and alternative evaluation, they first must have information about it among their market segments. There are several pieces of the information-processing puzzle that they should seek to fill in (assuming that search activity is engaged in by a significant segment of their market). First, they need to determine what sources of information are actually used by people. Next, they must determine each source's influence.

Evaluation of Alternatives. In order for marketers to develop a successful marketing mix, there must be an understanding of what criteria are used by individuals in making an exchange decision for this object, as well as how important each criterion is, and how the person rates each object on the various criteria. Marketers will first need to determine which evaluative criteria people in an exchange decision use. This may be accomplished by *directly asking* people what factors they consider when they compare alternatives. If the marketers believe that individuals cannot or will not directly reveal their evaluative criteria, then an *indirect* approach may be utilized. In this situation the marketers may, for instance, ask the individual what evaluative criteria he/she thinks someone else would use. Once the evaluative criteria are known, a second measure that marketers will find useful is the relative importance individuals place on these criteria.

Choice and Post-Choice. If you discover your organization or its ministries are at a disadvantage based on the evaluative criteria being used by your targeted group, then several options are available: (1) make changes in the organization or its programs to perform better on these criteria, (2) alter beliefs about your organization or its ministries—sometimes people have formed the wrong impressions based on faulty or inadequate information, (3) alter the importance weights—perhaps people do not appreciate the real value of some of the characteristics you've designed into your offering, (4) call attention to neglected attributes of your offering, (5) shift the person's ideals for one or more of the attributes. There are several marketing implications that arise from our discussion of cognitive dissonance. To avoid dissonance, it is important for the product to conform to expectations. Similarly, it is imperative for marketers not to generate unrealistic expectations by promising more than can be delivered. Marketers should first design products that will fulfill people's expectations insofar as possible. How can the advertiser counter this potential problem? One way is to develop promotions that are consistent with what the product can reasonably deliver. Another way is to develop specific plans for reinforcing the new member's decision to join your organization. Don't think that the marketing job is done when the initial exchange has been completed (e.g., join organization, use the ministry, etc.). Successful organizations have a plan to continue interactions with the exchange partners so that meaningful long-term relationships are forged. Research has demonstrated that such actions taken by marketers reduces dissonance[50] and increases loyalty rates.[51]

----

[1] A single chapter devoted to coverage of human behavior obviously is only briefly skimming what is a very comprehensive topic. Interested readers should examine one of the standard *Consumer Behavior* texts devoted to the subject. In this chapter we draw primarily from David Loudon, Bruce Wrenn, Robert Stevens, and Albert Della Bitta, *Consumer Behavior: Putting the Theory Into Practice* (New York: Routledge, forthcoming), and chapter 6 of Philip Kotler and Kevin Lane Keller, *Marketing Management,* 13th ed. (Upper Saddle River, N.J.: Pearson Prentice-Hall, 2009).

[2] Kotler and Keller.

[3] For more on consumer goals and goal setting, see Richard P. Bagozzi and Utpal Dholakia, "Goal Setting and Goal Striving in Consumer Behavior," *Journal of Marketing* 63 (Special Issue, 1999): 19-32; Alexander Chernov, "Goal Orientation and Consumer Preference for the Status Quo," *Journal of Consumer Research*, December 2004, pp. 557-565; and James A. Roberts and Stephen F. Pirog III, "Personal Goals and Their Role in Consumer Behavior: The Case for Compulsive Buying," *Journal of Marketing Theory and Practice*, Summer 2004, pp. 61-73.

[4] Abraham H. Maslow, "A Theory of Human Motivation," *Psychological Review* 50 (1943): 370-396.

[5] Abraham H. Maslow, *Toward a Psychology of Being* (New York: Van Nostrand Reinhold, 1968).

[6] Jacques E. Brisoux and Emmanuel J. Cheron, "Brand Categorization and Product Involvement," in Marvin Goldberg, Gerald Gorn, and Richard Pollay, eds., *Advances in Consumer Research* (Provo, Utah: Association for Consumer Research, 1990), vol. 17, pp. 101-109.

[7] Richard E. Petty and John Cacioppo, *Attitudes and Persuasion: Classic and Contemporary Approaches* (New York: McGraw-Hill, 1981).

[8] Bernard Berelson and Gary A. Steiner, *Human Behavior: An Inventory of Scientific Findings* (New York: Harcourt, Brace, Jovanovich, 1964), p. 88.

[9] Raymond Bauer and Stephen Greyser, *Advertising in America: The Consumer's View* (Cambridge, Mass.: Harvard University Press, 1968), p. 178.

[10] J. Edward Russo, Margaret G. Meloy, and T. J. Wilks, "The Distortion of Product Information During Brand Choice," *Journal of Marketing Research* 35 (1998): 438-452.

[11] Leslie de Chernatony and Simon Knox, "How an Appreciation of Consumer Behavior Can Help in Product Testing," *Journal of Market Research Society,* July 1990, p. 333.

[12] Much of this section is based on John Dollard and Neal Miller, *Personality and Psychotherapy* (New York: McGraw-Hill, 1950), pp. 25-47.

[13] Winfred F. Hill, *Learning: A Survey of Psychological Interpretations* (San Francisco: Chandler, 1963), p. 225.

[14] See Ernest R. Hilgard and Gordon H. Bower, *Theories of Learning*, 3rd ed. (New York: Appleton-Century-Crofts, 1966), for a comprehensive review of these theories.

[15] Ivan Pavlov, *Conditioned Reflexes, an Investigation of the Psychological Activity of the Cerebral Cortex*, ed. and trans. G. V. Anrep (London: Oxford University Press, 1927).

[16] See I. Kirsch, S. J. Lynn, M. Vigorito, and R. R. Miller, "The Role of Cognition in Classical and Operant Conditioning," *Journal of Clinical Psychology*, April 2004, pp. 369-392.

[17] See Terence A. Shimp, "Neo-Pavlovian Conditioning and Its Implications for Consumer Theory and Research," in Thomas S. Robertson and Harold H. Kassarjian, eds., *Handbook of Consumer Behavior* (Englewood Cliffs, N.J.: Prentice-Hall, 1991), pp. 162-187, for a review of Pavlovian conditioning, which argues that much greater cognitive activity is involved in this form of conditioning than was previously thought.

[18] See James Bettman, *An Information Processing Theory of Consumer Choice* (Reading, Mass.: Addison-Wesley, 1979), pp. 139-143.

[19] See Joel Saegert, "A Demonstration of Levels-of-Processing Theory in Memory for Advertisements," in William L. Wilkie, ed., *Advances in Consumer Research* (Ann Arbor, Mich.: Association for Consumer Research, 1979), vol. 6, pp. 82-84; Leonard N. Reid and Lawrence C. Soley, "Levels-of-Processing in Memory and the Recall and Recognition of Television Commercials," in James H. Leigh and Claude R. Martin, Jr., eds., *Current Issues and Research in Advertising*, (Ann Arbor, Mich.: University of Michigan, 1980), pp. 135-145; Joel Saegert, "Comparison of Effects of Repetition and Levels of Processing in Memory for Advertisements," in Andrew Mitchell, ed., *Advances in Consumer Research* (Ann Arbor, Mich.: Association for Consumer Research, 1982), vol. 9, pp. 431-434.

[20] Joan Meyers-Levy and Alice M. Tybout, "Schema Congruity as a Basis for Product Evaluation," *Journal of Consumer Research* 16 (June 1989): 39-54.

[21] James R. Bettman, "Memory Factors in Consumer Choice: A Review," *Journal of Marketing* 43 (Spring 1979): 37-53.

[22] See John G. Lynch, Jr., and Thomas K. Srull, "Memory and Attentional Factors in Consumer Choice: Concepts and Research Methods," *Journal of Consumer Research* 9 (June 1982): 18-36; and Kevin Lane Keller, "Memory Factors in Advertising."

[23] See John R. Rossiter, "Visual Imagery: Applications to Advertising," in Mitchell, ed., *Advances in Consumer Research,* vol. 9, pp. 101-106.

[24] See, for example, James T. Heimbach and Jacob Jacoby, "The Zeigarnik Effect in Advertising," in M. Venkatesan, ed., *Proceedings of the Third Annual Conference* (College Park, Md.: Association for Consumer Research, 1972), pp. 746-756.

[25] Alan G. Sawyer and Daniel J. Howard, "Effects of Omitting Conclusions in Advertisements to Involved and Uninvolved Audiences," *Journal of Marketing Research* 28 (November 1991): 467-474.

[26] See Naresh K. Malhotra, "Mnemonics in Marketing: A Pedagogical Tool," *Journal of the Academy of Marketing Science*, 19 (Spring 1991): 141-149 for a review of this memory aid.

[27] See Bernard Weiner, "Attributional Thoughts About Consumer Behavior," *Journal of Consumer Research* 27, no. 3 (December 2000): 382-387.

[28] For an excellent explanation of attribution theory, including the foot-in-the-door technique see Leon G. Schiffman and Leslie Lazar Kanuk, *Consumer Behavior,* 9th ed. (Upper Saddle River, N.J.: Pearson Prentice-Hall, 2007), chap. 8.

[29] Berelson and Steiner, p. 453.

[30] Richard P. Coleman and Lee Rainwater, *Social Standing in America: New Dimensions of Class* (New York: Basic Books, Inc., 1978), p. 29.

[31] Edward B. Tylor, *Primitive Culture* (London: Murray, 1891), p. 1.

[32] Linda C. Ueltschy and Robert F. Krampf, "Cultural Sensitivity to Satisfaction and Service Quality Measures," *Journal of Marketing Theory and Practice*, Summer 2001, pp. 14-31.

[33] James F. Engel and Roger D. Blackwell, *Consumer Behavior*, 4th ed. (New York: Dryden Press, New York, 1982), p. 300.

[34] Dell Hawkins, Kenneth A. Coney, and Roger J. Best, *Consumer Behavior* (Dallas: Business Publications, Inc., 1980), p. 388.

[35] John A. Howard, *Consumer Behavior: Application of Theory* (New York: McGraw-Hill, 1977), p. 29.

[36] Henry Assael, *Consumer Behavior and Marketing Action* (Boston: Kent, 1981), p. 38.

[37] Jagdish N. Sheth, "An Investigation of Relationships Among Evaluative Beliefs, Affect, Behavioral Intention, and Behavior," in *Consumer Behavior: Theory and Application*, ed. John U. Farley, John A. Howard, and L. Winston Ring (Boston: Allyn & Bacon, 1974), pp. 89-114.

[38] Martin Fishbein, "Attitudes and Prediction of Behavior," in Readings in *Attitude Theory and Measurement*, ed. Martin Fishbein (New York: John Wiley, 1967), pp. 477-492.

[39] B. Shiv and A. Fedorikhim, "Heart and Mind in Conflict," *Journal of Consumer Research*, December 1999, 278-291, and M. T. Pham et al., "Affect Monitoring and the Primacy of Feelings in Judgment," *Journal of Consumer Research*, September 2001, pp. 167-187.

[40] M. T. Pham, "Representativeness, Relevance, and the Use of Feelings in Decision Making," *Journal of Consumer Research*, September 1998, pp. 144-159.

[41] J. A. Ruth, "Promoting a Brand's Emotional Benefits," *Journal of Consumer Psychology* 11, no. 2 (2001): 99-113.

[42] B. Shiv and J. Huber, "The Impact of Anticipating Satisfaction on Consumer Choice," *Journal of Consumer Research*, September 2000, pp. 202-216.

[43] Ralph L. Day, "Toward a Process Model of Consumer Satisfaction," in M. Keith Hunt, ed., *Conceptualization and Measurement of Consumer Satisfaction and Dissatisfaction* (Cambridge, Mass.: Marketing Science Institute, 1977), pp. 163-167.

[44] Gerald Linda, "New Research Works on Consumer Satisfaction/Dissatisfaction Model," *Marketing News*, Sept. 21, 1979, p. 8.

[45] Robert A. Westbrook, "Intrapersonal Affective Influences on Consumer Satisfaction With Products," *Journal of Consumer Research* 7 (June 1980): 49-54.

[46] Diane Halstead and Cornelia Droge, "Consumer Attitudes Toward Complaining and the Prediction of Multiple Complaint Responses," in Rebecca H. Holman and Michael R. Solomon, eds., *Advances in Consumer Research* (Provo, Utah: Association for Consumer Research, 1991), vol. 18, pp. 210-216.

[47] Marsha L. Richins, "Negative Word-of-Mouth by Dissatisfied Consumers: A Pilot Study," *Journal of Marketing* 47 (Winter 1983): 68-78.

[48] Jerry Plymire, "Complaints as Opportunities," *Journal of Services Marketing* 5 (Winter 1991): 61-65.

[49] See William H. Cummings and M. Venkatesan, "Cognitive Dissonance and Consumer Behavior: A Review of the Evidence," in Mary Jane Schlinger, ed., *Advances in Consumer Research*, 2nd ed. (Chicago: Association for Consumer Research, 1975), pp. 21-31; and Leonard A. LoSciuto and Robert Perloff, "Influence of Product Preference on Dissonance Reduction," *Journal of Marketing Research* 4 (August 1967): 286-290.

[50] Shelby D. Hunt, "Post-Transaction Communications and Dissonance Reduction," *Journal of Marketing* 34 (July 1970): 46-51.

[51] James H. Donnelly, Jr., and John M. Ivancevich, "Post-Purchase Reinforcement and Back-Out Behavior," *Journal of Marketing Research* 7 (August 1970): 399, 400.

WORKSHEETS: CHAPTER 5

Factors Influencing Human Behavior

A. Intrapersonal Factors

List the key understandings you have for the following intrapersonal aspects of the people you intend to engage in exchange:

Needs, Motives, Goals

_____

_____

_____

Marketing Implications

_____

_____

_____

Involvement Level

_____

_____

Marketing Implications

_____

_____

_____

Perceptions

_____

_____

_____

Marketing Implications

_____
_____
_____

Learning Processes

_____
_____
_____

Marketing Implications

_____
_____
_____

Attributions

_____
_____
_____

Marketing Implications

_____
_____
_____

B. Interpersonal Factors

List the key understandings you have for the following interpersonal aspects of the people you intend to engage in exchange:

Reference Groups

_____
_____
_____

Marketing Implications

_____

_____

_____

Social Class

_____

_____

_____

Marketing Implications

_____

_____

_____

Culture and Subculture

_____

_____

_____

Marketing Implications

_____

_____

_____

C. Decision-making Process

List the key understandings you have of your exchange partner for each stage of the decision-making process.

Problem Recognition

_____

_____

_____

Marketing Implications

_____
_____
_____

Information Search

_____
_____
_____

Marketing Implications

_____
_____
_____

Evaluation of Alternatives

_____
_____
_____

Marketing Implications

_____
_____
_____

Choice Decision

_____
_____
_____

Marketing Implications

_____
_____
_____

Post-Choice Behavior

_____

_____

_____

Marketing Implications

_____

_____

_____

Overall Marketing Implications:

_____

_____

_____

Plan the Marketing Strategy

Part 4:

THE EFFECTIVE MARKETING PROCESS

Adopting a Marketing Philosophy

↓

Develop an Understanding

↓

Plan the Marketing Strategy
CHAPTER 6 *Think Like a Marketing Strategist:
Fundamental Marketing Concepts*
CHAPTER 7 *Market Segmentation, Targeting, and Positioning*
CHAPTER 8 *Strategic Marketing Planning*

↓

Design and Implement the Marketing Tactics

↓

Connect With Exchange Partners

What we learned about our exchange partners in part 2 of the book—*How* and *What* to Understand—has prepared us for the next step in the effective marketing process, which is to plan marketing strategies. Chapter 6 begins the three-chapter sequence devoted to this task by putting some marketing fundamentals in place upon which we can construct our strategies. Then in chapter 7 we discuss the three-step process of segmenting, targeting, and positioning that is considered to be the "bricks and mortar" of modern marketing strategy. Finally, in chapter 8 we describe in detail the steps to be followed in constructing a marketing plan, including an example to illustrate how you can put together a plan for your organization. As always, worksheets at the end of each chapter are included to help guide your team through each step of the process.

CHAPTER 6:

Thinking Like a Marketing Strategist:
FUNDAMENTAL MARKETING CONCEPTS

"Our people should not have unproductive lives. They must learn to do good by helping others who have urgent needs" (TITUS 3:14, NLT).

In this chapter we will address the following questions:

1. What are the components of our organization's mission?

2. How should we conceptualize the exchange relationships we have with our various publics?

3. How can we group people into homogeneous segments to serve them better?

4. What is our image among the people in the segments, and how can we improve it?

5. How can we best satisfy our publics' needs through our missions?

In this chapter we begin the process of *Developing a Plan* based upon the *Understanding* we obtained from conducting the chapter 4 and 5 activities. We discuss the central building blocks, or fundamental concepts, of modern marketing plans. These provide the foundation for making those decisions that allow you to solve your marketing problems or take advantage of your opportunities.

Essential Marketing Concepts

1. Each congregation has a mission.

2. In carrying out the mission of the congregation, the leaders will engage in exchanges with a large number of publics.

3. The congregation will segment the populace into groupings, and target those it will serve from among the great many publics in its environment.

4. To perform its mission, the congregation needs to attract resources through exchange.

5. The publics will respond in terms of their image of the congregation.

6. The congregation and its ministry team can take concrete steps to improve the satisfaction of its target publics with its ministries/programs.

We will now consider more closely the set of marketing concepts that are essential for building societal marketing oriented, fully responsive congregations. These concepts, when applied, are almost certain to make a ministry more effective. They are described here, and will be used extensively in later chapters of this book. Each concept serves as an important tool for understanding and improving organizational responsiveness, and for developing marketing plans.

The Concept of Mission

Every effective organization starts with a mission. In fact, an organization can be defined as a human collectivity that is structured to perform a specific mission through the use of largely rational means. Its specific mission is usually clear at the beginning. However, unless it is continually being clarified in response to the changes going on within the organization and its environment, the mission will soon become forgotten, irrelevant, or banal.

The mission should be thought of as that to which the congregants or God is calling the congregation to *be* and *do* at this particular time, in its particular place. A clear understanding of a congregation's mission requires that the people discover the relationship among four distinct concerns:

1. What do Scripture and our own faith tradition tell us about our mission?

2. What unique and specific needs and interests do our members want the congregation and its programs to satisfy?

3. What specific needs in our community can and should we address?

4. What specific needs in society and the world can and should we address?[1]

It is in the interrelationship of these four concerns that a congregation comes to understand its mission. Some religious traditions tend to focus only on item 1 in seeking to understand their mission, while others tend to focus more on items 2, 3, and 4. But all 4 must be held in tension if the congregation is to correctly understand its mission.

An example of a congregation broadening its missional understanding may be found in the First Nazarene Church of Salem, Oregon.

When Tom Wilson became the pastor of the First Nazarene Church in Salem, Oregon, he dedicated three months in studying the community, its people, and their predominant needs and interests. Wilson rode with the police on their rounds, with paramedics responding to emergency calls. He spent many days going door to door, he talked to social service workers and to people on the street, and he also studied his Sunday and Wednesday congregations to see who *wasn't* there. And then throughout the week Wilson frequented the businesses in the town.

By this survey Wilson discovered there was a large gap in the ministries of Salem's churches in meeting the needs of two large and growing groups: the divorced and the singles by choice. Having reached this conclusion, Wilson encouraged the congregation's ministry team to develop programs and services targeted to the needs and interests of these two groups.

He reviewed the church's newspaper, radio, and television advertising from the point of view of what singles and divorced people would listen to and read, and then designed the church's weekly newspaper advertising to accentuate programs for single and divorced persons. He placed the ads not in the religious section, but in the sports and entertainment sections, reasoning that few singles and divorced persons were sitting around reading the religious section of the newspaper.

As Easter Sunday approached, the congregation rented the city's largest coliseum for their Easter worship services, reasoning that the unchurched folk of Salem would be more willing to attend Easter worship if the services were offered on more "neutral" territory than in the church's sanctuary.

This was not an easy decision for the congregation—they loved their church and its building. However, they were more interested in reaching the community's unchurched than they were in enjoying the beauty and solace of their beloved sanctuary.

The church launched a heavy media campaign to welcome the unchurched to worship with them in the city coliseum. On Easter Sunday 6,000 people filled the coliseum to capacity. An estimated 3,000 people were turned away. The congregation's largest Easter attendance prior to this was 2,500. The results of these adjustments to their ministries and "packaging" were that over the next year some 1,000 single, divorced persons, and young married couples joined the congregation.

The original mission of the Salem First Church of the Nazarene was to deepen religious faith among believers through offering worship, religious training, and fellowship. With Tom Wilson as its pastor, the church added another dimension to its mission: that of meeting the needs and interests of singles, divorced persons, and children of single-parent households. It is no longer so easy to distinguish between the church's core mission and its peripheral missions. Is the church basically a religious center, a social center, or a mental health center? The church's growing responsiveness to other needs is changing its character and its membership composition.

Every church and synagogue that wants to be responsive must answer two questions: Responsive to whom? Responsive to what? No congregation can serve everyone and every need. If it tries to serve everyone, it will serve no one well. From time to time each congregation must reexamine its mission to see whether it is still on target with the needs of its members and the expectations of those it is trying to reach.

Exhibit 6.1 depicts the components of a congregation's mission statement as stemming from two contexts, the eternal and the timely.[2]

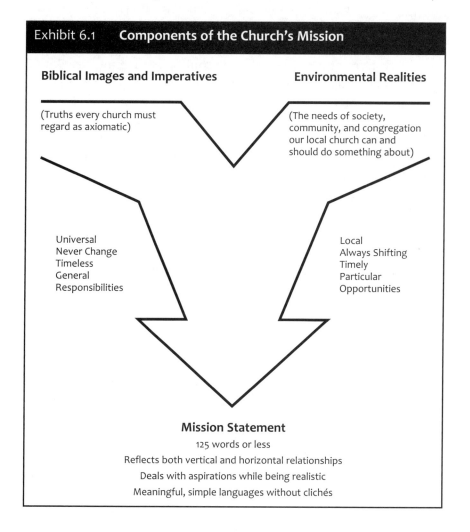

Exhibit 6.1   Components of the Church's Mission

Biblical Images and Imperatives

(Truths every church must regard as axiomatic)

Universal
Never Change
Timeless
General
Responsibilities

Environmental Realities

(The needs of society, community, and congregation our local church can and should do something about)

Local
Always Shifting
Timely
Particular
Opportunities

Mission Statement
125 words or less
Reflects both vertical and horizontal relationships
Deals with aspirations while being realistic
Meaningful, simple languages without clichés

Years ago Peter Drucker pointed out that organizations need to answer the following questions: 1. What is our business (mission)? 2. Who is the customer? 3. What is of value to the customer? 4. What will our business be? 5. What should our business be?"[3] Although the first question ("What is our business?") sounds simple, it is actually the most profound question an organization can ask itself. The "business" of a religious organization is defined as its mission.

You should not define your mission by listing the particular services your congregation offers. Rather, you should identify the group(s) you want to serve and the needs and interests of the group(s) that you will try to satisfy.

Ultimately you must decide what your mission is, so as not to lose sight of your targeted publics or confuse your ministries with a host of intermediate goals and services that you might provide. An example of this is found in Willow Creek Community Church, which holds as its focus to target Unchurched Harry for its Sunday services, so they include in their mission statement exaltation, edification, evangelism, and extension (i.e., all four cells of Exhibit 1), all of which are actions in concert with whom they want to be and whom they want to reach.

Clarifying the congregation's mission is a soul-searching and time consuming process. Different members will have different views of what the church or synagogue should be about. It is not uncommon for a searching congregation to hold numerous meetings over a one- or two-year period before membership consensus is developed regarding the mission.

A helpful approach to defining mission is to establish the congregation's scope along three dimensions. The first is its *target groups*—namely, *who* are to be served. The second is its *mission components*—namely, *what* are we called to do as a congregation. The third is *alternative technologies*—namely, *how* we will deliver and communicate the mission components.[4] For example, consider a church serving mainly senior citizens who want only a simple weekly worship service. (The small cube in Exhibit 6.2A represents this church's mission scope.) Now consider another, larger congregation in Exhibit 6.2B. This church serves all age groups, meets at least four

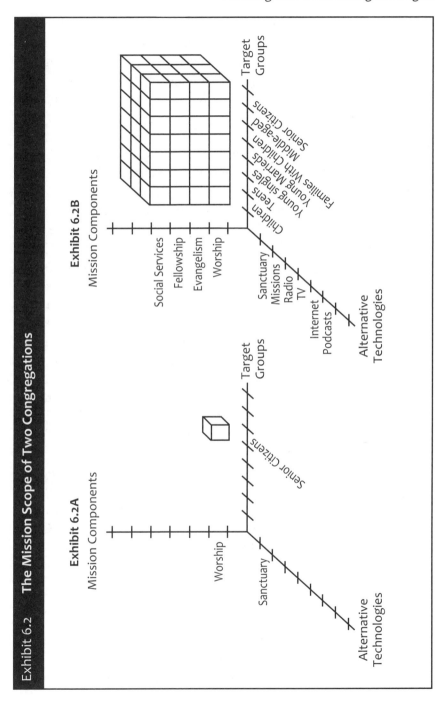

Exhibit 6.2   **The Mission Scope of Two Congregations**

Exhibit 6.2A
Mission Components

Exhibit 6.2B
Mission Components

parts to its mission, and provides services through the church building (sanctuary), missions (e.g., going where needed to deliver social services), and uses radio, TV, and Podcasts to deliver its messages to the target groups, and the Internet to maintain two-way communications with these groups, utilizing Web 2.0 technology (Web site, blogs, and discussion forums).

Still other congregations will have a different mission scope. A campus church will serve primarily students of a particular religious faith and meet a wide variety of needs (for belief, sociability, counseling, and so on) within the four walls of a religious house. On the other hand, the Garden Grove Community Church in Garden Grove, California, meets a wide variety of needs of more than 10,000 members and other interested individuals. Its *Hour of Power* video ministry by Robert Schuller is available via television, podcasts, downloadable streaming video, CDs or DVDs. An online gift store includes books, music CDs, and DVDs of special programs at the Crystal Cathedral. A variety of "club" membership packages, audio books, gifts for special occasions (e.g., Mother's Day), products for children (including video and music), links to the Robert Schuller Institute, New Hope Now crisis counseling, Possibility Thinking Coaches Network, and numerous ministries targeted to specific needs (e.g., a wedding ministry) are available. There is also a Crystal Cathedral Memorial Gardens cemetery/mausoleum, and an online forum called One Community.[5]

You should strive for a mission that is *feasible*, *distinctive*, and *motivational*. In terms of being feasible, you should avoid a "mission impossible." Pastor Robert Schuller wants his church to grow to 25,000 members. While this may be feasible for Garden Grove Community Church, it would likely prove infeasible for most congregations. To accomplish this mission, Schuller's followers must believe in the feasibility of this goal if they are to lend their support. An institution should always reach high, but not so high as to produce incredulity in its publics.

A mission serves best when it is distinctive. A well-stated mission allows people to make differential comparisons, allowing members and seekers to see how and why this church is different from the other churches in the community, thus helping persons to decide whether this is the church for them, The mission identifies the church's uniqueness, sets it apart from other churches, strengthens its boundaries, and helps members know "who we are," and why "this is the congregation for me."

The mission should also be motivational. Those working for the organization should feel that they are worthwhile members of a worthwhile endeavor. A congregation whose mission includes helping the poor is likely to inspire more support than one whose mission is meeting the social, cultural, and athletic needs of its current members. Your mission should be something that is faithful to all aspects of your calling.

The Concept of Publics

Every organization has to address at least one public in order to carry out its mission. An organization may have only one public, but growth or expansion will almost always cause the organization to relate to more than one. Publics may be internal, that is, inside the organization, or external, outside the formal structures of the organization.

A public is a distinct group of people or organizations that have an actual or potential interest or impact on an organization.

Since each public has a different relationship with the church, they have different expectations and are experiencing different needs and interests. Therefore, the church leaders must communicate differently and hold different expectations of each group. The concept of publics may be new to many readers. To illustrate this concept, an example from a familiar organization, McDonald's, is used to clarify two familiar terms, *customers* and *consumers*.

McDonald's is a franchise corporation. As such, the people who purchase a franchise and open a McDonald's restaurant are the corporation's customers—they have purchased something from McDonald's and will continue to purchase many items from the company. However, the owners of McDonald's restaurants do not consume the many products on the menu. Here, then, is another of McDonald's Corporation's publics—the people who buy and eat (consume) the products.

These two distinct groups constitute two publics of the McDonald's Corporation: its customers and its consumers. The two publics experience differing needs and interests, which McDonald's Corporation seeks to satisfy, and by so doing hopes to receive in exchange certain values for the corporation.

The company must communicate differently to each public, even though it is talking about the same thing—hamburgers. To its customers (franchisees) the company communicates profits, while to its consumers it communicates taste. This is necessary because the customer has different interests and needs from those of the consumer—even though both are interested in the hamburger.

The Ronald McDonald House offers another illustration. Each McDonald's franchise owner is expected to contribute a certain percentage of sales to support the house. In order to keep its restaurant owners feeling good about this, the company must convince them that this is an exchange of value, and so the company emphasizes high publicity, consumer goodwill, and increased sales. But to the consumer, the company communicates "the house that love built."

The leaders of such well-known churches as Willow Creek Community Church, Saddleback Valley Community Church, and the Crystal Cathedral make it very clear who are their "customers" and "consumers." The leaders do not try to communicate a one-size-fits-all message. Rather, they communicate specific messages to specific publics.

Both Willow Creek and Saddleback devote the entire weekend program to communicating with their *consumers*—the unchurched and the, as of yet, uncommitted.

Also, both churches devote the entire midweek services to communicating with their *customers*—members who have bought into the church's philosophy and are committed to growth and maturity in their religious journey.

Undoubtedly the ability to distinguish between their customers and consumers, and to interact with each appropriately, is one of the success secrets of these churches.

Even a small congregation faces many publics, often more than a local business firm. A local congregation has many internal and external publics whom the leaders must seek to satisfy—and *each public can be satisfied only in terms of its own unique needs and interests.*

It is fairly easy to identify the key publics that surround a particular congregation; Exhibit 6.3 shows several major publics with which a local church relates. The diagram is intended to illustrate that a congregation generally has its *internal publics* and its *external publics.* Marketing must take place *within* the congregation and also *outside* its own organizational structures—through its interactions with those publics it is trying to reach or serve beyond its own membership groups.

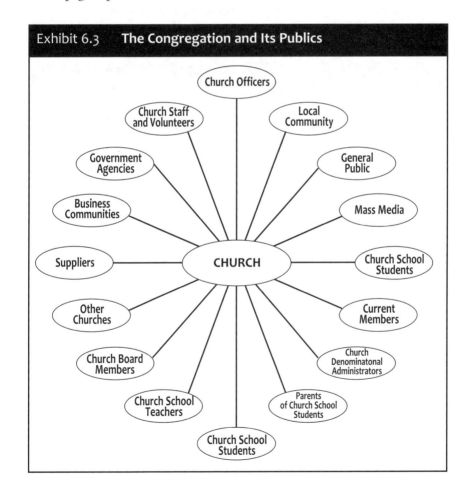

Exhibit 6.3   The Congregation and Its Publics

Not all publics are equally active or important to a religious organization. Publics come about because the organization's activities and policies can draw support or criticism from inside and outside groups. A *welcome public* is one that likes the organization and whose support the organization welcomes. A *sought public* is one whose support the organization wants, but which is currently indifferent or negative toward it. An *unwelcome public* is one that is negatively disposed toward the organization and that is trying to impose constraints, pressures, or controls on it.

Their functional relationship to the organization can also be the basis for classifying publics. Exhibit 6.4 presents such a classification. An organization is viewed as a resource-conversion machine in which certain *input publics* supply resources that are converted by *in-*

Exhibit 6.4   The Main Publics of a Religious Organization

Input Publics

Donor
Supplier
Judicatory

Internal Publics

Trustees
Ruling
Board
Ministry Team
Volunteers

Intermediary Publics

Internet Agencies
Publishers
Broadcast Media
Agents
Marketing Firms

Consumer Publics

Members
Other Participants
Service Recipients

External Publics

Local Activist
General Media
Competitive

ternal publics into useful goods and services that are carried by *intermediary publics* to designated *consuming publics* and influenced by various external publics. We will look at the various publics more closely.

Input Publics

Input publics mainly supply original resources and constraints to the organization, such as donors, suppliers, and judicatory agencies.

Donor publics are those who make gifts of money and other assets to the organization. A synagogue's donors consist of constituents, friends of the synagogue, foundations, and Jewish religious organizations.

Supplier publics are those organizations that sell needed goods and services to the organization. Religious organizations often try to obtain price concessions or even donations of goods and services, but don't always succeed.

Judicatory publics are agencies that impose rules of conduct upon the congregation. The *regulatory publics* of a church or synagogue include federal, state, and local government agencies, ecclesiastical hierarchies, and various academic accreditation associations for schools. The church or synagogue must keep in close contact with these ecclesiastical and regulatory organizations and be ready to argue against regulations that will harm its ability to provide high-quality programs and ministries to its members and external publics.

Internal Publics

The various inputs are managed by the organization's internal publics to accomplish its mission. The *internal publics* of a congregation consist of several groups, including trustees, ruling boards, ministry teams, volunteer leaders and workers, and paid staff. They prepare and serve the congregation's *product*—its services and ministries.

Trustees are a legal entity charged with the responsibility of managing the organization's financial and real assets within the constitution of the state, the ecclesiastical hierarchy, and the local body.

The ruling board is charged with the management of the organization's goals, programs, and ministries. Further, the board is charged with the public trust of the organization and its external publics. When members do not trust the leadership and their decisions, the board is responsible. In addition, the board establishes the policies by which the programs and ministries will be administered.

The ministry team is composed of the paid and volunteer leaders and workers who share responsibility for carrying out the congregation's ministries and programs. The lead pastor or rabbi is generally charged with the administrative oversight of the congregation's paid and volunteer personnel, which is carried out within the policies established by the ruling board and the congregation.

Volunteer leaders and workers. In almost any religious organization volunteer workers constitute a major part of the ministry's workforce and, as such, are a highly important public. In this group are persons who are often more experienced in program planning and management, financial management, personnel supervision, and the like than are the clergy and other paid staff. Adequately marketing to this public is of prime importance to the success of the religious organization.[6]

Intermediary Publics

Marketing intermediaries assist the organization in promoting and distributing its goods and services to the final consumers. They are described below.

Internet. Many congregations now use their own Web site or "local" search engines by Yahoo, Google, etc., for their announcements or to carry their blogs.

Publishers. Most congregations depend on local newspapers, the yellow pages, and similar services to announce themselves to the public.

Radio, television, and podcasts. Many congregations also utilize the airwaves and iTunes podcasts to carry their announcements and entire services to the public.

Agents. Congregations and national-level religious organizations depend on parachurch agencies to assist in mission projects. For example, many congregations rely on such organizations as World

Vision, Compassion, Young Life, Campus Crusade for Christ, Prison Fellowship, and InterVarsity to assist in carrying out their mission projects.

Facilitators. These are organizations—such as transportation companies, real estate firms, and media firms—that assist in the distribution of products, services, and messages, but do not take title to or negotiate purchases. Thus the congregation will use the telephone company (including facsimile), the post office, and overnight delivery services to send messages and materials. These facilitators are paid a normal rate for their transportation, communication, and storage services.

Marketing firms. These are organizations—such as advertising agencies, graphic design firms, marketing research firms, and marketing consulting firms—that assist in identifying and promoting the organization's products and services to the right markets. The congregation may hire the services of these marketing firms to investigate and promote to new member markets.

Consuming Publics

Various groups consume the outputs of a church or synagogue. They are described below.

Members. The members are those who are committed to the organization and its mission and who carry responsibility for its overall success. They *are* the organization. In a local church or synagogue, however, the members are also a major consuming public. They receive and utilize a great amount of the congregation's ministry.

Other participants in the congregation's ministries and programs. They include visitors who attend its services, who participate in its programs, and who may even contribute financially to those programs in which they hold greatest interest.

Recipients of services. These people benefit from the congregation's ministries, often without attending any of its religious services or feeling a part of the congregation. These include patients at a free clinic, the guests of a soup kitchen, and the person asking for financial help.

The internal and consuming publics represent the religious organization's primary publics, its raison d'être. Drucker insists that the only valid definition of a business is to create a customer (a public that the organization might serve).[7] He says that hospitals exist to serve patients, colleges to serve students, opera companies to serve opera lovers, and social agencies to serve the needy.

Various names are used to describe consumers, such as clients, buyers, constituents, patients, and members. In some cases the appropriate term is *elusive*. Clearly, you can have multiple sets of customers and consumers, and one of your tasks is to distinguish these groups and their relative importance to your organization.

Consider this issue in relation to a church or synagogue: Who is its primary consumer? The current members who pay for and "consume much of the product"? Inactive members, whom the leaders might desire to bring back "into the fold"? Prospective new members whom the church is attempting to interest in joining the congregation? People in the local community who benefit from the social service ministries of the congregation? In other words, which of the various types of marketing—adherent, fellowship, or social services—are you needing to engage at any one point in time?

In formulating its services and policies, a congregation must take into account the interest of all of these groups. At times you will aim to increase your service to one group more than to another. At times membership growth may be a top priority, and so resources are shifted to carry the message to prospective new members. At other times the goal may be to involve more current members in your programs, to increase the congregation's sense of community, as well as to broaden shared responsibilities. Often you are engaging in all three times of marketing to various consumer groups simultaneously.

External Publics

Local publics. Every congregation is physically located somewhere and comes in contact with local publics, such as neighborhood residents and community organizations. These groups may take an active or passive interest in the congregation's activities. Thus community residents often get concerned about traffic congestion

and other things that go along with living near a church or synagogue.

However, many local congregations are not responsive to the
community's situation. Rather, they expect the community to ac-
cord it a favored status because it is a religious organization. Yet the
church or synagogue that targets one or more local publics and
wholeheartedly serves their needs and interests will attract more
members than if it seeks only to serve its internal groups and to convert the community to its beliefs.

Members of the Trinity Church of the Nazarene, Lompoc,
California, congregation report that the key to its quite phenomenal
growth was Pastor Tom Wilson's success in turning its attention to
serve human needs within the local community. The congregation
adopted as its mission the statement "We will find a need and fill it,
find a hurt and heal it." Wilson maintained, "If a congregation sets
out to find hurts and heal them, it will never have to plead for
money or search for new people. People and money will come."
This responsive approach to ministry and marketing the church certainly seems to have worked at the Trinity Nazarene Church in
Lompoc. In reflecting upon Pastor Wilson's tenure of six years, one
member told us, "Every day the driveway of our church was lined
with ambulances, police cars, and even an occasional fire truck. The
emergency-care providers of the community knew where they
could find help to assist anyone in need. People who passed by wondered what was happening inside. Every hospital, social worker, and
police officer thought first of Tom when they needed a pastor. We
didn't have to advertise. People just came because this church had a
reputation for caring for hurting people."

As in the case of Pastor Wilson's later tenure at the First Church
of the Nazarene in Salem, Oregon, we see that when these congregations became genuinely responsive to the needs of targeted
publics, they experienced phenomenal growth. Growth and ministry
continue at both of these churches, even after Pastor Wilson left
(Wilson passed away in June 2006 in Phoenix, Arizona).

Activist publics. Religious organizations are increasingly peti-
tioned by consumer groups, environmental groups, minority orga-

nizations, and other public-interest groups for certain concessions or support. In congregations, activist publics often arise from within the membership. We know of several congregations in which dissatisfied members have joined in petition campaigns to remove the pastor or the ruling board, thus becoming an activist public. Likewise, on a larger scale, within ecclesiastical bodies, members from across the nation are joining together as activist publics to protest or change denominational edicts.

Religious organizations would be foolish to attack or ignore demands of activist publics. Responsive organizations can do two things. First, they can train their leaders and administrators to include social criteria in their decision-making in order to strike a better balance between the needs of the members, community populations, and the organization itself. Second, they can assign a staff member to stay in touch with these groups and to communicate the organization's goals, activities, and intentions more effectively.

General publics. An effective organization must be concerned with the general public's attitude toward its activities and policies. The general public does not act in an organized way toward the organization, as activist groups do. But the members of the general public form images of the organization, which affect their patronage and legislative support. Every congregation should monitor how it is seen by the general public, and should take concrete steps to improve its public image where it is weak. Managing the organization's image will be discussed later in this chapter.

Media publics. Media publics include media companies that carry news, features, and editorial opinion—specifically, newspapers, magazines, other journals, and their Web sites. Religious organizations are acutely sensitive to the role played by the press in affecting their capacity to achieve their marketing objectives. Congregations normally would like more and better press coverage than they get. Getting more and better coverage calls for understanding what the press is really interested in.

The person responsible for press coverage at the national level of a denomination will make it a point to know most of the editors in the major media and will systematically cultivate mutually beneficial relations with them. The same is true for pastors and rabbis at the local level. They will make it a point to know the religious editors and the managing editors of the local newspapers and related Web sites. They will offer interesting news items, informational material, and quick access to religious information. In return, the media editors are likely to give the congregation more and better coverage.

Competitive publics. In carrying out the task of producing and delivering services to a target market, one will typically face competition. Many congregations deny the importance or the existence of competition. Some think that competition is evil. Some feel that it is more characteristic of business firms. Thus congregations do not prefer to think of other congregations as competitors, for fear of treating each other as winners and losers. They would rather think of all congregations as providing needed services.

Nonetheless, one must be sensitive to the competitive environment operated in. The competitive environment does not consist only of similar organizations or services. Perhaps the major competition facing many congregations today is such things as professional sports, leisure activities, and competing philosophies of life.

A local congregation may experience itself in competition with another congregation nearby. If so, that congregation, in order to provide effective services, must decide how it will position itself as unique from the other congregation. For example, if a small congregation is living in the long shadow of a megachurch, it must market itself in some way as "the alternative church."

You may face up to four major types of competitors in trying to serve your target market.

1. *Desire competitors*: other immediate needs that the publics might want to satisfy.

2. *Generic competitors*: other basic ways in which the publics can satisfy a particular need.

3. *Service form competitors*: other service forms that can satisfy the public's particular needs.

4. *Enterprise competitors*: other enterprises offering the same service form that can satisfy the public's particular need.

Exhibit 6.5 illustrates these four types of competitors in relation to the selection of a congregation. Consider Mary Jones, a young woman working to clarify her worldview. She faces several competing desires (desire competitors): organized religion, humanism, New Age philosophy, and so on. Suppose, because of her upbringing, she is inclined toward organized religion. She then considers the best way to pursue this interest (generic competitors): Christianity, Judaism, Islam, or an Eastern religion. She decides in favor of Christianity. She then considers what type of Christian religion (service form competitors): Baptist, Methodist, Catholic, Lutheran, and so on. She favors the Roman Catholic Church. This leads her to consider a specific church to attend (enterprise competitors): St. John's, St. Mary's, St. Paul's, and so on. Thus, St. Paul's Catholic Church faces different levels of competition in attempting to meet the needs of this young woman. These levels are not meant to simulate the decision to join a church, nor to suggest that marketing would provide the primary means of addressing all of these "competitive" situations. Rather, we seek to make the point that churches and synagogues hoping to influence such a decision will face various forms of competition, which they must meet in different ways.

Another type of competition, not included in the exhibit, but that may appeal to Mary, comes from do-it-yourself religion, when people unhappy with the choices of established congregations start one of their own. "From Christian gatherings that emphasize post-sermon discussions to small Jewish congregations that aren't centered around a synagogue, worshipers are crafting special-interest prayer groups to supplement or even replace services offered by their regular houses of worship."[8] Some of these groups follow a more orthodox version of religious practice than the denominations from which they split.

Different strategies and skill sets are needed to successfully compete at each of these levels, including with alternative "religious delivery systems," such as the do-it-yourself groups and the Web.

The best marketers in the for-profit world do not think in terms of "beating the competition," but rather in terms of "making the competition irrelevant" and "owning the market."[9] For example,

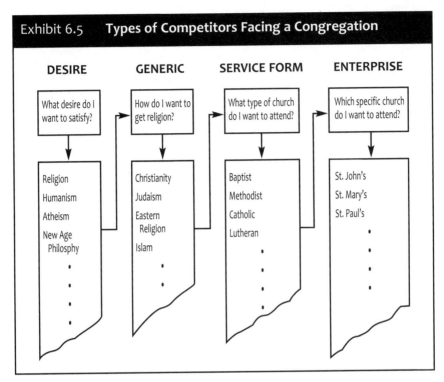

Exhibit 6.5	Types of Competitors Facing a Congregation

Jaguar thinks of owning the market for car buyers interested in classic Old World elegance and sophisticated styling in a luxury automobile, while BMW wants to own the market for those desiring a technologically sophisticated high-performance driver's car (the "Ultimate Driving Machine"). Hence, they want car buyers who desire that set of characteristics to see their models as the "obvious choice"—no other car make is directly competitive. These types of marketers are successful with this approach to competing because they are able to "push back" the choice decision for customers in their targeted market segment from the enterprise level (i.e., comparisons of brand to brand), to the generic or even desire level. The parallel for you would be to have people who determine that once they determine that religion is their choice to satisfy the desire for finding meaning to their life, or to fill the "God-sized hole" that exists in their life, your congregation would be their one and only choice (i.e., you have no generic, form, or enterprise competition).

Needless to say, while all marketers would love to operate under these conditions, only a select few ever attain such status. You should prepare strategies enabling you to compete at each competitive level. Using the tools and knowledge gained from chapters 4 and 5 should help you to understand the nature of your competitive environment better. In the following chapters we will help you develop your competitive strategies.

The Relationship Between a Public and a Market

Having demonstrated that every organization is surrounded by a multitude of publics, we can now pose this question: What is the relationship between a public and a market? The term *market* has a different origin than does the term *public*, and yet has several affinities with it.

The Connected Congregation

In response to opportunities to meet demand in religious markets, cell phone companies have developed phones with only basic voice service for ultra-Orthodox Jews who don't want the distractions of Internet service, text messaging, MP3 players, or cameras in their phones. In Israel there are more than 20,000 subscribers for these "kosher" phones. For Christians, Good News Holdings launched FaithMobile phone service with scriptures, Wallpaper backgrounds, Christian ring tones, and one-minute-long inspirational videos (ad slogan: "Have you talked to God today?"). The service, available on T-Mobile, Verizon, Sprint, Nextel, and AT&T's Cingular, costs $5.99 a month. Also offered are daily devotional text messages from "your favorite ministries," such as Promise Keepers and Mary-Mary. Muslim-related cell phone services include timers that remind worshippers of prayer time, with an alarm that features an actual muezzin's voice, internal compasses that tell the direction of Mecca, a Hijri, the Gregorian calendar, and complete versions of the Quran with English translation. Sikhs and Hindus can choose cell phone services that offer special religious ringtones.[10]

A market is a distinct group of people and/or organizations that have re-sources they want to exchange, or might conceivably be willing to exchange, for distinct benefits.

From the point of view of an organization, a market is a potential arena for the exchange of resources. For an organization to operate, it must acquire resources through trading other resources. In each case, it must offer something to the market if it is to receive in return the resources it seeks.

We can now see the affinities between a market and a public. *A public* is any group that has an actual or potential interest or impact on your organization. If you wish to attract certain resources from that public through offering a set of benefits in exchange, then you are taking a *marketing viewpoint* toward that public. Once you begin thinking in terms of *exchanging something of value* with that public, you are viewing the public as a *market*. You are attempting to determine the best marketing approach to that public.

The Concepts of Segmentation and Targeting

The first step in the process that leads to the development of a strategy for serving the needs of a specific group is to identify the relevant groups in the "market" you are trying to serve. Famously, both Willow Creek Community Church and Saddleback Valley Community Church conducted marketing research in their communities to discover the various groups (segments) and their interests and needs. Once you have successfully grouped people into appropriate segments you are able to select the best segment(s) to target with your ministries. From a review of the various groups, Willow Creek decided to target "Unchurched Harry," and Saddleback decided to target "Saddleback Sam."

Segmentation: identifying groups (segments) in the population who have different wants and needs.

Targeting: choosing the segments who will become the organization's focus for one or more of its programs or ministries. That specific segment becomes the target the organization will aim to reach with its message and activities, and from whom it will seek a mutual exchange of value.

Targeting involves learning the unique needs and interests of the target group, developing specific resources to meet their unique needs and interests, and promoting the resources in such a way that the information will connect with the persons you wish to attract and serve. Targeting is a wise move whenever you do not have enough resources to reach and minister to the unique needs and interests of every public represented in the internal and external communities, or when it is felt that concentrating on a particular segment might produce results beyond the ordinary.

Many local congregations never experience anything beyond the ordinary, or perhaps fail altogether, because they feel they must try to be all things to all people. Thus they fail to seize the extraordinary opportunities God puts before them. The truth is that there isn't a congregation in the world that has sufficient resources to minister to the unique needs of each of the many publics represented in its community. It is by targeting some of the specific publics that the dynamics are put in place to capture the attention, support, and/or response of other publics.

Remember two things about segmenting and targeting. First, targeting a ministry to one group does not mean all other groups will be cut off or denied that ministry. "Unchurched Harry" is the *target* of Willow Creek's Sunday service, Christianity 101, and its evangelism efforts. However, this does not cut off or exclude the thousands of women and children who attend the same Sunday service, and for whom many special ministries are offered. Second, targeting may cause growth or ministry to expand among segments of the population. If the congregation's resources are too meager to be all things to all groups and to do it well, it makes sense that the congregation should begin by targeting one (or more) groups that, by focusing its resources, it might serve with excellence. Success with the targeted group may then generate resources that allow for other groups to be targeted.

The process of segmentation and targeting will be discussed in greater detail in chapter 7, including how some congregations use state-of-the-art techniques to reach chosen population segments efficiently and effectively.

The Connected Congregation

Marketing-related uses of the Internet by congregations with Web sites:
  recruiting new members
  serving a global community of believers
  staying in touch with far-flung former members
  online activities for children or teenagers
  posting frequently asked questions (FAQs)
  "Ask the Pastor" services
  conducting searches for new clergy and staff
  promoting presence in a community
  promoting scheduled events
  posting photos of congregational events
  promoting missionary/evangelical work
  recruiting volunteers for church or temple functions
  signing up for classes or programs
  online fund-raising
  Webcasting of services
  fostering a sense of community through listserves and discussion
    groups

---

www.pewinternet.org

The Concept of Exchange

The concept of exchange helps us to understand how one can fulfill a mission by interacting with various targeted publics. Two key dimensions underlie the concept of exchange. The first is that each party believes the other party can offer something of genuine value and benefit—so that both parties feel mutually benefited and satisfied in the transaction. The second important dimension in exchange is that both parties are free in deciding to participate in the exchange. *Without value and free choice, there can be no exchange.* There may be extortion, manipulation, acquiescence, or accommodation,

211

but not exchange. Exchange occurs when "something of value" is given and received between two parties.

All religious organizations have reason to be leery of working toward exchanges that are merely transactional in nature: "You give us your tithes, and we'll give you a good sermon and Sunday school." The business of the church is a transformed person, and exchanges that are *transformational*, rather than merely *transactional*, are healthy for the religious organization and the individual alike.

Conditions Underlying Exchange

Exchange assumes four conditions:

1. There are at least two parties. In the simplest exchange situation, there are two parties. If one party is more actively seeking an exchange than the other, the first party becomes the *marketer* and the second party the customer or *consumer*. The religious "marketer" is seeking to affect exchanges between individuals and the organization.

2. Each party can offer something that the other perceives to be of value. If one of the parties has nothing that is valued by the other party, exchange will not take place. Each party must consider what it has to offer that may be perceived as benefits by the other party. "Something of value" may be various "products" or a "response."

Products offered in an exchange can consist of:

Goods: Sunday school materials, worship bulletins

Services: counseling, church school classes

Events: a Christmas concert, a speech by well-known author

Experiences: Vacation Bible School, family week at religious camp

Persons: rabbi, pastor, counselor

Places: spiritual retreat center, synagogue, holy sites

Properties: real estate owned by religious organization

Organizations: congregation, Scouts, women's club

Information: blogs by rabbi or pastor, grief recovery information pamphlet

Activities: stop smoking, sports program, sing in a choir

Ideas: volunteering is virtuous; faithful tithing is a matter of conscience

Responses to products may consist of:

Money.

Another product: exchanging a skill, helping to install plumbing in a new church

A social behavior: the performance of some desirable activity or nonperformance of some undesirable activity

Acceptance or adoption of a person, an idea, value, or view of the world

Use of a blog, Web site, YouTube video clip, printed information, or physical facility

3. *Each party must be capable of communication and delivery.* For exchange to take place, the parties must be capable of communicating with each other. They must be able to describe what is being offered and when, where, and how it will be exchanged. Each party must state or imply certain expectations or guarantees about the expected performance of the exchanged objects. In addition to communicating, each party must be capable of finding means to deliver the things of value to the other party.

4. *Each is free to accept or reject the offer.* Exchange assumes that both parties are engaging in voluntary behavior. There is no coercion. For this reason, every transaction is normally assumed to leave both parties better off. Presumably each party ends up with more value than it started with, since they entered the exchange freely.

Exchange is best understood as a process rather than an event. Two parties can be said to be engaged in exchange if they are anywhere in the process of moving toward an exchange. The exchange process, when successful, is marked by an event called a transaction, or an outcome, called a relationship or a transformation.

Transactions are the basic unit of exchange. A transaction takes place at a time and place and with specified amounts and conditions. Thus when a minister agrees to accept a new church position, a transaction takes place. Every organization engages in countless transactions with other parties—clients, employees, suppliers, distributors, etc. Transactions themselves are a subset of a larger number of events called interactions, which make up the exchange process. Transactions are interactions that involve the formal trading of values. *Marketing* is when either party is actively trying to create or influence the nature or terms of an exchange.[11]

An exchange process will result in a transaction whenever the target recipient perceives that the benefits of the transaction exceed the "costs" or sacrifices the exchange entails—and that the ratio of benefits to costs is greater than what can be hoped to be achieved by "spending" the costs in any other conceivable way. For example, the absent member will begin attending weekly worship services when he or she perceives that the personal benefit of participating in the worship services exceeds the benefits of whatever it is he or she is in the habit of doing at that hour. The "costs" that the absent member has to spend in this instance are time plus whatever he or she would be doing at that hour.

Types of Exchanges

It is possible to categorize exchanges as resulting from two kinds of exchange processes.

1. Unilateral exchange processes, in which only one party seeks to influence the outcome of the exchange process. For example, the congregation of Salem First Church of the Nazarene carried out a unilateral exchange process when it decided to give up its traditional Easter worship services in its sanctuary to make it possible for unchurched persons to "come back" to church in a more neutral, less threatening setting.

2. Bilateral exchange processes, in which both sides seek to influence the outcome of an exchange process. For example, the founders of Willow Creek Church entered into a bilateral exchange process when they first asked unchurched persons what there was about attending church services that made them most uncomfortable and kept them away and then designed a style of Sunday service that intentionally stays clear of those things.

Exchanges also vary in whether they are *two-party* or *multiple-party*, and whether they lead to transactions that are of *continuing* or *fixed* duration. Multiple-party exchanges in a religious organization can occur in a number of contexts. The additional party may be:

   (a) *allied with the recipient of the services*—for example, other
   family members, other members of the neighborhood, or

other members of a buying group

(b) allied with the religious organization—for example, an advertising agency or consulting firm

(c) independent of either primary party but necessary to facilitate the transaction—for example, a state education official regulating a church elementary school

(d) independent of either party but seeking to influence the existence or content of an exchange—for example, a chamber of commerce seeking to convince a synagogue to open a day-care center in the business district.

These additional parties are unique in the exchange process in that they do not bear any of the direct costs in the transaction but are involved because they expect to reap benefits, depending on the nature of the outcome.

"Continuing transactions" are those in which one or more parties must perform some continuing behavior as their part of the exchange agreement. Most exchanges sought by churches and synagogues are continuing transactions that require the party to change *permanently* some behavior or set of behaviors. Examples include tithing; requiring members to stop using alcohol, tobacco, or drugs; and sending children to church school.

Implicit in continuing transactions—and therefore crucial to religious marketing—is the fact that marketing does not stop, and *should not stop*, with the parties' agreement to the transaction or when the exchange is first performed under the terms of the transaction. The church's mission is accomplished as new behaviors become habits and persons are transformed thereby. Just as marketing helped to bring the person to new behavior, so also marketing is needed to inform, sustain, and strengthen the person's resolve to stay with the behavior until it becomes fixed in his or her actions and attitudes.

Analyzing Exchange Flows

Whenever two social units are engaged in exchange, it is useful to develop a diagram or map showing what is actually or potentially being exchanged between the two parties. An exchange between a

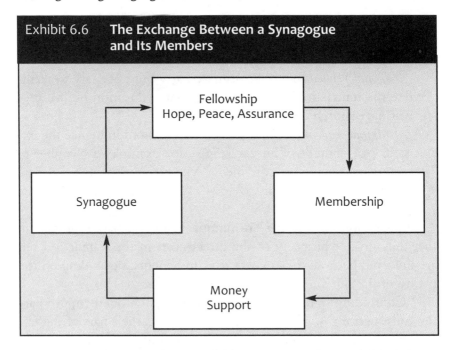

Exhibit 6.6   The Exchange Between a Synagogue and Its Members

synagogue and its members could be represented in Exhibit 6.6.

To give a sense of how an exchange framework can be used in the development of a marketing strategy, suppose a rabbi of a synagogue seeks to persuade a couple who have recently joined the congregation to send their 7-year-old son to the synagogue's elementary day school instead of sending him to public school. We could represent this situation in the following abstract way.

$$X \xleftarrow{\quad W \quad} Y$$

This says that X wants W from Y. In the concrete case, this is expanded to read.

$$\textit{Synagogue's School} \xleftarrow{\quad W \quad} \textit{Parents}$$

The synagogue wants from parents:

    (1) parents' acceptance of the importance of religious-based education

    (2) child's enrollment in school

    (3) tuition

Thus, the school wants the parents to enroll their child in the synagogue's school, support the ideals of religious-based education, and pay the required tuition.

In turn, the parents hope to satisfy certain wants by the school's education. We can diagram these as follows:

Synagogue's School $\xrightarrow{\text{\hspace{0.5em}w\hspace{0.5em}}}$ Parents

Parents want from the school:
(1) training in parents' values and religious beliefs
(2) education in academic subjects exceeding that of public schools
(3) healthy, safe environment
(4) socialization with other "quality" children

It would be helpful for the rabbi (teachers and principal) to know the relative importance that parents attach to each of these wants.

These diagrams illustrate an important aspect of exchange: Value is in the eye of the beholder. It does not matter how much value we see in the product we are offering; what matters is the perception of the party who we wish to engage in exchange.

Many religious organizations adopt a selling or product orientation that assumes that everyone will recognize the obvious and inherent value of their product. This is an *inside-out* perspective. In contrast, a marketing orientation, as we saw in chapter 2, always takes an *outside-in* perspective by looking at the congregation's programs and ministries from the perspective of the other party (the consumer). We may think that the value of religious education is real, significant, and obvious, but an exchange will not take place unless parents perceive that its value, *as they define value*, equals or exceeds the value of what they must offer in response.

Elaborating the Exchange Process

We have examined the exchange process as though it involved only two parties. But an exchange process may involve multiple parties. We can illustrate a multiple-party exchange process by introducing the child into our example. In Exhibit 6.7 we see three sets of wants and/or values being considered in the exchange process.

217

The child wants to feel loved and cared for by the parents, including parental concern for doing what is good for the child in the long run. *The school* is looking for children who have the capacity and desire to learn, who will be well behaved, and who can be used as examples of the type of children enrolled in the day school. The synagogue values this type of student in order to encourage other parents to enroll their children in its school. *The parents* want a happy, well-adjusted child with the values and beliefs they prize, as well as an academic training that prepares the child for further education.

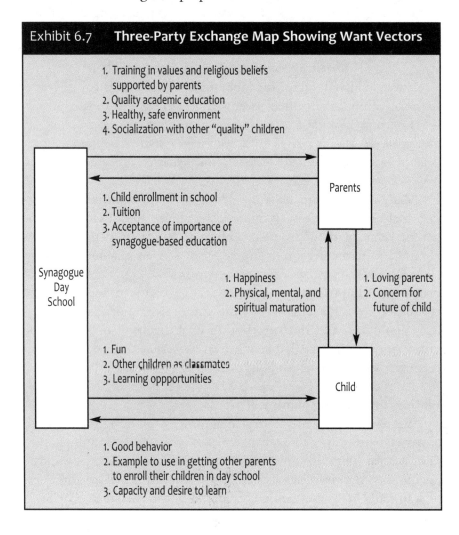

Exhibit 6.7   Three-Party Exchange Map Showing Want Vectors

Not included in the diagram but still pertinent parties to the three-way exchange would be, on the school's side, accrediting associations and other agencies that could affect the parents' perception of the value of the school's program. On the parents' side would be other institutions, such as financial institutions, that might affect the parents' financial ability to enroll their child in the day school. Clearly the synagogue, as marketer, must take these various needs and weightings of value into consideration when formulating strategies to attract students to its school.

When marketers are anxious to consummate a transaction, they may be tempted to exaggerate the actual product benefits. Thus the rabbi may be tempted to overstate the competence of the teachers or understate the total costs to the parents, financial and otherwise. By doing so, he may succeed in getting the parents to enroll their child, but the parents and/or child will become dissatisfied because of the difference between their expectations and the school's performance. As unhappy participants in this exchange, they can be expected to complain a great deal, talk negatively about the school to other parents or playmates, or leave the school and synagogue. In the case of the day school, these dissatisfactions could carry over into other exchanges between the synagogue and the family.

The best transactions are those in which it is realized that both (or all) parties are not simply seeking a single transaction but a continuing expected behavior on the part of the other party, and where parties behave in such a way as to ensure the other will receive the expected values from the exchange.

Good marketing will not *compensate for an inferior ministry or program.* A church or synagogue cannot market a value its product does not have. Marketing can never be a substitute for the diligent effort required to build an effective ministry. Members and outside targeted publics are too sophisticated to be taken in for very long. If an inferior program or ministry is marketed, the results will always be worse than before. Effective marketing must begin with a product of sufficient value (as perceived by the targeted public, not by the organization) to convince the consumers that the benefits to their lives will outweigh the costs. Here again, it is obvious that we must *understand* before we *plan* and *act*.

The Cost of an Exchange

In the consumers' perspective of an organization's programs, they are being asked to incur cost or make sacrifices (that is, to give up something of value) in return for promised benefits. There are four types of "costs":

1. *Economic costs*—e.g., to give up money or goods as tithes or offerings, or simply to buy a product or service.

2. *Give up old ideas, values, or views of the world*—e.g., to stop believing that you shouldn't accept charity when in need, to undergo marriage counseling and change your expectations of marriage, to change your perception of what it would be like to join a large church.

3. *Give up old patterns of behavior*—e.g., to stay drug free, receive home budget counseling, go to divorce recovery group meetings once a week.

4. *Give up time and energy*—e.g., to perform a voluntary service or give blood to a church blood drive.

In return for these types of sacrifices, consumers of ecclesial services receive benefits of four basic kinds: *goods, services, social, and psychological*. The combination of these kinds of sacrifices and benefits yield the matrix outlined in Exhibit 6.8. We have presented this discussion of exchange theory because it is central to a responsive congregation. To be responsive requires analyzing the other party's needs and interests and determining how far the organization can go toward satisfying them. A congregation that is oblivious or indifferent to the needs of the other party cannot, by definition, be responsive.

The key understanding you should get from this extensive discussion of exchange is this: Whenever you find yourself in an exchange situation (i.e., you want something from someone and must give up something valued by the other party in exchange), you will benefit from "thinking like a marketer." That is, you will enhance the possibility that the desired exchange will take place if you put into practice the principles inherent in the societal marketing orien-

Exhibit 6.8	Cost/Benefit Matrix for Religious Organizational Exchanges			
Costs	**A Good**	**A Service**	**Social**	**Psychological**
give up economic assets	buy a CD of sermons	church school education	donate to building fund	church tithes and offerings
give up old ideas, values, opinions	receive free clothing donated by church members	premarital counseling, marriage counseling	prison ministry by laypersons	what joining a church will be like, talking in front of people
give up old behaviors, undertake or learn new behaviors	stay drug-free and receive a "how to" videotape	participate in stop-smoking program, home budget counseling	go to divorce recovery group once a week	dependence on alcohol or tobacco, attend church services
give up time or energy	come to a committee meeting and get a free lunch	attend a free religious concert	volunteer for Vacation Bible School	give blood in church blood drive

tation. Extensive research in both the for-profit and not-for-profit sectors have consistently demonstrated that organizations that are marketing oriented outperform those that are not.[12] So try to see things from your exchange partner's point of view—what do you have that they will see as valuable, how can you add value to it, how can you communicate to them so that they will see even more value, and how can you reduce its "cost" in terms of what they have to give up to get it. Also, be sure to identify the other parties that play a role in influencing the exchange and think about how an exchange of values can be achieved with those parties. You'll be amazed at how much more successful you'll be once you adopt this approach to thinking about your exchanges with others (remember, we aren't saying that everything you do involves exchange, just some of the components of your mission).

The Concept of Image

One consequence of the exchanges between a church or synagogue and its targeted audiences is that the audiences develop an image of the congregation. Every congregation has an image. *Your* congregation has an image. Do you know what it is?

The most important point about the image of a religious organization is "To market a positive image, you need a product worth marketing. Without that, you are doomed to failure. Image makers' efforts and resources would be better spent on needed improvements in the product."[13] To put it simply, *you cannot market what you do not have.*

Responsive religious institutions have a strong interest in how their publics view their structures, ministries, and services. It is your institution's image, not necessarily its reality, that people initially respond to. Publics holding a negative image of you will avoid or disparage everything you do, while those holding a positive image will be drawn to you. You have a vital interest in learning about your image and in seeking to create a more positive image in the minds of your members and nonmembers alike.

You do not acquire a favorable image simply through public relations work. Your image is a function of your *deeds* and its *communications.* Good deeds without good words, or good words without good deeds, will not work. A strong favorable image is achieved when you create real satisfaction for your members and other users of your ministries and services, and let others know

---

The Connected Congregation

Amital Etzioni wrote a thought-provoking piece in *Tikkun* (15, no. 1 [January-February 2000]: 30, 31) entitled "The Internet Versus the Sabbath." The full version of the article is available online through the ATLAReligion database.

Netministries.com and Forministry.com offer free, template-based Web page development for congregations desiring to post their own sites.

about this. Here are some things you likely want to know about image:

1. What is an image?
2. How can an image be measured?
3. What determines the image?
4. How might an image be changed?
5. What is the relationship between the person's image of a program or ministry and his or her behavior toward the church or synagogue?

Definition of Image

The term *image* came into popular use in the 1950s. It is currently used in a variety of contexts: organization image, corporate image, national image, brand image, public image, self-image, and so on. Its wide use has tended to blur its meaning.

Our definition of image is:

Image is the sum of the feelings, beliefs, attitudes, impressions, thoughts, perceptions, ideas, recollections, conclusions, and mind sets that a person or group has of another person, organization, or object.[14]

This definition enables us to distinguish an image from similar-sounding concepts, such as *impressions, attitudes,* and *stereotypes.*

An image is more than a simple impression. The impression that the Roman Catholic Church takes a strong stand against abortion would be only one element in a large image that might be held about the Roman Catholic Church. An image is a whole set of impressions about an object.

On the other hand, people's images of an object do not necessarily reveal their attitudes toward that object. Two persons may hold the same image of the Catholic Church and yet have different attitudes toward it. An attitude is a disposition toward an object that includes cognitive, affective, and behavioral components.

How does an image differ from a stereotype? A stereotype suggests a widely held image that is highly distorted and simplistic, and that carries a favorable or unfavorable attitude toward the object. An image, however, is a more personal perception of an object that can vary among groups. Actually, a specific religious organization will have several images, depending on the particular group.

Image Measurement: Discovering the Organization's Image

We will describe a two-step approach to measuring a congregation's image.[15] The first consists in measuring how familiar and favorable the congregation's image is. The second consists in measuring the organization's image along major relevant dimensions. These approaches are suggestions only.

Familiarity-favorability measurement. The first step is to establish how familiar each public is with the congregation and how favorable they feel toward it. To establish the degree of familiarity, respondents are asked to check one of the following:

Never heard of	Heard of only	Know a little bit	Know a fair amount	Know very well

The results indicate the public's level of awareness of the congregation. If most of the respondents check the first two or three categories, the congregation has a serious awareness problem.

If most of the respondents indicate they know the congregation "a fair amount" or "very well," they are then asked to describe how favorable they feel toward it by checking one of the following:

Very unfavorable	Somewhat unfavorable	Indifferent	Somewhat favorable	Very favorable

To illustrate these scales, suppose the residents of an area are asked to rate four local congregations: A, B, C, and D. Their responses are averaged and the results displayed in Exhibit 6.9.

Exhibit 6.9	Familiarity-Favorability Analysis

	Favorable Attitude	
A		B
	Low	High
	Familiarity	Familiarity
C	Unfavorable Attitude	D

The exhibit depicts congregation B as having the strongest image; most people know it and like it. Congregation A is viewed favorably, but too few know about it. The people who know it negatively view congregation C; fortunately not too many people know about it. Congregation D is in the weakest position; it is seen as an undesirable congregation, and everyone knows it.

Clearly, each congregation faces a different task. Congregation B must work at maintaining its good reputation and high community awareness. Congregation A must bring itself to the attention of more

---

New Light
Why People Switch Religions

Up to one third of the people practicing religion in the U.S. switch religious faiths at least once during their lives. Why do people switch their religious identification? Matthew Loveland's research into this question led him to the following conclusion.

1. Childhood socialization (attendance at a religious school, Sunday school, saying grace before meals) has little affect on religious preferences later in life. Those whose childhoods included religious involvement and education are no less likely to switch religions than those with less religious socialization.

2. It is true, however, that those people who joined a church during childhood are significantly less likely to switch religions later in life than those who did not join a church.

3. Lapses in religious practice increase the likelihood of switching to a significant degree. Those who spend little time with relatives are also more likely to switch.

4. Members of distinctive denominations and Catholics are less likely to switch religions. It is speculated that religious bodies that create preference for unique religious goods make it difficult for individuals to find satisfactory religious "products" elsewhere.

Matthew T. Loveland, "Religious Switching: Preference Development, Maintenance, and Change," *Journal of the Scientific Study of Religions* 42, no. 1 (2003): 147-157.

people, since those who know it find it to be a good church. Congregation C needs to find out why people dislike the church and take steps to mend its ways, while keeping a low profile. Congregation D would be well advised to lower its profile (avoid news), mend its ways, and when it is a better church, it can start seeking public attention again.

Semantic differential. Each congregation needs to go further to re-search the *content* of its image. One of the most popular tools for this is the semantic differential.[16] It involves the following steps.

1. Developing a set of relevant dimensions. The researcher first asks people to identify the dimensions they would use in thinking about the object. People could be asked what things they think of when they consider a church. If someone suggests "quality of preaching," this would be turned into a bipolar adjective scale, with "inferior preaching" at one end and "superior preaching" at the other. This could be rendered as a five- or seven-point scale. A set of additional relevant dimensions for a church is shown in Exhibit 6.10.

2. Reducing the set of relevant dimensions. The number of dimensions should be kept small to avoid respondent fatigue in having to rate several congregations on a number of scales. Osgood and his coworkers feel that there are essentially three types of scales.
- evaluation scales (good-bad qualities)
- potency scales (strong-weak qualities)
- activity scales (active-passive qualities)

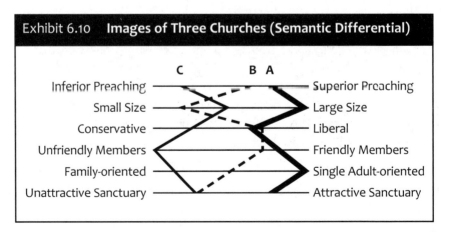

Exhibit 6.10 Images of Three Churches (Semantic Differential)

	C	B A	
Inferior Preaching			Superior Preaching
Small Size			Large Size
Conservative			Liberal
Unfriendly Members			Friendly Members
Family-oriented			Single Adult-oriented
Unattractive Sanctuary			Attractive Sanctuary

Using these scales as a guide, the researcher can remove redundant scales that fail to add much information.

3. Administering the instrument to a sample of respondents. The respondents are asked to rate one organization at a time. The bipolar adjectives should be arranged so as not to load all of the negative adjectives on one side.

4. Averaging the results. Exhibit 6.10 shows the results of averaging the respondents' impressions of congregations A, B, and C. A line that summarizes how the average respondent sees that institution represents each congregation's image (i.e., if the line is a seven-point scale, all the responses for each congregation are totaled, then divided by number of respondents, and the resulting average for each congregation is plotted on the seven-point scale). Thus congregation A is seen as large, liberal, friendly, singles-oriented with superior preaching. Congregation C, on the other hand, is seen as a moderate-sized, conservative, unfriendly group with inferior preaching. Congregation B is seen as small, liberal, friendly, with good preaching.

5. Checking on the image variance. Since each image profile is the result of averaging the respondents' answer, it does not reveal how variable the image is among different respondents. If there were 100 respondents, did they all see congregation B, for example, exactly as shown, or was there considerable variation? If the responses were very similar, the image is highly *specific*. If the responses were greatly varied, the image is highly *diffused*.

An institution may or may not want a very specific image. Some religious organizations prefer a diffused image so that different groups can project their needs onto it. The organization will want to analyze whether a variable image is really the result of different subgroups rating the organization, with each subgroup having a highly specific image.

The semantic differential is a flexible image-measuring tool that can provide the following useful information:

1. The congregation can discover how a particular public views the organization and its major competitors. It can learn its image strengths and weaknesses, along with those of the competitors, and take remedial steps toward creating a more desirable image.

2. The congregation can discover how different publics and market segments view it. One can imagine that the image profiles in Exhibit 6.10 represent the images of one congregation held by three different publics. The congregation would then consider taking steps to improve its image among those publics who view it most unfavorably.

3. The congregation can monitor changes in its image over time. By repeating the image study periodically, the congregation can detect any significant image slippage or improvement. Image slippage signals that the organization is doing something wrong. Image improvement, on the other hand, verifies that the organization is performing better as a result of some steps it has taken.

Image Causation

What determines the image a person holds of your organization? A theory of image determinants will help you understand the factors that have shaped your present image and help in planning to change the image. Two opposite theories of image formation prevail. One holds that image is largely object-determined—that is, persons simply perceive the object's reality. If an attractive church is located next to a lake and is surrounded by beautiful trees, then it is going to strike people as a beautiful church. A few individuals might describe it as ugly, but this would be dismissed as the peculiarity of certain individuals. The object-determined view of images assumes that: (1) people tend to have firsthand experience with objects; (2) people get reliable sensory data from the object; (3) people tend to process the sensory data in a similar way in spite of having different backgrounds and personalities. These assumptions imply that organizations cannot easily create false images of themselves.

The other theory holds that images are largely *person-determined.* Those holding this view argue that: (1) people have different degrees of contact with the object; (2) people viewing the object will selectively perceive different aspects of the object; (3) people have individual ways of processing sensory data, leading to selective distortion. This set of assumptions implies that people are likely to hold quite different images of the object. That is, there is a weak relation between the image and the actual object.

The Connected Congregation

The American Bible Society in 1998 committed $5 million to providing a free Web page for each of the 300,000 congregations in North America. ABS's http://www.forministry.com Web site offers free help in assisting congregations setting up a Web site. As of spring 2009, more than 25,000 Web sites had been established using this service. More than 150,000 churches are in the ABS's directory.

The truth lies somewhere in between. An image is influenced both by the object's objective characteristics and the perceiver's subjective characteristics. We might expect people to hold rather similar images of a given object mainly under the following conditions: when the object is simple rather than complex; when it is frequently and directly experienced; and when it is fairly stable in its real characteristics over time.

Conversely, people may hold quite different images of an object if it is complex, infrequently experienced, and changing through time. People have quite different images of a particular church or synagogue because it is complex, infrequently experienced in direct contact, and changes through time.

Image Modification

The leaders of an organization are often surprised and disturbed by the measured image. Thus you might be upset that the public sees you substantially different from your own perceptions. Your immediate reaction might be to disbelieve the results by complaining that the number of persons interviewed is too small or unrepresentative. But if the results can be defended as reliable, you need to consider what you should do about your image problem.

The first step is to develop a picture of the *desired image that you would like to earn in the general public's mind—in contrast to the current image.*

The second step is to decide which image gaps you want to

work on initially; for example, is it more desirable to improve the congregation's image of friendliness (through staff training, etc.) or to improve the condition of the facilities (through renovation)?

Each image dimension should be reviewed separately in terms of the following questions:

1. What contribution to your overall favorable image would be made by closing the image gap in this dimension?

2. What strategy (combination of real changes and communication changes) would be used to close the particular image gap?

3. What would be the cost of closing that image gap?

4. How long would it take to close that image gap?

For example, you might decide it would be more apparent, quicker, and less costly to improve your image of friendliness than to improve the buildings' physical facilities. An overall image modification plan would involve planning the sequence of steps through which you would go to transform your current image into your desired image.

An organization seeking to change its image must have great patience. Images are "sticky" and last long after the reality of the organization has changed. Thus a congregation may be more family-oriented and yet continue to be considered singles-oriented in the public mind. Image persistence is explained by the fact that once people have formed a certain image of an object, they tend to be selective perceivers of further data. Their perceptions are oriented toward seeing what they expect to see. It will take highly disconfirming stimuli to raise doubts, and open them to new information. Thus an image enjoys a life of its own for a while, especially when people are not likely to have new firsthand experiences with the changed object.

The Organization's Image and the Way Persons Respond

You should be interested in image measurement and modification because there is a close relationship between the public's image of you and their behavior toward you. Organizations can obtain better public response by acquiring a better image.

However, the connection between image and behavior is not as close as you might think. Images are only one component of attitudes. Two people may view a church as large and have opposite attitudes toward a large church. Furthermore, the connection between attitudes and behavior is also tenuous. A person might prefer a large church to a small one, and yet end up in the small one because it is closer to home, or their friends go there.

Nevertheless, one should not dismiss image measurement and planning simply because images are hard to change and their effects on behavior are unclear. Quite to the contrary, measuring your image is a very useful step in understanding what is happening to you, what results your efforts are achieving, and in planning steps toward changing your image. Furthermore, though the connection between image and behavior is not always strong, it does exist. The connection should be neither overrated nor underrated. You should attempt to make an investment in developing the best image you can for the advantages this might bring.

The Concept of Satisfaction

A responsive organization is one that makes every effort to sense, serve, and satisfy the needs and wants of its members and publics. Each organization must determine how responsive it wants to be, and develop the appropriate systems for measuring and improving its satisfaction-creating ability.

Since responsive organizations aim to create satisfaction, it is necessary to define the term *satisfaction*. Our definition is:

Satisfaction is a state felt by a person (or group) who has experienced a performance (or outcome) that has fulfilled his or her expectation.

Thus, satisfaction is a function of the relative levels of expectation and perceived performance. A person will experience one of three states of satisfaction: If the performance exceeds the person's expectations, the person is *highly satisfied*. If the performance matches the expectations, the person is *satisfied*. If the performance falls short of the expectations, the person is *dissatisfied*.

In the last case, the amount of dissatisfaction depends on the person's method of handling the gap between expectations and performance. Some members and participants try to *minimize* the felt dissonance by imagining better performance than there really is, or reasoning that they set their expectations too high. Other persons will exaggerate the perceived performance gap because of their disappointment.[17] They are more prone to reduce or end their contacts with the organization.

Measuring Satisfaction

Member or participant satisfaction, in spite of its central importance, is difficult to measure. Religious organizations use various methods to make an inference about how much member or participant satisfaction they are creating. The major methods are described below.

Performance-related methods. Many congregations feel that the extent of member and participant satisfaction created by their activities is revealed by such objective measures as:

Growth statistics: the increase or decline of the number of persons attending or participating in their programs and ministries

Market share: the number of members and of persons participating, as compared to the other congregations nearby

Repeat ratio: the percentage of persons who attend more than once, and how long they keep returning

Active ratio: the percentage of active members out of the total membership ("active" must be defined)

If these measures are rising, the leaders draw the conclusion that the organization is satisfying its members and participants. Thus if congregation X is crowded at the worship services and 100 percent of its members subscribe to support the budget, the leaders conclude that the members must be satisfied. If a Sunday school class attracts more teenage students each year, even though the number of teenagers in the congregation is declining, it implies that the teenagers in the congregation must be satisfied.

These indirect measures are important but hardly sufficient. In situations of no competition, or of excess demand, these measures may be high and yet not reflect actual satisfaction, because members have no alternatives. In other situations, attendance at the worship service can remain strong for a while, even after the levels of satisfaction have started to decline, because dissatisfied members might continue to participate for a period of time out of habit, or inertia.

Complaint and suggestion systems. A responsive congregation will make it easy for its members and others to complain if they are disappointed with the service. Leaders will want complaints to surface, on the theory that members who are not given an opportunity to complain might reduce their level of participation and/or support for the organization, bad-mouth it, or abandon it completely. Not collecting complaints represents a loss of valuable information that the organization could have used to improve its services.

To facilitate the opportunity for persons to register complaints,

---

Becoming Doers
Measuring Member Satisfaction

One recent study of member satisfaction at a mainstream denominational church in the Midwest organized 37 individual satisfaction measures into 10 categories, or "factors":

satisfaction with church programs and social and service opportunities

satisfaction with worship service and social interaction and member support

importance of physical and social ambience of the worship service

opinions of congregational harmony

satisfaction with church time and place

preferences for Sunday school content

Sunday school leadership opportunities

community obligations of the church

church convenience and image

administrative communication with members

Administrators interested in conducting a survey of their congregation to measure satisfaction levels will find a suggested methodology as well as the 37 questions used in this study included in the article listed below.

Paula M. Saunders, "Increasing Member Satisfaction and Retention," *Journal of Ministry Marketing and Management* 5, no. 2 (2000): 51-82.

you can set up systems that make it easy for dissatisfied (or satisfied) persons to express their feelings. Several devices can be used in this connection. For example, you could place *suggestion boxes* in convenient areas. It could supply members and participants with a *comment card*, allowing responses to several of the congregation's services. These cards encourage the submission of complaints, compliments, suggestions, and requests for information.

You should try to identify the major categories of complaints. You might count the number of complaints about the timing of worship services, sermon topics, and youth ministry and focus your corrective actions on those categories showing a high frequency, high seriousness, and/or high remediability.

A good complaint management system will provide much valuable information for improving your performance. At the same time, a complaint system tends to understate the amount of real dissatisfaction felt by members and by participants. The reasons are (1) many people who are disappointed may choose not to complain, either being too angry or feeling that complaining would do no good. (One study found that only 34 percent of a group of dissatisfied people said they would complain); (2) some people overcomplain (the chronic complainers), and this introduces a bias into the data.

Some critics have argued that complaint systems do more harm than good. When given an opportunity—indeed, an incentive—to complain, people are more likely to feel dissatisfied. Instead of ignoring their disappointment, they are asked to spell it out. They are also led to expect redress. If the latter is not forthcoming, they will be more dissatisfied than ever. Even though this might happen, it is our view that the value of the information gathered by soliciting complaints far exceeds the cost of possibly overstimulating dissatisfaction.

Consumer panels. Some organizations set up a consumer panel to keep informed of member and participant satisfaction. The panel consists of a small group of members and participants who are periodically sampled about their feelings toward the organization or any of its services.

Some provision is usually made to rotate membership of the panel, in order to get fresh views from new people. The panel is typically a source of valuable information to the organization. At the same time, the information may not be completely reliable. The panel's representativeness can be called into question. People who do not like to be members of panels are not represented. Those who join the panel may be more loyal to the organization, and thus less likely to see its faults.

Member and participant satisfaction surveys. Many organizations supplement the preceding devices with direct periodic surveys of members and participants. They send questionnaires or make telephone calls to random samples of volunteer workers, members, and participants to find out how much they like or dislike a particular program or ministry. In this way they avoid the possible biases of complaints systems, on the one hand, and consumer panels, on the other.

The level of satisfaction a group holds for a particular program or service can be measured in a number of ways, three of which will be described here.

1. Directly Reported Satisfaction. You could distribute a questionnaire to a representative sample of members, asking them to state their felt satisfaction with the organization as a whole, and with specific components. The questionnaire is distributed on a periodic basis either in person, by mail, or through a telephone survey.

The questionnaire might contain questions of the following form:

Indicate how satisfied you are with _____
on the following scale:

1	2	3	4	5
Highly Dissatisfied	Dissatisfied	Indifferent	Satisfied	Highly Satisfied

Here, five intervals are used. When the results are in, a bar graph (histogram) can be prepared, showing the percentage of respondents who fall into each group.

If the histogram is highly skewed to the left, you are in deep trouble. If the histogram is bell-shaped, then you have the usual number of dissatisfied, indifferent, and satisfied members. If the histogram is highly skewed to the right, you can be satisfied that are a responsive organization, meeting your goal of delivering high satisfaction to the majority of your members and participants.

The survey should be repeated at regular intervals to spot any significant changes in the distribution. Furthermore, the respondents should check scales for other components of your organization, such as your community service activities, youth programs, choir, and the like. It would help to know how the various components of satisfaction relate to overall satisfaction.

2. Derived Dissatisfaction. The second method of satisfaction measurement is based on the premise that a person's satisfaction is influenced by his or her expectations and perception of the object. The respondent is asked two questions about each component of the organization—for example, the quality of the youth program:

A. How much quality is there now?
minimum　　1　2　3　4　5　6　7　　maximum

B. Considering costs, how much quality should there be?
minimum　　1　2　3　4　5　6　7　　maximum

Suppose the respondent circles 2 for part A and 5 for part B. Subtracting the weight given to part A from that given to part B can then derive a "need deficiency" score. In this instance the difference would be 5 minus 2, or 3. The greater the need deficiency score, the greater the respondent's degree of dissatisfaction (or the smaller his or her degree of satisfaction).

This method provides more useful information than the previous method. By averaging the scores of all the respondents to part A, you learn the average perceived level of that attribute of the object. The dispersion around the average shows how much agreement there is among the members. If all members see your youth program at approximately 2 on a seven-point scale, the program is quite deficient. If members hold widely differing perceptions of the program's actual quality, this will require further analysis of why the perceptions differ so much and what individual or group factors might be related to the differing perceptions.

It is also useful to average the scores of all the respondents to part B. This will reveal the average member's view of how much quality is expected in the youth program. The measure of dispersion will show how much spread there is in member opinion regarding the desired level of quality.

By finding the need deficiency score for each program or ministry, the leaders will have a good understanding of current member and participant moods, and where to make the necessary changes. By repeating this survey at regular intervals, the leaders can detect new need deficiencies as they arise, and take timely steps to remedy them.

3. Importance/Performance Ratings. Another satisfaction-measuring device is to ask members and participants to rate several programs and ministries provided by your congregation in terms of (1) the importance of each service and (2) how well you perform each service. Exhibit 6.11 shows how church members rated 14 services. A service's importance was rated on a four-point scale of "extremely important," "important," "slightly important," and "not important," The congregation's performance was rated on a four-point scale of "excellent," "good," "fair," and "poor."

For example, the first service, "youth program," received a mean importance rating of 3.83 and a mean performance rating of 2.63, indicating that members felt it was highly important, although not being performed all that well.

The ratings of all 14 services are displayed in Exhibit 6.11. The figure is divided into four sections.

Quadrant A shows important services that are not being offered at the desired performance levels. You should concentrate on improving these services.

Quadrant B shows important services that the church is performing well. Its job here is to maintain the high performance.

Quadrant C shows minor services that are being delivered in a mediocre way, but do not need any attention since they are not very important.

Quadrant D shows a minor service that is being performed in an excellent manner, a case of possible "overkill."

This rating of services according to their perceived importance and performance provides the church with guidelines as to where it should concentrate its efforts for increasing levels of satisfaction.

Consumer Satisfaction and Other Goals

Many people believe that the marketing concept calls upon the organization to *maximize* the satisfaction of its members and participants. This, however, is not realistic. The marketing concept says the organization should strive to create a *high level* of satisfaction among its members and participants. The reasons for this are explained below.

First, consumer satisfaction can always be increased by incurring additional cost. Thus you might hire more associate pastors, build better facilities, and institute more programs to increase the satisfaction of your members. But obviously you face a financial constraint in trying to maximize the satisfaction of a particular public.

Importance and Performance Ratings for Several Church Services

Service	Service Description	Mean Importance Rating[a]	Mean Performance Rating[b]
1	Youth Program	3.83	2.63
2	Premarital Counseling	3.63	2.73
3	At-Home Visitation	3.60	3.15
4	Sermon Quality	3.56	3.00
5	Community Service	3.41	3.05
6	Evangelistic Outreach	3.39	3.29
7	Church School Quality	3.38	3.03
8	Sunday School Classes	3.37	3.11
9	Bible Camp	3.29	2.24
10	Vacation Bible School	3.27	3.02
11	Midweek Prayer Meeting	2.52	2.25
12	Pastoral Counseling	2.43	2.49
13	Social Events	2.37	2.35
14	Infant and Toddler Care	2.05	3.13

[a]Ratings obtained from a four-point scale of "extremely important," "important," "slightly important," and "not important."

[b]Ratings obtained from a four-point scale of "excellent," "good," "fair," and "poor." A "no basis for judgment" category was also provided.

Second, you have to satisfy many publics. Increasing the satisfaction of one public might reduce the satisfaction available to another public. You owe each public some specific level of satisfaction. Ultimately, you must operate on the philosophy that you are trying to satisfy the needs of different groups at levels that are acceptable to these groups within the constraint of your total resources. This is why you must systematically measure the levels of satisfaction expected by your different constituent publics and the current levels they are, in fact, receiving.

You hope to derive a number of benefits as a result of creating high satisfaction in your publics. One benefit is that your members will participate with a better sense of purpose and pride. Another benefit is that you create loyal publics. This reduces the costs of market turnover. Finally, the loyal publics say good things to others about you. This attracts new participants without requiring as much direct effort on your part. In chapter 12 we will discuss in greater detail various ways to create satisfied customers and consumers.

Exhibit 6.11	Plot of Importance and Performance Ratings

Summary

Religious organizations that adopt a societal marketing orientation exist to be responsive to the needs of their members and constituents, and responsive to the needs of society. A responsive congregation is one that makes every effort to sense, serve, and satisfy the needs and wants of its members and participants within the constraints of its budget. The concept of a responsive congregation rests on the concepts of mission, publics, segmentation and targeting, exchange, image, and satisfaction.

Every organization starts with a *mission* that answers these questions: What is our business? Who is the customer? What is of value to the customer? What will our business be? What should our business be? A mission is best when it is feasible, motivating, and distinctive. Congregations interact with several *publics*. A public is a distinct group of people and/or organizations that has an actual or potential interest and/or impact on an organization. Publics can be classified as input publics (donors, suppliers, judicatory agencies), internal publics (trustees, board, ministry team, volunteers), intermediary publics (facilitators, publishers, agents, radio and TV media, Internet agencies, marketing firms), consuming publics (members, other participants, recipients of services), and external publics (local publics, activist publics, general public, media publics, and competitive publics).

When an organization seeks some response from a public, this public is called a market. A market is a distinct group of people and/or organizations that has resources it (or they) want to exchange, or might be willing to exchange, for distinct benefits.

No single organization can serve all the needs and interests of all the people surrounding it. A congregation that attempts to do so will likely dissipate its resources and accomplish little. Therefore it is important that the congregation *segment* the population into identifiable groups in order to decide those that it will *target* with its programs and ministries.

To carry out its mission with targeted publics, a religious organization needs resources. A congregation can attract resources through self-production, force, begging, or *exchange*. Marketing is based on exchange, and it assumes that there are at least two parties; each able to offer something of value to the other, each capable of communication and delivery, and each free to accept or reject the offer. Exchanges take place when both parties expect to be better off after a transaction is completed.

Responsive religious organizations are interested in their image, because it is their image to which people respond. An organization's image is the sum of the beliefs, ideas, and impressions that a person or group has of it. Images can be measured by scaling techniques. Organizations can work to modify undesirable aspects of their image through changing their practices and their communications.

The acid test of a congregation's responsiveness to its members, and society's physical and social needs, is the *satisfaction* it creates among the publics it serves. Religious organizations range from those that are unresponsive and casually responsive to those that are highly responsive and fully responsive.

The more highly responsive religious organizations make use of complaint systems, surveys of satisfaction, surveys of needs and preferences, person-oriented personnel, and empowered members and participants. Responsive organizations create more satisfaction for their publics. Satisfaction is a state felt by a person or group that has experienced organizational performance that has matched their expectations.

---

[1] For further discussion of mission clarification in religious organizations, see Rick Warren, *The Purpose Driven Church: Growth Without Compromising Your Message & Mission* (Grand Rapids: Zondervan, 1995); Alvin Lindgren and Norman Shawchuck, *Management for Your Church* (Schaumburg, Ill.: Spirtual Growth Resources, 1985) and *Let My People Go: Empowering Laity for Ministry*; Lloyd Perry and Norman Shawchuck, *Revitalizing the 20th Century Church* (Chicago: Moody, 1986); and Peter F. Drucker, "Mission and Leadership," *The Nonprofit Drucker Tape Library*, vol. 1.

[2] The sketch is adapted from Perry and Shawchuck, pp. 13-30.

[3] See Peter F. Drucker, *Management: Tasks, Responsibilities, Practices* (New York: Harper & Row, 1973), chap. 7.

[4] See Derek F. Abell, *Defining the Business: The Starting Point of Strategic Planning* (Englewood Cliffs, N.J.: Prentice-Hall, 1980), chap. 2, esp. p. 17.

[5] Accessed from crystalcathedral.org and links on that Web site on March 29, 2007.

[6] See David L. Sills, *The Volunteers: Means and Ends in a National Organization* (Glencoe, Ill: Free Press, 1957). Also note that the National Center for Voluntary Action, 1785

Massachusetts Ave. NW. Washington, D.C. 20036, researches, conducts seminars, and disseminates up-to-date information for managing volunteers.

[7] See Drucker, *Management*, p. 61.

[8] Elizabeth Bernstein, "Do-It-Yourself Religion," *Wall Street Journal*, Jun.11, 2004, p. W1.

[9] This strategic approach has been referred to as "blue ocean strategy." See W. Chan Kim and Renee Mauborgne, *Blue Ocean Strategy: How to Create Uncontested Market Space and Make the Competition Irrelevant* (Cambridge, Mass.: Harvard University Press, 2005).

[10] Sarmad Ali, "New Cell Phone Services Put God on the Line," *Wall Street Journal*, Mar. 27, 2006, p. B1.

[11] For additional discussion of the concept of exchange in marketing, see Richard P. Bagozzi, "Marketing as an Organized Behavioral System of Exchange," *Journal of Marketing*, October 1974, pp. 77-81; and "Marketing as Exchange," *American Behavioral Scientist*, March-April 1978, pp. 535-556.

[12] See Ahmet H. Kirca, Satish Jayachandran, and William O. Bearden, "Market Orientation: A meta-analytic Review and Assessment of Its Antecedents and Impact on Performance," *Journal of Marketing* 69 (April 2005): 24-41.

[13] See Robert S. Topor, *Institutional Image: How to Define, Improve, Market It* (Washington, D.C.: Council for the Advancement and Support of Education, 1986), p. vii.

[14] *Ibid.,* p. 1.

[15] Topor's book gives many suggestions for image measurement.

[16] C. E. Osgood, G. J. Suci, and P. H. Tannenbaum, *The Measurement of Meaning* (Urbana, Ill.: University of Illinois Press, 1957).

[17] See Ralph E. Anderson, "Consumer Dissatisfaction: The Effect of Disconfirmed Expectancy on Perceived Product Performance," *Journal of Marketing Research*, February 1973, pp. 38-44.

WORKSHEETS: CHAPTER 6

Identifying Marketing Concepts
That Can Be Put to Use for Your Organization

A. Mission
Identify the key components of your mission:

Focus of Relationships

		Internal			External
Vertical		Worship	1	2	Evangelism
Direction of Relationship		Community (Adherent and Fellowship)	3	4	Social Services
Horizontal					

Describe the aspects of your mission for each cell:

1. Worship

_____

_____

_____

2. Evangelism

_____

_____

_____

3. Community

_____

_____

_____

4. Social Service

_____

_____

_____

B. Publics

Describe the key publics for your organization.

1. Input Publics

_____

_____

_____

2. Intermediary

_____

_____

_____

3. Consuming Publics

_____

_____

_____

4 External Publics

_____

_____

_____

These publics should be reflected in your mission statement.

C. Competition
Describe your competition at each of the competitive levels:
1. Desire

_____

_____

_____

2. Generic

_____

_____

_____

3. Service Form

_____

_____

_____

4. Enterprise

_____

_____

_____

5. "Do-It-Yourself" Groups

_____

_____

_____

6. Internet-based

_____

_____

_____

D. Exchange

In the table below fill in the cells where you are engaged in exchange, indicating the intersection of costs and benefits involved in those exchanges.

Cost/Benefit Matrix for Religious Organizational Exchanges

BENEFITS

Costs	A Good	A Service	Social	Psychological
give up economic assets				
give up old ideas, values, opinions				
give up old behaviors, undertake or learn new behaviors				
give up time or energy				

Diagram exchange maps for your key publics identified in the table above. Be sure to include in the diagram all the parties to each exchange and the wants (the "something of value") sought by each party. Complete individual maps for each key public. Devote considerable thought to the something-of-value (SOV) lists. How much do you really know about that public's SOVs? Are you speculating or do you know this for a fact? If you don't know the wants, use the methods described in chapter 5, marketing research, to learn of the wants. These can change over time, so be certain your understanding of the wants for the parties is up-to-date.

Public   What We Need to Know

_____   _____

_____   _____

_____   _____

_____   _____

_____   _____

Exchange Maps

E. Image

Describe the Image of your organization. Use the semantic differential method described in the chapter to measure the image of your organization and that of your primary competitors. Construct a graph similar to Exhibit 6.10 to display the images. What about your image needs changing?

Image Graph

F. Importance/Satisfaction

Using the method described in the chapter, create a graph similar to Exhibit 6.11 to display the position of your ministries/programs with regard to their performance and satisfaction ratings. The existing programs positioned in quadrant A are prime candidates for the marketing planning activities discussed in the following chapters.

Importance/Satisfaction Graph

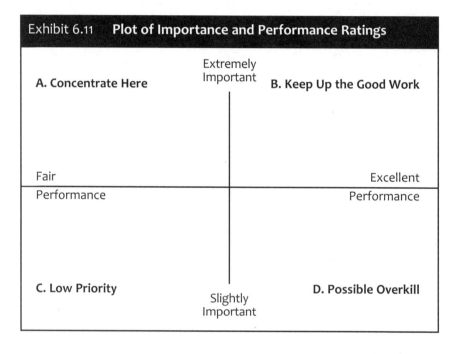

Exhibit 6.11	Plot of Importance and Performance Ratings

A. Concentrate Here

Extremely Important

B. Keep Up the Good Work

Fair
Performance

Excellent
Performance

C. Low Priority

Slightly Important

D. Possible Overkill

CHAPTER 7:

Market Segmentation, Targeting, and Positioning

"He will sort the people out, much as a shepherd sorts out sheep and goats, putting sheep to his right and goats to his left" (MATTHEW 25:32, 33, MESSAGE).

In this chapter we will address the following questions:

1. What is the rationale for segmenting religious organizational "markets"?

2. What are the three methods for segmenting markets?

3. How can existing segmentation "systems" be used to segment religious organizational "markets"?

4. What strategies can be used to choose a target(s) among the segments?

5. How can a religious organization position its programs to the targeted segment?

Youth ministers who had believed that reaching teenagers required wrapping religion in a pop-culture package have now begun offering young people a message grounded in Bible study and doctrinal teaching about their denomination. This change in type of appeal was sparked by a growing recognition that the sugarcoated Christianity, popular in the 1990s and early 2000s, that centered on entertainment was causing a growing number of kids to turn away from both church youth-fellowship activities and practicing their faith at all. One research study reported in 2006 found that more than 60 percent of adults in their 20s said they had participated in church activities as teenagers, but no longer do. To fight this trend, some churches are focusing less on amusement and more on Scripture and religious doctrine, using the model developed by youth pastors at the Saddleback Church centering on evangelism, fellowship, discipleship, ministry, and worship. Using this approach, the Calvary Baptist Church in Bellflower, California, has seen its youth rolls grow from 70 to 200+ in recent years. Other churches report similar gains. Changes have occurred in nonquantitative ways as well—one teen at Calvary says, "Before attending Calvary, I believed in God and prayed at night, but I was still very bitter and unhappy about many things in life. I've learned what it means to be a Christian, and now I wake up smiling every morning."[1]

This report illustrates this chapter's trio of topics: segmentation, targeting and positioning. Here, pastors had segmented their "market" using age as their segmentation base, selected the age segment of teenagers as a target, and then positioned a message toward that segment. Actually they repositioned a message toward that group, changing their strategy when it became apparent that a previous strategy no longer generated the results they desired. These three topics were introduced in the previous chapter as essential marketing concepts. In this chapter we describe how you can use them to increase both the efficiency and effectiveness of your marketing strategies.

Market segmentation is the process of classifying a population into groups that exhibit differing needs, interests, values, and behaviors that will affect their reactions to a religious program or ministry that is offered to them.

Target marketing is the process of selecting one or more of these segments and developing ministries and marketing plans designed to meet the unique needs and interests of each chosen segment.

Positioning is the art of developing and communicating meaningful differences between one's offer and those of other organizations serving the same target market.

Market Segmentation

Segmentation Rationale. Our discussion of market segmentation begins with the following somewhat surprising bits of due diligence:

• Segmentation itself achieves nothing. You achieve your marketing goals when you successfully engage others in long-term highly satisfying mutually beneficial exchange relationships. Market segmentation is merely a device created by marketers in order to generate such relationships more efficiently and effectively.

• Market segments do not actually exist. Or perhaps it is more accurate to say that marketers try to impose structure upon a market that has no universal, naturally occurring structure to it. Markets are not like the animal kingdom, with its universally understood natural segments of genus, subgenus, and species. If segments exist in a market, they are there because a marketer has constructed them, hopefully by tapping into consumer behavior realities.

The truthfulness of this second point is supported by your own experience as a consumer—you have been classified by marketers into hundreds if not thousands of market segments by domestic and foreign marketers, yet do not define yourself in any way by these segment memberships. You are simultaneously a member of the heavy cell phone-using segment, the price shopper clothing segment, the outdoor sports activist segment, and hundreds of other segments because marketers have found it useful to categorize you in such a way for marketing planning purposes. Sometimes you are grouped in the same segment as your neighbors; sometimes you are put in different segments. In every case, marketers understand how to better think about a market's structure in ways that reflect the realities of how consumers can be grouped together so that a marketing appeal can connect with the people in the targeted segment. The rationale for segmenting a market as a prerequisite for marketing planning is therefore based on the following assumptions:

1. The diversity of consumer behavior means that not everyone

in the market is looking for the same things from what you offer. That is, a specific marketing appeal will not connect equally well with all people in a market.

2. It is better to establish very successful connections with a portion of the people in a market than only marginally successfully connect with everyone, leaving you vulnerable to another organization who very successfully connects with them (i.e., if you try to be something to everyone, you'll end up being nothing to anyone).

3. To be very successful with your portion of the people in a market, you must be able to identify them, understand them in depth, and then use that understanding to develop highly satisfying offerings for them.

4. People will prefer to give their loyalties to those organizations that seek to understand the members of the market segments, and then develop highly satisfying marketing offerings based upon that understanding.

If any of these four assumptions are invalid, market segmentation may not prove as advisable as mass marketing appeals (i.e., treating all people as the same and marketing the same way to everyone in the market). However, it should be obvious that these assumptions hold true for the vast majority of markets, including many of the groups of people you are interested in gaining as exchange partners.

In addition to these assumptions, marketers also use a set of criteria to determine if segmentation, targeting, and positioning are worthwhile in developing marketing programs.[2]

1. *Mutual Exclusivity.* Each segment should be separable from all other segments. Another way to think of this assumption is that each person should be a member of only one segment. So you would not want to segment congregational members into past tithers and present tithers, for example, since a member could appear in both segments.

2. *Exhaustiveness.* Every potential target member should be included in some segment. If, for example, you are segmenting by age, then your age categories should include people of all ages (e.g., under 2, 2-4 years, 5-9 years, . . . 80+ years).

3. *Sizeable.* Any segmentation of a market must generate segments of a size sufficient to be of interest to you. If the resulting seg-

ments are too small, segmentation may not be worthwhile.

4. *Identifiability.* Segments arising from the segmentation process should have characteristics that allow for easy description and correspond to your general observations of the market.

5. *Reachability.* Marketers want to be able to not only identify the segments, but also to be able to reach them selectively, that is, without having to talk to the entire market in order to reach a particular segment's consumers. So if you want to reach the middle-aged singles segment looking for a new church family, you would look for media patterns that these people have in common, allowing for a promotional campaign that could speak to them without wasting resources on people who have no interest in your programs directed to this group.

6. *Different Response.* Marketers want to develop a segmentation scheme for the market that results in different "sweet spots" for the segments. In other words, what appeals to the members of one segment will be common within that segment, but different from what consumers in another segment find appealing. If several segments respond exactly alike to several ministries, although it may be *conceptually* useful to develop separate segments, it would not be useful in terms of ministry effectiveness. In this case you would aggregate these segments for planning purposes.

7. *Coherence.* Ideally, members within a particular segment are homogeneous along several attitudinal, behavioral, and other dimensions useful in developing marketing programs, but are heterogeneous with respect to other segments. In this way you can maximize effectiveness by choosing a customized appeal for each segment that is uniquely capable of connecting with the segment's members.

8. *Stability.* While this criteria is not absolute (no segment will stay perfectly stable forever), it is desirable that the formation of the segments and the resulting marketing programs will have a lifetime sufficiently long to allow for successful connections over a reasonable length of time.

If, by segmenting a market, you correctly assume the four assumptions hold true, and you find the resulting segments pass these eight criteria, then segmentation can provide several benefits to you:

Effectiveness—you'll be better able to connect with a group of people whose common needs are better understood and are not highly diffuse.

Efficiency—you'll get more "bang for the buck" when you can concentrate on smaller, more responsive segments instead of larger diverse groups of people.

Loyalty—Developing marketing programs that communicate to your target audience that you really understand them and then used that understanding to deliver highly satisfying offerings leads to loyal exchange partners seeking to maintain long-term relationships with you. (i.e., you have "connected" with your target audience, to use the terminology of Exhibit 2.1's Effective Marketing Process).

Methods of Segmenting Markets

Segmentation is done by one of three methods:

Research-based Segmentation. In this method, typically people are screened to ensure they are members of the market under study, and then surveyed to determine their attitudes, behaviors, motives, preferences, etc. Multivariate statistical analysis of the research results is conducted to then reveal the number and characteristics of market segments. However, the research-based approach need not be so complex (and expensive) as this to be of value in helping you identify market segments, as will be described below.

Existing Segmentation Systems. Here the marketer uses an existing segmentation service or system to identify market segments that can be evaluated for making targeting decisions. These systems are typically commercial systems, such as the geodemographic systems or VALS. In either case, the segments are already established before the marketer buys the information, so this approach lacks the customization of the research-based method.

Managerial Judgment. The marketer uses his or her knowledge of the market to identify segments. The marketer's insight and skill at using existing information is key in generating good results from this approach.

Each of these approaches is successfully used by organizations for segmentation purposes, and while each has its advantages and disadvantages, no single approach can be said to be best under all circumstances. Each of these methods will be described below.

Research-based Segmentation

Research-based segmentation offers a highly customized method of segmentation based upon extensive up-to-date market data. When conducted by commercial firms, this approach demands a high degree of expertise in research methodology and analysis, and can be very expensive and time-consuming. It can be adapted to your purposes, however, with minimal costs and complexity. For example, if you conducted a research study using the methods described in chapter 4, you might use a simple cross-tabulation program to help you segment your audience. This could be done by first using an answer to a question regarding level of interest in a potential new program to categorize the market into high, medium, and low interest. Then you can profile the three groups using cross tabulations to discover the characteristics of the high-interest group (e.g., their media habits, demographics, location, behaviors, attitudes, etc.) in order to better develop a marketing plan to attract them to the program. This means you would have a research question such as "What segments exist in this market?" and would need to incorporate survey questions into your questionnaire to identify the presence of segments, and questions that would provide a profile of those segments.

Use the eight conditions cited above as a guide when determining what questions to incorporate into your questionnaire. For example, a question such as "Please rate the following attributes in importance to you when choosing a day-care center" could be used to determine how people would *respond differently* to day-care center services offered. One segment may be willing to pay more for longer hours, while another segment values a center with religious-oriented activities.

Existing Segmentation Systems

Marketers who seek to segment their markets for planning purposes but who do not have the resources or inclination to use a customized research study to identify segments might turn to existing segmentation systems. These systems have been developed by commercial firms to sell to companies for use in making marketing plans. Companies buying these services get "standardized" market segmentation schemes—the segments do not vary in composition by market or product type (e.g., you get the same segmentation scheme whether your organization is a bicycle manufacturer, wireless communications supplier, real estate company, or religious organization). The advantage to using such a system is the wealth of information available describing the people that occupy each segment. The best known of these systems for the consumer market are the geodemographic systems and SRIC-BI's VALS system. These two systems are described below.

Geodemographic Systems. Congregational marketers may turn to inexpensive and easily obtainable objective measures, such as the census demographic data, to segment populations and try to infer what needs might exist among the local population so that specific ministries are designed to meet those needs. This approach has met with limited success. For example, consider the following demographic data for census tract 1051 in Oklahoma City, Oklahoma.

Census tract 1051 appears to be fairly "middle America" in its demographic profile. What ministry would you direct toward this census tract? Now consider the description of the two dominant types of people located in census tract 1051 shown in Exhibit 7.2. Notice that the demographic averages shown in Exhibit 7.1 masked the fact that

Exhibit 7.1	Demographic Data

Oklahoma City Census Tract 1051

Population	2,387
Percent White	59
Percent Black	36
Percent Other	5
Median Age	46
Average Years School	13
Average Family Size	2.97
Median Income	$31,390
Percent Housing Owned	54
Percent White Collar	57
Percent Blue Collar	26

two dramatically different groups live in this census tract. Unless you have some means of identifying the presence of *lifestyle segments* living within a geographic area, demographic averages alone might give a very distorted picture of the people groups living there.

What ministry(s) would you now use in this census tract? Chances are you have changed your mind based on the new information. This "new information" (which is, by the way, actual data for this census tract) is called *geodemography*. Geodemography represents a major step forward for religious marketers seeking to address conceptualization, quantification, and strategizing segmentation issues in order to target their ministries.

Geodemography is a "hybrid" segmentation method intended to identify households characterized by "lifestyle"—demographics, financial means, consumption patterns, social class, tastes, interests, and similar variables. It is a database method for linking a variety of demographic information (e.g., age, sex, race, income, household size,

Exhibit 7.2	Comparison of Two Segments Present in Tract 1051	
	Affluent Singles	**Low-Income Single Retirees**
Description	Apartment and Condominium, High Rent, Above-Average Income, Well-educated, Professionally Employed, Mobile, Singles, Few Children, Urban Areas	Old, Few Children, Low Income, Below-Average Education, One-Person Households, Retirees
Product Preferences	High-Quality Clothing, Bottled Water, Movies, Cordials and Liqueurs, Burglar Alarm, Car Rentals	Cigars, Relatively Low Weekly Grocery Expenditures, Fast-Food Restaurants
Selected Demographics Median Age Median Income Median Years School Percent Professional Percent Moved Past 5 Years	40.1 top third 14 36.4 63	54.8 bottom third 12 20.7 50

etc.) to units of geography (e.g., census tracts, zip codes, towns, etc.), leading to the coining of the word "geo-demography." All of the firms offering geodemographic segmentation services begin by subjecting U.S Census data to multivariate statistical analysis to identify clusters of people who share a common set of socioeconomic characteristics. These clusters, or segments, of society share both a common set of these characteristics and proximate geographic location. The phrase "birds of a feather flock together" is often invoked to describe this phenomenon—we see people with similar demographic and economic profiles living in neighborhoods that are close to one another.

Each geographic supplier has created a segmentation scheme for the U.S. population, with the total number of segments varying by supplier. The suppliers then use other databases, including public records, surveys, and the third-party databases, to enrich the profiles of the people occupying each segment. Each of the geodemographic companies assigns every U.S. household to one of its segments based on the household's street address. Since census data are available at the block group/enumeration district level (approx. 340 households per BG/ED), these companies can utilize a person's street address to attach a "geo-code" to that location, signifying the socioeconomic segment that best describes what the census data reveal about people living in the BG/ED of that street address. Your residential address therefore identifies you as a member of a specific segment for each geodemographic firm, although the names and composition of the segments will vary from company to company. This assignment process then allows an organization to learn what segments are present within a specified geographic area, such as a circle with a five-mile radius with your church at the center, or within a ZIP+4 area.

One purpose for using a geodemographic system would be to gain more insight into the types of people living in an area where a congregation might be planning to do some types of outreach ministry. The Oklahoma City census tract example illustrates this application. However, it would be even more useful if we could enhance the lifestyle description of these people by learning whether they were very similar, or different from those people who had responded favorably to types of ministries similar to ours in the past. In this way we can identify whether an area is "fertile ground," whether it contains many people similar to those who have joined the congregation, or whether it represents "rocky soil" with few people similar to new members.

How do we know what types of people have joined your congregation? In the same way that geodemographic firms can profile an area to determine the concentration of the population by clusters, they can take a list of new members with their street addresses and, based on what their constantly updated databases tell them about people living at that address, determine a profile of new members along the same clusters. Therefore, the Presbyterian Church (USA) could profile its membership (or just newly joined members) in central Indiana to determine the types of people who have been attracted to the Presbyterian Church (USA). They could then examine areas where they were considering locating a new church to determine if there were many unchurched (i.e., adherents without a church home) people who were similar to those who have joined the church in central Indiana (i.e., from the same lifestyle clusters). This list profiling could be done successfully for any list with several thousand names and, therefore, could be done at an entire denominational level for all members, new adult members, or for new adult members in a geographic area, etc.

While geodemographic marketing is a major advance for religious organizations, much remains to be done. The congregation needs to identify attitudes for each cluster that are related to the adoption of religious "products." The more directly applicable the cluster descriptions are to religious organizations, the more effective segmentation, targeting, and positioning strategies will be. Additionally, work is needed to discover appropriate outreach strategies for each of the different segments.

Geodemography may prove to be a useful segmentation approach for persons considering any of the following objectives.[3]

1. Planting new congregations is considered by church growth experts to be the best way to reach target populations. Many denominations use a very capital-intensive model for planting new congregations. Making a poor decision can cost up to $100,000 or more.

Therefore, they use the best demographic data available to pick the location for the new church. However, data on the lifestyle characteristics of the targeted population would dramatically increase the probable success of the venture.

2. If a church wants to relocate, decisions can again be guided by having in-depth information on the population living in the area.

3. Churches that are located in transitional neighborhoods can use this data to understand the factors that motivate the new residents of a different ethnic background to attend religious services. This could revive a church that does not want to relocate, but instead begin new ministries with the new population.

4. Outreach is a high priority for many denominations. Having data on the lifestyles of the targeted group can be very valuable. Lifestyle characteristics can help suggest modifications in the church's image and services, as well as help to target the appeal.

5. Fund-raising campaigns may be enhanced by knowing the types of people living in an area, in addition to demographic data on the number of people by income category.

6. Stratified sampling designs for image research or other types of marketing research could be better planned if lifestyle segments were identified in a particular area. After the introduction of a new church program follow-up research will help determine whether the church had been more successful with some segments than others in improving the church's image.

7. Geodemographic data firms can provide the media characteristics of the various segments: mailing lists and phone numbers for people in selected segments of a specified geographic area for churches interested in cost-effective ways to reach households in targeted segments.

Some of the better-known geodemographic companies are Claritas' PRIZM, CACI's Acorn, ESRI's Community Tapestry, Experian's MOSAIC, and MapInfo's PSYTE U.S. Advantage system (other systems are available in Canada and the United Kingdom). We will describe in more detail the services available from two of the better-known geodemographic suppliers serving the needs of religious organizations—Claritas and Percept.

Claritas

Claritas, a Nielsen company (http://www.claritas.com/MyBest Segments/Default.jsp), is the most widely used of all the geodemographic suppliers. Claritas represents thousands of client organizations within restaurants, real estate, retail, automotive, financial, telecommunications, media/newspapers/advertising agencies, energy/utilities, and nonprofit organizations. Their segmentation scheme uses 39 factors in five categories in the formation of segments: (1) education and affluence, (2) family life cycle, (3) urbanization, (4) race and ethnicity, and (5) mobility. The latest version of its segmentation scheme for U.S. households, PRIZM NE, consists of 66 segments. Claritas is now able to identify which of the 66 segments are present in geographic areas as small as ZIP+6 (i.e., essentially individual household levels). Using a ZIP-based geographic unit has some advantages, since it couples the lifestyle profiling of PRIZM with postal geocoding. This would, for example, permit a church to target direct mail pieces to individual households in many cases. Claritas maintains that organizations seeking to accomplish the following would benefit from using its system:

- Identify the key characteristics of the target audience.
- Quantify the number of each type of customer group in a given market area.
- Locate where target audience members live.
- Target them through an understanding of media preference or residential address.

You can profile a specific area (i.e., a census tract, zip code, city, county, circle of set radius, polygon of specified boundaries [such as four city streets bounding a four-square-mile area], block group, etc.) to determine the number of households in that area that "belong" to each of the 66 segments. A high-rent district census tract may have representation of only four or five segments, all of which are low numbered (i.e., high socioeconomic standing), while a county may have 25 or 30 segments spread out among the 66 clusters because a greater variety of lifestyles would be represented in the larger geographic area. An analysis of a given area provides greater enriched information for program planners than demographics alone can provide. This is because PRIZM segments capture more information about lifestyles than does a large set of demographic statistical averages. Obviously, different ministries may be needed to appeal to two segments that might share similar demographics, but vastly different lifestyles.

Exhibits 7.3 and 7.4 provide some selected statistics for three of the largest PRIZM segments occupying zip code 46280 in Carmel, Indiana. (An index of 100 is average, above 100 is higher than average. For example, an index of 200 means that characteristic occurs in that segment at twice the national average.) These statistics are just a small sample of what is available from PRIZM to profile an area of interest. A brief thumbnail sketch of the three segments follows the exhibits. Below is a listing of the 66 PRIZM segments.

01 Upper Crust	23 Greenbelt Sports	45 Blue Highways
02 Blue Blood Estates	24 Up-and-Comers	46 Old Glories
03 Movers and Shakers	25 Country Casuals	47 City Startups
04 Young Digerati	26 The Cosmopolitans	48 Young & Rustic
05 Country Squires	27 Middleburg Managers	49 American Classics
06 Winner's Circle	28 Traditional Times	50 Kid Country, USA
07 Money and Brains	29 American Dreams	51 Shotguns and Pickups
08 Executive Suites	30 Suburban Sprawl	52 Suburban Pioneers
09 Big Fish, Small Pond	31 Urban Achievers	53 Mobility Blues
10 Second City Elite	32 New Homesteaders	54 Multi-Culti Mosaic
11 God's Country	33 Big Sky Families	55 Golden Ponds
12 Brite Lites, Li'l City	34 White Picket Fences	56 Crossroads Villagers
13 Upward Bound	35 Boomtown Singles	57 Old Milltowns
14 New Empty Nests	36 Blue-chip Blues	58 Back Country Folks
15 Pools and Patios	37 Mayberry-ville	59 Urban Elders
16 Bohemian Mix	38 Simple Pleasures	60 Park Bench Seniors
17 Beltway Boomers	39 Domestic Duos	61 City Roots
18 Kids and Cul-de-sacs	40 Close-in Couples	62 Hometown Retired
19 Home Sweet Home	41 Sunset City Blues	63 Family Thrifts
20 Fast-track Families	42 Red, White & Blues	64 Bedrock America
21 Gray Power	43 Heartlanders	65 Big City Blues
22 Young Influentials	44 New Beginnings	66 Low-Rise Living

Claritas PRIZM NE. Used by permission.

Exhibit 7.3 PRIZM Segments in Carmel, Indiana 46280

Movers and Shakers	Percent	Index	Kids and Cul-de-sacs	Percent	Index	Home Sweet Home	Percent	Index
HH's Householder age								
45-54	27	126	25-34	19	121	25-34	18	112
55-59	11	128	35-44	29	142	35-44	23	111
60-64	8	118	45-54	25	117	45-54	22	104
Education								
bachelor's degree	31	194	some college, no degree	28	130	some college, no degree	24	113
master's degree	14	229	associate degree	9	142	bachelor's degree	22	138
professional degree	5	244	bachelor's degree	21	132	master's degree	7	125
Home Value								
$300-400k	19	194	$100-150k	21	111	$150-200k	23	163
$400-500k	13	290	$150-200k	24	166	$200-300k	30	179
$500-750k	18	348	$200-300k	29	172	$300-400k	12	137
$750-1.0m	7	375						
$1.0m+	7	326						
HH's Income								
$100-150k	25	231	$50-75k	27	138	$50-75k	25	127
$150-250k	16	362	$75-100k	24	166	$75-100k	18	152
$250-500k	5	383	$100-150k	18	105	$100-150k	17	151
$500k+	3	426						
HH Composition								
household size: 2	58	158	household size: 3 or 4	70	248	household size: 2	62	170
married/no children <18	33	124	children 6-11 years old	51	353	married/no children<18	28	104
Ethnicity								
White	88	103	White	86	101	White	85	100
Asian	4	226	Black	8	71	Black	12	93
Occupation								
management/business/finance	36	290	management/business/finance	19	155	management/business/finance	18	150
professional	30	227	professional	22	166	professional	27	203

Claritas PRIZM NE. Used by permission.

Exhibit 7.4	Lifestyle and Media Habits of Selected PRIZM Segments				
Movers and Shakers		**Kids and Cul-de-sacs**		**Home Sweet Home**	
	Index		Index		Index
Lifestyle					
own/lease new BMW	553	buy toys by Internet	343	play soccer	317
business travel	471	buy children's athletic shoes	333	go in-line skating	315
shop at Bloomingdales	408	shop at Disney store	292	go snowboarding	284
order from Eddie Bauer	397	go to zoo	242	go mountain biking	268
buy watches $300+	360	drive minivan	234	own/lease new VW	256
domestic vacation/play golf	343	play soccer	223	buy MP3 player	225
buy Apple iPod	322	play softball	202	shop at Express	225
travel to Caribbean islands	305	own mountain bike	194	eat at Cheesecake Factory	218
domestic vacation/spa	291	own tent	191	shop at Banana Republic	197
buy collectibles by Internet	289	visit theme park	181	eat at Houlihan's	194
Media Habits					
read *Wall Street Journal* daily	343	read *Parenting*	270	listen to rock music	228
read *Men's Health*	256	watch Disney Channel	222	read *Rolling Stone*	183
read *Travel & Leisure*	227	soft contemporary radio	188	watch VH1	170
listen to radio on Internet	223	listen to ESPN radio	183	watch *The Simpsons*	161
soft contemporary radio	208	religious TV	150	listen to ESPN radio	154
radio MLB regular season	198	ABC Family Channel	148	watch HBO	151
National Public Radio	196	read *People*	143	read *Vibe*	150
read *New Yorker*	189	watch Nick at Nite	139	read *Popular Science*	143

Claritas PRIZM NE. Used by permission.

Wealthy, Suburban Boomer Couples
03 Movers and Shakers

Movers and Shakers is home to America's up-and-coming business class: a wealthy suburban world of dual-income couples who are highly educated, typically between the ages of 35 and 54, often with children. Given its high percentage of executives and white-collar professionals, there's a decided business bent to this segment: Movers and Shakers rank number one for owning a small business and having a home office.

Wealthy $97,100 Age 35-64 White, Asian

Upper-Middle-Class Suburban Families
18 Kids and Cul-de-Sacs

Upscale, suburban, married couples with children—that's the skinny on Kids and Cul-de-Sacs, an enviable lifestyle of large families in recently built subdivisions. With a high rate of Hispanic and Asian Americans, this segment is a refuge for college-educated, white-collar professionals with administrative jobs and upper-middle-class incomes. Their nexus of education, affluence, and children translates into large outlays for child-centered products and services.

UpperMid $68,900 Age 25-54 White, Asian, Hispanic

Middle-aged, Upscale Suburbanites
19 Home Sweet Home

Widely scattered across the nation's suburbs, the residents of Home Sweet Home tend to be upper-middle-class married couples living in midsized homes with few children. The adults in the segment, mostly between the ages of 25 and 54, have gone to college and hold professional and white-collar jobs. With their upscale incomes and small families, these folks have fashioned comfortable lifestyles, filling their homes with toys, TV sets, and pets.

UpperMid $63,700 Age 25-44 White

Claritas PRIZM NE. Used by permission.

Percept

Percept was established in 1987 to serve the needs of congregations for demographic and geodemographic information. They use Claritas' Microvision's 50 lifestyle clustering system instead of PRIZM's 66 clusters as their segmentation database. (Note: Claritas no longer sells Microvision data to the open market.) Percept refers to the Microvision database as "US Lifestyles" in their literature. Percept also uses Global Insight for their data forecasting service. More than 300 denominations and 30,000 churches have used Percept's services. The "value added" aspect of Percept, beyond what could be obtained by using Claritas and Global Insight directly, is that their products are specifically designed for use by religious organizations. Some of the more significant of these are described below:

Ethos Survey Series: Through a survey instrument designed to measure the "beliefs, attitudes, and behaviors" of the American public toward religious issues, Percept has established an extensive database to use in concert with their U.S. Lifestyles geodemographic segmentation system. This integration of databases permits Percept to profile local geographic areas with regards to faith preferences, community issues, and religious involvement, in addition to the standard geodemographic lifestyle information.

Revision: This is a self-guided process that takes a congregation through a series of visioning and planning exercises using a survey instrument. The resulting data provide an assessment of a congregation's concerns and satisfactions with their personal lives, the congregation's programs, and their leadership and worship style preferences. Ethos sample surveys of national populations inferred to local areas permit comparison between the congregation and its community along these same dimensions. This comparison helps a congregation match their strengths and desires with the community's needs and preferences.

NeighborArea Analysis: For use by large local congregations or multicongregation associations (e.g., regional or national denominational organizational units), this service provides demographic and geodemographic information for custom studies of geographic areas of interest.

266

Percept offers other information and analysis services to regional and national denominational agencies through their Percept (http://www.perceptgroup.com/) and Link2Lead (http://www.link2lead.com/GettingStarted/Home.aspx) products. An example of the use of Percept is described below.

The fact that the Donegal Presbyterian Church in Mount Joy, Pennsylvania, is more than 280 years old did not mean that they were content to rest on their laurels. Donegal members realized as a new millennium dawned that they had lost focus in their missions. Their missions methodology could best be described as the proverbial "shotgun approach"—lots of good ideas taking them in a hundred directions at once. Ruthann Dwyer, a deacon at Donegal, assessed this approach this way: "Many churches, including Donegal, have tons of good ideas . . . but you often just end up doing a little bit here and a little bit there. And while they're wonderful ideas and worthy of being done, the fact is that not all ideas are really what your church should be doing, because that is not what God intends for that church."

The Presbytery of Donegal suggested that the church use Percept's *Revision* to:

(1) help discover God's mission for this church

(2) help locate their target ministry area

(3) determine what type of ministries they needed to launch that would reach both existing and potential church members

Based on what the Percept data revealed about the people living within a seven-mile radius circle around the church, several ministries were started. One of these was a second service that was called "The Back Door Church," offering a more contemporary, intimate worship experience, compared to the more traditional, formal service the church offered in the other worship service. The success of targeting this segment became apparent immediately—the new service attracted 50 people in the first week, twice as many as they had expected. The people attracted to the "Back Door" service represented a totally new segment of worshippers for Donegal, but reflected the needs of those living near the church. The church used two different worship service styles to target the two different segments, successfully hitting the "sweet spots" of both groups. A "rifle" had replaced the "shotgun" approach to ministry, with results that exceeded expectations.[4]

VALS

SRI Consulting Business Intelligence's (SRIC-BI) VALS (values, attitudes, and lifestyles) (http://www.sric-bi.com/VALS/) was first established in 1978 as a consumer segmentation system based on lifestyle characteristics. Later large national surveys of consumer opinions in 1987 and 1992 allowed SRI to identify psychological characteristics and key demographic variables that have a high correlation with a wide range of consumer preferences for products, activities, and media, thus having relevance for advertising and marketing applications. The current VALS system categorizes the U.S. adult population into eight mutually exclusive groups based on their personality traits. "Rather than looking at what people do and segregating people with like activities, VALS uses psychology to segment people according to their distinct personality traits."[5] They promote their segmentation service as allowing marketers to:[6]

- identify who to target
- uncover what your target group buys and does
- locate where concentrations of your target group lives
- identify how to communicate with your target group
- gain insight into why the target group acts the way it does

A survey of attitudinal and demographic questions are used to classify people into one of the eight segments. Product usage and media data for the segments is available through VALS link with Mediamark Research Inc.'s *Survey of American Consumers* database and other client specific databases. VALS differs from the geodemographic segmentation systems by classifying people into segments based upon attitudinal surveys of a sample of the population that permits classification into the eight segments, rather than the use of census and other databases by geodemographic firms. The geodemographic systems typically have up to 60+ "lifestyle" segments, offering finer distinctions among segments compared to the eight offered by VALS. VALS can be divided into 34 microsegments for firms wanting redefined targets. GeoVALS estimates the proportion of the VALS types by zip code or block group. Both types of systems have been used successfully for market segmentation, targeting, and positioning purposes.

Exhibit 7.5 provides a diagram of the eight VALS segments with the columns signifying the primary motivation (what in particular about the self or the world is the meaningful core that governs his or her activities) of the segments, and the rows indicating the amount of resources (energy, self-confidence, intellectualism, novelty seeking, innovativeness, impulsiveness, leadership, and vanity, along with key demographics) available to the members of the segment. The segments on the top (Innovators) and bottom (Survivors) have primary motivations independent of those for the three columns, but are located vertically according to the resources available to the

Exhibit 7.5   Summary Diagram of SRI VALS Segments

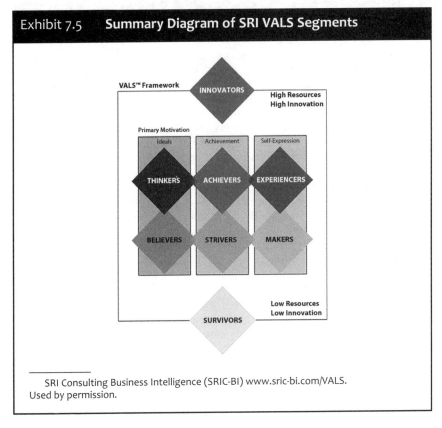

SRI Consulting Business Intelligence (SRIC-BI) www.sric-bi.com/VALS.
Used by permission.

members of the two segments (i.e., the higher the segment on the graph, the greater its access to resources).

Exhibit 7.6 describes the people occupying the segments. As with the Claritas PRIZM segments, the composition of the VALS segments does not vary according to the markets of interest by the VALS client—your VALS segments are the same as Verizon's, Nissan's, Kraft Foods', Fox TV's, *Christianity Today*'s, or any other organization that uses this segmentation scheme. In other words, these "off the shelf" segmentation systems have segmented the U.S. adult population using a segmentation base (lifestyles for Claritas and Percept, personality types for VALS), and it is up to the potential client to determine whether that means of segmenting the market is an appropriate base for segmenting the client's market(s).

Exhibit 7.6   VALS Segments

Innovators (formerly Actualizers)
   Innovators are successful, sophisticated, take-charge people with high self-esteem. Because they have such abundant resources, they exhibit all three primary motivations in varying degrees. They are change leaders and are the most receptive to new ideas and technologies. Innovators are very active consumers, and their purchases reflect cultivated tastes for upscale, niche products and services.
   Image is important to Innovators, not as evidence of status or power but as an expression of their taste, independence, and personality. Innovators are among the established and emerging leaders in business and government, yet they continue to seek challenges. Their lives are characterized by variety. Their possessions and recreation reflect a cultivated taste for the finer things in life.

Thinkers (formerly Fulfilleds)
   Thinkers are motivated by ideals. They are mature, satisfied, comfortable , and reflective people who value order, knowledge, and responsibility. They tend to be well educated and actively seek out information in the decision-making process. They are well-informed about world and national events and are alert to opportunities to broaden their knowledge.
   Thinkers have a moderate respect for the status quo institutions of authority and social decorum, but are open to consider new ideas.

Exhibit 7.6   VALS Segments—continued

Although their incomes allow them many choices, Thinkers are conservative, practical consumers; they look for durability, functionality, and value in the products they buy.

Believers
Like Thinkers, Believers are motivated by ideals. They are conservative, conventional people with concrete beliefs based on traditional, established codes: family, religion, community, and the nation. Many Believers express moral codes that are deeply rooted and literally interpreted. They follow established routines, organized in large part around home, family, community, and social or religious organizations to which they belong.

As consumers, Believers are predictable; they choose familiar products and established brands. They favor American products and are generally loyal customers.

Achievers
Motivated by the desire for achievement, Achievers have goal-oriented lifestyles and a deep commitment to career and family. Their social lives reflect this focus and are structured around family, their place of worship, and work. Achievers live conventional lives, are politically conservative, and respect authority and the status quo. They value consensus, predictability, and stability over risk, intimacy, and self-discovery.

With many wants and needs, Achievers are active in the consumer marketplace. Image is important to Achievers; they favor established, prestige products and services that demonstrate success to their peers. Because of their busy lives, they are often interested in a variety of time-saving devices.

Strivers
Strivers are trendy and fun-loving. Because they are motivated by achievement, Strivers are concerned about the opinions and approval of others. Money defines success for Strivers, who don't have enough of it to meet their desires. They favor stylish products that emulate the purchases of people with greater material wealth. Many see themselves as having a job rather than a career, and a lack of skills and focus often prevents them from moving ahead.

Strivers are active consumers because shopping is both a social activity and an opportunity to demonstrate to peers their ability to buy. As consumers, they are as impulsive as their financial circumstance will allow.

| Exhibit 7.6 | **VALS Segments—continued** |

Experiencers

Experiencers are motivated by self-expression. As young, enthusiastic, and impulsive consumers, Experiencers quickly become enthusiastic about new possibilities but are equally quick to cool. They seek variety and excitement, savoring the new, the offbeat, and the risky. Their energy finds an outlet in exercise, sports, outdoor recreation, and social activities.

Experiencers are avid consumers and spend a comparatively high proportion of their income on fashion, entertainment, and socializing. Their purchases reflect the emphasis they place on looking good and having "cool" stuff.

Makers

Like Experiencers, Makers are motivated by self-expression. They express themselves and experience the world by working on it—building a house, raising children, fixing a car, or canning vegetables—and have enough skill and energy to carry out their projects successfully. Makers are practical people who have constructive skills and value self-sufficiency. They live within a traditional context of family, practical work, and physical recreation and have little interest in what lies outside that context.

Makers are suspicious of new ideas and large institutions such as big business. They are respectful of government authority and organized labor, but resentful of government intrusion on individual rights. They are unimpressed by material possessions other than those with a practical or functional purpose. Because they prefer value to luxury, they buy basic products.

Survivors (formerly Strugglers)

Survivors live narrowly focused lives. With few resources with which to cope, they often believe that the world is changing too quickly. They are comfortable with the familiar and are primarily concerned with safety and security. Because they must focus on meeting needs rather than fulfilling desires, Survivors do not show a strong primary motivation.

Survivors are cautious consumers. They represent a very modest market for most products and services. They are loyal to favorite brands, especially if they can purchase them at a discount.

———

SRI Consulting Business Intelligence (SRIC-BI) www.sric-bi.com/VALS. Used by permission.

Managerial Judgment

Another approach to segmenting markets is by exercising managerial judgment. This is not to suggest that using a research-based or existing segmentation system method does not also involve the judgment of marketing decision-makers, because clearly marketers must make choices in either of those approaches. What managerial judgment means here is that administrators use their judgment, based upon experience with the market in question, to identify the base for segmenting markets and for the number of segments the market contains. Some typical bases for use in specifying market segments are shown in Exhibit 7.7[7]

Exhibit 7.7	Major Segmentation Variables

MAJOR SEGMENTATION VARIABLES	
Variable	**Typical Breakdowns**
Geographic Region	Pacific, Mountain, West North Central, West South Central, East North Central, East South Central, South Atlantic, Middle Atlantic, New England
Country size	A, B, C, D
City or MSA size	Under 5,000; 5,000-20,000; 20,000-50,000; 50,000-100,000; 100,000-250,000; 250,000-500,000; 500,000-1,000,000; 1,000,000-4,000,000; 4,000,000 or over
Density	Urban, suburban, rural
Climate	Northern, southern
Demographic Age	Under 6, 6-11, 12-19, 20-34, 35-49, 50-64, 65+
Generation	Baby boomers, Gen X, Gen Y, Gen Z
Gender	Male, female

Exhibit 7.7	**Major Segmentation Variables—continued**
Family size	1-2, 3-4, 5+
Family life cycle	Bachelor; young, married, no children; young, married, youngest child under 6; single parent, youngest child 6 or over; older, married, with children; older, married, no children under 18; older, single; other
Income	Under $10,000; $10,000-$24,999; $25,000-$39,999; $40,000-$54,999; $55,000-$69,999; $70,000-$84,999, $85,000-$100,000; $100,000 and above
Occupation	Professional and technical; managers, officials, and proprietors; clerical, sales; craftsmen, foremen; operatives, farmers; retired; students; housewives; unemployed
Education	Grade school or less; some high school; high school graduate; some college; college graduate; some graduate school; graduate degree
Religion	Catholic, Protestant, Jewish, other
Race	White, Black, Asian
Nationality	American, British, French, German, Scandinavian, Italian, Latin American, Middle Eastern, Japanese
Psychographic Social class	Lower lowers, upper lowers, lower middles, upper middles, lower uppers, upper uppers
Lifestyle	Outdoor active, home body, sophisticate
Personality	Compulsive, gregarious, authoritarian, ambitious
Behavioral Use occasion	Regular occasion, special occasion
Benefits sought	Inspiration, fraternity, comfort

Exhibit 7.7	Major Segmentation Variables—continued
Member status	Nonmember, ex-member, potential member, new member, regular member
Attendance rate	Light attender, medium attender, heavy attender
Loyalty status	None, medium, strong, absolute
Readiness stage	Unaware, aware, informed, interested, desirous, intending to commit
Attitude toward program	Enthusiastic, positive, indifferent, negative, hostile

The choice of any variable used as a base to segment a market, whether by the exercise of managerial judgment, discovery by research, or adoption by use of an existing segmentation system, must reflect the primary motivator of market response to the exchange object. Consider these examples:

Product	Segmentation Base Variable
Toothpaste	Benefits sought (decay prevention, whitening, etc.)
Music	Age/generation (toddler, teenager, baby boomer, etc.)
Vacation site	Social class (lower, middle, upper)

In each case, the segmentation base is the "best" variable for capturing the differences between members of the market that reflect the way they will respond to marketing appeals. That is, you are a member of a segment in each case because that characteristic best describes your "sweet spot" when it comes to that type of product. For toothpaste it could be that the fact that you are a "worrier" makes you respond most favorably to brands that provide the best decay prevention. For music, you listen to XM Radio channels that play music from the sixties, the baby boomers' golden age of rock. For vacationing, members of your upper social class will go to the Four Seasons hotel in Nevis, knowing they will find "people like us" there. Each of the markets for these products could have been segmented by other variables (e.g., geography, race, use occasion, etc.), but those variables reflect differences that have nothing to do with the segments' "sweet spots" for those products. In other words, the eight conditions for segmentation listed above are directly related to your goals in choosing a segmentation base—it is the means by which you achieve both efficiency and effectiveness for your marketing program. Choosing a base variable by managerial judgment can be an effective way of achieving those twin goals *if* you can choose correctly. The other two methods of segmentation can be combined with managerial judgment in segmenting a market (e.g., using managerial judgment to identify the variables to measure in a research study to identify the best segmentation base). We will now discuss the categories of segmentation base variables at greater length.

Alternative Segmentation Base Variable Categories

Geographical Segmentation. In geographical segmentation the market is divided into different geographical entities, such as nations, states, regions, countries, cities, or neighborhoods, based on the notion that consumer needs or responses vary geographically.

Saddleback Community Church, for example, has started dozens of "sister" congregations, each planning its own program to fit the particular needs and interests of its congregations and community. This is in contrast to structuring the churches so that they would all be carrying out identical programs. A local church may select specific census tracts or zip codes in which to operate within a geographic area.

The organization decides to operate in either one or a few parts of the country as a specialist in meeting the needs of the populace, or to operate broadly but pay attention to variations in the population's needs and preferences within the various geographical areas.

Demographic Segmentation. In demographic segmentation the market is divided into different groups on the basis of demographic variables, such as age, gender, family size, family life cycle, income, occupation, education, religion, race and nationality.

Demographic variables have long been a popular base for distinguishing target groups. One reason is that an individual's or a group's wants and preferences are often highly associated with demographic variables. Another reason is that demographic variables are easier to measure than are other types of variables.

Even when the target market is described in nondemographic terms, such as a personality type, the link back to demographic characteristics is necessary in order to know the size of the target market and how to reach it efficiently.

We will illustrate how certain demographic variables have been applied creatively to market segmentation.

Age. A person's wants and capacities change with age. Congregations develop different programs for children, youth, singles, married adults, and senior citizens. Congregations try to "customize" the religious and social experiences to the interests of the different age groups. Some congregations go further to subsegment the senior citizens into those between 55 and 70, and 70 years and up. Others distinguish between the psychological and physical differences among older individuals; the "go-goes," the "go-slows," and the "no-goes." There is a strong correlation between a person's age and time spent in religious activity. According to Azzi and Ehrenberg, the number of hours devoted to religious activity increases with age. We should also note that there is a limit to this correlation, since the very oldest parishioners are sometimes unable to attend church or other religious activities because of poor health. There is also an interaction between age and gender variables with respect to religious activity. As they age, females devote more time to religious activities than do males.[8]

Generation. Each generation is profoundly influenced by the times in which it grows up—the music, movies, politics, and defining events of that period. Demographers call these groups *cohorts*. Members of a cohort share the same major cultural, political, and economic experiences. They have similar outlooks and values. The vignette that began this chapter was an example of targeting the

277

Generation Y cohort. Yet, while a distinction can be made between different cohorts, generational cohorts also influence each other. For instance, because so many members of Generation Y—"echo boomers"—are living with their boomer parents, the parents are exhibiting what demographers are calling a "boom-boom effect." The same things that appeal to 21-year-olds are appealing to youth-obsessed baby boomers.

Meredith, Schewe, and Karlovich developed a framework called the lifestyle analytic matrix, which combines information on cohorts, life stages, physiographics, emotional effects, and socioeconomics in analyzing a segment or individual.[9] For example, two individuals from the same cohort may differ in their *life stages* (having a divorce, getting remarried), *physiographics* (coping with hair loss, menopause, arthritis, or osteoporosis), *emotional effects* (nostalgia for the past, wanting experiences instead of things, seeking a sense of contribution to others' lives), or *socioeconomics* (losing a job, receiving an inheritance). The authors believe this analysis will lead to a more complete understanding of your segments, leading to more effective marketing appeals.

Gender. Gender segmentation appears in many nonprofit sectors, such as male and female colleges, service and social clubs, prisons and military services. Men and women tend to have different attitudinal and behavioral orientations, based partly on genetic makeup and partly on socialization. For example, women tend to be more communal-minded and men tend to be more self-expressive and goal-directed; women tend to take in more of the data in their immediate environment; men tend to focus on the part of the environment that helps them achieve a goal. Research has shown that women participate in religious activities (including church attendance) more than men.[10]

Within a single sex, further segmentation may be applied. The Christian education department of a congregation segments the female adult learners into "at home" and "working outside the home." The "at home" are subdivided into "homemakers" and "displaced homemakers." Homemakers are attracted to courses for spirituality of children, self-enrichment, and improved homemaking skills, while displaced homemakers are more interested in fellowship, spirituality for women, and career preparation.

The "working outside the home" segment breaks into two sub-segments, "married working" and "single working." Each segment has a different set of motivations and fellowship/learning interests. Furthermore, each segment faces certain problems not common to the other. By addressing the specific problems and interests of each segment, the Christian education department is in a better position to attract more women to its programs.

Family Life Cycle. The family life cycle concept is based on the notion that throughout one's lifetime, there are critical transition points when major changes in consumer and other behaviors take place. These transition points are generally defined in terms of objective variables, such as marital status, workforce status, and the presence and age of children. A modern family life cycle is described as consisting of 13 stages:[11]

1. Bachelor I: head is 18-34, single (never married, divorced, separated, widowed), no dependent children.

2. Young Couple: female head is 18-34, couple (married or unmarried), no children.

3. Full Nest I: female head is 18-34, couple (married or unmarried), youngest child under 6.

4. Full Nest II: female head is 18-34, couple (married or unmarried), youngest child 6 or over.

5. Single Parent I: head is 18-34, single (never married, divorced, separated, widowed), youngest child under 6.

6. Single Parent II: head is 18-34, single (never married, divorced, separated, widowed), youngest child 6 or over.

7. Bachelor II: head is 35-64, single (never married, divorced, separated. widowed), no dependent children.

8. Childless Couple: female head is 35-64, couple (married or unmarried), no dependent children.

9. Delayed Full Nest: female head is 35-64, couple (married or unmarried), youngest child under 6.

10. Full Nest III: female head is 35-64, couple (married or unmarried), youngest child 6 or over.

11. Single Parent III: head is 35-64, youngest child 6 or over.

12. Bachelor III: head is 65 or older, single (never married, divorced, separated, widowed), no dependent children.

13. Older Couple (Empty Nest): female head is 65 or older, couple (married or unmarried), no dependent children.

Studies have shown that people go through *psychological* life-cycles as well—with adults experiencing certain "passages" or "transformations" as they go through life.[12] Literature suggests that age and life-cycle stages interact when influencing religious participation, and that this could be correlated to the organized social groups within a church: "Our results suggest that an aging hypothesis and the Family Life Cycle hypothesis are not incompatible. We find that age effects are an integral part of family formation effects, and vice versa. . . .We think that this interaction between parents' ages and a child's ages occurs because churches deliver many of their benefits to members through informal interpersonal networks."[13] Research also found that church attendance increases after marriage if the couples have school-age children then declines again after the children leave home.[14] Church attendance is also higher for those living in conventional nuclear families.[15] Marriage and parenthood increase the likelihood that men who had gone away from the church would return; this was not true in the case of women, however.[16]

Income. Income segmentation is another longstanding practice in the nonprofit sector. Religious organizations, including congregations, segment the membership into income levels for fund-raising purposes. In addition, the amount of income and how it is earned—wage earner, self-employed, new money, old money, etc.—suggests unique interests and needs that the religious organization may want to focus on in ministries and program offerings to each group. By doing so, the church or synagogue is able to assist persons within each segment to connect stewardship with spirituality and responsibility.

Psychographic Segmentation

Marketers also segment markets on the basis of variables that suggest more about the psychological orientation of the particular group.

Social Class. Social classes are relatively homogeneous and enduring divisions in society that are hierarchically ordered and whose members share similar values, interests and behavior. Social scientists have distinguished six social classes: (1) upper uppers (less than 1 percent); (2) lower uppers (about 2 percent); (3) upper middles (12 percent); (4) lower middles (30 percent); (5) upper lowers (35 percent); and (6) lower lowers (20 percent), using objective variables such as income, occupation, education, and type of residence. Denominational preference seems to vary closely with social class variations.[17] Research has found that "only weak relationships are found between income (or social class) and church attendance. Usually the relationship is positive, but some investigators find it backward bending (participation is highest for the middle-income groups)."[18]

Lifestyles. Lifestyle segmentation is based on the notion that "we do what we do because it fits into the kind of life we are living or want to live." There are several different approaches to identifying lifestyle groups in the population. However, most are based on measures of consumers' activities, interests and opinions (AIOs). Lifestyle segmentation measures developed from these data can be general or more specific, as in the case of one's leisure lifestyle. In using a lifestyle segmentation scheme, your objective is to relate specific lifestyle patterns to religious behavioral patterns. In this way you can use membership in a lifestyle category to predict how a person will react to a specific marketing program or religious product.

Behavioral Segmentation. In behavioral segmentation people are divided into groups on the basis of their knowledge of, attitude toward, use of, or response to a religious organization. Such behavior can be manifested in several ways of interest to religious leaders.

Benefits. A powerful form of segmentation is the classification of people according to the different benefits they seek from exchanges with the religious organization. Some simple marketing research can identify what the various internal and external markets are seeking. It is then possible to profile the benefit-seeking groups with respect to their demographic, behavioral and psychographic characteristics. Each segment will also have attitudes toward various religious organizations as well as other benefit-delivering agencies (i.e., government agencies, community groups, self-help groups. etc.). Religious organizations will necessarily need to determine which benefit group it will seek to satisfy.[19]

Loyalty Status and Decision Process. A market can be segmented by the loyalty patterns and behavioral processes used by people in choosing a church or synagogue. To illustrate, consider the hypothetical example of four families searching for a new church after moving to a moderate-sized Southern city from their home in the Northeast. Different levels of loyalty patterns and complexity of decision processes are used by these archetypal people as they select a new church.

Joyce Evans, 23, illustrates a pattern of highly complex decision-making. Joyce attended the ecumenical campus church at the private college from which she recently graduated. While in her senior year she had a spiritual awakening, brought on by a search for a meaning to life and talks with the church's associate pastor for campus ministries. She is eager to find a church in the Southern city with people who share her enthusiasm for her newfound faith. Her dad grew up as a Northern Baptist, but went to church only at Easter and Christmas, and her mother belonged to a Pentecostal congregation. Joyce never felt comfortable with the people at either of her parents' churches. At her new job she talks to people about where they go to church, what the people are like, the size of the church, whether there are other young singles, and if the church is reasonably close to her apartment complex. Engaging some of the young women in conversation in the laundry room of her apartment complex, she learns of several more churches that have a large number of active young people who share her religious fervor.

She begins to attend a variety of churches—some Catholic, some mainline Protestant, some Evangelical—on her own and with new friends from work and from her apartment complex, and with a few women she met at the health club. She also reads the churches' material and is asked to dinner by several church members after weekend services. She notes that some churches are more family-oriented, while others seem to have a special ministry for singles. Some large churches actually seem more warm and friendly than some smaller churches. Some people seem to have the same sort of deep spiritual feelings she first felt in college, and seem to live their faith, while others seem to be uncomfortable when she starts asking about their beliefs. Joyce, after three months, finally chooses a moderate-sized, interdenominational, independent church with many young couples and singles who are active in Bible study and social events with the church. She drives by seven other churches every Sunday to get to her new church family.

The Kingmans, Frank and Theresa, both 32, and their children, Jason, 16, Casey, 15, and the twins Kate and Bailey, 8, are an example of a family undergoing simplified decision-making. Frank has accepted a transfer and promotion to a job in a Southern city and is eager to fit in with the other executives where he works. Theresa ran a catering business in the Northeastern city they moved from, and wants to open another catering business, but not until they get settled.

Both Frank and Theresa are concerned that their children be brought up with a strong moral foundation and traditional values. They each grew up in different Protestant faiths and attended the churches of their parents, but are now seeking to enroll their children in a church school and start attending the same church together as a family. Frank asks his fellow executives what church they attend, whether it has a church school, and how the officials of the school care for the children. He is pleased to learn that there are two Episcopal executives with children enrolled in their church school (Theresa is Episcopalian) and that the Lutheran school is highly regarded. They attend a few other Protestant churches near them to see what they are like, but finally settle on the Episcopal church and Lutheran school suggested by Frank's fellow workers. The Kingmans' decision-making process could be characterized as simpler than that of Joyce Evans, but not as routine as is the case of the Bells.

Kevin and Ginger Bell, whose children are married with homes of their own, have decided to move to the South after Kevin took early retirement at his plant. They have been lifelong Southern Baptists and are looking for a Southern Baptist church in their new city. They do not have to look very far—the phone book's yellow pages list 18 Southern Baptist churches within 10 miles of their home. They decide to visit four that are conveniently located and about the size of their previous church. After several weeks their choice is narrowed to two churches. After receiving phone calls from several church members and a visit from the pastor, they decide upon a congregation that will be their church home.

Before Tanya and Stanley Goldman and their son, Cooper, 14, packed for their move to Atlanta, they asked the rabbi of their synagogue whether he was aware of a nearby synagogue. Their rabbi knew the rabbi at a congregation near their new home and said he was sure they would like it there. The Goldmans are glad not to worry about finding a synagogue and plan to transfer their membership there once they are settled in their new home. The Goldmans are considered largely uninvolved decision-makers.

As these four examples suggest, you need to understand whether target segments are undergoing complex, simple, or routine evaluations, or are simply uninvolved. Your approach to each family would be very different simply because of the way they went about making decisions.

Several points need to be made about people's decision styles:

1. The fact that a potential member adopts a particular style for a particular exchange does not mean that the member would use the same process for other decisions. Thus, the Goldmans might exhibit high involvement (chapter 5) with regard to some decisions at the synagogue because they feel strongly about the issue. At the same time, Joyce Evans might show low involvement in some issues at her church because she does not feel that it would make much difference which way her church decided.

2. The fact that a consumer adopts a decision style on one occasion

does not necessarily mean that he or she will adopt it the next time for the same decision. Three kinds of circumstances could alter the decision style. First, the consumer could simply acquire more experience; and a highly complex decision could become simplified and more routine. If the Kingmans move again, they may choose a church the same way the Bells did. Second, the consumer could change in his or her perceptions, needs, and wants. If Kate were to die from leukemia, Frank and Theresa Kingman may question their faith and stop going to church. Third, circumstances surrounding the next decision occasion could change. Some churches lose members when questions are raised about the church founders' authenticity, when the church takes a stand on an explosive issue counter to that of the individual believer, or when church leaders are found to have embezzled church funds.

3. Although the consumers in a market at a given time will undoubtedly represent all four decision styles, the majority may be characterized as one type or another. This may be the case when a crucial subject is at issue and everyone must choose for the first time (for example, when a new church is being formed by members of one congregation and everyone chooses between the old and new churches). Or it may just be that although the decision is not new or unique, the behavior in question is one that is almost always routine (for example, perhaps contributing to the annual Christmas offering) or always highly complex (for example, choosing a new faith).

4. Although a certain type of exchange may frequently involve a particular decision style for most consumers, virtually everyone in the market may change their decision-making style before the next time they decide. Again, this may be because of the passage of time and the maturing of a market over its life cycle. Thus, when consumers were first asked many years ago to consider relatively narrow

---

The Connected Congregation

A church offering apartments for travelers and church groups reported a 95 percent increase in occupancy rate once it began publicizing their availability on its Web site. (www.pewinternet.org).

New Light
Bases for Market Segmentation

Several other bases have been suggested for segmenting religious markets in addition to those outlined in Exhibit 7.7:

"Churched" Versus "Unchurched." The classic case of doing this was the Willow Creek experience of conducting door-to-door research to find the "Unchurched Harrys and Marys" in the local area. Finding that the unchurched had a dislike for traditional services, they designed "seeker services" to appeal to this group with more emphasis on drama, contemporary music, and integrating aspects of popular culture in the sermons. The "churched" segment was targeted with services called "New Community," which uses a more traditional worship format.

Stage in Spiritual Growth. Similar to the churched/unchurched segmentation base, here we are segmenting the market based on the degree of spiritual maturity exhibited by the members of the market. While people at different spiritual levels can become successfully integrated into the same congregation, they will likely need different programs or ministries designed to engage them and encourage continuous spiritual growth.

Adapted from James A. Muncy, "Market Differentiation Strategies for Church Growth," *Journal of Ministry Marketing and Management* 2, no. 2 (1996): 1-13.

---

antismoking ordinances, the decision for many was highly complex. Today, as society seems to have accepted such restrictions on individual freedom, voting on similar ordinances are simpler for the members of our society.

Behavioral segmentation could prove very useful to religious leaders seeking to identify and understand how and why certain congregations are selected by people in different market segments to satisfy their needs. However, great care must be taken when interpreting this behavior and drawing implications from it.

Target Marketing

Market segmentation provides you with segment opportunities

for targeting. At this point you must decide between three broad market selection strategies.

1. *Undifferentiated marketing*: The organization can decide to go after the whole market with one offer and marketing mix, while attempting to attract as many new members as possible. This is another name for mass marketing.

2. *Differentiated marketing*: The organization can decide to go after several market segments, developing an effective offer and marketing mix for each.

3. *Concentrated marketing*: The organization can decide to go after one market segment, and develop the ideal offer and marketing mix. We will now describe the logic and merits of each of these strategies (see Exhibit 7.8).

Undifferentiated Marketing

In undifferentiated marketing, the congregation chooses to ignore the different market segments making up the market. It treats the market as an aggregate, focusing on what is common in the needs of consumers rather than on what is different. It tries to design a marketing program that appeals to the broadest number of people. A church that has only one weekend service for everyone, or a bishop who travels throughout the area, preaching the same sermon to all groups, could exemplify this type of targeting approach.

Undifferentiated marketing is typically defended on the grounds of cost economies. It is the marketing counterpart to standardization and mass production in manufacturing. Program, research, media and training costs are kept low through promoting only one church ministry to everyone the same way. The lower cost, however, is accompanied by reduced satisfaction because of the failure of a program to address everyone's needs equally well.

Differentiated Marketing

Under differentiated marketing, a congregation decides to operate in two or more segments of the market, but designs separate ministries and/or marketing programs for each segment. By offering ministry and marketing variations, it hopes to attain a higher num-

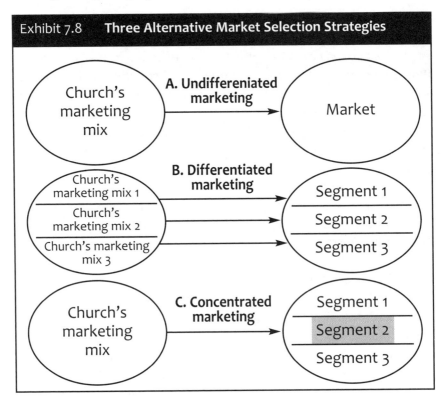

Exhibit 7.8   **Three Alternative Market Selection Strategies**

ber of exchanges, and a deeper position within each segment. It hopes that a deep position in several segments will strengthen the exchange partners' overall association of the congregation with the ministry (i.e., the ministry becomes "branded" by the congregation in that community). Furthermore, it hopes for greater loyalty because the ministry's offerings have been bent to the exchange partners' desires rather than the other way around.

The net effect of differentiated marketing is to create more exchanges for the congregation than undifferentiated marketing can provide. However, it also tends to create higher costs of fulfilling your mission. The leaders and workers have to spend more time and money in ministry development, marketing research, communication materials, and advertising and training. Since differentiated marketing leads to more exchanges and higher costs, nothing can be said in advance about the optimality of this strategy. Some organizations

push differentiated marketing too far in that they run more segmented programs than are economically feasible; some should be
pruned. The majority of religious organizations, however, probably
err in not pushing differentiated marketing far enough, in the light
of varying needs of their exchange partners.

Concentrated Marketing

Concentrated marketing occurs when an organization decides to
divide the market into meaningful segments and devote its major
marketing effort to one segment. Instead of spreading itself too thin
in many parts of the market, it concentrates on serving a particular
market segment well. Through concentrated marketing the organization usually achieves a strong following and standing in a particular market segment. It enjoys greater knowledge of the market
segment's needs and behavior; it also achieves operating economies
through specialization in program development, distribution, and
promotion. Churches that concentrate on reaching single adults or
young families or white-collar managers are examples of concentrated targeting. Concentrated marketing does involve higher-than-
normal risk in that the market may suddenly decline or disappear. In
this case the congregation is faced with relocation, a change of focus,
or a broadening of its targeted groups.

Saddleback Valley Community Church is an example of a congregation that from its beginning utilized concentrated marketing.
Part of the genius of Pastor Rick Warren is displayed in the fact that
he not only named the target segment (Saddleback Sam), but he also
helps the members and ministers to see the segment by providing a
pictorial description of Saddleback Sam (aka Mr. Orange County).

Choosing Among Market Selection Strategies

The actual choice among these three marketing strategies depends on the specific factors you face. If you have *limited resources*,
you will probably choose concentrated marketing because you do
not have enough resources to relate to the whole market and/or to
tailor special services for each segment. If the market were fairly *homogeneous* in its needs and desires, you would usually choose an un-

differentiated marketing approach, because there is little gained from differentiated offerings. If you aspire to be a leader in several segments of the market, you will choose differentiated marketing. If *competitors* have already established dominance in all but a few segments of the market, you might try to concentrate your marketing in one of the remaining segments. Many churches and synagogues begin with a strategy of undifferentiated or concentrated marketing; and, if they are successful, they evolve into a strategy of differentiated marketing.

If you elect to use a concentrated or differentiated marketing strategy, you must evaluate carefully the best segment(s) to serve. The best way to do this is to follow the Effective Marketing Process approach described in this book. Each segment should be rated on its intrinsic market attractiveness in relation to the congregation's particular strengths. You should focus on the needs of market segments that you are capable of satisfying. This would occur either by virtue of having an inherently good match of capabilities with exchange partner needs, or as a result of your research providing you with an understanding of how to acquire that capability.

Positioning Your Ministries

Having selected its target market, you will now need to develop a strategy to create a competitive position vis-à-vis other congregations serving the same segment. Positioning is act of designing the organization's offering and image to occupy a distinctive place in the minds of the target market.[20]

Positioning describes the efforts of an organization to locate itself in the *minds* of the people it is attempting to attract or serve. Positioning is attempting to find a niche in the mind of the exchange partner that hits his/her "sweet spot."[21]

Perhaps an illustration from the frozen pizza business will shed light on how an organization can position itself to find a "niche" in the market, a "hole in the mind" of the potential customer.

DiGiorno's is a frozen pizza whose crust rises when the pizza is heated. Instead of putting it in the frozen pizza category, the marketers positioned it in the delivered pizza category. One of their ads shows party guests asking which pizza delivery service the host used. Then he says: "It's not delivery, it's DiGorno!" This helped highlight DiGiorno's fresh quality and superior taste. Through this clever positioning, DiGiorno's sales went from essentially nothing in 1995 to $382 million in 2002, making it the frozen pizza leader.[22]

To a church or synagogue, there is no greater importance than knowing what position it occupies in the minds of the people it is attempting to attract to its services and ministries. Temple Beth Schul, discussed below, offers insight into the position a rabbi might occupy in persons' minds, and possible attempts to *reposition* the rabbi. The story also reveals the position of a synagogue, and the effects of this upon its programs.

Temple Beth Schul (the name is fictional to protect confidentiality), an established synagogue in a major metropolitan area, began to lose members. A dynamic high-profile "competitor" began to dominate the "local market." Temple Beth Schul clearly needed information and a marketing plan.

To identify the major issues, the synagogue organized a series of focus groups involving current members, former members, and nonmembers from the Jewish community at large. Following this, it developed a questionnaire for phase 2 of the research process: a phone survey targeting the same three population groups.

The key issues, it turned out, ran the gamut from the purely practical to the purely emotional. They ranged from the amount and quality of the religious education offered by the institution to whether the respondents liked the rabbi.

On most of the key issues Temple Beth Schul received high ratings from its current members. However, it seriously lagged behind ifs chief "competitor" on these same issues, in the estimation of nonmembers.

Was this because Temple Beth Schul had somehow acquired a "bad" reputation in the community? Not at all. Much of the synagogue's problem stemmed from the Jewish community's overall lack of information about the synagogue's programs and practices, even though these same people were much more familiar with the programs and practices offered by its competition.

One major issue was the importance of available educational programs and activities for children. Although Temple Beth Schul offered many excellent programs and activities for children, few respondents outside the congregation were aware of them. The result: a higher number of "don't know" and generally lower ratings on this key issue for Temple Beth Schul.

The same lack of knowledge was also partially responsible for the comparatively low ratings given to Temple Beth Schul's rabbi by nonmembers. In the focus groups and phone survey, the rabbi was named as the most important aspect of any synagogue and was considered by many as the one factor that could persuade them to change from one synagogue to another.

While the rabbi at the main competitor had a high recognition factor and received high ratings from the general Jewish population, the rabbi at Temple Beth Schul, while receiving high ratings from members of his own congregation, was not nearly as well known by nonmembers.

During the focus groups involving Temple Beth Schul members, it was also noted that the synagogue's rabbi was much more effective at relating to people on a one-to-one basis than at services. Another logical conclusion was that even nonmembers who said they were familiar with the rabbi might not have seen him at his "best."

To help Temple Beth Schul solve its recognition and familiarity problems, some simple "repackaging" and "repositioning" strategies were proposed.

First, it was suggested that the synagogue initiate a campaign of targeted communications emphasizing its many family- and youth-oriented programs and activities to nonmembers with children.

It was also recommended that Temple Beth Schul organize and encourage its members to participate in a "bring a friend" program of small, informal gatherings hosted by the rabbi. These gatherings would also present the rabbi in his best environment, and allow him to establish a personal rapport with prospective members.

However, repackaging and repositioning could solve only one part of the temple's problems. In at least one basic and very sensitive area, it became clear that the synagogue would need to undergo some "reformulation" as well.

Because reformed synagogues attract members from all types of Jewish upbringing (reformed, conservative, and orthodox), it is crucial for these institutions to be aware of and sensitive to the practices and traditions that are most prevalent in the communities they serve.

In the community served by Temple Beth Schul, most people had come from orthodox or conservative backgrounds and were brought up with their more formal traditions. Although a significant portion of the general Jewish population identified itself as reformed, most of those who were familiar with Temple Beth Schul perceived it as too reformed for them. On the other hand, they perceived the synagogue's leading competitor, also a reformed temple, as being much more successful at blending reformed liberalism with tradition.

If Temple Beth Schul hoped to survive in the community, it would have to reformulate its atmosphere and practices to attract the more tradition-oriented prospects. At the same time, reformulation had to be subtle enough to avoid sacrificing the open, relaxed atmosphere that was so important to its less-traditional current congregation.

To accomplish these goals, the temple, it was recommended, needed to make a concerted communications effort, emphasizing its long history in the community and, indirectly, its high regard for and adherence to basic traditional standards and customs.

At the same time, more traditional elements, such as wearing traditional garb, could be introduced as options for congregants, with emphasis on how the synagogue's openness and acceptance of a wide range of customs and traditions make if possible for Jewish people of all backgrounds to worship and socialize together.[23]

The Temple Beth Schul story is one of repositioning an existing institution. Positioning, however, is also an important concern for a new institution, which as of yet occupies no position in persons' minds.

When Rick Warren decided to start a new church in the Saddleback Valley of southern California, no less than seven of the largest churches, served by some of the most popular preachers and

Bible teachers in the United States, were located within driving distance of the location he had chosen. The list of pastors included Chuck Swindoll, Robert Schuller, John MacArthur, Jack Hayford, and John Wimber.

Rick reasoned that if he was to establish a strong congregation, surrounded by these great churches, he needed to position his church as being different, an alternative to the great churches in the valley. He further reasoned that the people attending these great churches were there because they wanted the style of service and preaching that was offered. Therefore, he would organize a church whose style could be seen as different from the surrounding congregations. Thus came a church for Saddleback Sam, the unchurched baby boomer turned off by religious ceremony and structure.

By doing this, Rick succeeded in positioning Saddleback Valley Community Church as the place for people searching for spiritual values but who felt organized religion had nothing to offer them in their search. He succeeded in positioning Saddleback Church as the place where spiritual values are taken seriously, and where religion is unorganized and informal.

It would have done little good to the seven people who started Saddleback Valley Community Church in the Warrens' condo to have presented the church as another Crystal Cathedral or Vineyard. Those niches were already "owned" in the mind of the potential "customer." So they went looking for a place in the mind of their potential customer, Saddleback Sam, that was not yet taken—and they found it by positioning themselves as a church for those who do not like church.

Positioning is akin to *image*, but different from *attitude*. One person may fully understand that Saddleback Church is very different from the other large churches surrounding it (position), and at the same time believe it to be a "cheap grace" church, at which everything goes (attitude). Another person may see Saddleback Church as very different from the other large churches in the area, and believe it is the best place to go in order to discover and strengthen one's spiritual values within an informal, relaxed atmosphere (attitude).

What we learn from these examples is that a responsive church will actively take steps to develop its image and position because this determines the target publics it will attract. Responsive churches will think through the position they wish to occupy in the minds of their target publics.

Positioning Strategy Statement

To communicate your organization's positioning, marketing plans (chapter 8) often include a positioning strategy statement.[24]The statement should follow this form: To *(target group and need)* the *(brand, organization, or ministry)* is a/an *(concept)* that *(distinguishing characteristic)*. An example from the commercial field: "To busy professionals who need to stay organized, the Palm Pilot is an electronic organizer that allows you to back up files on your PC more easily and reliably than competitive products." Sometimes the statement is more detailed:

Mountain Dew: To young, active soft-drink consumers who have little time for sleep, Mountain Dew is the soft drink that gives you more energy than any other brand because it has the highest level of caffeine. With Mountain Dew you can stay alert and keep going even when you haven't been able to get a good night's sleep.

A positioning statement for a ministry might look something like this:

To young childless couples who want to become more involved in the church and experience spiritual growth, our Growing Together small group ministry offers a nonthreatening, informal social setting for scriptural study and bonding that provides you with opportunities to interact with other like-minded couples.

Executing the Positioning Strategy
Through the Marketing Mix

The final step in market segmentation, target marketing, and positioning is the development of a "marketing mix" that supports and reinforces its chosen position (see Exhibit 7.9). This describes the "four P's" of the marketing mix—*product, promotion, price,* and *place*—that an organization puts together in order to attain its cho-

| Exhibit 7.9 | **Components of the Marketing Mix** |

sen position in the minds of those it is trying to reach. In other words, the chosen competitive position dictates the elements of the marketing mix that will be emphasized. These four elements are more fully discussed in chapters 9 and 10.

[1] Sonja Steptoe Bellflower, "In Touch With Jesus," *Time*, Oct. 31, 2006.

[2] Donald R. Lehman and Russell S. Wines, *Analysis for Marketing Planning* (Chicago: Irwin, 1997), pp. 118, 119.

[3] Several of these objectives were suggested by Ric Olson, local church ministries consultant, Iowa Conference, United Methodist Church, in an interview with the authors.

[4] Source: Adapted from *Digging Deep in Donegal,* Percept Web site: http://www.link2lead.com/L2L/MyWorld/FullStory/F_v1n9.asp.

[5] http://www.sric-bi.com/VALS.

[6] http://www.sric-bi.com/VALS/about.shtml.

[7] Adapted from P. Kotler and K. L. Keller, *Marketing Management.*

[8] Corry Azzi and Ronald Ehrenberg, "Household Allocation of Time and Church

Attendance," *Journal of Political Economy* 83, no. 1 (February 1975): 27-56. The authors have benefited from the literature review done by Jen Birney that found this, and several other sources, discussed in this section of the chapter.

[9] Geoffrey E. Meredith and Charles D. Schewe with Janice Karlovich, *Defining Markets, Defining Moments* (New York: Hungry Minds, Inc., 2002).

[10] Donald R. Ploch and Donald W. Hastings. 1993. "Graphic Presentations of Church Attendance Using General Social Survey Data" (working paper). Knoxville, Tenn.: University of Tennessee.

[11] Mary C. Gilly and Ben M. Enis, "Recycling the Family Life Cycle: A Proposal for Redefinition," in Andrew Mitchell, ed., *Advances in Consumer Research,* (1982), vol. 9, p. 274.

[12] Rex Y. Du and Wagenr A. Kamakura, "Household Life Cycles and Lifestyles in the United States," *Journal of Marketing Research* 48 (February 2006): 121-132.

[13] Ross M. Stolzenberg, Mary Blair-Loy, Linda J. Waite, "Religious Participation in Early Adulthood: Age and Family Life Cycle Effects on Church Membership," *American Sociological Review* 60, no. 1 (February 1995): 84-103.

[14] H. M. Bahr, "Aging and Religious Disaffiliation," *Social Forces* 49, no. 1 (1970): 59-71.

[15] Mark Chaves, "Family Structure and Protestant Church Attendance: The Sociological Basis of Cohort and Age Effects," *Journal for the Scientific Study of Religion* 30, no. 4 (1991): 501-514.

[16] John Wilson and Darren E. Sherkat, "Returning to the Fold," *Journal for the Scientific Study of Religion* 33, no. 2 (June 1994): 148-161.

[17] For an extensive discussion of denominational variations based on geography, social class, church attendance, education, and attitudinal, as well as denominational, switching patterns, see Robert Wuthnow, *The Restructuring of American Religion* (Princeton, N.J.: Princeton Unversity Press, 1988), pp. 83-91.

[18] Azzi and Ehrenberg, p. 40.

[19] For a discussion of benefit segmentation see Russell I. Haley, "Benefit Segments: Backwards and Forwards," *Journal of Advertising Research* 24 (February/March 1984): 21.

[20] Al Ries and Jack Trout, *Positioning: The Battle for Your Mind,* 20th Anniversary Edition (New York: McGraw-Hill, 2001).

[21] For an advanced discussion of positioning strategy, see Kevin Lane Keller, Brian Sternthal, and Alice Tybout, "Three Questions You Need to Ask About Your Brand," *Harvard Business Review* 80 (September 2001): 80-89.

[22] Alice M. Tybout and Brian Sternthal, "Brand Positioning," in *Kellogg on Marketing*, ed. Dawn Iacobucci (New York: John Wiley and Sons, 2001), p. 35; Theresa Howard, "DiGiorno's Campaign Delivers Major Sales," *USA Today,* Apr. 1, 2002.

[23] See Patrick M. Baldasare, "True Believer Puts Its Faith in Marketing Research," *Marketing News* 24, no. 1 (June 8, 1990): 29, 31.

[24] See Bobby J. Calder and Steven J. Reagan, "Brand Design," and Alice M. Tybout and Brian Sternthal, "Brand Positioning," in *Kellogg on Marketing,* pp. 54,61.

WORKSHEETS: CHAPTER 7

Segmentation, Targeting, and Positioning

Segmentation

1. Assumptions about segments:

To the best of your knowledge, does the segmentation of the market(s) of interest conform to these assumptions:

mutual exclusivity	_____
exhaustiveness	_____
sizeable	_____
identity	_____
reachability	_____
different response	_____
coherence	_____
stablity	_____

2. Choice of Segmentation Method:

By which method will you establish segments?

research based	_____
existing segmentation system	_____
managerial judgment	_____

3. Describe what your research (chapters 4 and 5 worksheets), segmentation system, or secondary data tell you about the profile of people in each segment:

Segmentation Base: _____

Name	**Profile**

Segment 1: _____ _____
_____ _____
_____ _____
_____ _____

Segment 2: _____ _____
_____ _____
_____ _____
_____ _____

Segment 3: _____ _____
_____ _____
_____ _____
_____ _____

Segment 4: _____ _____
_____ _____
_____ _____
_____ _____

Segment 5: _____ _____
_____ _____
_____ _____
_____ _____

Segment 6: _____ _____
_____ _____
_____ _____

_____   _____

Targeting

1. Identify the segments that you will target:
   segments targeted: _____

2. Describe your targeting strategy:
   undifferentiated marketing   _____
   differentiated marketing   _____
   concentrated marketing   _____

Positioning

Describe your positioning strategy statement for each targeted segment:

Targeted Segment   *Positioning Strategy Statement*

_____   _____

_____   _____

_____   _____

CHAPTER 8:

Strategic Marketing Planning

"Careful planning puts you ahead in the long run; hurry and scurry puts you further behind" (PROVERBS 21:5, MESSAGE).

"Plans fail for lack of counsel, but with many advisers they succeed" (PROVERBS 15:22, NIV).

In this chapter we will address the following questions:

1. How does an organization benefit from planning?

2. What are the characteristics of a good plan?

3. What are the objectives of a marketing plan?

4. What are the components of a marketing plan?

The first thing to realize about marketing planning is that, if you have read the chapters and completed the worksheets for the preceding chapters, you have already been doing it! Or at least you have begun to create the pieces that, when fit together, form the picture puzzle that is a marketing plan. In this chapter we'll develop a few more critical pieces, and then provide the template for fitting the pieces together. But first we need to stress some very important aspects of the planning process.

Dwight D. Eisenhower once said, "In preparing for battle I have always found that plans are useless, but planning is indispensable." This enigmatic statement contains some truths of real significance for you. How does the planning *process* contribute to what you are trying to achieve through the marketing *plan*? The planning process helps you several ways:

• By involving key people in the planning process you are able to diffuse the societal marketing orientation (SMO) throughout the leadership of the organization. The marketing planning process forces people to adopt the "outside-in" perspective. This will help you to achieve your goals by concentrating on helping your exchange partners achieve theirs. Using the planning process to spread an SMO throughout the organization will pay dividends beyond the quality of the plan itself that emerges from the process.

• People are forced to think deeply and realistically about the organization's future that they are trying to create.

• Limited resources mean that people must arrive at a consensus about your priorities, and be realistic in setting goals and expectations.

• Planning energizes and stimulates people to become more engaged in your organization. A greater sense of purpose emerges from thinking about directing the future of the congregation.

Research has shown that planning is most likely to take place when a congregation perceives its environment to be complex and dynamic—conditions that confront an increasing number of churches and synagogues today.[1]

Strategic Planning and Marketing Planning

Religious organizations are increasingly turning to formal planning methods as the way to adapt to the rapid environmental changes they face. Large and growing churches tend to be more formal planners.[2] It is not clear, however, whether formal planning is the cause or the consequence of being a large church. Nevertheless, a planning approach has caused some churches or denominations to become large.

The authors hold four principles of utmost importance to the success of developing a marketing plan:

1. *Keep It Simple.* Einstein is credited with saying that everything "should be kept as simple as possible but no simpler." This, of course, includes planning. The simpler the planning process, the easier it is for members to participate in it, and the less resistance it will encounter.

2. *Keep It Natural.* The planning processes used in any congregation should take into consideration the culture, work experiences, and abilities of its people. What feels natural to one congregation's members may not feel natural in another congregation.

3. *People Tend to Support What They Have Helped to Create.* Any person or group whose support is needed to carry out the plan should be involved in making the plan. Where this is not possible, they should be kept fully informed throughout the planning process, and invited to comment on it.

4. *Stay Focused.* Always keep in mind the ultimate objective for your plan—to facilitate the creation of long-term mutually beneficial exchange relationships. All of your analyses, each step of the planning process, and all of your resources should be contributing to this goal. This focus provides a good benchmark for you to use whenever anyone suggests adding an expense or a new component to the plan.

Most religious organizations pay more attention to *budgeting* than they do to planning. For many religious organizations, budgeting comes so naturally that when they are building the budget they think they are planning. Planning is not the same as budgeting or forecasting, although both would find a place in a good plan.

Planning, from a marketing perspective, can be thought of as two processes:

1. *Strategic planning* is the process of developing and maintaining a *strategic fit* between the organization's goals and resources, and its changing marketing opportunities. It seeks to answer these questions: What kind of church are we? What kind of church do we want to be? (mission and goals)

2. *Marketing planning* is the process of selecting *target markets* (groups to be focused upon), choosing a *strategic position*, and devel-

oping an effective *marketing mix* to reach and serve the target groups and achieve organizational goals. It seeks to answer these questions: What ministries do we want to offer? (strategy) and How do we implement these ministries? (tactics).

Admittedly, drawing a distinction between strategic and marketing planning is more for illustration than for operational purposes. For our purposes, we will use a marketing plan to show how strategic planning and marketing planning may be used by a religious organization to help identify and accomplish its goals. We will describe the objectives of a marketing plan and the steps in developing one.

Objectives of the Marketing Plan

William Cohen specifies seven marketing plan objectives for any marketing plan.[3]

1. Act as a road map. A marketing plan should act as a road map, telling you how to get from the point of launching the planned ministry to reaching your objectives. Like a road map, the plan must describe the environment in which you find yourself along the way. A marketing plan will embrace four environs that will have influence upon the ministry plan. They are:

> *a. The organization itself.* The congregation becomes a very important and influential environment for any of its plans and ministries. The congregation may act as a resource, providing needed resources for the plan, or it may act as a constraint, failing to provide the needed resources to sustain a healthy, vibrant institution.

As consultants to congregations, the authors often discover that the staffs and ruling boards of all types of churches fail to consider the membership as an environment. They fail to "bring the members along." They make plans without the members' involvement, input, or understanding—then they blame the members for the failure of the programs.

A cardinal rule in planning is "people tend to support what they have helped to create." If the staff or ruling board relies upon the congregation for financial support, final approval, and so on, it only makes sense that the planning process should involve the congregation. We are not talking about rubber-stamp involvement, but about having input and influence on the plan as it is developed.

What has been said about the membership as an environment can also be said about any group or agency within the organization whose responsibilities or activities are relevant to the plan. For example, doesn't it make sense for a congregation building committee to involve young parents in deciding the location, space requirements, toys, and furnishings of a new or remodeled nursery? Yet in our experience very few building committees satisfy this test. Then they complain when, "after we spent all this money to remodel the nursery, the young parents refused to put their children there."

b. The competitors: The congregation, in general, has its competitors (see chapter 6). However, each new ministry will likely have its specific competitors. The marketing plan must identify the general and the specific competitors and decide how to neutralize, or control, the effects of the competition.

c. Neutral environs: The environment in which a planned ministry will be launched is composed, in part, of a number of "neutral" entities with which the congregation must contend (i.e., ecclesiastical judicatories; local, state, and federal governments; media; and special-interest groups). Any one of these "neutral" entities may become a very important resource or constraint on a particular plan or ministry. For example, if the congregation is planning to launch a day-care center for children of working parents in the surrounding downtown area, the state may suddenly become an important environmental factor by way of imposing several code restrictions. In this instance the state environment becomes a constraint. On the other hand, several financial institutions, or the chamber of commerce, may provide ample finances for remodeling building space and equipment, thus becoming a resource.

d. Situational environs. The situational environment—which includes politics, laws and regulations, economic and business conditions, technology, demand, social and cultural factors, and demographics—will have an impact on the planned ministries.

At any point in time a number of these environs may be acting as resources to the plan, while others are acting as constraints. The planning of any significant ministry should include a review of all the environs. This will go a long way to strengthening the plan and avoiding many unpleasant surprises along the way.

The problem in dealing with all of these environs is how to do it well, while at the same time keeping it simple and natural. If an effort is not made to do this, the average volunteer planning group will become bogged down, overwhelmed, angry, and the like.

2. Assist in administrative control and monitoring of implementation of strategy. A marketing plan assists in administrative control and allows better decisions to be made, and to be made much more quickly than might otherwise be the case.

3. Inform new participants in the plan of their role and function. All individuals involved in carrying out the plan should be familiar with the plan in its entirety. Individuals need to know what they are responsible for, what actions they will be required to take, and how their part is necessary for the success of the ministry. Everyone, especially volunteers, wants to know the ultimate goal for the ministry and exactly how their efforts will help accomplish it.

4. To obtain resources for implementation. The implementation of any marketing strategy requires a congregation to allocate the resources necessary for its accomplishment. No plan is complete until the resource decisions are clearly decided and agreed upon.

Resources are not automatically made available. Therefore, those who have the authority to provide the resources—whether financial groups, volunteer workers, denominational hierarchy, or the congregation—must be convinced that this is the best use of the resources. A marketing plan is the "sales" vehicle to assist in persuading the resource providers that the plan will help them meet their *personal* goals in supplying the resources, as well as helping the organization accomplish an important ministry.

5. To stimulate thinking and make better use of resources. Developing a marketing strategy depends on building on one's strengths and making one's weaknesses irrelevant. As one develops a marketing plan, thinking is stimulated. Therefore the plan is often changed and modified. As a result of this, the strategy and tactics necessary to achieve the marketing objectives and goals of the marketing plan are continually improved as the plan develops.

6. Assignment of responsibilities, tasks, and timing. Any marketing plan is only as good as those who implement it. Therefore, it is absolutely crucial that the responsibilities of everyone be indicated and that tasks be thoroughly understood by all individuals who have roles to play in implementation. Further, these actions must be scheduled so that the overall plan is executed in a coordinated fashion.

There is an old adage that "if *everyone* is responsible for accomplishing a task, then *no one* is responsible." The marketing plan must assure that every task is assigned to someone who is responsible, and the scheduling is coordinated to maximize the effectiveness of what is done.

7. Awareness of opportunities and threats. The preparation of a marketing plan requires investigation into the environs in such a fashion that opportunities and threats are precisely identified. The more one plans (instead of shooting from the hip), the more one understands the nature of these opportunities and threats, and what can be done about them.

In no case should opportunities or threats be ignored. Rather, the marketing plan should have enough flexibility in it to allow for modifications along the way—so that the organization can take advantage of the opportunities and avoid or overcome unanticipated threats.[4]

Steps to Developing a Marketing Plan

We will now examine the basic components of a marketing plan (see Exhibit 8.1), using the following hypothetical example.

The First Presbyterian Church of Carmel, Indiana, has a membership of approximately 500 on the church books, with a typical attendance of fewer than 300 at worship services on Sunday (less in Sunday school). Dan Carmichael, 31, has only recently been appointed to the head pastor position at First Church. He was pleased

---

Exhibit 8.1   Marketing Plan Format

A. Mission Statement (*Who are we? Who do we want to be?*)
Purpose of your church (what it is we are trying to accomplish?)
Objectives of the church consistent with the purpose

B. Situation Analysis (*Where are we now?*)
1. Internal Environment
Describe your experiences relative to the financial, human, and capital resources, and strengths and weaknesses of your internal publics (administration, board, staff, members, ministry team volunteers; see chapter 6's discussion of internal publics). Take a "spiritual gifts inventory" to determine what your members can contribute to achieving the church's objectives. Keep in mind the four planning principles.
2. Input Environment
Describe the aspects of the donor, supplier, and judicatory publics that could impact on your objectives (see chapter 6's discussion of input publics and intermediary publics). Also, list your expectations for intermediary publics, such as financial, marketing, or other facilitator publics intended to help you achieve your objectives. Ask such questions as:
- How does the availability or nonavailability of funds affect the situation?
- How will judicatory action or anything else in current or future state, federal, or local government actions likely affect this plan?
- Does current media publicity favor or disfavor church activities?
3. External Environment
Describe the cultural, societal, economic, and demographic trends existing on a national and local scale that could positively or negatively impact the ability to achieve your objectives. These environmental trends or events are categorized as opportunities or threats. Also, in addition to these social trends you should also describe any trends occurring within your External Publics (see chapter 6) that have an impact on achieving your objectives. Incorporate an understanding of the competitive, neutral, and situational environs.

C. Target Market (*Where do we want to go?*)
Describe your target group by using detailed information on demographics, geo-demographics, lifestyle and lifecycle, needs, psychographics, or whatever is the most appropriate basis for segmentation (see chapter 7 on segmentation and targeting decisions, and chapter 5 on behavioral factors). Why are you interested in this group rather than some other segment?

Exhibit 8.1   Marketing Plan Format—continued

D. Marketing Strategy *(How are we going to get there?)*
  1. Goals
  What are the quantifiable goals for the church's programs? How will they be measured? What constitutes "success"?
  2. Positioning Strategy
  How do we intend to position ourselves to the Target Market and against our competition?

E. Design and Implement Marketing Tactics *(What and when?)*
  1. Design Marketing Tactics
    • What program services will we offer to satisfy target market needs? (product, chapter 9)
    • How and where will the target market make use of the service? (distribution, chapter 9)
    • What must the target market give up to use the services offered? (price, chapter 9)
    • What communications will be sent to the target market and how will they hear them? (promotion, chapter 10)
  2. Implement Marketing Tactics
  Give a detailed breakdown of how each aspect of the strategy will be put into operation, who will be responsible for the tactical implementation of each task, and when it must be accomplished.

F. Marketing Budget *(How much, where, and who?)*
  Who will be involved in the program? How much time will each person involved have to devote in order to make the program successful? How much money will each task take, when must the money be available, and what is the allocation priority?

G. Marketing Control *(How did we do?)*
  What are the results of the program's implementation? How do they compare to our stated objectives? What corrections are necessary to improve performance?

---

to find that his personal desire to reach out to the adherents without a church home in Carmel was shared by the Sunday school superintendent and other church leaders. There was also a deep concern for reviving the church's current inactive members. The current membership could best be described as relatively homogeneous economically (upper middle class), but ethnically diverse (mix of white,

Asian, and some families of northern European heritage) and spread over several generation groups. While some members were content with the status quo, there seemed to be a sizable number of members who were eager to reach out to the community and build a more vibrant, spirit-filled congregation. To that end, Dan met with the church leaders to put together a marketing plan that would help the church accomplish its objectives.

It is important to go beyond merely collecting and recording the information described in the situation analysis section of the plan. This information must be analyzed for the *implications* it has for the selection of a target market, a strategy and tactics, and a budget. Write down the Implications as you conduct each analysis section, and then write an implications summary and conclusions as an input to the selection of a target market, the development of strategy and tactics, and establishment of a marketing budget. Your common sense, understanding of chapter 5's discussion of human behavior, and a growing ability to "think like a marketer" will help you factor these implications into your marketing decisions.

We will now describe the development of the marketing plan for the First Church in Carmel, Indiana.

Mission Statement

Responsive religious organizations seek to clarify two questions: *responsive to whom and to what?* These questions help the religious organization to define its mission the *guiding principle* to what it does. In chapter 1, Exhibit 1 we identified four mission goals related to internal and external focus, and vertical and horizontal relationships in order to distinguish those aspects of religious organizations that are marketable from those that are not. Those four components were for expositional purposes, but are common to many congregational missions (see the example below). There are many resources available to help you establish a mission if you do not already have one (see note 5 for some of these sources).

Suppose that after much soul searching and prayerful discussion, the planning group of the First Presbyterian Church settles on the following mission statement. [5]

First Presbyterian Church Mission

WE EXIST TO PRAISE GOD

through celebrating new life in Jesus.

through responding to His presence in our lives.

through allowing His Holy Spirit to lead us.

Praise is our way of expressing our deep love for God. In worship we submit to His lordship in our lives and reflect His majesty, glory, and power.

WE PREPARE OURSELVES FOR SERVICE

through the study and application of Scripture.

through developing our talents and spiritual gifts.

through becoming mature in Jesus Christ.

Preparation and growth are vital. It is not merely an option. However, growth is not an end in itself. Therefore, we seek to grow and become mature so that we can be prepared for service to our Lord, Jesus Christ.

PROVIDE LOVE AND CARE FOR ONE ANOTHER

through sharing each other's needs, burdens, and joys.

through serving each other in a sacrificial way.

through learning how to love and be loved.

God, in His grace, has given us to each other. An integral part of our life as His body is caring for and supporting each other.

PROCLAIM CHRIST TO THE WORLD

through the penetration of our society.

through reproducing ourselves by evangelism and discipleship.

through applying ourselves and our resources in reaching out to
our community, our nation, and our world.

We take seriously our Lord's command to go and make disciples.
Mission is the bedrock of our reason for being.

Situation Analysis

Following the mission statement, the planning group prepares a situation analysis consisting of examining the internal environment, the input environment, and the external environment.

Internal Environment. In addition to information gathered on their internal publics, the planning team collected membership and attendance data. Exhibit 8.2 shows the background data for First Church's performance and resources. It would appear from the information in Exhibit 8.2 that the church has had a decline in both membership and attendance over the past 3 years, although the percentage of members attending services is holding at around 50 percent, above the national average of 42 percent. This leads to the next major section of internal analysis—listing the church's strengths and weaknesses.

Resources and Constraints. Following the background study on the congregation's performance, planners should undertake an analysis of the church's resources and capabilities. An organization should pur-

Exhibit 8.2	Background Data for First Presbyterian Church		
	2009	**2010**	**2011**
Membership	550	530	500
Average Worship Attendance	290	275	250
Attendance as Percentage			
of Membership	53%	52%	50%
Annual Capacity*	39,000	39,000	39,000
Main Worship Attendance†	15,080	14,300	13,000
Worshippers as Percentage			
of Capacity	39%	37%	33%
Operating Income	$58,000	$53,360	$48,720
Operating Expenses			
and Transfers	$58,250	$52,785	47,200
Balance	$250	($575)	($1520)

*Church sanctuary capacity is 750 multiplied by 52 Sundays.
†Average attendance per week multiplied by 52 weeks.

sue goals, opportunities, and strategies that are suggested by, or congruent with, its strengths/resources, and avoid those where its resources are insufficient.

We understand that God's people have always been called upon to accomplish tasks quite beyond their normal ability. This is part of the meaning of being "faith-full," and living by faith. However, there is a big difference between faith and presumption. An example follows.

The authors worked with a congregation of 75 members whose pastor led them into a half-million-dollar debt to establish a Christian day school, saying that God had instructed them to teach their children the laws of God and to protect them from the evils of public education. The members mortgaged personal property, borrowed against pensions, and tried other means of raising money. In addition, the congregation mortgaged the parsonage and sold junk bonds to relatives and friends. The school failed, the denomination had to assume the debt, the pastor left the scene, and the congregation was left with the pain and sorrow.

A resource is whatever the organization has of value in accomplishing its plans. Resources may be money, good will, people, skill, or common sense. A constraint is whatever the organization does not have enough of to accomplish its plans. Exhibit 8.3 shows a form that the congregation can use to develop an analysis of its resources (strengths) and constraints (weaknesses). The major resource areas are people, money, facilities, systems, and image. The analysis is to indicate whether the church's position with respect to each constitutes a strength (high, medium, low), is neutral, or constitutes a weakness (low, medium, high).

Suppose the checks reflect First Church's evaluation of its resources. The church believes that it has an adequate number of members who are highly enthusiastic, loyal, service-minded, and imbued with hospitality and teaching spiritual gifts.[6] As for money, the church is somewhat short of funds, and almost all funds are committed. Therefore, the church does not have the flexibility to take on many new projects. The church's facilities are adequate, but not flexible for multipurpose uses. Also, the church location is somewhat inconvenient. The church's management system for planning and information is reasonably good, but it is weak in feedback (control) systems. Finally, the church's image with the general public is neutral, as it is with the targeted groups. (The congregation would fill in the image ratings with survey responses after selecting target segments, discussed in chapter 7.) Several organizations have developed other tools for taking an inventory of a congregation's resources and constraints. A few of these are listed below:

www.vitalevangelicalleadership.org (vital congregation profile)

http://www.search-institute.org/congregations/basf/ (building assets, strengthening faith)

http://www.uscongregations.org/survey.htm (U.S. congregational life survey)

http://www.perceptgroup.com/Products/ReVision/ REVISIONfront.aspx (Revision)

Remember to write down the implications of what your situation analysis reveals.

Input Environment. The relevant input publics should be evaluated to determine the possible impact they will have on achieving the church's objectives; for example, the donors, community, judicatories, suppliers, and so on.

External Environment. The major components of the external environment should be analyzed to determine their impact on the church's ability to achieve its objectives. The procedure is (1) listing the major factors and subfactors making up the environment component, (2) describing the major trends in each factor, (3) converting the implications of these trends into specific opportunities and threats, and (4) assessing the threats—by their probability of occurrence and potential severity—and assessing the opportunities by their potential attractiveness and probability of success.

Threat Analysis. Every organization needs to identify the major threats it faces.

An environmental threat is a challenge posed by an unfavorable trend or specific disturbance in the environment that, in the absence of purposeful marketing action, would lead to the stagnation, decline, or demise of a religious organization or one of its ministry programs.

	Strength				Weakness		
Resource	**H**	**M**	**L**	**N**	**L**	**M**	**H**
People 1. Adequate number? 2. Spiritual gifts? 3. Enthusiastic? 4. Loyal? 5. Service-minded?	 ✓ ✓ ✓	 ✓ ✓ 					
Money 1. Adequate? 2. Flexible?					 ✓ 	 ✓	
Facilities 1. Adequate? 2. Flexible? 3. Location quality?			 ✓ 		 ✓		 ✓
Systems 1. Information system quality? 2. Planning system quality? 3. Control system quality?		 ✓ 	 ✓ 		 ✓		
Image 1. General reputation? 2. Among target group?				 ✓ ✓			
Notes: H=high; M=medium; L=low; N=neutral							

Exhibit 8.3   Strengths/Weaknesses Analysis

Suppose the congregation's planning committee identified the following four threats:

1. Another Presbyterian congregation about four miles away, with a sizable number of young families as members, has been considering opening a church school. This might attract some of First Church's members away.

2. The congregation's cost of operation—heating, lighting, salaries, and so on—might rise 15 percent next year.

3. A donor/member has retired and is talking of moving to

Arizona. This might cause the congregation to lose $20,000 a year in contributions.

4. A local radio station might stop broadcasting the church's main worship hour on Sunday.

These threats must be weighed to determine their potential severity and probability of occurrence. Suppose the results are those shown in Exhibit 8.4. For those threats that are most severe and highly probable, contingency plans should be made (upper left cell). Threats that are quite severe but of lower probability should be monitored (upper right cell). Those that are neither very severe nor probable can be ignored (bottom cells). By identifying and classifying threats, the organization knows which environmental developments to plan for, monitor, or ignore.

Opportunity Analysis. While threat analysis is important, opportunity analysis is much more important. Managing threats and problem solving is maintenance-oriented—it will not develop a quality organization or facilitate growth and expansion. But by managing its opportunities successfully, the congregation will grow and strengthen its ministries. Here we are concerned mainly with marketing opportunities.

A marketing opportunity is an attractive arena of relevant marketing action in which a congregation can apply its strengths to satisfy significant needs of a target group.

Exhibit 8.4	**Threat Matrix**	
	Probability of Occurrence	
	High	Low
Potential Severity High	1, 2	3
Low		4

Exhibit 8.5	**Opportunity Matrix**

		Probability of Success	
		High	Low
Potential Attractiveness	High	1	3
	Low	4	2

Suppose the planning committee perceived the following opportunities, which are located in the four cells of Exhibit 8.5, according to their probability of success (measured by the ability of the church to develop the opportunity) and potential attractiveness (measured by the likelihood of achievement of church objectives.)

1. The church could develop programs to satisfy the needs of adherent segments who did not currently have a church home. (Through geodemographic analysis [see chapter 7], the planning committee learned which lifestyle segments lived in or near Carmel. See target market discussion below).

2. The church could start a small group ministry that would help to get more people to become involved in the life of the congregation.

3. The church could open a day school for grades 1-9.

4. The church could start a branch Sunday school at the large local nursing home.

Starting some outreach programs to meet the needs of adherent families without a church home seems to be the best opportunity for the church, since it fits nicely with the church's objectives, its "market" conditions, and the ability of the church to capitalize on their current strengths of enthusiasm, service-mindedness, and related spiritual gifts. The idea of a church school fits church objectives well, but lack of funds, an insufficient "critical mass" of children in each grade, and strong competition from other private schools locally gives it little chance of success. A branch Sunday school at the local nursing home could prove successful, and will be pursued by some of the older members. The small group ministry is a pet project of a few parishioners, and will be assigned for development by the core group eager to start this ministry.

In considering opportunities, congregations should generally avoid those for which necessary resources are weak or inadequate. But a weakness is not fatal to a project if the congregation can see a way to acquire the needed resources. Therefore, what is an opportunity for one church may not be a possibility for another, and what is a mediocre idea at one point in time may become an attractive possibility at another time.

Target Market

The first step in preparing a marketing strategy is to gain a thorough understanding of the target market(s). Selection of a target market(s) follows a segmentation of the entire market, in which different segments are identified and evaluated for attractiveness (see chapter 7).

You might have an "open door policy" and welcome (and, in fact, desire) all people from a diverse spectrum of ages, cultures, ethnicities, etc. to come to your congregation to worship. However, you are likely to have a more narrow range of that spectrum living in neighborhoods around you. The segmentation, targeting, and positioning (STP) process we are describing here is not intended to be exclusive in its approach to your outreach activities. Rather, it is intended to help you identify, focus on, and effectively reach those people who are most likely to respond positively to your appeal. The concern with both effectiveness and efficiency that underlies the STP process is part of what most congregations see as a missional duty (e.g., being effective witnesses and faithful stewards of resources). Once you learn who lives in your "service area," you can begin to make decisions on which groups to focus on in priority order (i.e., targeting decisions) and how to best address their needs (i.e., positioning decisions). Your success with these segments then builds the financial and human resources needed to reach out to those more difficult to reach but no less desirable segments.

In the case of First Church, suppose the segmentation approach was to use geodemography to identify the households in the various lifestyle segments. They might have used both Claritas' PRIZM NE segmentation scheme, along with Percept's First View database to profile the people in the Carmel area (zip codes 46268, 46280, and 46033).

Analysis of Claritas PRIZM Segments. As can be seen in Exhibit 8.6, while the Carmel area has a number of lifestyle segments living in the area, three segments are among the top five most numerous in more than one zip code: Movers and Shakers, Kids and Cul-de-Sacs, and Home Sweet Home.

Clearly, from a quick analysis of these segments the area has a concentration of relatively young, well-educated, high-income professionals who are largely Caucasian and Asian homeowners with a mix of children and childless families. This appears to mirror the current church membership. Based on these findings, the planning

Exhibit 8.6	Clartas PRIZM Top 5 Most Numerous Segments in Zip Code		
	Zip Code		
Segment	46280	46033	46268
01 Upper Crust		✓	
03 Movers and Shakers	✓	✓	
06 Winner's Circle		✓	
10 Second City Elite		✓	
13 Upward Bound		✓	
14 New Empty Nests	✓		
18 Kids and Cul-de-Sacs	✓		✓
19 Home Sweet Home	✓		✓
21 Gray Power	✓		
22 Young Influentials			✓
30 Suburban Sprawl			✓
44 New Beginnings			✓

committee decided to use a differentiated targeting strategy (chapter 7) to target three groups: Movers and Shakers, Kids and Cul-de-Sacs, and Home Sweet Homes, all of whom closely resemble many of the current member families, and those members on the books that have stopped coming to church. These three segments were profiled in detail in Exhibits 7.3 and 7.4 in chapter 7's section on Claritas.

Note: For a free sample of Claritas' PRIZM segments in any zip code, go to:

http://www.claritas.com/MyBestSegments/Default.jsp?ID=20 &SubID=&pageName=ZIP%2BCode%2BLook-up.

More detailed information, at a cost, for the zip codes and PRIZM segments is available from Claritas at (800) 234-5973.

Analysis of Percept First View Data. In addition to the Claritas PRIZM profile of this area, First Church purchased a *First View* profile of the area from Percept. This revealed the profile on the following pages for a five-mile radius circle around the church.

These First View reports are available for $85 from Percept at: http://www.perceptgroup.com/Products/FirstView/FVfront.aspx.

When the Claritas and Percept data sources are combined, a picture of the targeted groups begins to emerge:

Target 1: *Young Upwardly Mobile Middle-Class Families.* This group is upscale suburban married couples with children who live an enviable lifestyle of families in recently built subdivisions. With a higher-than-average incidence of Asians, college-educated white-collar professionals with managerial jobs and upper-middle-class incomes populate this largely Caucasian segment. This group is expected to grow by about 9 percent in this area by 2011. Primary household concerns are for parenting, having a satisfying career, having time to enjoy leisure and recreation, and long-term financial security. Faith receptivity of this group is about average, which is also the level of preference for a Presbyterian faith affiliation. Worship style is about evenly split among this group between contemporary and more traditional, and there is a preference among this segment for church programs that are recreational, as well as for day-care services.

Precept First View™ Data Report, PAGE 1

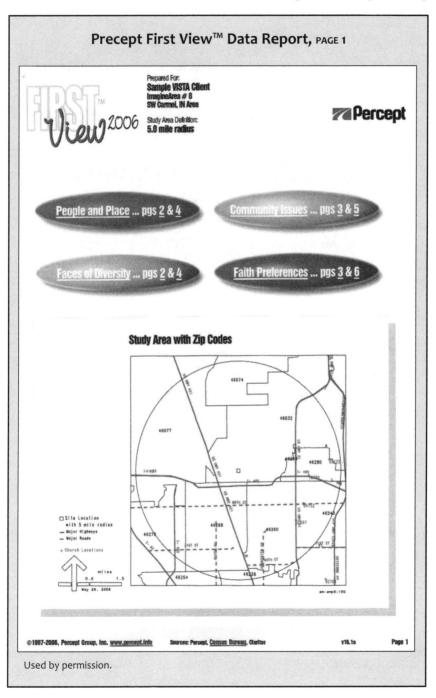

Prepared For:
Sample VISTA Client
ImagineArea # 8
SW Carmel, IN Area

Study Area Definition:
5.0 mile radius

Percept

People and Place ... pgs 2 & 4

Community Issues ... pgs 3 & 5

Faces of Diversity ... pgs 2 & 4

Faith Preferences ... pgs 3 & 6

Study Area with Zip Codes

46074

46032

46077

46280

46240

46268

46260

46277

46254

46228

☐ Site Location
with 5 mile radius
— Major Highways
— Major Roads

+ Church Locations

miles
0.0   1.5

May 26, 2006

©1997-2006, Percept Group, Inc. www.percept.Info   Sources: Percept, Census Bureau, Claritas   v16.1a   Page 1

Used by permission.

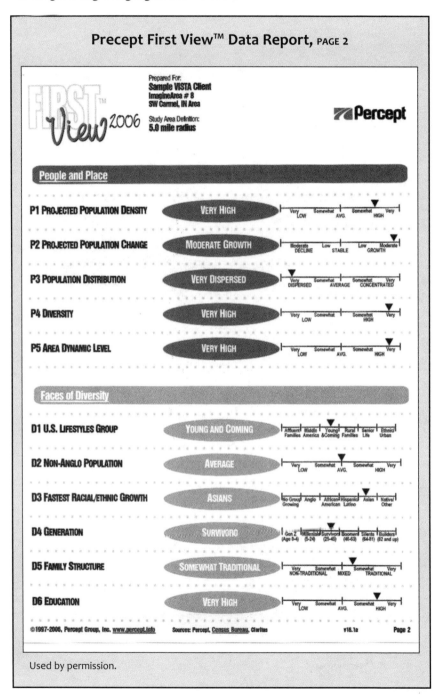

Precept First View™ Data Report, PAGE 2

Prepared For:
Sample VISTA Client
ImagineArea # 8
SW Carmel, IN Area

Study Area Definition:
5.0 mile radius

Percept

People and Place

P1 PROJECTED POPULATION DENSITY — VERY HIGH — Very LOW · Somewhat AVG. · Somewhat HIGH · Very

P2 PROJECTED POPULATION CHANGE — MODERATE GROWTH — Moderate DECLINE · Low STABLE · Low GROWTH · Moderate

P3 POPULATION DISTRIBUTION — VERY DISPERSED — Very DISPERSED · Somewhat AVERAGE · Somewhat CONCENTRATED · Very

P4 DIVERSITY — VERY HIGH — Very LOW · Somewhat · Somewhat HIGH · Very

P5 AREA DYNAMIC LEVEL — VERY HIGH — Very LOW · Somewhat AVG. · Somewhat HIGH · Very

Faces of Diversity

D1 U.S. LIFESTYLES GROUP — YOUNG AND COMING — Affluent Families · Middle America · Young &Coming · Rural Families · Senior Life · Ethnic Urban

D2 NON-ANGLO POPULATION — AVERAGE — Very LOW · Somewhat AVG. · Somewhat HIGH · Very

D3 FASTEST RACIAL/ETHNIC GROWTH — ASIANS — No Group Growing · Anglo · African American · Hispanic/ Latino · Asian · Native/ Other

D4 GENERATION — SURVIVORS — Gen 2 (Age 0-4) · Millennials (5-24) · Survivors (25-45) · Boomers (46-63) · Silents (64-81) · Builders (82 and up)

D5 FAMILY STRUCTURE — SOMEWHAT TRADITIONAL — Very NON-TRADITIONAL · Somewhat MIXED · Somewhat TRADITIONAL · Very

D6 EDUCATION — VERY HIGH — Very LOW · Somewhat AVG. · Somewhat HIGH · Very

©1997-2006, Percept Group, Inc. www.percept.info   Sources: Percept, Census Bureau, Claritas   v16.1a   Page 2

Used by permission.

Precept First View™ Data Report, PAGE 3

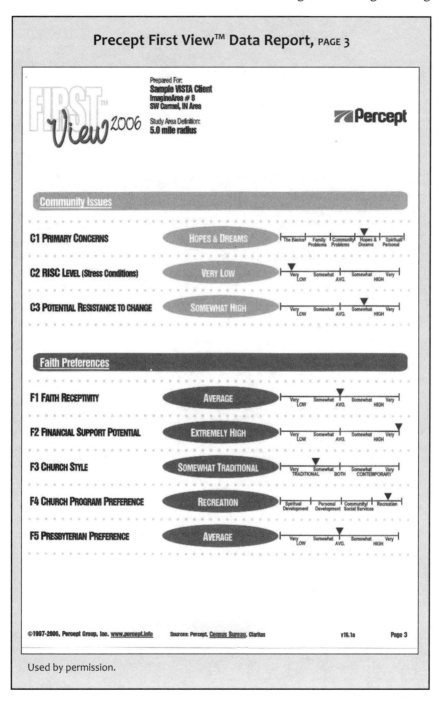

Precept First View™ Data Report, PAGE 4

Prepared For:
Sample VISTA Client
ImagineArea # 8
SW Carmel, IN Area

Study Area Definition:
5.0 mile radius

People and Place Detail

P1: How many people live in the defined study area?
Currently, there are 160,980 persons residing in the defined study area. This represents an increase of 47,818 or 42.3% since 1990. During the same period of time, the U.S. as a whole grew by 18.7%. (see MAP page 4)

Population History & Projection	1990 Census	2000 Census	2006 Update	2011 Projection
Study Area	113,162	147,992	160,980	175,151

P2: Is the population in this area projected to grow?
Yes, between 2006 and 2011, the population is projected to increase by 8.8% or 14,171 additional persons. During the same period, the U.S. population is projected to grow by 4.9%. (see MAP page 4)

Population Change	Actual Change From 1990 to 2000	Actual Change From 2000 to 2006	PROJECTED Change From 2006 to 2011
Study Area	31%	9%	9%
U.S. AVERAGE	13%	5%	5%

P3: How spread out is the population in the study area?
In the study area, the top three quarters of the population resides in approximately 44% of the geographical area. In the U.S. as a whole and in the average community, the top 75% of the population resides in just 25% of the populated geographical area. In comparison, the study area population is *more dispersed* within the overall area.

P4: What is the overall level of diversity in the area?
Based upon the number of different lifestyle and racial/ethnic groups in the area, the overall diversity in the study area can be described as *very high*. See D1 and D2 below.

P5: How dynamic is the study area?
As the population density and overall diversity in an area increase, the environment becomes more complex and challenging. Given these factors, the study area dynamic level can be described as *very high.*

Faces of Diversity Detail

D1: How much lifestyle diversity is represented?
The lifestyle diversity in the area is *extremely high* with a considerable 33 of the 50 U.S. Lifestyles segments represented. Of the six major segment groupings, the largest is referred to as *Young and Coming* which accounts for 42.0% of the households in the area. The top individual segment is *Rising Potential Professionals* representing 19.6% of all households. (see MAP pages 13 and 14)

Households By U.S. Lifestyles Group	Affluent Families	Middle American Families	Young and Coming	Rural Families	Senior Life	Ethnic & Urban Diversity
Study Area	35%	13%	42%	< 1%	5%	4%
U.S. AVERAGE	15%	31%	15%	13%	7%	18%

D2 & D3: How do racial or ethnic groups contribute to diversity in this area?
Based upon the total number of different groups present, the racial/ethnic diversity in the area is *very high*. Among individual groups, *Anglos* represent 74.9% of the population and all other racial/ethnic groups make up only 25.1% which is somewhat below the national average of 33%. The largest of these groups, *African-Americans*, accounts for 15.0% of the total population. *Asians* are projected to be the fastest growing group increasing by 42.0% between 2006 and 2011. (see MAP pages 4 and 7)

Population By Race/Ethnicity	Anglo	African-American	Hispanic	Asian	Native Am. and Other
Study Area	75%	15%	4%	4%	2%
U.S. AVERAGE	67%	12%	14%	4%	3%

D4: What are the major generational groups represented?
The most significant group in terms of numbers and comparison to national averages is *Survivors* (age 25 to 45) who make up 31.7% of the total population in the area compared to 29.8% of the U.S. population as a whole. (see MAP page 4)

Population By Generation	Gen Z 0 to 4	Millenials 5 to 24	Survivors 25 to 45	Boomers 46 to 63	Silents 64 to 81	Builders 82 & up
Study Area	7%	27%	32%	22%	9%	3%
U.S. AVERAGE	7%	28%	30%	22%	10%	3%

Used by permission.

Precept First View™ Data Report, PAGE 5

Prepared For:
Sample VISTA Client
ImagineArea # 8
SW Carmel, IN Area

Study Area Definition:
5.0 mile radius

◢◢Percept

Faces of Diversity Detail (cont.)

D5: Overall, how traditional are the family structures?
The area can be described as *somewhat traditional* due to the above average presence of married persons and two-parent families. (see MAP page 6)

Population By Marital Status (15 and older)	Single (never married)	Divorced or Widowed	Married
Study Area	26%	16%	58%
U.S. AVERAGE	27%	16%	57%

D6: How educated are the adults?
Based upon the number of years completed and college enrollment, the overall education level in the area is *very high*. While 93.6% of the population aged 25 and over have graduated from high school as compared to the national average of 80.4%, college graduates account for 50.5% of those over 25 in the area versus 24.4% in the U.S. (see MAP page 8)

Households with Children by Marital Status	Single Mothers	Single Fathers	Married Couples
Study Area	19%	5%	75%
U.S. AVERAGE	23%	7%	69%

Adult Population By Education Completed	Less than High School	High School	Some College	College Graduate	Post Graduate
Study Area	6%	18%	26%	33%	18%
U.S. AVERAGE	20%	29%	27%	16%	9%

Community Issues Detail

C1: Which household concerns are unusually high in the area?
Concerns which are likely to exceed the national average include: *Satisfying Job/Career, Time for Recreation/Leisure, Neighborhood Gangs, Retirement Opportunities, Aging Parent Care and Long-term Financial Security*. As an overall category, concerns related to *Hopes & Dreams* are the most significant based upon the total number of households and comparison to national averages. (see MAP page 10)

Households By Primary Concerns Group	The Basics	Family Problems	Community Problems	Hopes and Dreams	Spiritual/Personal
Study Area	22%	10%	17%	34%	14%
U.S. AVERAGE	24%	11%	16%	30%	15%

C2: What is the overall community stress level in the area?
Conditions which can contribute to placing an area at risk (particularly the children) are at an overall *very low* level. This is evidenced by noting that on the whole the area is significantly below average in the characteristics known to contribute to community problems such as households below poverty line, adults without a high school diploma, households with a single mother and unusually high concern about issues such as community problems, family problems, and/or basic necessities such as food, housing and jobs. (see MAP pages 5, 6, 8, 9 and 10)

Regionally Indexed Stress Conditions (RISC)	Households Below Poverty (<15,000)	Households with Children: Single Mothers	Adult Pop.: High School Dropouts	Primary Concerns: The Basics	Primary Concerns: Family Problems	Primary Concerns: Community Problems
Study Area	7%	19%	6%	22%	10%	17%
U.S. AVERAGE	14%	23%	20%	24%	11%	16%

C3: How much overall resistance to change is likely in the area?
Based upon the assumption that as a group of people become older and more diverse the potential for resistance to change becomes more significant, the area's potential resistance is likely to be *somewhat high*. (see MAP pages 4-6, 13-14)

Population By Age and Diversity	Average Age	Overall Lifestyle and Racial/Ethnic Diversity
Study Area	36.6	9
U.S. AVERAGE	37.0	6

©1997-2006, Percept Group, Inc. www.percept.info   Sources: Percept, Census Bureau, Claritas   v16.1a   Page 5

Used by permission.

Precept First View™ Data Report, PAGE 6

Prepared For:
Sample VISTA Client
ImagineArea # 8
SW Carmel, IN Area

Study Area Definition:
5.0 mile radius

⌐ Percept

Faith Preferences Detail

F1: What is the likely faith receptivity?
Overall, the likely faith involvement level and preference for historic Christian religious affiliations is *about average* when compared to national averages. (see MAP page 15)

Households By Faith Involvement Level	Not Involved	Somewhat Involved	Strongly Involved
Study Area	37%	31%	32%
U.S. AVERAGE	35%	30%	35%

F2: What is the likely giving potential in the area?
Based upon the average household income of $89,894 per year and the likely contribution behavior in the area, the overall religious giving potential can be described as *extremely high*. (see MAP page 4 and 17)

Households By Religious Giving Potential	Average Annual Household Income	Households Contributing More Than $500 per Year to Churches
Study Area	$89,894	35%
U.S. AVERAGE	$64,816	31%

F3: Do households prefer an overall church style which is more traditional or contemporary?
Based upon likely worship, music and architectural style preferences in the area, the overall church style preference can be described as *somewhat traditional*. (see COMPASS pages 3 and 4)

Households By Church Styles Preferences	Worship: Traditional	Music: Traditional	Architecture: Traditional	Worship: Contemporary	Music: Contemporary	Architecture: Contemporary
Study Area	25%	29%	29%	26%	22%	18%
U.S. AVERAGE	20%	24%	27%	20%	20%	16%

F4: Which general church programs or services are most likely to be preferred in the area?
Church program preferences which are likely to exceed the national average include: *Church Sponsored Day-School, Sports and/or Camping Programs, Cultural Programs (Music, Art, etc.)* and *Adult Theological Discussion Groups*. As an overall category, programs related to *Recreation* are the most significant based upon total number of households and comparison to national averages. (see COMPASS page 2)

Households By Church Program Preference Category	Spiritual Development	Personal Development	Community/ Social Services	Recreation
Study Area	22%	9%	20%	40%
U.S. AVERAGE	25%	10%	20%	38%

F5: How likely are people to express a Presbyterian/Reformed preference?
In the study area, 4.7% of the households are likely to express a Presbyterian/Reformed preference, about the same as the national average of 4.6%. (see MAP page 15)

Households By Religious Preference	No Preference	Non-"Historic Christian" Groups	"Historic Christian" Groups
Study Area	15%	6%	80%
U.S. AVERAGE	15%	8%	77%

Target 2: *Upper-Middle-Class Professional Couples.* Compared to Target 1, this group is somewhat older, and has fewer households with children present. They are similar in that they are largely employed in well-paying managerial-level jobs and have the same ethnic profile. The population living this comfortable lifestyle in the area is expected to grow by 21 percent by 2011. Primary concerns are for caring for aging parents, career satisfaction, and long-term financial security. Like Target 1, faith receptivity and preference for Presbyterian affiliation with this group is average, but worship style preference leans more to traditional with this group than with Target 1.

Target 3: *Inactive Church Members.* An analysis of this group revealed no particular patterns of demographic or psychographic membership. People who had become inactive seemed to have done so for a variety of reasons. The planning committee thought it best to think of this group as a diverse group that should be appealed to somewhat differently than the two new targets.

Understanding Your Target Markets

It is at this point that you would want to obtain a thorough understanding of your target markets. This understanding, putting chapters 4 and 5 research materials into practice, is not something you can get secondhand from a quantitative demographic report. Or we should say that the kind of understanding you get from such a report is not the same as that you get from doing the qualitative investigation of seeing, hearing, and experiencing your target market members face to face. If you want to reach these people "where they live" and establish long-term relationships with them, you'll want to begin that process now by understanding their hopes, dreams, fears, needs, etc. The better you understand them, the better you'll be able to develop an effective marketing strategy.

This is also the point at which you should conduct *image measurement* research and draw your *exchange maps* (chapter 6) to help you determine their perceptions of your organization and the something-of-value they would look to receive in their exchange with you. Also, you should consider the level and nature of *competition* (chapter 6) that you face in getting each targeted segment to engage in exchange with you. A *member satisfaction survey* such as shown in Exhibit 6.11 would allow you to compare active with inactive members to determine where some potential problem areas lie with the inactive member target. This information, along with an understanding of other aspects of the inactive group, will help you in developing your strategy for this targeted segment.

Marketing Strategy

For each targeted market you must develop a marketing strategy for succeeding with that segment. Marketing strategy represents your "game plan" to achieve your goals with that segment. Marketing strategy consists of specifying marketing goals and setting your positioning strategy.

Goals. Specific goals need to be set for each targeted group. In the case of Target 1, the young families target market, the goals may read as:

• To provide at least one program ministry that will prove successful in helping young parents cope with the stresses of caring for small children, in the next 12 months. For example, a parent's-day-out program, or a day-care program for children of working couples might be started.

• To provide a training program of at least 12 sessions for parents of hyperactive children, to be followed by an ongoing support group for the parents.

• To provide nursery services during Sunday school and worship hours, and on Wednesday evening, to allow young parents to participate in Sunday and Wednesday evening services without concern for the care of their children.

Positioning. Using the format described in the previous chapter, let's say that First Church had the following positioning strategy for Target 1, Young Families:

To young upper-middle-class families who want to find a church home with other people like themselves and who are looking for a deepening spiritual relationship with their creator, First Church offers a warm, caring, Christ-centered environment and the opportunity to interact with other active lifestyle-oriented families.

Positioning strategy statements should be developed for each targeted segment. While the positioning strategy indicates how you can best appeal to the target group (i.e., hit their "sweet spot" revealed in your efforts to better understand them), you obviously must already have or be able to develop the ability to deliver on the promises made in the positioning statement.

Design and Implement Marketing Tactics

The next step in marketing strategy is to develop your tactical implementation of your strategy—your marketing mix. We define marketing mix as follows.

Marketing mix is the particular blend of controllable marketing variables that the religious organization uses to achieve its objectives in the target segment. This is the means by which the organization implements its positioning strategy.

Although many variables make up the marketing mix, they can be classified into a few major groups. McCarthy formulated a popular classification called the "four P's: *product, price, place, and promotion.*[7] These variables can be translated for religious marketing as follows:

Product—the program(s) and ministries that the religious organization offers a target segment (covered in chapter 9).

Price—the sacrifices or commitments that the target group must make to use or adopt the organization's program(s) (covered in chapter 9).

Place—the means or location by which the program is delivered to the target segment (covered in chapter 9).

Promotion—the means used to communicate the attributes of the organization's program(s) to the targeted segment (covered in chapter 10).

In the case of First Church, it might have a marketing mix consisting of several programs, with different "prices" or "costs," (see Exhibit 6.8) delivered through a variety of means and communicated with different messages using several media. For example, young families are found to move frequently. The marketing mix for this target group might, therefore, include the following elements:

Product—A "Welcome to Carmel" program, in which new families are identified and given welcome baskets with information, gifts, and offers of help in getting the new family settled.

Price—Targeted families may be asked to give up time to come to a welcome dinner for recently arrived residents.

Place—The congregation might rent a hall instead of using the church facility for the welcome dinner.

Promotion—A printed invitation, followed by a personal phone invitation to the welcome dinner. Claritas will supply the mailing lists for all households in the Kids and Cul-de-Sacs segment within the Carmel zip codes.

The product in this case is capitalizing on one of First Church's existing assets—the spiritual gift of hospitality, discovered when conducting a spiritual gift inventory as part of the assessment of the congregational strengths and weaknesses. When delivering the welcome basket, informal marketing research might be done, consisting of a few questions to determine the needs and interests of the young family, including their entertainment/recreation interests. If certain entertainment activities frequently surface during these welcome visits/interviews, some specific recreation-based ministries might be developed to satisfy those needs. For example, we saw in Exhibit 7.4 that some of the activities frequently enjoyed by the Kids and Cul-de-sacs and Home Sweet Home groups were soccer, softball, in-line skating, and mountain biking. Some programs might be directed at the parents, others at the entire family. By asking a few questions and making simple observations, this informal marketing research could prove valuable in suggesting other specific outreach programs to this targeted segment. First Church would want to be sure to send people from its congregation who fit the profile of the Kids and Cul-de-sacs segment they are targeting.

The objective of developing the marketing mix is to put together the most *effective* and *efficient* means possible to achieve the marketing goals. This means developing an action program or set of tactics and establishing a marketing budget.

Exhibit 8.7 Implementation Plan Control Sheet

Time	Responsibility	Goal	Results	Deviance From Goal
1. Call Apartment Complexes and Housing Authority for names of new residents. Determine which are young families, ethnic composition.				
Every Wednesday	J. Smith	6/3 6/10 6/17 6/24		
2. Fill Welcome Baskets with materials.				
Every Saturday	R. Jones H. Brown	6/6 6/13 6/20 6/27		
3. Have baskets delivered by young couples of simiar ethnic background. Dinner invitations made.				
Every Tuesday or Thursday	A. Couple B. Couple C. Couple D. Couple	6/2 6/12 6/16 6/18 6/25	50 percent acceptance of dinner invitation	60 percent acceptance for June

Implementation Action Plan

The marketing strategy and related tactics need to be turned into a specific set of actions for accomplishing the marketing goals. Each element should be elaborated into appropriate actions. For example, the element "reach newly arrived young families" could lead to the actions of obtaining the names and characteristics of new young families moving into the community, preparation of the welcome baskets, delivery of the welcome baskets by church couples, and so on. (See Exhibit 8.7.)

Marketing Budget

The goals, strategies, and planned actions allow the planners to build a budget. A schedule should be prepared such as in Exhibit 8.8, where each task is listed, along with its cost and time of occurrence.[8]

331

| Exhibit 8.8 | **Marketing Budget and Plan Schedule** | | | | | | |

WEEK

Task	1	2	3	4	5	6-8	TOTAL
Program Development	$25						$ 25
Material		$100	$100	$100	$100	$100	700
Printing			75	75	75		225
Promotion					80	80	320
COST TOTALS	$25	$100	$175	$175	$225	$180	$1270

Marketing Control

Plans are useful only if they are implemented and monitored. The purpose of a marketing control system is to maximize the probability that the organization will achieve the short-term and long-term objectives of the organization's ministries. It accomplishes this purpose by measuring the ongoing results of a plan against the plan's goals, indicating where corrective action should be taken before it is too late. See chapter 13 for a more thorough discussion of how to evaluate the success of your programs.

The marketing plan for the First Presbyterian Church of Carmel, Indiana, described above was an example of adherent marketing. The same planning process could be used for developing marketing plans for fellowship marketing (i.e., ministries targeting current members) or for social services marketing (i.e., delivery of services to external groups). Following the format of the EMP, the key in all these cases will be to first *understand,* before you *plan* and *act.*

Again, planning is necessary to the success of any major effort. However, it need not be overwhelming in complexity. Neither does planning have to be boring. Keep it natural; keep it simple. Remember: a plan should be kept as simple as possible, but no simpler.[9]

---

[1] See Randall Y. Odom and W. Randy Boxx, "Environment, Planning Processes, and Organizational Performance of Churches," *Strategic Management Journal* 9 (1988): 197-205.
[2] *Ibid.,* p. 202.

[3] This section is adapted from William A. Cohen, *The Practice of Marketing Management* (New York: Macmillan, 1988), pp. 44-47.

[4] See William A. Cohen, *The Marketing Plan,* 5th ed. (New York: John Wiley and Sons, 2006), and *Developing a Winning Marketing Plan* (New York: John Wiley and Sons, 1987), pp. 2-6.

[5] This mission statement is based on that of the Crossroads Community Church in Camarillo, California, as quoted in Michael T. Dibbert, *Spiritual Leadership, Responsible Management* (Grand Rapids: Zondervan, 1989), p. 45. For more information on the development of a church's mission, see chapter 4 of Dibbert's book, chapter 6 of our book, and Rick Warren's *The Purpose Driven Church.* For examples of church mission statements, go to http://www.missionstatements.com/church_mission_statements.html. Also see our resource guide for more resources to help you prepare a mission statement.

[6] There are numerous instruments for measuring the spiritual gifts of a congregation. See Fuller Institute, *Spiritual Gifts and Church Growth: Modified Houts*; D.W. Hoover and R.W. Leenerts, *Enlightened With His Gifts: A Bible Study on Spiritual Gifts* (St. Louis: Lutheran Growth, 1979); *Discover Your Gifts: Workbook* (Grand Rapids: Christian Reformed Home Missions, 1981); Fuller Institute, *Trenton Spiritual Gifts Analysis*; and an empirically tested instrument, Roy C. Naden and Robert J. Cruise, *The Spiritual Gifts Inventory* (Berrien Springs, Mich.: Institute of Church Ministry).

[7] See William D. Perreault, Joseph P. Cannon, and E. Jerome McCarthy, *Basic Marketing: A Marketing Planning Strategy Approach,* 16th ed. (Homewood, Ill: R.D. Irwin, 2008).

[8] See Cohen, *The Practice of Marketing Management,* p. 55.

[9] For an excellent resource on planning and strategies, see Peter F. Drucker, "Planning and Strategies," *The Nonprofit Drucker* (Tyler, Tex.: The Leadership Network, 1989), vol. 2. *The Nonprofit Drucker* is a five-volume cassette tape library. Each volume contains five audiocassette tapes. Volume 3 of the library is devoted to marketing planning and strategies.

• •

WORKSHEETS: CHAPTER 8

Strategic Marketing Planning

Using what you have done in previous worksheets as input where possible, develop your marketing plan using this format:

A. Mission Statement (from chapter 6 worksheet)

_____

_____

_____

B. Situation Analysis

Include material from chapter 6 worksheets plus additional insights from analysis conducted for this chapter.

1. Internal Environment/Publics

_____

_____

_____

   a. Background Data

	Year 1	Year 2	Year 3
Membership			
Average Worship Attendance			
Attendance as Percent of Membership			
Annual Capacity			
Main Worship Attendance			
Worshippers as Percent of Capacity			
Operating Income			
Operating Expenses and Transfers			
Balance			

b. Resources and Constraints

_____

_____

_____

Exhibit 8.3 Strengths/Weaknesses Analysis							
	Strength				**Weakness**		
Resource	H	M	L	N	L	M	H
People 1. Adequate number? 2. Spiritual gifts? 3. Enthusiastic? 4. Loyal? 5. Service-minded?							
Money 1. Adequate? 2. Flexible?							
Facilities 1. Adequate? 2. Flexible? 3. Location quality?							
Systems 1. Information system quality? 2. Planning system quality? 3. Control system quality?							
Image 1. General reputation? 2. Among target group?							
Notes: *H=high;* *M=medium;* *L=low;* *N=neutral*							

2. Input Environment/Publics

_____

_____

_____

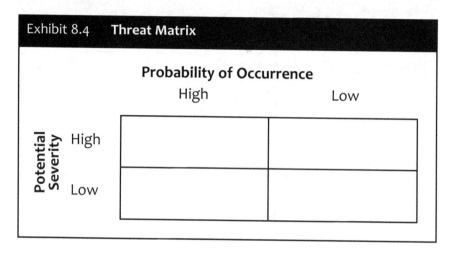

3. External Environment/Publics

_____

_____

_____

_____

a. Threat Analysis Matrix

Exhibit 8.4	Threat Matrix

Probability of Occurrence

		High	Low
Potential Severity	High		
	Low		

b. Opportunity Analysis Matrix

Exhibit 8.5	Opportunity Matrix

Probability of Success

		High	Low
Potential Attractiveness	High		
	Low		

C. Target Market

_____
_____
_____

1. Identify the segments that you will target:
   Segments Targeted: Describe in detail each targeted segment using chapter 5 and chapter 7 worksheets, plus insights gained from discussion in chapter 8.

   Target 1: _____
   _____
   _____

   Target 2: _____
   _____
   _____

   Target 3: _____
   _____
   _____

2. Describe your targeting strategy:
   undifferentiated marketing   _____
   differentiated marketing   _____
   concentrated marketing   _____

3. Image of organization by targeted segment (from chapter 6 worksheet):
   Target 1 image: _____
   _____
   _____

   Target 2 image: _____
   _____
   _____

Target 3 image: _____

_____

_____

4. Exchange maps for target markets (from chapter 6 worksheet)
   Target 1 map:

   Target 2 map:

   Target 3 map:

D. Marketing Strategy
1. Goals

_____

_____

_____

2. Positioning
   Describe your positioning strategy statement for each targeted segment (from chapter 7 worksheet):

Targeted Segment	**Positioning Strategy Statement**
_____	_____
_____	_____
_____	_____

E. Marketing Tactics
1. Design Marketing Tactics
   a. Product/program/ministry (see chapter 9)

   _____
   _____
   _____

   b. Distribution of product/program/ministry (see chapter 9)

   _____
   _____
   _____

   c. Price (see chapter 9)

   _____
   _____
   _____

   d. Promotion (see chapter 10)

   _____
   _____
   _____

2. Design Implementation Plan Control Sheet (similar to Exhibit 8.7)

   _____
   _____
   _____

F. Budget

   _____
   _____
   _____

G. Control (see chapter 13)

   _____
   _____
   _____

Part 5: Design and Implement Marketing Tactics

THE EFFECTIVE MARKETING PROCESS

Adopting a Marketing Philosophy

↓

Develop an Understanding

↓

Plan the Marketing Strategy

↓

Design and Implement the Marketing Tactics
CHAPTER 9: *Product, Price, and Place Decisions*
CHAPTER 10: *Advertising and Public Relations*
CHAPTER 11: *Fund-raising Decisions*

↓

Connect With Exchange Partners

In part 1 of this book we detailed the dynamic environmental forces leading some religious organizations to recognize the potential for marketing to contribute to achievement of their mission. This led to a description of the appropriate role for marketing in religious organizations. We then discussed how the marketing orientation philosophy is consistent with certain components of the mission of many congregations. The effective marketing process (EMP) was introduced as a model for helping organize and implement marketing programs.

In part 2 we discussed the first step of the EMP model, adopting a marketing philosophy. We indicated what a highly responsive, marketing-oriented organization looks like in describing this stage of the process.

The next step of the EMP (understanding) was described in part 3. This involved both *how* to understand (marketing research) as well as *what* to understand (the factors influencing our behavior).

Part 4, developing a marketing plan, then described the third step of the model. Here we indicated what it means to think like a marketing decision-maker, and how to segment a market, choose segments as targets, and then position your offerings to those targeted segments. The final act in this step was the planning process itself, with the output being a strategic marketing plan for your organization.

In part 5 we continue our discussion of the EMP model by describing its fourth step, "doing" marketing (designing and implementing marketing tactics), by focusing on the "marketing mix"—the mix of product (ministries or programs), price (what target audiences must give up in terms of time, money, and psychological or social costs), place (the location or means of delivering the ministry), and promotion (the message and media by which we communicate the product's benefits). These four tactical tools are the means of carrying out the position we planned to occupy in the minds of the targeted segment. These tools are discussed in chapter 9 (product, place, price) and chapter 10 (promotion—i.e., advertising and public relations). A further "doing" activity is the object of chapter 11—fund-raising.

CHAPTER 9:

Product, Price, and Place Decisions

"Forget the former things; do not dwell on the past" (ISAIAH 43:18, NIV).

In this chapter we will address the following questions:

1. What are the three levels of our "products"?
2. What products should be contained in our portfolio?
3. What branding opportunities exist for us?
4. By what process might we develop new products?
5. How should we "price" our products?
6. How should we "distribute" our products?

Throughout the previous chapters we have described the previous steps of the Effective Marketing Process—establishing a philosophy, developing an understanding of your exchange partners, and creating a marketing plan. We are now ready to discuss developing and implementing marketing tactics—the marketing mix of product, price, place, and promotion.

This chapter will focus on the first three P's of the marketing mix: product, price and place. The following chapter will address the last P, the promotional component.

Part 1: Product Decisions

Hundreds, if not thousands, of religious organizations across the United States have begun to drastically alter the "product" they offer to their "markets." A few examples are described below.

• Hot Metal Bridge Faith Community is a Pittsburgh-based congregation composed of "an eclectic group of drunks and college kids, suburbanites and street people, Catholics and scrawny punk artists with New Testament citations tattooed on their chests." The young pastors, a United Methodist and a Presbyterian, also sport religious tattoos. Dramatic plays, in which the congregation plays the roles of biblical characters, replace sermons in the worship service. Hot Metal is an example of the "emergent church" movement, in which ministries have sprung up around a central interest such as yoga, dance, art, or other passions (one Minneapolis group attracts drummers). The pastors at Hot Metal Bridge maintain the dramas are tools to teach people about God.

• St. Francis Episcopal Church in Stamford, Connecticut, is but one example of congregations who have attracted new members and gotten dormant members to return to services by welcoming people with their pets. At St. Francis people bring their pets to the altar when taking Holy Communion. Congregants at Temple Beth Shir Sholom, in Santa Monica, have an animal prayer sung to Sabbath Prayer from *Fiddler on the Roof.* All Saints Episcopal Church in Fort Lauderdale doubled attendance at Sunday evening services when it invited members to bring their pets once a month. Rabbis in Palm Beach, Florida, and Baltimore have noted the popularity of pet blessings conducted at their synagogues. Pet services are aiming to draw in the elderly individuals, among others, whose pets are their only companions.[1]

These examples, while extreme by some standards, illustrate the efforts some congregational leaders are taking to change their products in order to make them relevant to their markets. We do not want to imply that such radical methods are always necessary for congregations to generate products capable of helping them achieve their goals. We do, however, want to help you identify how you might benefit from adjusting what you offer to the target markets selected in chapter 8 that you desire to serve. The major topics of this chapter will provide some ideas for how you can design, price, and deliver products that help you implement a strategy to connect with your target audience.

A special word to the reader. When presenting new ideas to an audience, the burden is on the writer to translate the ideas into the reader's vocabulary, and to demonstrate how to apply to his or her institution. Writing a text on marketing for leaders of religious organizations is not a simple task.

The religious world has few corollaries for many of the marketing terms that are familiar to other institutions, such as *market, customer, consumer, product,* and *price.* Having noted this, we will alert the reader to the fact that in this chapter we will use marketing terms borrowed from a secular marketing vocabulary, without any attempt to cast them in "religious" terms. We do this for the sake of simplicity in reading, and because we assume that by now you have progressed in your understanding of marketing concepts to the point where "secular" marketing terms will cause no problems, and may add to the learning.

The Nature of Products

Chapter 6 stated that products can consist of goods, services, events, experiences, people, places, properties, organizations, information, activities, or ideas. We will use the term *product,* rather than *service* or *ministry,* in this chapter because it is the more inclusive term. *A product is anything that can be offered to a market to satisfy a need. Other names for a product would be a value package or benefit bundle. For a religious organization, these products are sometimes called ministries, programs, services, or offerings.*

Exhibit 6.8 indicated that your congregation is engaged in offering different products or benefit bundles whose consumption incurs different types of costs for the consumer of those products. In the definition below, as well as in Exhibit 6.8, it is important to note that products are to be viewed from the perspective of the *consumer* rather than the *producer*. You must determine what type of product will have value in the eyes of the product's consumers, if you are to successfully engage them in exchange.

A producer's sense of a product's value is determined not by its intrinsic characteristics, but rather by what *results* it can produce (see Exhibit 9.1). Sometimes a pastor or rabbi will see a ministry as important because he or she has a personal desire to offer it, even though this same opinion is not shared by the congregation or by the target consumers. Exhibit 9.1, however, suggests that the value a pastor or rabbi places on a product should be based on its abilities to provide true need satisfaction for the consumer and to satisfy other mission related objectives, not because it is someone's "pet" project.

Research that produces findings such as in Exhibit 9.1 will help to determine which ministries are perceived as most important and satisfying to your target market.

Levels of Products

Products that are completely contained within chapter 1's Exhibit 1 worship and evangelism cells (cells 1 and 2) are not subject to marketing efforts, and are not the object of product management decision-making. However, some products have components that fall within these unmarketable cells and some that fall within the

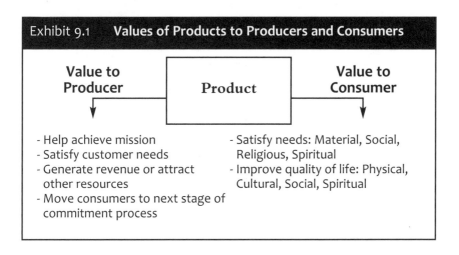

Exhibit 9.1   Values of Products to Producers and Consumers

Value to Producer	Product	Value to Consumer

- Help achieve mission
- Satisfy customer needs
- Generate revenue or attract other resources
- Move consumers to next stage of commitment process

- Satisfy needs: Material, Social, Religious, Spiritual
- Improve quality of life: Physical, Cultural, Social, Spiritual

marketable cells of the exhibit. It is these products that we will now discuss. We will then discuss those products that fall completely within the marketable cells of Exhibit 1 (cells 3 and 4).

Religious organizations differ from other types of organizations with respect to the ability and willingness of decision makers to alter products to fit market conditions. This is because at least some of the products of the religious organization are composed of both sacred and non-sacred components. What is "sacred" may itself be sacred by its nature (e.g., sacred scripture, religious doctrine) or be sacred by tradition (e.g., the type of music considered appropriate to be used in a worship service). Products that have these sacred components sometimes also have a nonsacred component as well. It is this nonsacred component that might be most easily (in terms of gaining consensus by key decision-makers) be adjusted to fit market needs (see Exhibit 9.2)[2].

1. Sacred core (i.e., sacred by nature or by doctrine [God/ Scripture] [nonnegotiable])

2. Sacred by tradition (i.e., how our faith community has done this over time [negotiable])

3. Nonsacred (i.e., the aspects of the product seen as most readily adjustable to fit the market)

It is important to think of approaching negotiating the marketing decisions related to your products in the same way as Fisher and Ury described the way to approach negotiation in their famous book

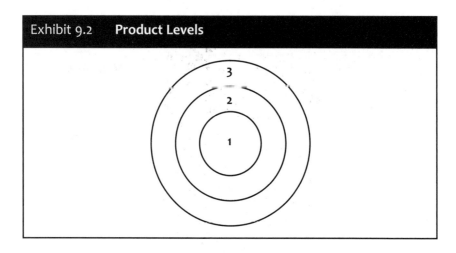

Exhibit 9.2	**Product Levels**

Getting to Yes (see Exhibit 9.3): be hard on *merits* or principles at stake, but soft on *people*. That is, you should not alter the "sacred" component of your product, but should gently guide people to help them become willing to be innovative and flexible when it comes to adjusting these aspects of the product that fall outside the sacred core

---

Exhibit 9.3   How to Negotiate the Negotiable Aspects of Your Product

In their best-selling book *Getting to Yes*, Roger Fisher and William Ury of the Harvard Negotiation Project, provide some useful advice for those leaders trying to make adjustments in the negotiable aspects of their products (i.e., levels 2 and 3 of Exhibit 9.2). They maintain that the typical negotiation process involves positional bargaining (i.e., each side takes a position, argues for it, and makes concessions to reach a compromise), and produces unwise agreements. Positional bargaining is not the best way to achieve the goals of any negotiation. Negotiations:

- should produce a wise agreement if agreement is possible
- should be efficient, and
- should improve or at least not damage the relationship between the parties.

(A "wise agreement" is defined as "one which meets the legitimate interests of each side to the extent possible, resolves conflicting interests fairly, is durable, and takes community interests into account" [p. 4].) Fisher and Ury recommend a four element alternative to positional bargaining:

1. People: Separate the people from the problem. People's egos become entangled with their positions, and emotions run high. Instead, participants should see themselves as working together to attack the problem, not each other: i.e., separate the people from the problem.

2. Interests: Focus on interests, not positions. "Your position is something you have decided upon. Your interests are what caused you to so decide" (p. 42).

3. Options: Generate a variety of possibilities before deciding what to do.

4. Criteria: Insist that the result be based on some objective criteria.

These four elements can be applied to a variety of types of negotiations, including your attempts to make changes in the negotiable and adjustable aspects of your products to make them more attractive to your market.[3]

(level 1) boundary. The implication is that you can collectively de-termine where to draw those boundary lines between the three lev-els of products. We suggest that a leadership team, rather than a single individual, would best explore this topic. Once you have suc-cessfully determined those boundaries through consensus, you'll have a base of support, as well as ideas, for instituting innovative marketing plans for your products.

Conflicts that have occurred in some congregations, with regards to adopting marketing thought and practice, have been over where the boundary lines should be drawn. Some congregations have had an exodus of members who believe the line has been drawn beyond where they think it should. This fracturing can occur when the per-ception exists that an attempt is being made to "market religion" rather than to "market the congregation."[4] Congregations might have internal conflict in determining what is "marketable," and how to market the marketable aspects of a product. For example, *Worship* (cell 1 of Exhibit 1) falls into the un-marketable aspects of Exhibit 1, but some aspects of the *worship service* are considered changeable to fit the needs of exchange partners. *Worship* is considered sacred core (level 1), *worship service* is considered tangible (levels 2 and 3), and therefore marketable. Here is how some congregations might see the 3 levels for their main worship service:

Worship Service
1. Sacred core (non-negotiable): contents of service (scripture, sermon, sacraments, etc.)
2. Sacred by tradition (negotiable): order of service, time of ser-vice, type of music and instruments, etc.
3. Nonsacred (adjustable): proper dress, recording of service, de-sign of bulletin, etc.

But some people see the entire worship service as the sacred core, and will leave the congregation rather than be willing to use the societal marketing orientation (SMO) to guide the structuring of any part of the worship service. Such people might be willing to use the SMO to guide other programs (e.g., a grief ministry, such as was described in the supplement to chapter 2), so they aren't opposed to marketing or the SMO, they just see the boundary line differently than others who are willing to make those changes.

How do congregational leaders avoid this type of dysfunctional conflict? By educating the congregation on the source of the conflict (i.e., a difference of opinion of what is contained in each of the 3 levels), and using a negotiation process, such as Fisher and Ury's, to arrive at a consensus of where lines can be drawn. We suggest a meeting during which the interested parties' interests are put on a "whiteboard" or "flip charts," indicating what is core and what is tangible for "products" that are controversial marketing objects. Where controversy continues, segmenting the market and designing products that address the needs of the segments is advised wherever possible.

When people disagree over where to draw the boundary line between the levels, they are merely confirming the phenomenon of market segmentation, described in chapter 7. Solutions can be found by acknowledging that each segment deserves a "product" capable of delivering satisfaction that segment needs (e.g., scheduling a "traditional" early service and a "contemporary" later service). It is important to understand that we are not advocating division within the congregation here. Each of us are members of different segments within our congregation based on our age, gender, marital status, whether we are a couple with or without children, etc., so segmentation already exists in many forms in our congregation. Segmentation based on different opinions about where to draw boundaries surrounding the sacred and nonsacred levels is merely one more instance of segmenting that can lead to an amicable solution. People who disagree with one another should be able to acknowledge that neither position is right or wrong—just different. Segmentation followed by solutions that address both positions can result in satisfaction without dissolution. Remember the point made by Fisher and Ury: separate people from the problem.

Marketing Products to Satisfy Needs

In developing a product for an external or internal market, the organization must distinguish between the need and the product, and first focus on the need that the product is intended to address.

The Need. At the most fundamental level stands the need that the product is satisfying. Needs are states of felt deprivation. As such, they should not be thought of as existing in a tangible (i.e., product) form. For example, people don't need youth camp, but they need to expose their children to entertainment and educational experiences that will enhance their children's spiritual life. People don't need Vacation Bible School, but they need to have a means of enjoyable religious education for children and adolescents during the summer. The classic example given, which illustrates this point, is that people don't need drill bits; they need holes! Sometimes the need is a complex combination of biogenic, psychogenic, and sociogenic forces (see chapter 5). For example, what is the need that people have that is satisfied by a cup of Starbucks coffee? One might say that it is a combination of thirst, a desire to pamper oneself, and a desire to interact with others in a social setting. Thirst, which on the surface might appear to be the primary need, may in fact be the least motivating of the three need components for many people. You don't just consume a cup of Starbucks *coffee*—you consume the Starbucks *experience.* Starbucks confirms this "need" when they refer to Starbucks as "the third place" (work and home being the other two places we spend our time). You'll have to "dig deep" to uncover the needs that motivate people in your markets to seek satisfaction.

Tangible Products. The product is always made available to the consumer in some tangible form. The *need* for spiritual inspiration can be provided through the *tangible products* of a sermon, a Sunday school lesson, a midweek prayer service, religious literature, and the like. The point is that needs may evolve, but are enduring, and that there is more than one product that could be developed to fit the need. People don't *need* products. They *want* products to satisfy a need. This is an important distinction, because it spells the difference between mistakenly concentrating on improving the characteristics of the product (making better drill bits) rather than finding ways of satisfying enduring needs (making holes).

Organizations that believe that consumers "need our product" tend to have product orientations (see chapter 2) to the marketplace. They believe that by making their product "better," as they define better, will guarantee that they will always have a ready market for whatever they decide to make. These organizations commonly wonder what happened when the market begins to desert them for an organization that focused on customer needs first rather than the organization's product. You need only to examine your own behavior as a consumer to recognize the verity of this statement. As your need for, say, self-expression in photography evolves over time, you will favor those companies that are producing products capable of growing with your skill level. A company that concentrated on producing more sophisticated film cameras might find their market share being lost to such a market needs-oriented company producing digital cameras and photo modification software. It would be cold comfort indeed to know that you had "the best product" on the market if no one wanted it to satisfy his or her need.

Consequently, all present or potential ministries should be subjected to this test: Does this program do the most effective and efficient job of satisfying the core need that the consumer is seeking to satisfy at this point in time?

In addition to satisfying the core need, the tangible product must also satisfy several other criteria of importance to the religious organization. Organizations typically need a portfolio of products in order to achieve these multiple objectives.

Product Portfolios

The introduction or continuation of any ministry, program, or activity should be based on that ministry's potential for accomplishing some basic objectives growing out of a marketing plan. These objectives are related to balancing the product portfolio from three perspectives: the organization's mission, the decision processes of target consumers, and concern for resource attraction.

Missional Objectives. The first step in developing a strategic marketing plan is to establish the organization's mission. The intent here is not to discuss how a mission might be developed,[5] but rather to indicate how a church's products should relate to that mission. In the

351

previous chapter the mission statement of the hypothetical First Presbyterian Church contained four major components: praise, prepare, provide, and proclaim, roughly corresponding to the four cells in Exhibit 1. If the church is to fulfill such a mission, it needs a balanced *product portfolio*, which would include products for each of these four missional objectives—products relating to the worship and disciplining experience, products intended to edify members and enhance their talents, products that permit the church to foster loving fellowship among all its constituents, and outreach products that use the church's resources to meet the spiritual, physical, and social needs of the world around the church.

A product portfolio is the set of all product lines that a religious organization makes available to consumers, internal and external to the organization.

A product line is a group of products, within a product portfolio, that are closely related in the organization's objectives, target audience, or function.

Developing a balanced product portfolio requires having products related to each missional area, specifically designed for each targeted consumer group.

A religious organization's identity is, to a large degree, dependent on how it defines and carries out its mission. It is important, therefore, that the organization plans product portfolios to enhance the organization's identity along the relevant four dimensions. Of course, not every religious organization may have a mission statement that stresses all four cells of Exhibit 1.

An example will help to illustrate these concepts. Exhibit 9.4 lists a few of the major products (ministries) offered by Willow Creek Community Church (Willow Creek has more than 100 ministries or programs; only a sampling of them are listed here). For each major component of a hypothetical mission for their church, a product line is listed consisting of products targeted at different age groups. The entire set of product lines comprises the product portfolio. Every religious organization should establish a mission that reflects its answers to the question of why the organization exists.

Exhibit 9.4	Willow Creek Community Church—Product Portfolio			
Missional Objectives *Ministries by Age Group*	**Worship** *Product Line:*	**Fellowship** *Product Line:*	**Evangelism** *Product Line:*	**Social Action** *Product Line:*
All Ages	Saturday night service Sunday service translations in Spanish, Korean, Chinese	Sports Ministry—sports activities for different age groups. Camp Paradise—camping for all ages	Wednesday night service verbal witnessing by lay members	Protection—providing safe environments for all ages Food Pantry—emergency food and clothing for families in need
Children	Promiseland—nursing care and creative playtime for toddler during adult service	PromiseTowne—6 weeks through 6 years Bible classes, other activities		Grief Support for Children
Youth	Heroes—teaching those in their 20s spiritual lessons Earth—Friday night worship community	Metro 212—small group ministry for youth	Elevate—worship services intended to reach young people	Axis—those in their 20s serving neighbors in need
Single Adults and Couples	Marriage Ministry—committed to building Christ-centered marriages	Bravehearts—women getting together in adventures to share life experiences.	Seeker Small Group—singles curious about God	Eagle's Nest—small groups for parents of children with special needs

353

Failure to carefully plan a product portfolio that is consistent with the missional objectives will result in an identity that is vague and confusing to internal and external publics alike.

Influencing Behavior in Faith and Practice. A portfolio of products should also have as its objective the leading of persons along toward increasing maturity in their faith (e.g., disciplining). Individual ministries should be planned with regard to how they contribute to a commitment of persons to enter a process by which they will become aware of the church or synagogue, develop interest in its offerings, go through a period of exposure to its offerings, and experience spiritual and social growth. Products should be targeted to meet the needs of people at each stage of this process, and to move them to the next stage. For example, at Willow Creek the Sunday morning service is intended to appeal to the general public with a sermon, drama, and music, while the Wednesday night service is intended to prepare those who have moved from curiosity to a more serious interest in membership through a study of the Bible and church doctrines.

Securing Financial and Volunteer Resources. Some products of a church or synagogue have the objective of attracting volunteers, funds, or donated resources. Annual fund drives, sales of goods, stewardship programs, and the like are products designed with the objective of attracting resources necessary for the congregation's continued operation. Just as a product portfolio must be balanced to achieve missional objectives and to fulfill consumer needs at various stages of a commitment/assimilation process, so also churches and synagogues must have a balance of products that generate and absorb resources.

Failure to design attractive products that generate revenues can result in the perception that a church or synagogue is constantly begging for money. Such a perception may well inhibit the consumption of other products by people who are afraid to come near the place for fear of being asked to contribute funds for its operations.

Branding Religious Institutional Products

The idea of branding the products of religious organizations has gained increasing popularity in the past few years.[6] We will attempt to provide some guidance for those interested in pursuing a branding strategy for their institution.[7]

What Is a Brand? A brand is a product that adds dimensions that differentiate it in some way from other products or services designed to satisfy the same need. These differences may be functional, rational, or tangible, but they might also be symbolic, emotional, or intangible. Not all of our needs are rational or tangible, and brands may be powerful motivators when we seek to satisfy our desires for intangibles. Branding has been used since the medieval guilds required craftspeople to put trademarks on their products to protect themselves and consumers against inferior quality. Likewise, when an artist signs his/her work, they are branding it. Branding is used virtually anywhere individual choice exists. For example, you can brand a physical good (NIV Bibles, Baldwin pianos), a service (Thrivent Financial for Lutherans), a retail establishment (Disney Store, Zondervan Bookstore), a person (Peter Drucker, Rick Warren), a place (Lourdes, Crystal Cathedral), an organization (Willowcreek Association, Leadership Network), an idea (Right to Life, Purpose Driven), events (National Bible Bowl), experiences (Family Camp), or information (*Christianity Today*).

Role of Brands. Brands help simplify our decision-making process. As our lives become more complicated, rushed, and time-starved, the ability of a brand to take the place of all the information search and evaluation we would need to do for unknown products is invaluable. Brands signal a certain level of quality and need fulfillment based on past experiences that provides risk reduction and assurance to the buyer. Successful brands may be a powerful means of making the organization's competition irrelevant to the brand loyal user—reducing the cost of competition and raising the entry barrier for new competitors.

Building Strong Brands. Research has shown that the world's strongest brands share 10 attributes:[8]

1. The brand excels at delivering the benefits that consumers truly desire.

2. The brand stays relevant.

3. Customers perceive real value in the offering (i.e., the ratio of what's received in exchange for what they have to give up to get it).

4. The brand is properly positioned.

5. The brand consistently sends clear messages about its position.

6. The brand portfolio and hierarchy makes sense.

7. The brand makes use of and coordinates a full repertoire of marketing activities to build brand equity.

8. The brand's managers understand what the brand means to consumers.

9. The brand is given proper, sustained support.

10. The organization monitors sources of brand equity.

The implications of this list are that the desirable benefits that accrue to an organization and its consumers come at a price. Branding involves more than just attaching a clever name to a product and reaping rewards—building a strong brand takes persistent, knowledgeable effort on the part of the brander.

How then do you "brand" a product? Although organizations provide the impetus to brand creation through marketing programs and other activities, ultimately a brand is something that resides in the minds of consumers. A brand is a perceptual entity that is rooted in reality but reflects the perceptions and perhaps even the idiosyncrasies of consumers. To brand a product, it is necessary to teach consumers "who" the product is—by giving it a name and using other brand elements to help identify it—as well as what the product does and why consumers should care.

For branding strategies to be successful and brand value to be created, consumers must be convinced that there are meaningful differences among brands in the product category. The key to branding is that consumers must not think that all the brands in the category are the same. The challenge for building strong brands is ensuring that the experiences that consumers have with the brand are so uniquely satisfying that they distinguish that brand in a positive way from the other products they might have selected.

Some brands are capable of connecting with consumers at an emotional level to provide a satisfying experience that goes beyond functional performance. Apple Computer epitomizes this type of brand in the commercial world. While there are functional differences between Apple's products and their competitors, the brand's success in connecting with consumers at an emotional level has been equally impactful in their resurgence after almost going under in the 1990s. Apple's loyal consumers have a missionary zeal in promoting

Brand Logos

The churchrelevance.com Web site, operated by Bombay Creative, creators of church logos (among other things), had this advice for those seeking to create a church logo:

"A good logo design is . . . Distinctive. Memorable. And timeless. It is aesthetically pleasing. It is scalable, looking good while as large as a billboard or as small as a dime. It looks good in color as well as black and white. And it is simple enough that it can be applied to a media spectrum as broad as paper to plastic and T-shirts to Web sites. Most importantly, a good logo communicates the unique qualities of its brand." Here are some of their favorite church logos:

the brand to nonusers. In fact, it is not uncommon for an Apple enthusiast to appeal to a Windows user to "come over from the dark side into the light" and convert to the Apple computer. If a brand can generate such devotion to a company's products made of inanimate plastic, steel, and glass, how much more possible is it that religious institutions should be able to do it for their products, which are inherently emotion-laden and objects of devotion?

Brand Elements. Brand elements are those devices that serve to identify and differentiate the brand. Many strong brands employ multiple brand elements: for example, Nike as the distinctive "swoosh" logo, the empowering "Just Do It" slogan, and the mythological "Nike" name based on the winged goddess of victory. There are six criteria in choosing brand elements.

1. *Memorable.* How easily is the brand element recalled? How easily is it recognized?

2. *Meaningful.* To what extent is the brand element credible and suggestive of the corresponding category? Does it suggest something about a product characteristic or the type of person who might use the brand? Consider the inherent meaning in names such as Die-Hard auto batteries and Lean Cuisine low-calorie frozen entrées.

3. *Likability.* How aesthetically appealing do consumers find the brand element? Is it inherently likable visually, verbally, and in other ways?

4. *Transferable.* Can the brand element be used to introduce new products in the same or different categories?

5. *Adaptable.* How adaptable and updatable is the brand element?

6. *Protectable.* How legally protectable is the brand element? How competitively protectable? Can it be easily copied?

What Are You Branding?

What might your organization brand? Branding could be done for all three types of marketing discussed in chapter 1: adherent, fellowship, and social service marketing. In fact, widely recognized "brands" already exist for each of these forms of religious organizational marketing:

Adherent: Willowcreek Church, Saddleback Church

Fellowship: See Exhibit 9.4 for examples of this for Willowcreek. Your congregation likely has similar branded products for its small groups, Sunday or Sabbath school classes, midweek prayer service, main worship service, etc.

Social Service: ADRA (Adventist Disaster Relief Agency), JSSA (Jewish Social Service Agency)

While it is possible to establish your institution or any of its programs as brands (whether targeting internal or external audiences), it is important to remember a brand is more than just a catchy memorable name. Revisit the list of 10 attributes for the world's strongest brands. It is obvious that a brand's marketing power, that is, its ability to establish long-lasting mutually beneficial exchange relationships, is derived from more than clever wordsmithing. You must have a clear plan for *managing* the brand over time to achieve your marketing goals.

Managing a brand is not the same thing as managing a product. *Product Management* involves making the key marketing mix decisions (product design, pricing, distribution, and promotion) for a product to establish a competitive advantage for it in a target market. *Brand Management* involves creating mental structures and helping consumers organize their knowledge about a brand over time. Brand elements must be established that meet the criteria (see list) and that continue to resonate with the target market. Managing a *brand* requires you to remain relevant while adapting to a changing market, while retaining the core brand identity that is meaningful to your consumers. Managing a *product* requires you to alter the attributes of the product to deliver satisfaction to your market better than the competition.

Strong marketing organizations, such as Apple, Coca-Cola, Nike, and Procter and Gamble, are good at both brand and product management. The Tide detergent you see on the shelf in the grocery store bears no physical resemblance to the original product (it has been reformulated more than 60 times), and its marketing mix has undergone constant and dramatic alteration. However, it has retained its core brand identity over its lifetime. Your decision to brand your congregation, programs, and/or social services might make a significant contribution to achieving your marketing goals for those products, but it will demand an ongoing effort on your part long after you have established brand names and logos for the products.

Service Marketing

We believe that several lessons learned by service enterprises might be applicable to religious organizations. The concept that comes most readily to mind is *Service Quality*—what it is, and recommendations for improving it.[9] Extensive research among service providers has led to the following five determinants of service quality:[10]

1. *Reliability.* The ability to perform the promised service dependably and accurately.

2. *Responsiveness.* The willingness to help customers and to provide prompt service.

3. *Assurance.* The knowledge and courtesy of employees and their ability to convey trust and confidence.

4. *Empathy.* The provision of caring, individualized attention to customers.

5. *Tangibles.* The appearance of physical facilities, equipment, personnel, and communication materials.

Recommendations for improving service quality include:[11]

1. *Listening.* Understand what customers really want through continuous learning about the expectations and perceptions of customers and noncustomers.

2. *Reliability.* Reliability is the single most important dimension of service quality and must be a service priority.

3. *Basic service.* Service organizations must deliver the basics and do what they are supposed to do: keep promises, use common sense, listen to customers, keep customers informed, and be determined to deliver value to customers.

4. *Service design.* Develop a wholistic view of the service while managing its many details.

5. *Recovery.* To satisfy customers who encounter a service problem, service organizations should encourage customers to complain (and make it easy for them to do so), respond quickly and personally, and develop a problem resolution system.

6. *Surprising customers.* Although reliability is the most important dimension in *meeting* customers' service expectations, process dimensions (e.g., assurance, responsiveness, and empathy) are most important in *exceeding* customer expectations, for example, by surprising them with uncommon swiftness, grace, courtesy, competence, commitment, and understanding.

7. *Fair play.* Service organizations must make special efforts to be fair and to demonstrate fairness to customers and employees.

8. *Teamwork.* Teamwork is what enables large organizations to deliver service with care and attentiveness by improving employee motivation and capabilities.

9. *Employee research.* Conduct research with employees to reveal why service problems occur and what companies must do to solve problems.

10. *Service leadership.* Quality service comes from inspired leadership throughout the organization; from excellent service-system design; from the effective use of information and technology; and from a slow-to-change, invisible, all-powerful internal force called organization culture.

Change some of the terminology in these lists, and you can easily imagine its direct application to your organization and its programs, ministries, and social services. Maintaining high-quality services is an important step in achieving the end goal of the effective marketing management process—*connecting* with your exchange partners. See chapter 12 for more on service delivery.

Developing New Products

A religious organization that wishes to develop new products to achieve a balanced portfolio must establish a process that will lead to successful new product launches.

The Bethel African Methodist Episcopal Church, located in a low-income area of Baltimore, was stagnant. Only half of its 600 members attended Sunday services. That was before John Bryant, 32, arrived with dreams of what a city church could do. Pastor Bryant envisioned a church that would reach out to the "whole person" and the surrounding community. Among the church programs started were sign language instruction for about 50 deaf parishioners; a prison missionary project for adults and youth; an outreach center that provides job counseling, clothing, food, and vouchers for emergency payment of rent and utility bills; an energy cooperative that sells fuel oil at reduced prices; and a 2,000-member food cooperative. The Senior Citizens Eating Together program serves free meals to members and nonmembers alike.

Yet the religious message was not forgotten. In addition to three Sunday services, Bethel sponsors Sunday school classes for all ages and daily Bible classes and discussion groups. Bryant's spirit has spread to his congregants, one of whom recently gave money to start a ministry for cancer patients and their families—a program that several other churches have copied. In less than 10 years membership climbed to 6,000, with a paid staff of 31 and dozens of volunteers. As one church member noted: "We're not just adding people to the church rolls. Reverend Bryant has shaken our consciousness and awakened us as Christians."[12]

While the marketing plan will specify to whom the product will be marketed, how it will be offered, and what the offering's objectives will be, the organization must first be capable of generating new product ideas, and then be able to screen the ideas so that the best ones can be incorporated into the marketing plan. These steps of idea generation and screening are described in the following sections.

Generating New Ideas

Religious organizations differ in their need for new product ideas. Some are quite busy carrying out their current activities and do not need new things to do. Others need one or two big new ideas to balance their product portfolio. Still others need several new ideas simply to keep up with the changing local environment. Shifting demographic compositions of the population surrounding an urban congregation, for example, may require substantial changes in its portfolio.

The idea generation stage is most relevant to you if you need one or more ideas to maintain or expand your ministries. It may be argued that the more ideas you generate—and the more diverse they are—the greater chance you will have of finding successful ideas. Ideas can occur spontaneously from the following "natural" sources:

- Personal inspiration of one or more members.
- Serendipitous stimuli from the environment—for example, learning of a new idea from another congregation or in discussion with religious workers from other parts of the country or the world on a church related blog.
- Requests for new offerings or modification of existing offerings from persons in a target market or key public.
- Suggestions from a participant in one of your program offerings.

Ideas that arise spontaneously should not be ignored. They indicate areas in which "something is trying to be born." However, spontaneous ideas are not the only approach you should rely on for new ideas—for at least two reasons. First, they rely on a chance combination of an idea's appearing *and* someone's alertness in recognizing it.

These casual approaches have a second problem. As noted by Crompton: "There is a great deal of evidence that suggests that many efforts to produce new programs that meet client needs are incestuous. That is, there is a tendency to reach for prior experiences, prior approaches, or moderate distortions of old answers, as opposed to really searching for new ideas. We become victimized by habit."[13]

Therefore, you should create a climate in which spontaneous ideas are welcomed, and at the same time employ a systematic methodology for generating ideas. A systematic process requires four steps.

1. A *commitment* must be made to routinely and formally search for new ideas.

2. *Responsibility* for this task must be specifically assigned to someone or some group.

3. A *procedure* must be put in place for *systematically* seeking new ideas.

4. The procedure must contain a *creative* component if truly new ideas are sought.

The Connected Congregation

Since San Francisco's Grace Cathedral started an audio Webcast of Sunday services in 2002, the 1,500 typical Internet "congregation" outnumbers those in the pews by two to one.

"More Prayer, Less Hassle," *Wall Street Journal*, June 27, 2003, pp. W1, W4.

The Connected Congregation

A random sample of 500 churches and ministries reported that virtually all used a computer, 70 percent had Internet access, and of those that did, 37 percent had a Web page. Of those who did not, 58 percent plan on having one within a year. The following were mentioned as the most common ways churches use their Web sites:

1. Describing features of the church such as service times or event schedules.

2. Having a way to communicate with church publics.

3. Providing a means for others to contact the church via electronic mail.

4. Image management.

Several benefits were cited for maintaining a Web site:

1. Improved communication.

2. Increased knowledge by members of church programs.

3. Increased attendance at church activities (because of dispensing information over the Web site).

Robert E. Stevens, "A Study of Church/Ministry Internet Usage," *Journal of Ministry Marketing and Management* 7, no. 1 (2001): 23-32.

Procedures for Gathering New Ideas

Establishing the idea generation procedure involves the entire organization in listing all possible sources for new ideas, and then developing a strategy for generating or collecting ideas routinely from each source. Major sources and procedures for mining them are listed below.

1. Similar organizations
    a. A jointly funded clearinghouse could be established to share new ideas among congregations in the same denomination or a group of independent congregations.
    b. Scheduled, routine visits or telephone conversations with similar organizations on specific dates; for example, the first Tuesday of every February and July.
2. Journals, newspapers, magazines, Internet
    a. Probable written sources of ideas should be identified, subscriptions acquired, and someone (or several people) assigned to peruse these sources routinely.
    b. A clipping service might be subscribed to.
    c. A librarian might be hired and assigned these tasks.
    d. A computer-based information retrieval system could be subscribed to, or RSS (Really Simple Syndication, a group of Web feed formats that can put frequently updated content on your PC) could be used to scan blogs, news entries, podcasts, etc. for new product ideas for your congregation. RSS subscription can be as easy as clicking on a RSS icon in a browser to initiate the subscription process.
3. Conferences, lectures
   People should be routinely assigned to attend important gatherings to collect ideas and useful literature.
4. Members
   You should solicit members for their ideas rather than waiting until they spontaneously offer them. Many religious organizations obtain most of their best new ideas by soliciting or actively listening to members and other stakeholders, whether internal or external.
5. Evaluation of market data

Idea suggestions may surface when market data is evaluated (e.g., how to best serve the needs of newly arrived young families for First Church in Carmel, Indiana).

Three features should characterize the idea-generation system. First, specific dates should be set for carrying out each information gathering technique. Second, a formal reporting and assessment mechanism should be developed to assure that each idea comes before the appropriate group for consideration. Finally, the system should be *unblocked*. A few vocal persons should not be able to kill ideas as "too outrageous" or "not really appropriate for us right now." This stage is intended to generate, not evaluate, ideas.

One technique for improving the emergence of new ideas is to assign responsibility to someone who might be called a *ministry idea manager*. A ministry idea manager would perform five major functions:

1. *Idea finding.* The ministry idea manager would conduct an organized and continuous search for new ideas by reading journals, blogs, and newsletters, listening to podcasts, frequenting Web sites that have proven to be good sources for ideas, attending conferences, and talking to consultants.

2. *Idea stimulating.* The ministry idea manager would use creativity-generating techniques to stimulate others to create new and useful ideas.

3. *Idea collecting.* The ministry idea manager would serve as a receiving station for the good ideas spotted by others. Everyone would know that good ideas should be sent to this person.

4. *Idea evaluating.* The ministry idea manager would do a preliminary analysis and evaluation of the ideas and identify the really good ones.

5. *Idea disseminating.* The ministry idea manager would know to whom each worthwhile idea should be sent. The ministry idea manager would act as an idea champion of the better ideas.

This important responsibility should be assigned to someone who has some power and stature in your congregation.

Generating ideas involves both spontaneous and systematic techniques for routinely scanning or prodding various systems for ideas.

This will yield a high proportion of ideas. If an organization seeks "breakthrough-quality" ideas, it can utilize a number of proven techniques. Individuals can use some techniques; others are best done in groups where persons can spark ideas off each other.[14]

Brainstorming. This is probably the best-known technique for forcing creativity. Brainstorming involves putting five to nine people, preferably of diverse backgrounds, together and giving them a very broad problem mandate. They are then told (1) to come up with as many solutions as possible; (2) that no solution is too wild to suggest; (3) that no one is to evaluate—most particularly, criticize—any idea at this stage; and (4) that it is possible to build upon another's idea. The objective is to place the participants in a nonthreatening environment where they can let their imaginations soar as they use one another's input to suggest new and increasingly creative solutions.

Attribute listing. Here the major attributes of the idea, product, or service are listed, and each attribute is scrutinized to see if it can be adapted, modified, magnified, substituted, rearranged, reversed, or combined.

Forced relationships. Here several objects or elements are listed, and each is considered in relation to the other. Thus, a product portfolio for children might include a Saturday afternoon storytelling hour and picnic, a children's worship service, and a Sunday school "preconfirmation series" dealing with the sacraments of the church. An analysis of possible relationships might suggest stories to be told to children to indirectly teach them what the sacraments are, and how they fit into worship. Perhaps the stories might be of children in other cultures i.e., American Indian, and sacraments and worship in that culture.

Morphological analysis. Start with a problem, such as "getting something from one place to another via a powered vehicle." Now think of dimensions, such as the type of platform (cart, chair, sling, bed), the medium (air, water oil, rails), and the power source (compressed air, electric motor, magnetic fields). By breaking the problem into its component parts, thinking of different means of achieving that part of the activity, and listing all the possible combinations for those separate solutions, you can generate many product ideas for overcoming the problem.

Reverse assumption analysis. List all the normal assumptions about an entity and then reverse them. Sometimes what has been the "way it has always been done" might not be the best way of doing it. By reversing the assumptions, you might discover new product ideas. For example, at one time all luggage was carried. By reversing the assumptions, designers were able to imagine luggage that could be pushed or pulled (i.e., wheeled luggage) instead of carried, and transformed the luggage industry.

New contexts. Take familiar processes, such as people-helping services, and put them into a new context. Imagine day care for pets, instead of people, for example. Instead of having someone park your car for you, they pick you up in a golf cart and take you to and from where you parked the car, etc.

Mind-mapping. Start with a thought, such as an emergency food pantry, write it on a piece of paper, then think of the next thought that comes up (say vegetables), link it to the pantry, then think of the next association (say garden), and do this with all associations that come up with each new word. Perhaps a whole new idea will materialize.

Idea Screening

As ideas accumulate, an effort must be made to identify the most promising and to eliminate those that do not warrant further attention. There is some chance that screening might result in an excellent idea's being prematurely dropped (a *drop*-error). What might be worse, however, is accepting a bad idea for further development (a *go*-error) as a result of poor screening. Each idea that is developed consumes substantial paid or volunteer time and money. The purpose of screening is, therefore, to eliminate all but the most promising ideas.

Several steps are necessary to ensure effective idea screening:

1. *A screening committee should be established to evaluate new ideas.* The committee should include representatives of each key program area and ministry department. Selection of those to serve on the

committee should assure that the committee represents experience and expertise on the proposed new ministries and programs.

2. *Regular meetings should be scheduled to evaluate new ideas.*

3. *Criteria should be developed against which the ideas are to be evaluated.* The criteria would be consistently applied over many evaluation sessions. You will want to establish criteria most appropriate for your circumstances. Weights for the criteria should be developed prior to each evaluation session. The ministry leaders and ruling board should set these weights since they will directly affect where the organization wishes to go in the future. Every new product idea should be able to pass the criteria of being capable of satisfying the need that motivates the consumer to want the product (see part 1 above), and fit the positioning statement developed in chapter 7.

4. *Prior to the evaluation meeting, committee members should prepare briefs on each idea, as a basis for group discussion.* The briefs should present data that is relevant to each of the major criteria.

5. *The group should meet and discuss each idea.* Afterward, they should rate each idea, either individually or collectively, on each criterion. (A form should be devised for this purpose.)

It is not enough to generate and screen product ideas. It is also important to understand the process by which people will adopt the new product, so that an implementation plan can be devised with maximum likelihood of success.

The Innovation Adoption Process

Rogers and Shoemaker have identified four steps that individuals typically go through in adopting some new pattern of behavior.[15]

1. *Knowledge.* First, the targeted consumer must (a) become aware of the program or new life pattern, and (b) learn enough about it to deduce whether it has relevance for his or her needs, wants, and lifestyle.

2. *Persuasion.* Next, the target consumer must move from simple awareness and vague interest to being motivated to take action. This is primarily a matter of attitude change. However, it is also possible that a *behavioral response* could be achieved through offering incentives, with relatively little *attitude change.*

3. Decision. At some point the target consumer thinks through the probable consequences of the proposed behavior change and makes a decision to adopt or reject it.

4. Confirmation. After the initial decision, it is hoped that the target consumer will continue the behavior. This can be a major problem for social change agents. For example, more than 70 percent of those who have stopped smoking resume the habit within a year.

The value of the Rogers-Shoemaker adoption model is three-fold. First, it points to the *sequence* of tasks necessary to move a given target group to adopt a product. Thus early messages must create awareness and interest, subsequent messages persuade, and later messages secure and reinforce decisions.

Second, the Rogers-Shoemaker adoption model provides a monitoring device to identify reasons for a slow rate of acceptance. For example, research on how persons quit smoking shows that many smokers are blocked at the decision stage. For these persons, attempts to persuade them to stop smoking are no longer necessary, and effort should focus on inducing a decision.

Innovation Characteristics

The innovation's characteristics will affect the rate of adoption. Five characteristics have an especially important influence on the adoption rate.

The first is the innovation's *relative advantage*, the degree to which it appears superior to previous ideas. The greater the perceived relative advantage (higher quality, lower cost, and so on), the more quickly the innovation will be adopted.

For example, a five-evening Vacation Bible School, with transportation that charges tuition of $10 per child and that is being offered in a neighborhood with a high percentage of single-parent households will be *adopted* (utilized) by more households than a school providing no transportation with a tuition of $5. Even though one costs less, which will certainly be appreciated by the working parent, the other may have more appeal because of the convenience of the parent not having to rush the child off to church after just returning from work.

The second characteristic is the innovation's *compatibility*—the degree to which it is consistent with the values and experiences of the individuals in the social system. Thus persuading women in developing nations to practice birth control when they believe that their number of children is "in God's hands" will take more time than persuading them to boil water before drinking it, because the latter has no religious significance.

The third characteristic is the innovation's *divisibility*—the degree to which it may be tried on a limited basis. The evidence of many studies indicates that divisibility helps to increase adoption. For example, a prospective member may more readily sign up to attend a three-month Sabbath series on spiritual formation than to pledge lifelong allegiance to God for all affairs of one's life.

When Rick Warren publicly launched Saddleback Valley Community Church, the congregation (15 people) hand-addressed and hand-stamped 15,000 letters to homes in the neighborhood. The letters announced that the church's first public service would be held on Easter Sunday, two weeks after the letters were mailed.

The letter also stated that Rick would be doing a trial run of the service, in the high school, on the Sunday prior to Easter. Sixty people came to the trial run by accident, thinking it was the real service, and five of them committed their lives to Christ that day and joined the church.

By inviting people to attend the trial-run service, Rick Warren made it possible for persons to give the new church "a try" on a limited, one-shot basis. If they didn't like the trial run, they would never attend the church once it was started. Also, attending the practice session was much less threatening than attending the Easter service, where many more people might be present and the service would be "for real."

The fourth characteristic is the innovation's *complexity,* the degree to which it is relatively difficult to understand. More complex innovations take a longer time to diffuse, other things being equal.

The fifth characteristic is the innovation's *communicability*—the degree to which the results are observable or describable to others. Innovations whose advantages are more observable will diffuse more quickly throughout the social system. Thus new believers will adopt regular attendance habits faster than tithing 10 percent of their income, because the benefit of tithing can be understood or experienced only over a long time of faithful practice.

The planning team should research how the target market will perceive any proposed innovation in terms of these five characteristics before the marketing plan is developed. The committee can then proceed to make the innovation relatively more advantageous, more compatible, more divisible, less complex, and more communicable.[16]

Part 2: Price Decisions

Another element of the marketing mix, which must be planned along with the product, is *price*. In chapter 6 we discussed the cost of an exchange (see Exhibit 6.8). Consumers balance the expected benefits of an exchange against the expected costs. Money payment might be only one of these costs or sacrifices.

A perceived cost is any negative outcome of a proposed exchange perceived by a target consumer.

Consider the case of a man who is deciding whether to begin attending Sabbath worship services regularly. His wife has begun attending, and he is noticing a marked difference in her demeanor and conversation. Further, he has been reading some of the materials about the congregation and its many programs. He knows regular attendance will cost him a significant amount of money because he can work overtime several Saturdays a year at the car rental service where he is employed. He would have to give this up. Further, he imagines that being faithful to worship means one contributes money regularly. He is aware of another "cost." On most Saturday mornings, when he is not working overtime, he plays golf with his buddies. Regular worship attendance would wipe out Saturday morning golf.

There is yet another "cost" with which he is struggling. His crew at the rental office loves to tease, and nickname, anyone who attends religious services. This seems to him to be the greatest "cost." The family can get along well enough without his Saturday overtime, and he might possibly be able to pick up some Sunday overtime to compensate. He has long remembered his own father regularly contributing to the old family church. But he is not sure he could endure the taunts of his fellow workers.

For many persons considering joining a church or synagogue, the financial cost may not be the most important factor. A number of psychological costs may be of greater importance, including:

- awkwardness at having to ask for a change in work schedule or for time off.
- fear that turning down overtime might hurt chances for promotion.
- embarrassment at having to explain to coworkers why you aren't working overtime (or lying to them).
- regret of breaking up the golfing foursome.
- concerns of being ostracized by coworkers and friends.
- the social costs of being the only member of your social group who worships on Saturday instead of Sunday.

All of these perceived costs will run through one's mind. A church marketing portfolio that focuses primarily on promoting the responsibilities of bringing the family to worship and on the joy of worship will probably fail to motivate many persons whose situations parallel what is described above. Many persons know that it would be good to take the family to church. It is the vast array of perceived costs that keep them from taking the step.

Likewise, in many of the exchanges a religious organization seeks, managing the perceived costs is often much more important than managing the benefits. Furthermore, the nominal financial price tag on the exchange may be the least important perceived cost that concerns the individual. In many religious exchanges, there is no financial price tag at all.

Cost Management

Cost management (deciding a "price" for the organization's offering) presents a delicate problem for the religious marketing program. An optimal cost management strategy, from the organization's standpoint, is one that maximizes the number of exchanges for a given cost to the target market.

How can a cost management strategy be developed? The religious organization must begin by researching consumer perceptions of these costs. Otherwise, those who are planning the congregation's marketing portfolio may miss subtle but crucial barriers affecting particular consumer segments. Consider the following examples:

• The National Cancer Institute realized that a perceived cost keeping many people from trying to quit smoking is the fear of failure.

• In the rural areas of many countries women who want to practice contraception do not do so because all of the methods they know require that someone (or many people) become aware of their behavior.

• Some potential attendees of symphony concerts won't go because they believe they have to "dress up."

• Many elderly people do not attend theater in downtown areas because they believe they will be mugged or robbed.

• Many elderly people will not accept nursing home care because this involves admitting that they are old.

• Many alcoholics avoid treatment because they don't want to admit to themselves that they are alcoholics.

• Some males do not take medication for high blood pressure because they believe it will make them sterile.

• Many uneducated women do not use IUDs because they believe (1) an unexpected baby could be born with the IUD embedded in its body, or (2) the IUD will work its way through their bodies, causing all sorts of unimaginable problems.

• Some organizations won't hire consultants because to do so would be an admission that they lack some competence.

• Sanitary water systems are resisted in some villages in developing countries because they disrupt established social systems (for example, the twice-daily convening at the village well).

• Many potential theater, ballet, opera, and symphony attendees avoid going because they don't want to feel ignorant about what's being presented.

Costs may be incurred in several forms: 1. *Sacrifices of old ideas, values, or views of the world*—for example, to give up believing in reincarnation, that women are inferior, that God is vindictive, that you can't be forgiven. 2. *Sacrifices of old patterns of behavior*—for example, to start a daily discipline of prayer and Scripture reading or to attend church services. 3. *Sacrifices of time and energy*—for example, to perform a voluntary service or give blood to a church blood drive.

Once these costs are understood, the marketer can consider the following questions:

1. Are there strategies that can be used to reduce the perceived costs, while still avoiding the incorrect suggestion that costs are negligible?

2. What will be the effects on a product of reducing or increasing a perceived cost to the consumer?

3. What is the probable response of consumers to given levels of perceived cost reduction? Recognize that in rare cases, emphasizing that the costs are *high* might *increase* desire for the product ("few people will be willing to pay the price for this rare opportunity").

In summary, consumer responses to offers are usually a reaction to a *bundle* of costs (and, of course, a bundle of benefits). The problem in managing *costs* rather than *a cost* is to figure out *which* of many costs to reduce and *how much* to reduce them—if, indeed, the organization can reduce the costs to the consumer. Often this is not possible for a religious organization, since many perceived costs are not financial or tangible, but rather are psychological and intangible. Yet observations and other research methods (chapter 4) can, over time, provide decision-makers with answers to many of the cost-related questions discussed here.

Part 3: Place Decisions

Every organization must think through how it will make its products and services available and accessible to its target consumers. This is the *place*, or *distribution*, decision, and it is one of the key decisions in the marketing mix.

Religious organizations can be thought of as operating a religious service distribution system. Robert Buford and Fred Smith suggest that one way to view the local congregation is as a marketing organization, or as a distribution system. The congregation is the "manufacturer" or originator of its products. Its program departments and ministers com-

375

prise its "wholesale" or distribution operation, the workers (Sabbath school teachers, ministers, visitors, etc.) function as the "retailers," who come face to face with the "consumers"—the members, potential members, and other users of the congregation's products.

Large Congregations as Religious Retailers

Robert Buford of the Leadership Network, a resource group for large churches, uses a distribution model to contrast the nineteenth-century church with the large independent churches emerging at the end of the twentieth century. The early churches, he says, were like a corner grocery store, "serving a blue-collar or agricultural constituency that had little free time, and had one pastor for 200 or fewer people, because that was as many as the pastor could keep up with." As the country changed, the neighborhood church had to make way for what he calls parachurch organizations. Buford compares them to national chain stores, specializing in one part of church work: the Billy Graham Crusade, focusing on evangelism; Alcoholics Anonymous; youth groups, such as the InterVarsity Christian Fellowship. The successor to both the small church and the parachurch organization is the large church, which Buford describes as being like a shopping mall. It contains all the specialized ministries of parachurch groups under one roof. It is often suburban and its members are looking for a sense of community in a place that is often far from where they grew up. These large churches grow, according to Fred Smith of the Leadership Network, because they have identified their business differently. They see themselves as "delivery systems rather than as accumulators of human capital." The aim is to "distribute" ministry in the community rather than merely to get people to come to church. One thing they deliver better than small churches, paradoxically, is intimacy. Large churches are honeycombed with small "retail departments"—sharing groups, discipleship groups—organized around a subject, like caring for small children or growing older.[17]

When planning the distribution system for their products, congregations should pay careful attention to the characteristics of their target consumers and their possible reactions to the products. Some of Willow Creek's church products (Exhibit 9.4) would necessarily be distributed in locations more appropriate to the product type (e.g., a food pantry located in a low-income housing area for disadvantaged residents). The product's characteristics and the target market will combine to suggest the best form for the product's distribution.

Selection of Physical Facilities

Churches and synagogues must make decisions on the "look" of their facilities, because the facilities' appearance affects how persons see the congregation, its programs and priorities. Charles Sineath, pastor of the megachurch First United Methodist, Marietta, Georgia, said of the influence of the facility's exterior, "Every blade of grass is an evangelist. People see the lawns and gardens before they see the inside of the building."

Churches and synagogues must make decisions on the "look" of their facilities, because the appearance and "feel" of the facilities affect the attitudes persons develop about the congregations, its programs, and its priorities. Church leaders must become skilled in the use of atmospherics. Atmospherics describes the conscious designing of space to create or reinforce specific effects on members and other consumers; such as a feeling of well-being, safety, intimacy, or awe.[18]

A congregation that is designing a sanctuary for the first time faces four major decisions:

1. What should the building look like on the outside? The building can look awe-inspiring, ordinary, or intimate. The decision will be influenced by the type of message the congregation wants to convey about religion in general.

2. What should be the functional and flow characteristics of the building?

3. What should the building feel like on the inside? Every building conveys a feeling, whether intended or unplanned. The planners have to consider whether the facilities should feel awesome and somber, or bright and modern, or warm and intimate. Each feeling will have a different effect on the parishioners and their overall satisfaction of the services they attend in the building.

4. What materials would best support the desired feeling of the building? The feeling of a building is conveyed by visual cues (color, brightness, size, shapes), aural cues (volume, pitch), olfactory cues (scent, freshness), and tactile cues (softness, smoothness, temperature). The planners of the building have to choose colors, fabrics, and furnishings that create or reinforce the desired feeling.

When Doug Anderson (now at First United Methodist Church, Auburn, Indiana) came to serve as pastor of the United Methodist church in Wakarusa, Indiana, he found the church in about the same condition as the name of the little town implies. Wakarusa is an Indian term meaning "knee-deep in muck." The congregation was experiencing a period of long decline and much turmoil. He convinced the congregation that it could grow if it would position itself to reach the young couples who were moving into the area. After much discussion, the congregation decided to repair the outdoor sign; tidy up the outside areas; refurbish the entry, the women's restroom, and the nursery; and redecorate the little sanctuary. They did this assuming these were the building areas of greatest concern to the young couple with children. They then began to advertise the church as a place for little children and their parents, including a new community nursery school. In a few weeks young couples, new to the community, began to attend. The church experienced a significant growth in attendance and membership.

What has been said of the United Methodist churches in Marietta, Georgia, and Wakarusa, Indiana, can be said about dozens of large and small congregations who, in the past few years, have made the important discovery that the design and condition of the facilities either helps or hinders the ministry of the congregation—the effect is perhaps never neutral. The location, condition, cleanliness, smell, colors, acoustics, and so on are marketing decisions, either intentionally or by default.

E-Distribution: Blogs, Podcasts, Web sites, and Virtual Church

In Tiruchirapalli, India, a Hindu priest, adorned with yellow and red sacred paste, stands in front of a reclining Hindu god offering a plate of bananas and coconut. He chants Vishnu's name 108 times, asking for health, wealth, and good fortune—not on his own behalf, but for an Indian living in London who purchased the prayer with a credit card on a Hindu Web site.

Millions of Christians, Muslims, Jews, Hindus, Buddhists, Sikhs and countless other faiths have embraced the Internet as a place to pray, meditate, take confession, seek religious advice, and to attend "virtual" worship services. Some sites even offer "virtual" baptism services. For these cyber worshippers, accessing religious services over the Internet has replaced attendance at traditional churches, mosques, synagogues, or temples. For others, the Web constitutes their first experience with an organized religion. Millions of people reared on churchgoing are using the Internet as a new way of worshipping. "The first wave of religion online in the 1990s was mainly for nerds and young people and techies, but now it really is a mirror of society at large. This is providing a new forum for religious seekers," says Morten Hojsgaard, a Danish author who has written extensively about online religion. According to Hojsgaard, the increased interest in online religion is occurring when people, especially young people, are questioning traditional institutions. Many who are interested in religion desire the freedom to construct a personalized worship style and time for worship. "Old mechanisms of religious authority are changing," says Hojsgaard. "There is more emphasis on individualism. We want to decide for ourselves."[19]

In the spring of 2009 a search of Podcasts on Apple's iTunes Web site showed the following number of streams under Religion and Spirituality:

Category	Number of Streams
Buddhism	341
Hinduism	51
Islam	185
Judaism	523
Spirituality	1000s
Christianity	1000s

On iTunes radio, 138 religious "stations" were available. XM radio had three Christian channels. The number of Christian blogs alone on the Internet runs into the hundreds of thousands, if not millions (no documented estimate exists, and the number changes daily). A search on MySpace for "religion" got almost 19.1 million hits; Facebook had 500+ groups with religion in the title; a search on YouTube for "Islam" generated 350,000 video clips. A search on Second Life found the following numerous religious groups, including: Christian Church of Second Life, 759 members; Buddhists of Second Life, 798 members; Unitarian Universalists, 425 members; Roman Catholic Church, 523 members; Jews of Second Life, 265 members; Islamic Society, 425 members; Anglicans of Second Life, 567 members; Church of Elvis, 208 members (see boxed exhibit below). Many, if not most, congregations have developed Web sites for their church or synagogue. Some congregations have established online ordering of books and other material, and can register people for upcoming events, seminars, etc., online as well.

There have been obvious dramatic changes in the means that congregations use to deliver their services since we published *Marketing for Congregations* in 1992. Years ago the primary, and for many congregations the only, means of delivering their services was for the exchange partner to be physically present to complete an exchange (e.g., for a Sabbath service, or to receive a social service); nowadays many congregations have someone assigned to oversee multiple electronic channels for delivery of products such as those listed above.

Yet there is a concern that making it too easy for people to access congregational products may encourage some to use electronic media as the sole means of interacting with the congregation. There is some research that supports this concern for the privatization of faith. Barna, for example, estimates that over 10 million people who consider themselves "born again" do not attend any type of church or worship service.[21] Interestingly, he also reports that of all adults who do not participate in any type of formal religious services, 40 percent still report that their faith is "very important" in their lives. This suggests that there is definitely a "market" for online religious products, but highlights the conundrum of meeting this market de-

Religion in the Second Life

Second Life, the virtual, or online, world created in 2003 by Linden Lab, has gotten religion. More than 8.5 million people are "residents" of this world existing in cyberspace, operating businesses, establishing families and social contacts, practice politics, being educated or entertained, and in general leading a virtual life that is everything their life in the real world might not come up to. They do this by taking on the identity of an "avatar" (animated characters that serve as your identity in this cyberworld). Now residents have established religious congregations in Second Life. Ben Faust, an ordained evangelical minister living in Harrisonburg, Virginia, works as a Web site programming in the real world, but founded and pastors ALM Cyber Church in Second Life. Says Faust, "Worship is between you and God, wherever you are." Larry Transue, who works in the biotech industry, pastors the site's Northbound Community Church and sees SL as a mission field. His goal is to "practice what I preach no matter where I am."

Not all in the Second Life world is goodness and light, however. Synagogues, mosques, and churches have been sabotaged by "griefers"—slang for troublemakers who destroy the houses of worship or streak naked through religious services.

Frances Maier, chancellor of the Roman Catholic Archdiocese of Denver, who has written about the Internet and online role-playing games for Catholic publications, has a different take on this form of religion. He says that Second Life spirituality blasphemously perpetuates the idea that people control creation. "We aren't the ones in charge. God is in charge. I'm Catholic because I believe the Catholic Church teaches the truth. It's not just going through mumbo jumbo and dressing up." True religion requires submission to "beliefs and practices revealed by God and passed down by generations of believers. You can't phone that in."[20]

mand at the expense of encouraging corporate worship experiences.

While some commercial enterprises desire to move transactions to the Internet as much as possible, many congregations see achievement of their mission as requiring a complete mens/corpus/spiritus

The Connected Congregation

Here is a sampling of how digital technology is being used for religious purposes:

Pilotyid.com
Allows downloading of lists of kosher restaurants and Talmud selections to most PDAs. Also offers a virtual menorah for those without time to light a real one.

Time-it Right
A software program made by AutoTime that allows Orthodox Jews to preset lights, ovens, air-conditioning, electric window shades, etc. to operate on the Sabbath so that the observant doesn't have to manually operate them. Can be set for 50-year operating cycle.

Virtualrosary.org
A free 20-minute guided prayer with special instructions for beginners.

Islamicity.com
Can watch the Hajj in Mecca live.

ATMs in church lobbies
Allows tithe payment for those low on cash or who forget their checkbook.

Online confession
For those unable to physically go to the church for confession.

Cybermonkmro.org/zmm/cybermonk/index
A senior monastic available through e-mail to answer dharma questions.

_____

"More Prayer, Less Hassle," *Wall Street Journal*, June 27, 2003, pp. W1, W4.

(mind/body/spirit) involvement from members and other exchange partners, at least with respect to some exchanges. The admonition "Let us not give up meeting together, as some are in the habit of doing" (Hebrews 10:25, NIV) is often interpreted in a very literal way to mean the desirability of physically sharing time and place, and not just concurrently sharing a "virtual" space, or replaying a previously recorded service in private.

Contrast this concern with that of some commercial enterprises,

---

The Connected Congregation

A Pew Internet Project survey of 1,309 congregations who voluntarily responded to an e-mail invitation to fill out an online questionnaire found that the Internet has helped the spiritual life of their congregation:

83 percent said that the use of the Internet has helped congregational life—25 percent said it helped a great deal.

81 percent said that the use of e-mail by ministers, staff, and members helped spiritual life to some extent—35 percent a great deal.

63 percent said that e-mail has helped the church connect at least a bit more to the surrounding community—17 percent said it helped a lot.

The most commonly used features on congregational Web sites:

83 percent encourage visitors to attend their congregation's services.

77 percent post mission statements, sermons, or other text concerning their faith.

76 percent have a link to denomination and faith-related sites.

60 percent have links to Scripture studies or devotional material.

56 percent post schedules, meeting minutes, and other internal communications for the church.

"Wired Churches, Wired Temples: Taking Congregations and Missions into Cyberspace," Dec. 20, 2000; http://www.pewinternet.org/pdfs/PIP_Religion_Report.pdf.

such as banks, who use economic incentives to *discourage* customers from physically accessing services (e.g., paying to see a teller, being charged a fee to receive a statement in the mail, paying for printed checks instead of using a debit card, etc.). From their point of view, your physical presence is a cost that they would like to avoid whenever possible (a transaction at a bank branch costs 25 times what it does on the Internet: $1 versus $.04). The less often they *see* you (as opposed to servicing your needs electronically), the better.

Congregations, on the other hand, are seeking not to replace a physical presence with an electronic "transaction," but rather to supplement the sense of community fostered by face-to-face contact with enhanced connectedness via electronic media. That is, you desire to *increase* the points of contact between you and an exchange partner by using the Internet, not have him/her *substitute* the Internet for a physical presence. However, many congregations are using podcasts, blogs, Web sites, etc., to reach audiences that do not have a realistic opportunity to access the congregation's services by any other means. Such congregations see spreading their message to as wide an audience as possible as a fundamental part of their mission (see the Connected Congregation exhibit on page 385).

So how do you use the Internet to "spread the word" (projections are that 1.8 billion people will be using the Internet by 2010)[22] without encouraging some people to substitute private for public access to your products? There is no easy answer to this question, other than your ensuring that the act of being physically present to acquire the product(s) is a "value-added" activity. That is, your exchange partner must feel that there is no good substitute for collectively joining with others to receive the delivery of benefits from "consuming" the product. This is different from just advocating for their attendance. We are referring to *delivery* of benefits, not merely *promoting* benefits here. When developing your product portfolio, make certain that your products that require physical presence for consumption are fully capable of delivering the bundle of benefits that reward the consumer for expending that cost.

The products delivered electronically should likewise fit in the portfolio to accomplish the goals set for them. In other words, the portfolio is not redundant—each product is strategically targeted to its audience to achieve the goals set for it and contribute to the overall goals of the portfolio. For example, for the local nonmember market segment, Internet-based products might be used for customer attraction (i.e., attracting eyeballs and ears), and customer conversion (i.e., getting an Internet consumer to become a visitor to

---

The Connected Congregation

A national phone survey of more than 1,300 Internet users by the Pew Internet Project found that 64 percent of the nation's Internet users use the Internet for faith-relate reasons:

38 percent have sent or received e-mail with spiritual content.

35 percent have sent or received online greeting cards related to religious holidays.

32 percent have gone online to read news accounts of religious events and affairs.

21 percent have sought information about how to celebrate religious holidays.

17 percent have looked for information about where they could attend religious services.

7 percent have made or responded to online prayer requests.

7 percent have made donations to religious organizations or charities.

The Pew study's authors concluded, "Faith-related activity online is a supplement to, rather than a substitute for, offline religious life. The survey found that two thirds of those who attend religious services weekly use the Internet for personal or spiritual purposes. They are more likely to be women, White, middle-aged, college-educated, and relatively well-to-do. In addition, they are somewhat more active as Internet users than the rest of the Internet population."

"Faith Online: 64 percent of Wired Americans Have Used the Internet for Spiritual or Religious Purposes," Apr. 7, 2004; http://www.pewinternet.org/PPF/r/126/report_display.asp.

your congregation). Products consumed onsite at your physical facility then move the consumer along a path of escalating commitment to the organization, while satisfying consumer needs. For the nonlocal consumer, Internet products are used to establish a relationship with the consumer and perhaps generate interest in attending an affiliated congregation close by.

We suggest developing a positioning strategy statement (see chapter 7) for each electronic product as you did for every other product in your portfolio. Without a clear goal and positioning strategy for congregational Internet products, there is the danger that the consumer will treat them as just another bookmarked site to occasionally be used for convenient consumption of an educational/entertaining service. However, see the Connected Congregation exhibit on page 387 for some encouraging findings of people's use of the Internet for religious purposes.

If you envision developing online products as part of your portfolio that will be delivered via the Internet, we suggest making use of some of the related sources listed in the Resource Guide. They can help you take full advantage of what e-Delivery can accomplish for your congregation.

---

[1] Suzanne Sataline, "The Play's the Thing at Pittsburgh Church Targeting New Crowd," *Wall Street Journal*, Apr. 13, 2006, p. A1; Elizabeth Bernstein, "Houses of Worship are Reaching Out to a Flock of Pets," *Wall Street Journal*, Mar. 10, 2004, p. A1.

[2] The idea of three levels of religious products originated with Wendy L. Martin in her dissertation *Marketing My God: Adherent Perspectives on Marketing by Houses of Worship*, published by the University of Illinois at Chicago in 2007.

[3] Roger Fisher and William Ury, *Getting to Yes* (New York: Penguin Books, 1981).

[4] Here the use of "market" the verb is used to describe the societal marketing orientation (SMO), which means being willing to change the product to be more satisfying to the exchange partner. If you are using modern technology and are making sure you are effectively communicating the religious message, you are not necessarily marketing per se. Marketing is distinguished from communication, education, or other activities by the use of a marketing orientation (the desire to understand the exchange partner's needs and willingness to adjust your product so that it is capable of satisfying those needs).

[5] For models of developing a mission statement, see A. Lindgren and N. Shawchuck, *Management for Your Church*; L. Perry and N. Shawchuck, *Revitalizing the 20th Century Church*.

[6] See, for example these articles on church branding: http://www.chrisbusch.com/2004/09/church_branding.html; http://www.brandchannel.com/start1.asp?fa_id=254; http://www.churchexecutive.com/Page.cfm/PageID/2956.

[7] This section on branding is adapted from P. Kotler and K. L. Keller, *Marketing Management.*

[8] Kevin Lane Keller, "The Brand Report Card," *Harvard Business Review,* Jan. 1, 2000, pp. 147-157.

[9] This section on service quality is adapted from Kotler and Keller.

[10] Leonard L. Berry, and A. Parasuraman, *Marketing Services: Competing Through Quality* (New York: Free Press, 1991), p. 16.

[11] Leonard L. Berry, A. Parasuraman, and Valarie A. Zeithaml, "Ten Lessons for Improving Service Quality," *MSI Reports Working Paper Series, No. 03-001* (Cambridge, Mass.: Marketing Science Institute, 2003), pp. 61-82.

[12] "Spreading God's Word: Five Success Stories," *U.S. News and World Report,* Oct. 22, 1984, pp. 71-73.

[13] John Crompton, "Developing New Recreation and Park Programs," *Recreation Canada,* July 1983, p. 29.

[14] For a useful discussion of creativity techniques, see Michael Michalko, *Thinkertoys: A Handbook of Creative Thinking Tecniques, 2nd ed.* (Berkeley, Calif.: Ten Speed Press, 2006).

[15] See Everett M. Rogers and F. Floyd Shoemaker, *Communications of Innovation* (New York: Free Press, 1971).

[16] For an example of developing new products, see James L. Ginter and W. Wayne Talarzyk, "Applying the Marketing Concept to Design New Products," *Journal of Business Research* 6 (January 1978): 51-66.

[17] "Turning Around the Lord's Business," *Fortune,* Sept. 25, 1989, p. 128.

[18] Kotler and Keller, *Marketing Management,* pp. 453, 454, 521.

[19] K. Sullivan, "Linking Ancient and Modern, A Worldwide Web of Worship," Washington *Post,* Mar. 14, 2007, p. A01. For more on online religion see M. Hojsgaard, *Religion and Cyberspace*; L. L. Dawson, *Religion Online: Finding Faith on the Internet*; H. Campbell, *Exploring Religious Community Online*; S. M. Hoover, *Religion in the Media Age.*

[20] Source: Cathy Lynn Grossman, "Faithful Build a Second Life for Religion Online," available at http://www.usatoday.com/tech/gaming/2007-04-01-second-life-religion_N.htm

[21] George Barna, "2001 Church Attendance Survey"; http://www.adherents.com/rel_USA. Survey conducted from January 2000 to June 2001. N = 6,038 adults. Nov. 22, 2002.

[22] "Population Explosion! Internet," Mar. 12, 2006; http://www.clickz.com/showPage.html?page=3605776.

WORKSHEETS: CHAPTER 9

Product, Price, and Place Decisions

PRODUCT
Levels of Product (consensus from negotiations):
Product 1:
    Level 1 (sacred core): _____
    Level 2 (sacred by tradition):_____
    Level 3 (nonsacred): _____

Product 2:
    Level 1 (sacred core): _____
    Level 2 (sacred by tradition):_____
    Level 3 (nonsacred): _____

Product 3:
    Level 1 (sacred core): _____
    Level 2 (sacred by tradition):_____
    Level 3 (nonsacred): _____

Positioning (from chapter 8 worksheet):

Targeted Segment	Positioning Strategy Statement
1._____	_____
2._____	_____
3._____	_____

What is the need that the product you are positioning is really satisfying (levels 2 and 3 above, or the tangible, level 3, product for fully marketable products)? Review your SOV (Something of Value) from exchange maps in chapter 8 when answering this question. Also, keep in mind your target market characteristics.

Need:

1. _____
2. _____
3. _____

Describe the tangible product that will be offered to address this need. Include the new product if you have developed one to address this need.

1. _____
2. _____
3. _____

Product Portfolios

For each segment, list the products you are targeting to them for each of the mission components.

Targeted Segments	Worship	Evangelism	Community	Social Services
1. 2. 3.				

For each segment, list the products you are targeting to them for moving them toward stages of increasing commitment of the individual to your organization.

Targeted Segments	Stage 1	Stage 2	Stage 3	Stage 4
1. 2. 3.				

For each segment, list the products you are targeting to them for resource attraction.

Targeted Segments	Resource Sought
1. 2. 3.	

Branding:

If you are branding your products, how many of the characteristics of top brands does your brand possess?

	Yes	No
1. The brand excels at delivering the benefits consumers truly desire.	_____	_____
2. The brand stays relevant.	_____	_____
3. Customers perceive real value in the offering.	_____	_____
4. The brand is properly positioned.	_____	_____
5. The brand consistently sends clear messages about its position.	_____	_____
6. The brand portfolio and hierarchy makes sense.	_____	_____
7. The brand makes use of and coordinates a full repertoire of marketing activities to build brand equity.	_____	_____
8. The brand's managers understand what the brand means to consumers.	_____	_____
9. The brand is given proper, sustained support.	_____	_____
10. The organization monitors sources of brand equity.	_____	_____

Do your brand elements (name, symbols, etc.) have these characteristics?

	Yes	No
Memorable	____	____
Meaningful	____	____
Likability	____	____
Transferable	____	____
Adaptable	____	____
Protectable	____	____

Service Quality

To what extent do you have a strategy for the following characteristics of your services?

Reliability _____

Responsiveness _____

Assurance _____

Empathy _____

Tangibility _____

To what extent have you worked on the following service quality factors?

Listening _____

Reliability _____

Basic service _____

Recovery _____

Surprising customers _____

Fair Play _____

Teamwork _____

Employee research _____

Service leadership _____

PRICE

What costs will be incurred by your target market to obtain your product?

1. _____

2. _____

3. _____

Sacrifices of old ideas, values, views of the world
1. _____
2. _____
3. _____

Sacrifices of old patterns of behavior
1. _____
2. _____
3. _____

Sacrifices of time and energy
1. _____
2. _____
3. _____

Material sacrifices (money or resources)
1. _____
2. _____
3. _____

What can be done to reduce the perceived costs and increase the perceived value of obtaining the product?
1. _____
2. _____
3. _____

DISTRIBUTION

Atmospherics

Describe the desired atmospherics for your physical facility. Keep in mind the needs of the target audience and how you will use the atmospherics to convey your desired message to fulfill those needs.

_____
_____
_____

e-Distribution

Using resources from the Resource Guide, develop a strategy for the electronic products listed below.

Podcasts

Targeted Segment   **Product Strategy**

_____   _____

Blogs

Targeted Segment   **Product Strategy**

_____   _____

Web sites

Targeted Segment   **Product Strategy**

_____   _____

Other Electronic Products

Targeted Segment   **Product Strategy**

_____   _____

CHAPTER 10:

Marketing Communication Decisions

"It is better not to vow than to make a vow and not fulfill it" (ECCLESIASTES 5:5, NIV).

In this chapter we will address the following questions:

1. What are the characteristics of the major marketing communication methods?

2. What is meant by Integrated Marketing Communications?

3. What steps are involved in developing an advertising program?

4. How can the Internet be used for brand building and to help us achieve our advertising objectives?

5. How can we use viral and guerrilla marketing methods to our advantage?

6. How can we exploit the potential for public relations?

Michael Prewitt is chair and founding partner of Dana Communications, an advertising and marketing communications firm in New Jersey. He is also a 1999 graduate of the Princeton

Theological Seminary and an ordained pastor in the Presbyterian Church (USA). His 2003 article, "The True Worldliness of Advertising: *Apologia pro Vita Mea*," in *Theology Today*[1] provides an insider's look at how religious-minded people might view this most secular of professions.

After citing the case against advertising (e.g., crass, manipulative, materialistic, cynical, etc.), Prewitt quotes from the Vatican's Pontifical Council on Social Communications' "Ethics in Advertising," published in 1994. In it the council outlined the legitimate role for advertising in "informing people about the availability of rationally desirable new products and services and improvements in existing ones, helping them to make informed, prudent consumer decisions." Prewitt then goes on to quote their skeptical view of brand advertising: "The practice of brand-related advertising can raise serious problems. Often there are only negligible differences among similar products of different brands, and advertising may attempt to move people to act on the basis of irrational motives ("brand loyalty," . . .) instead of presenting differences in product quality and price as bases for rational choice."

In defense of his chosen profession, Prewitt says we need to appreciate the fact that, as Peter Drucker states, "the purpose of a business is to create a customer." Prewitt expands this to say, ". . . to create and *keep* a customer," which stresses relationship-building between the customer and the organization. *Branding* is the means by which an organization creates and keeps a customer. He makes the point that advertisers today see their job primarily as contributing to building the brand, rather than merely informing, persuading, or reminding customers about the organization's product. Advertising explicitly and implicitly makes promises about how the brand addresses the need that people are seeking to satisfy.

One of Prewitt's accounts was the Automobile Association of America (AAA). Whenever they did research and asked AAA members why they kept their membership, even when they had another roadside emergency service, they answered "trust." People who use AAA roadside service "need" more than the services themselves—they need to feel that they can trust AAA to be there for them or their loved one when they are vulnerable. Consequently, all AAA advertising stressed that brand promise: "You can trust AAA."

Brands deliver tangible and intangible benefits to consumers. A psychological benefit such as trust may be intangible, but is real, and important to consumers. The fact that it is intangible does not make it, to use the council's term, "irrational." Advertisers must understand all the needs that consumers seek to have satisfied, communicate how the brand promises to deliver satisfaction of those needs via the brand's benefits, and then ensure that those promises are kept.

It is important that the preceding chapter's topics—developing quality programs and ministries—come before this chapter's on promotion. Before you undertake the task of promoting your institution, you must be certain that your product is capable of satisfying the target group's needs and interests.

Nothing will kill a bad product faster than good promotion. *Advertising rule 1: Never advertise or claim what you do not have!* Being effective in making false claims about a product's ability to satisfy a target market's needs raises expectations and will only increase the target group's disappointment with the product and the organization. If a program or ministry cannot deliver on the promises, don't make the promises. "It is better that you should not vow than that you should vow and not fulfill it" (Eccl. 5:5, NRSV) is a good motto for advertisers. In other words, don't promote your church as "the friendliest place in town" if you aren't, even if you think you'll attract more people to your church with that slogan.

It is a wise principle, therefore, to *market-test* a new program or ministry among targeted consumers to ensure that it can deliver value to both the organization and the target group(s). Only after the product has been market-tested should a promotional campaign be designed for it. As regarding existing programs and ministries, methodical evaluation should be conducted to assure that the program is still of value to the target group(s), and to discover fine-tuning adjustments that will cause the program to deliver even greater satisfaction.

Note to anyone who bought this book and immediately turned to this chapter to learn how to advertise your organization: *There is a* *reason promotion is not discussed until chapter 10. Professional for-profit advertisers realize their money will be wasted if they develop a promotional campaign before developing a thorough understanding of their target audience, and go through the planning process we have been describing in the preceding chapters. You will not be able to sustain the kind of success you are striving for by promoting yourself via ill-conceived methods to an audience of strangers. It is vitally important that you get to this chapter's discussion after reading the first nine chapters.*

This chapter will examine the role and uses of marketing communications by religious organizations. We begin with a discussion of the communication methods used by marketers to promote the institution then address several of the most commonly used methods: advertising (including use of the Internet for search engine, contextual, and e-mail advertising), viral and guerrilla marketing, and public relations/publicity.

Marketing Communication Methods

The religious marketer has a large number of methods available for carrying a message to a target audience. There are six main methods:

1. *Paid advertising* is any paid form of nonpersonal presentation and promotion of an offer by an identified sponsor through a formal communications medium.

Paid advertising permits you total control over encoded message content and over the nature of the medium, plus substantial control of the scheduling of the message (and therefore its specific environment). On the other hand, paid advertising permits no control over message decoding by the audience and little (or, at best, lagged) feedback on the received message. Examples include print and broadcast ads, brochures and booklets, posters and leaflets, directories, billboards, display signs, audiovisual materials, symbols and logos.

2. *Unpaid (public service) advertising* is any form of advertising in which space or time for the placement of the advertisement is free. Your control is similar to that with paid advertising, except that there is very little control over the scheduling of the message. Many

public service radio or television advertisements appear after midnight or on Sunday mornings, when the audience is small and the media have unsold spots.

3. *Incentives* are short-term promotions to encourage the immediate exchange of a product or service, or the performance of a behavior. Your control is substantial, although the "message" or the "meaning" attached to the specific promotion by the receiver is not controllable. Examples include contests, games sweepstakes, lotteries, premiums and gifts, fairs, exhibits, demonstrations, and entertainment.

4. *Publicity* is nonpersonal stimulation of demand for an offering by securing the reporting of commercially significant news about the offer in a published medium or on radio, television, or the stage that is not paid for by the sponsor. Here the control you have over message encoding and the medium varies, depending on whether journalists will use and revise the message. Some feedback is possible from journalists or from selected target audiences. Examples include press kits, speeches, seminars, publications, community relations, lobbying, and an organization's own magazine.

5. *Person-to-person promotion* is oral presentation of information about an offering in a conversation with one or more prospective target audience members for the purpose of securing a desired exchange. In personal promotion, you have less control over encoding—that is, what the individual promoter (e.g., a current church member) actually says. The individual, however, has excellent opportunities to secure feedback on how the message is being received. According to this definition, sometimes a religious organization's leader or members will function as an individual promoter when engaged in conversation with a prospective new member. Person-to-person promotion is the method that most directly leads to a response from the other party—the person may or may not respond positively to an invitation, but they can't ignore it as they can do with the other methods. *Word-of-mouth marketing,* done face-to-face, by phone, or in chat rooms or blogs on the Internet is included in this category.

6. *Direct marketing* is the use of mail, telephone, fax, e-mail, or Web sites to communicate directly with, or solicit response from, specific individuals. *Interactive marketing* is online activities and pro-

grams designed to engage people in dialog and directly or indirectly raise awareness, improve image, or elicit exchange with them. Examples are blogs or chat rooms.

7. *Events and experiences* are organization-sponsored activities and programs designed to create a more special and personally relevant moment in the lives of your target audience. The intent is to increase the involvement of these people with the congregation in ways that are engaging and that broaden and deepen the relationship between them and you. People can be targeted geographically, demographically, psychographically, or behaviorally according to events. Event marketing is a good way to build or reinforce your congregation's brand image. Sponsoring, or just having a booth or tent at a local fair or festival, is a good way of saying "We are an important thread in the fabric of this community." Be sure that banners, signs, programs, etc., all portray a consistent brand image. For congregations, events often include fund-raising as well as activities that make a contribution to the welfare of the community.[2]

Characteristics of the Marketing Communications Mix

Each communication tool has its own unique characteristic and costs. We briefly review these below:

Advertising reaches a geographically dispersed audience. It can build up a long-term image, or trigger quick response (e.g., for a sacred music concert this weekend). It has several characteristics:

1. *Pervasiveness*—Advertising permits the seller to repeat a message many times, and also allows the receiver to compare the messages of many advertisers. A constant advertising program, even on a modest scale, suggests an organization is large and successful.

2. *Amplified expressiveness*—Advertising provides opportunities for dramatizing your organization and its ministries through the artful use of print, sound, and color.

3. *Impersonality*—The audience does not feel obligated to pay attention or respond to advertising. Advertising is a monologue in front of, not a dialogue with, the audience.

Incentives are used to draw stronger and quicker audience response, including short-run effects, such as highlighting product offers. There are three distinctive benefits to using incentives:

1. *Communication*—they gain attention and may lead the person to the ministry.

2. *Inducement*—They incorporate some concession, motive, or contribution that gives value to the individual (e.g., the first 25 people who sign up for the seminar get a $25 reduction on the next seminar they attend).

3. *Invitation*—They include a distinct invitation to engage in the exchange now.

Public Relations and Publicity are typically underused, yet a well-thought-out program coordinated with the other communications-mix elements can be extremely effective, especially if your organization needs to challenge audience misconceptions. The appeal of public relations and publicity is based on three distinctive qualities:

1. *High credibility*—News stories and features are more authentic and credible to readers than ads.

2. *Ability to catch the audience off guard*—Public relations can reach people who avoid paid forms of advertising.

3. *Dramatization*—Public relations has the potential for dramatizing your church or ministry.

Events and Experiences can have several advantages:

1. *Relevant*—A well-chosen event or experience can be seen as highly relevant because the consumer gets personally involved.

2. *Involving*—Given their live, real-time quality, events and experiences are more actively engaging for the audience.

3. *Implicit*—Events are an indirect "soft sell."

Direct and Interactive Marketing takes many forms—over the phone (including text messaging), online, or in person. They share three distinctive characteristics. The messages are:

1. *Customized*—The message can be prepared to appeal to the addressed individual.

2. *Up*-to-date—A message can be prepared very quickly.

3. *Interactive*—The message can be changed depending on the person's response.

Person-to-Person/Word-of-Mouth Marketing also takes many forms online or off-line. Three noteworthy characteristics are:

1. *Credible*—Because people trust others they know and respect, word of mouth can be highly influential.

2. *Personal*—Word of mouth can be a very intimate dialogue that reflects personal facts, opinions, and experiences.

3. *Timely*—It occurs when people want it to, and when they are most interested. And it often follows noteworthy or meaningful events or experiences.

Integrated Marketing Communications

As defined by the American Association of Advertising Agencies, integrated marketing communications (IMC) is a concept of marketing communications planning that recognizes the added value of a comprehensive plan. Such a plan evaluates the strategic roles of a variety of communications disciplines (for example, general advertising, direct response, incentives, and public relations) and combines these disciplines to provide clarity, consistency, and maximum impact through the seamless integration of messages.

Unfortunately, many organizations still rely on one or two communication tools. This practice persists in spite of the fragmentation of your markets into many segments, each requiring its own approach, the proliferation of new types of media, and the growing sophistication of your audience (regardless of their age). The wide range of communication tools, messages, and audiences makes it imperative that organizations, including religious organizations, move toward integrated marketing communications. Organizations must adopt a 360-degree view of individuals to fully understand all the different ways that communications can affect people in their daily lives. Media companies and ad agencies are expanding their capabilities to offer multi-platform deals for marketers. For example, newspapers and magazines have been frantically formulating digital strategies, such as adding video to their homepages, to increase advertising revenue. This type of expanded capabilities makes it easier for marketers to assemble various media properties in an integrated communications program.

IMC efforts are not necessarily the province of only large companies. For example, if you are using leaflets to announce an upcoming ministry for a targeted public, you can list your Web site on the leaflet and have more information that continues to "sell" the ministry there as well. Using a branding strategy for the ministry allows you to tie the different media used to promote the ministry, together with common graphics, logo and name, and message, when you use print, radio, billboards, posters, and electronic communication media.

We will now address one of the primary methods used by most congregations to promote themselves to their publics: advertising.

Advertising

Whether religious organizations should engage in marketing is not the question. Religious organizations are always doing marketing by attempting to satisfy needs via exchanges with internal and external markets and publics. Religious leaders can, however, choose not to do extensive advertising. In fact, some religious leaders have been outspoken in their criticism of secular advertising, and they have decried its use by any part of their organization.[3] On the other hand, other religious leaders have used bold advertising methods to promote their "product." The following example illustrates the Episcopal Church's advertising approach in the late 1980s, which was considered excellent strategy by some and controversial by others.

Likewise, many, but not all, critics have praised the television ads by the Church of Latter-Day Saints. Should religious organizations advertise their product, or does the use of advertising somehow di-

---

Admen for Heaven

"George Martin's office—the office of Saints Martha and Mary Episcopal Church—is in the basement of a funeral home. Public school gymnasiums, library auditoriums, and all the other public meeting spaces in Eagan, Minnesota, have been taken by other church-planting efforts. Thus every Sunday, in one of the funeral home's parlors, Martin erects a portable screen on which to hang a cross and a banner in order to help the brand-new 90-member congregation feel as if it has gone to church.

"In addition to his job as vicar, Martin is also executive director of

---

the Episcopal Ad Project, a high-quality, but low-budget, effort to get the attention of the unchurched. Appropriately, in a recent ad, the vicar of this funeral-home church appeared as one of a half-dozen pallbearers carrying a casket. The headline reads, 'Will it take six strong men to bring you back into the church?' The fine print explains that the church 'welcomes you no matter what condition you're in, but we'd really prefer to see you breathing.'

"Tom McElligott's office—the office of the ad agency that produces Martin's church ads—is in downtown Minneapolis, 18 miles from Martin's mortuary meeting space. The Fallon McElligott agency occupies the fifteenth and sixteenth floors of the blue steel-and-glass building." On its walls "ads for Bloomingdale's, the Wall Street Journal, and Lee jeans are mixed in with the more socially conscious pro bono work they have done for the Children's Defense Fund and the Episcopal Ad Project [this is now called the Church Ad Project, and can be found at churchad.com].

"'We're trying to stop people with these ads,' McElligott says of the Episcopal Church promotions. 'We're trying to make them open up their mental boxes. This is the first step in opening the possibility of regular church attendance.'

"The laid-back McElligott, relaxed in a green gingham-checked shirt and khakis, says he particularly enjoys beginning the ad brainstorming process with a piece of classical religious art. McElligott takes Titian's portrayal of Daniel in the lions' den as an example. 'People have closed their minds to that art. But by pulling it out of its original context and giving it a contemporary point of reference, we've made it meaningful again. Although,' admits McElligott sheepishly, 'I'm not sure I'd want to explain that to Titian.'

"What McElligott and Martin saw in Titian's painting was stress. Like the biblical Daniel, Christians have often been at odds with conventional values and have had to live with stress—and help each other cope. So Martin and McElligott put a headline above the painting: 'Contrary to conventional wisdom, stress is not a twentieth-century phenomenon.'"[4]

minish the very product it seeks to promote? William Lynch, a Jesuit expert on literacy images, suggests: "Nothing is more sacred than the intentions of life of man, and nothing is more offensive to the religious instinct than that this interior life should be twisted and maneuvered as though it were a vulgar, unimportant thing."[5]

It is our contention that it is not the *act* of promotion that "twists and maneuvers" the intentions of religious institutions. Rather the *way* in which a religious product is promoted determines whether the end result confers honor or ignominy on the advertiser and his or her product. Religious writers have commented that promotion does not, per se, go against scripture from the Bible[6] or the Talmud.[7]

In a sense, almost all religious organizations do some promotion, since a listing in the yellow pages or an outdoor sign with a sermon title on it constitutes promotion. Consider the following "promotion" at the bottom of the front page of the Friday New York *Times*: "JEWISH WOMEN/GIRLS Remember to light Shabbat candles 18 minutes before sunset. In NYC 8:09 PM. Information call 718-774-2060."

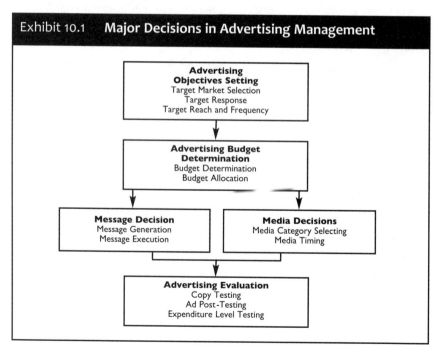

Exhibit 10.1   Major Decisions in Advertising Management

Martin Marty makes this point: "Who is kidding whom? Religious advertising goes on all the time. A religious group that offers no presentation of itself in a competitive, complex society will go undiscovered—or if it is already known, it will wane and disappear. The question is not 'Will churches advertise?' but 'How?'"[8]

Most clergy seem to agree that religious advertising is appropriate and necessary. In fact, a survey of 1,000 clergy and 1,250 members of the general population revealed that, if anything, clergy are more favorably disposed toward religious advertising than is the general populace.[9]

There are five major steps in developing an advertising program. They are detailed in Exhibit 10.1 and described below.

Determining Advertising Objectives

Before an advertising program and budget can be developed, advertising objectives must be set. These objectives must flow from prior decision-making on the target market, market positioning, and marketing mix. The marketing strategy defines advertising's job in the total marketing mix.

Developing advertising objectives calls for defining the target market, target response, and target reach and frequency.

Target Market Selection

A marketing communicator must begin with a clear target audience in mind. The audience may be potential new members, current members, or key publics. The audience may consist of individuals or groups. The target audience has a crucial influence on the communicator's decisions on *what* to say, *how* to say it, *when* to say it, *where* to say it, and *who* should say it.

Consider this in terms of First Presbyterian Church described in chapter 8. Suppose the church seeks to reach the Kids and Cul-de-Sacs segment located in Carmel, Indiana, based on the planning committee's assessment of market opportunity and the congregation's strengths and mission. Young couples with children, therefore, constitute one target market for the church.

Target Response

Once the target audience has been identified, you must define the target response that is sought. In this particular example, the First Church ultimately wants the targeted families to become a part of the First Church family. Any member of the target audience may be in one of six consumer readiness states with respect to the church or its members. These states—awareness, knowledge, liking, preference, conviction, and action—are described in the following paragraphs.[10]

1. *Awareness.* The first thing to establish is how aware the target audience is of the product (program, ministry, church, etc.). The audience may be completely unaware of the product, know only its name or one or two things about it. If most of the target audience is unaware, your task is to build awareness, perhaps just name recognition. This calls for simple messages repeating the name. Even then, building awareness takes time.

The First Presbyterian Church may be unknown to most of the young families, particularly those families who have just moved to Carmel. Some inexpensive marketing research can help determine their level of awareness. First Church may set, as its objective, making 70 percent of the young families aware of the church's name within one year.

2. *Knowledge.* The target audience may be aware of the product and yet not know much about it. In this case your goal is to transmit some key information. Thus, First Church may want its audience to know that it is a young, friendly church, with programs (products) that address the needs of young families. Following its advertising campaign, First Church can sample the target audience to measure whether they have little, some, or much knowledge of First Church, and to assess the content of their knowledge.

3. *Liking.* If the target audience members know the product, the next question is "How do they feel about it?" We can imagine a scale covering a range of responses, such as *dislike very much, dislike somewhat, indifferent, like somewhat,* and *like very much.* If the audience has an unfavorable view of First Church, they have to find out why, and then develop a communications program to build up favorable feelings. If the unfavorable view were rooted in real inadequacies of

the church (e.g., promoted as friendly, but when an interested prospect called the office she was treated rudely), then a communications campaign would not do the job and might make matters worse. The church would have to first improve and become the kind of congregation it claims to be, and then communicate this reality-based image.

4. *Preference.* The target audience may like the product, but may not prefer it to others. It may be one of several acceptable products available to the target audience. In this case your job is to build consumer preference. You will have to tout your quality, value, performance, and other attributes. In the case of First Church, it faces not only other churches, but also other generic competitors (i.e., other ways of spending time besides attending church services). This will influence the choice of messages intended to build preference for First over the alternative congregations. You can check on the success of the campaign by subsequently surveying the audience to see if its preference has grown stronger.

5. *Conviction.* A target audience may prefer a particular object, but may not develop a conviction about entering into an exchange with it. Thus some young families might prefer First to other churches, but never can get themselves out of bed in time on Sunday to make it to church. Your job is to build the conviction that going to church is the right thing to do. This requires an understanding of the benefits and perceived costs from the consumer's viewpoint. First Church must figure out how to generate conviction among its target audience that attending worship and Sunday school is the best thing they can do on a Sunday morning.

6. *Action.* Some target audience members may have conviction, but may not act. They may be waiting for additional information, may plan to act later, and so on. In this situation, you must lead the consumer to take the final step, which is called "closing the exchange." Among the action-producing devices are offering an incentive (e.g., the welcome dinner), offering an opportunity to try the object on a limited basis (e.g., Willow Creek's Wednesday evening worship service), and other means of inducing an urgency to act.

This model assumes that persons pass through a hierarchy of

states-of-readiness on the way to making a response decision to an offer. Your task is to identify the stage that most of the target audience is in, and develop a communication message or campaign that will move them to the next stage. From an advertiser's standpoint, the ideal ad campaign would ensure that:

(1) the right person is exposed to the right message at the right place and at the right time.

(2) the ad causes the person to pay attention to the ad but does not distract from the intended message.

(3) the ad properly reflects the person's level of understanding about your organization's programs or brand.

(4) the ad correctly positions your brand in concert with the other parts of the marketing mix.

(5) the ad motivates the person to become involved with your organization.

It would be efficient if one message could move the audience through all stages, but this rarely happens. Most communicators seek a cost-effective communication approach to move the target audience one stage at a time. The critical thing is to know where the main audience is and what the next feasible stage is.

Exhibit 10.2 Stages of Spiritual Growth and the Seven-step Philosophy of Willow Creek Church

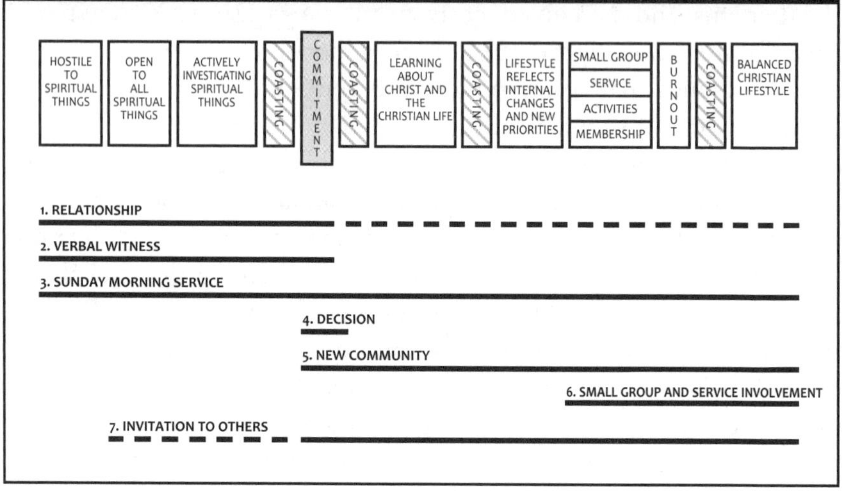

Willow Creek Community Church has developed a seven-step philosophy called "Stages of Spiritual Growth," which is their way of describing the stages persons pass through in their spiritual development (see Exhibit 10.2). The model identifies seven stages, from being "hostile to spiritual things" to adopting a "balanced Christian lifestyle." The leaders of the congregation use this model to track the growth of their parishioners and to inform the types of messages and experiences the person(s) should be receiving at each growth stage. Not only does this model suggest that different products are needed to meet the person's needs at different stages, but such a hierarchical model also assists in the planning of specific objectives for communications and advertising.

Saddleback Valley Community Church has also developed its unique model for understanding the hierarchy of states of readiness they see their parishioners passing through in their spiritual development. The religious organization's leaders have developed their ministry plan to move persons through the hierarchy of stages, and to inform their internal and external communications and advertising.

A careful study of the stages of growth models developed by the two churches makes it easy to understand that various advertising objectives can be developed for each stage—on the basis of whether their aim is to inform, persuade, or remind.[11]

The *inform* category includes such advertising objectives as telling the market about a new product, pointing out the benefits of a different religious behavior, informing the market of a "cost" change, explaining how the benefits of a ministry can be obtained, describing various available programs, correcting false impressions, reducing fears, and building an image. See Exhibits 10.3A, B, C for examples of informative ads.

The *persuade* category includes such advertising objectives as building preference for a church or synagogue's offering, encouraging switching to the advertiser's institution, trying to change the person's perception of the importance of different behavior attributes, persuading the member to act now, and persuading the unchurched person to receive a "sales call" (visit by clergy or layperson). See Exhibits 10.4A, B, C, D for examples of persuasive ads.

The *remind* category includes such advertising objectives as reminding persons that the religious organization will be there when they need it in the future, putting the person in touch with earlier religious inclinations and keeping the organization in their minds during holidays and other times during the year. See Exhibit 10.5A, B, C for examples of reminder ads.

Note: all ads in Exhibits 10.3-10.5 are used by permission of the Church Ad Project. More than 100 ads like these are available by contacting the Church Ad Project at http://www.churchad.com/ or (800) 331-9391.

Exhibit 10.3A Informative Ad

He died to
take away your sins.
Not your mind.

You don't have to stop thinking when you walk into
our church. Come and join us in an atmosphere where faith
and thought exist together in a spirit of fellowship.

Where women stand in our church.

If you believe that men and women should share equally in the sacraments and service of Christianity, join us where God's calling can be answered by anyone.

℗ © 2002 ChurchAd Project

Exhibit 10.3C Informative Ad

It's OK to dress casual for church. Jesus did.

Being comfortable with Jesus Christ starts with
being comfortable. Join us this Sunday, whatever you're wearing.

 © 2002 ChurchAd Project

Exhibit 10.4A Persuasive Ad

Sometimes it takes a miracle to get a couple into church.

After you've celebrated the wonder of birth, come join us as we
celebrate another miracle. The miracle of Jesus Christ.

Exhibit 10.4B **Persuasive Ad**

Without God, it's a vicious circle.

In a world too often ruled by war, hunger, disease and inhumanity, our church believes there is hope. Join us and grow in the faith and fellowship of Jesus Christ.

Exhibit 10.4C   Persuasive Ad

If you're looking for happiness here, you're just scratching the surface.

It takes more than luck to find happiness.
We suggest you try Jesus Christ. You'll find he's just the ticket for lasting joy.

Exhibit 10.4D Persuasive Ad

You're self-confident and self-reliant. But it never hurts to have a back-up.

You fearlessly push yourself to all kinds of achievements. So why do you find church so formidable? After all, Jesus Christ knows something about extremes himself. And he's waiting to show you some truly awesome things.

Do your kids think getting down the chimney is the miracle of Christmas?

Children should know there's more than one reason to celebrate Christmas. This year, introduce them to the real meaning of the Holiday season, and let Jesus give Santa Claus a little competition.

© 2002 ChurchAd Project

Exhibit 10.5B   Reminder Ad

What other meal can sustain you for a week?

Sometimes what we need most in life is not more physical nourishment, but spiritual nourishment.
Come join us in the weekly celebration of Holy Eucharist in our church.

Exhibit 10.5C Reminder Ad

Does Easter mean beans to your kids?

If you agree that Easter should do more for your children than raise their blood sugar level, we invite you and your family to experience the true miracle of Easter in our church.

See Exhibit 10.6 for an example of a reminder ad placed in a London subway station, and Exhibit 10.7 for a persuasive billboard ad placed along an interstate highway.

Exhibit 10.6   **Reminder Ad in London Underground (Subway) Station**

Target Reach and Frequency

The third decision that must be made is determining the optimal *target reach and frequency* of the advertising, Funds for advertising are rarely so abundant that everyone in the target audience can be reached, and reached with sufficient frequency. Religious marketers must decide what percentage of the audience to reach with what exposure frequency per time period.

First Presbyterian Church of Carmel, IN, for example, might decide to use direct mail, and decide on 500 advertising exposures. This leaves a wide choice available concerning target reach and frequency. First Church could send one letter to 500 different families, or it could send two different letters a week apart to 250 families, and so on. The issue is how much exposure is needed to create the desired response, given the market's (the target group) state of readiness. One exposure might be enough to move the targeted families from being unaware to being aware. It would not be enough to move families from awareness to preference.

Determining the Advertising Budget

Suppose First Church wants to send two letters to each of 250

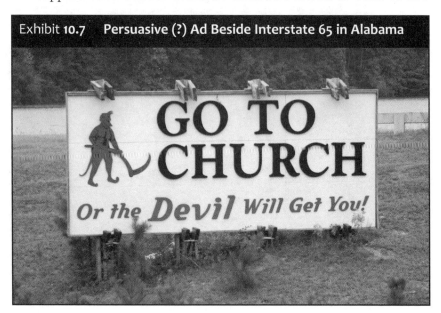

Exhibit **10.7**   Persuasive (?) Ad Beside Interstate 65 in Alabama

families. The gross number of exposures would be 500. Suppose that the average mailing piece will cost $.75 to design and mail. Then First Church will need a rough advertising budget of $375 to accomplish its objectives.

In addition to estimating the total amount of the required advertising budget, a determination must be made regarding how the budget should be allocated over different market segments, geographical areas, and time periods. In practice, advertising budgets are allocated to segments of demand according to their respective populations or response levels or in accordance with some other indicator of market potential (e.g., the presence of young families). It is common to spend twice as much advertising money in segment B as in segment A if segment B has twice the level of some indicator of market potential (e.g., young families without a church home).

How does one know whether one segment has twice as much potential for a positive response as another segment? In some cases, this judgment comes from experience—trial and error estimates of what works best with specific groups. Therefore, doing a bulk mailing to every home in census tract A versus census tract B makes sense if it is believed there are more young families in census tract A and if there is reason to believe young families will respond favorably to the promotion of the "product" designed with young families in mind. Geodemographics helps greatly in making such assumptions (see chapter 7). Geodemographic suppliers can also supply the mailing lists for your targeted segments for specific geographic areas, such as a zip code, a circle with a three-mile radius and your congregation at the center, a census tract, a one-mile-wide corridor on either side of a major road, etc.

Developing the Message

Once you have determined the objectives for the advertising program and established an advertising budget, the next step is to develop specific messages. Message generation involves developing a number of alternative messages (appeals, themes, motifs, ideas) from which the best one can be chosen.

When you selected the target segment and set the positioning strategy for it, you have already begun the design of the message you'll use in communicating to that segment. If, as described in chapters 7, 8, and 9, a specific ministry has been developed for a specific targeted group with a specific objective in mind that permits our mission to be achieved, you will already have a positioning strategy or promotional appeal in mind for the ministry. Even so, there are a variety of messages that could be developed around this basic theme.

Generating the Message

Messages can be generated in a number of ways. One approach is to talk with members of the target market and other influential parties to determine how they see the ministry or service, talk about it, and express their desires about it. A second approach is to hold a brainstorming session with laypeople in the church to generate several ideas. A third method is to use some formal deductive framework to tease out possible advertising messages. We will discuss one such framework—the rational, emotional, moral framework.

This framework identifies three types of messages that can be generated: rational, emotional, and moral.

Rational messages aim at passing on information, serving the audience's self-interest, or both. They attempt to show that the product will yield the expected benefits. Examples would be messages discussing a product's value or performance. In the case of the First Church, these might involve telling targeted Kids and Cul-de-Sacs segment about how children will enjoy learning about the Bible via the children's Sunday school classes, which focus on famous Bible characters.

Emotional messages are designed to stir up some negative or positive emotion that will motivate the desired behavior. Communicators have worked with fear, guilt, and shame appeals, especially in connection with getting people to start doing things they should do (e.g., attend church, hold a church office) or stop doing things they shouldn't do (e.g., smoke, over-imbibe, abuse drugs, or overeat). Advertisers have found that fear appeals work up to a point, but if there is too much fear the audience will ignore the message.[12]

Communicators have also used positive emotional appeals, such as love, humor, pride, and joy. Evidence has not, however, established that a humorous message, for example, is necessarily more effective than a straight version of the same message.[13] An emotional appeal for the First Church targeting young families might be showing a young family at worship with a message suggesting that the bond of a common faith enhances family cohesiveness.

Moral messages are directed to the audience's sense of what is right and proper. They are often used in messages exhorting people to support such social causes as a cleaner environment, better race relations, equal rights for women, and aiding the disadvantaged. A moral appeal for the First Church might focus on the need for parents to instill a strong sense of values based on biblical principles in their children to better ensure their future happiness and contribution to society.

Executing the Message

Once the basic message has been generated, it must find a style of execution. That is, a *style, tone, wording, order,* and *format* must be found to make the message effective.

Any message can be put across in different *execution styles*. Suppose a denomination is planning to launch a national campaign to get people to read their Bibles and wants to develop a 30-second television commercial to motivate people to start reading their Bibles and having family worship. Here are some major advertising execution styles they can consider:

1. *Slice of life.* A wife suggests to her husband that they might end the day right if they could contemplate some Bible passages together. He agrees, and the next frame shows them talking together on the couch with the TV off and an open Bible in front of them,

2. *Lifestyle.* A 30-year-old man pops out of bed when his alarm rings at 6:00 a.m. He races to the bathroom, races to the closet, races through breakfast, then slows down to take a few moments to read his Bible, then drives to work with a peaceful look on his face.

3. *Fantasy.* Parents read Bible stories to their children with the children imagining being in the lions' den or sitting on the lap of Jesus.

4. *Mood.* A jogger runs in a residential neighborhood on a beautiful spring day, noticing the beauty of nature. We hear Bible verses he is reciting to himself, which he read that morning from the book of Psalms, about God's handiwork. This ad creates a mood of beauty and harmony of humans with God's creation.

5. *Musical.* Ad depicts family singing hymns around the family piano with great joy and gusto.

6. *Personality symbol.* A well-known sports hero is shown reading his Bible with a smile on his face.

7. *Technical expertise.* A seminary professor or librarian discusses the variety of study Bibles currently available.

8. *Testimonial evidence.* The ad shows a variety of family members from different ethnic backgrounds telling how beneficial studying the Bible has been for them.

The communicator must also choose a *tone* for the message. The message could be deadly serious, chatty, humorous, and so on. The tone must be appropriate to the target audience and target response desired.

Words that are memorable and attention-getting must be found. This is nowhere more apparent than in the development of headlines and slogans to lead the reader into the message. There are six basic types of headlines: news, questions, narrative, command, 1-2-3 ways, and how-what-why.

The First Church, seeking to attract young families to their "welcome to your new home" dinner, might develop headlines using each of these styles.

News: "The Carmel First Presbyterian Church has been welcoming new neighbors to the area for years. Just listen to these glowing reports . . ."

Questions: "Why are these young families taking time from busy schedules to share a meal with strangers?"

Narrative: "The Campbell family didn't know a soul when they moved to Carmel, but that quickly changed when they attended a fellowship dinner last Wednesday night."

Command: "You've always said you wanted to get to know your new community. Well, do it now, and get a free meal in the bargain."

1-2-3 ways: "We have scheduled our fellowship dinners during different times to make it easy to get to know you."

How-what-why: "Getting to know your new community can begin tomorrow if you accept our invitation to meet your neighbors over dinner at the First Church."

Once the headline and the themes are determined, the communicator must consider the ordering of the ideas. There are three issues: conclusion drawing, one- or two-sided arguments, and order of presentation,

The first is the question of *conclusion drawing*, the extent to which the ad should draw a definite conclusion for the audience, such as telling them to "give their fair share," Experimental research seems to indicate that explicit conclusion drawing is more persuasive than leaving it to the audience to draw their own conclusions, There are exceptions, however, such as when the communicator is seen as untrustworthy or the audience is highly intelligent and annoyed at the attempt to influence them.

The second is the question of the *one- or two-sided argument*—that is, whether the message will be more effective if one side or both sides of the argument are presented. Two-sided arguments are of two types, First, there is the approach that admits that the offering has some defects. The classic example of this approach is the series of ads for the Volkswagen Beetle that admitted it was homely and that it didn't change its looks every model year, but that otherwise it was a marvelously sensible purchase. In the religious sector, there are many situations in which the target audience will know there is a negative side to a requested behavior:

- Potential tithers *know* that they are committing scarce financial resources on a regular basis to the church.
- Attendees to a midweek prayer service *know* that they are giving up leisure time and the comforts of home to attend,
- Potential blood donors to the church blood drive *know* that the needle will hurt and that they might feel faint.
- People who are asked to hold a church office *know* that they will have to devote time to carrying out those duties and may have to ask (beg, cajole, implore) others to carry out some responsibilities.

427

• Prospective new members *know* that giving up drinking or dancing to become new members will be a difficult change to make in their behavior.

• People *know* that being asked to observe the Sabbath means a major change in the way they spend their time on weekends.

The other kind of two-sided argument recognizes the fact that there are other alternatives. The burger and cola "wars" are message campaigns that fully recognize that there are tough competitors "out there." In the religious sector there are many parallel situations:

• Going to Sunday school means not being able to sleep in after being out late Saturday night.

• Paying tithe may mean not giving to the American Cancer Society or a university's alumni fund.

• Going to a church officers' meeting means not going bowling.

• Your child's choosing not to have sex before marriage means enduring the taunts of his or her peers.

• Not using artificial means of birth control means possibly having the economic pressures of a large family.

One-sided presentations are common in both the profit and religious sectors. They are often synonymous with what many would call a hard-sell approach. Yet social science research suggests that one-sided approaches may be relatively more effective in three situations: (1) when the audience is less educated; (2) when the audience already favors the message's central proposition; and (3) when the audience is not likely to be exposed later to counterpropaganda. Two-sided messages are said to be more effective when the opposite is true.

There is another, perhaps more compelling, factor that should influence whether two-sided messages are used. It is the degree of the audience's involvement in the behavior that the marketer is attempting to influence. In general we would argue the following: the higher the audience's involvement in the behavior, the more frequently the religious marketer should use two-sided messages.

There are several reasons for this: In high-involvement situations, target audience members are more likely to

• be very concerned about the costs of the behavior (see chapters 6 and 9).

- be opposed to the action advocated, if it means change.
- be aware of very attractive alternatives.

In high-involvement situations (see chapter 5) the target audience will engage in extensive internal cognitive activity, which will include considering costs and alternatives, They will engage in an extensive external search that will make available to them the "other side" of the argument. The religious communicator should seize the initiative and deal with the other side of the issue rather than leave it to the individual. A useful concept in this regard is what is called *inoculation theory*. If a communicator knows that a target audience member will *later* be exposed to counterpropaganda (the other side), a more favorable outcome will be achieved if the religious communicator deals with the counterarguments in advance, in effect "inoculating" the target audience against the later influence attempts.

Finally, it must be reemphasized that in situations in which a two-sided strategy would be appropriate, the religious communicator must go to great lengths to understand what *the target audience* perceives to be the key costs of the behavior and what they consider to be the reasonable alternative. Only with a solid research base can an effective two-sided strategy be developed.

A third issue for the communicator in cases where several ideas are to be conveyed is the best *order of presentation*. Social scientists have found that, other things being equal, people tend to remember the items in a message stream presented first (the primacy effect) and last (the recency effect). There are arguments for putting one's strongest statements in either position. Where one is using a two-sided message, the case is more complex. However, the following approach appears reasonable.

1. If the audience is likely to attend to the message under most circumstances (that is, not filter it out), it is probably best to place the message about the "other side" in the middle of the message where it is more likely to be forgotten and the arguments for one's own position in the first and last position.

2. If the audience is opposed to the message and likely to screen it out, then beginning with the other side of the issue or with the other alternative may disarm the audience into "hearing" the mar-

keter's message. Thus a religious marketer might say, "A night at home with the family watching TV by a warm fire would be great this winter. But First Church has some good reasons for you to consider other pleasures."

Format elements can make a difference in an ad's impact, as well as in its cost. If the message is to be carried in a print ad, the communicator must develop the elements of headline, copy, illustration, and color. Advertisers are adept at using such attention-getting devices as *novelty, contrast, arresting pictures,* and *movement.* Large ads, for example, gain more attention, and so do four-color ads, and this must be weighed against their higher costs. If the message is to be carried over the radio, the communicator must carefully choose words, voice qualities (speech rate, rhythm, pitch, articulation), and vocalizations (pauses, sighs, yawns). If the message is to be carried out on TV or given in person, then all of these elements, plus body language (nonverbal clues), must be planned. Presenters need to pay attention to their facial expressions, gestures, dress, posture, and hairstyle.

As we have already noted, individuals have a substantial background of experiences, categorization schemes, prejudices, association, needs, wants, and fears that can markedly affect what they "see" or "hear" in the message.

This potential for distortion can work to the communicator's advantage. Messages can be relatively economical in what they say by using association that they know people will bring to a symbol, a word, or an example. For example, readers need to see only one of these symbols depicted in an ad to know that a restaurant is *not* a fast-food outlet: a tablecloth, flowers on the table, silverware, a waiter taking an order, candles or subdued lighting, upholstered chairs, wine glasses, or china. Someone with glasses is supposed to be smarter than someone without them. Colors have symbolism: white is pure; gold is rich; blue is soothing; pastels are "modern"; and so on.

This is a major advantage to communicators. The problem, of course, is to choose the right symbols and to be assured that your audience sees them as you do. While the religious marketer should carefully plan the choice of association, one advantage of personal communication is that a sensitive communicator can secure feedback on how the message is actually perceived and fine-tune it so that it is perceived as intended.

Even if a message is perceived in an appropriate fashion, this does not guarantee that it will be retained or, more important, recalled at the moment it is "needed" to influence a particular behavior. One technique to reduce this possibility is, of course, repetition. Research has suggested that up to three repetitions will improve the probability of retention under high-involvement conditions. Another technique is to link the new information to existing cognition. Individuals are more likely to recall things that they can assimilate well.

Selecting the Media

Which Ads Don't Get Skipped? An ongoing research study by TiVo of 20,000 TiVo-equipped households (called TiVo Stop Watch), reveals some very interesting viewing habits of American households. The focus of the study is to determine which TV ads are fast-forwarded by the lowest number of viewers. The results are instructive about what "works" with regard to getting your ad noticed. The conclusion: it isn't the funniest, most creative, big-budget ads that are being viewed instead of being fast-forwarded past—it is "direct" ads. These are such ads as CORT Furniture Rentals and Bowflex home gyms, which present a message to people that relates directly to a felt need via a media placement that reaches them when the need is salient (e.g., the Bowflex ad appears during professional wrestling when a viewer is likely to reevaluate his own musculature and check out a home gym).

"Leaders on the overall least-fast-forwarded list . . . were often those that advertised during the daytime on cable, where shows have smaller, niche audiences, and it's easier to deduce the viewer, according to TiVo. Smart media planning, not creative ads, seems to be the key. . . . If TiVo owners are any guide, it seems that just reaching an interested audience and putting the product right out there sets you leagues ahead, no matter how banal or bludgeoning your spot is.[14]

As the findings of the study described above indicate, good placement of an "adequate" message may generate more positive results than adequate placement of a great creative ad. This suggests the importance of the next step in the advertising process—selecting the media.

Once the advertising budget and message have been set for a given market segment, region, and time period, the next task is to allocate this budget across media categories and vehicles. There are two basic steps in the media selection process: (1) choosing among major media categories and (2) timing.

Choosing Among Major Media Categories

The first step calls for allocating the advertising budget to the major *media categories*. These categories must be examined for their capacity to deliver reach, frequency, and impact. They are newspapers, television, direct mail, radio, magazines, outdoor (billboards, and other public spaces, such as on mass transit, in movie theaters, sports arenas, hotel elevators, restrooms, bicycle racks, gasoline pumps, bus benches, etc.), and the Internet. Religious marketers choose among these major media categories by considering the following variables.

1. *Target audience media habits.* For example, radio, television, and the Internet are the most effective media for reaching teenagers.

2. *Product or service.* Media categories have different potentialities for demonstration, visualization, explanation, believability, and color.

3. *Message.* A message announcing an emergency blood drive tomorrow requires radio or newspapers. A message containing a great deal of technical data might require specialized magazines, Internet, or direct mailings. Messages that would benefit from consumers adding their own inputs might be most effective on the radio.

4. *Cost.* Television is very expensive, and newspaper advertising is inexpensive. What counts, of course, is the cost per thousand relevant exposures, rather than the total cost. That is, if one media cost $80 and reaches 5,000 members of the target audience (cost per thousand = 1.6 cents), and another costs $70 and reaches 3,500 (cost

per thousand = 2.0 cents), then the more expensive medium is the "better buy." Keyword advertising (i.e., "pay per click") on the Internet can be a very low-cost way of advertising to people who have demonstrated an interest in subjects related to your organization based on their choice of keywords used in a search. See the discussion of Internet advertising below.

The organization's leaders must decide how to allocate its advertising budget to the major media categories.

Newspapers. Newspapers have definitely fallen on hard times in America. Even major newspapers in large cities have gone out of business (e.g., *The Rocky Mountain News*), declared bankruptcy (e.g., Chicago *Tribune*), or have reduced home delivery to three times a week (e.g., Detroit *Free Press*). With declining circulation threatening newspapers throughout the country, many newspaper publishers have started electronic editions to stave off closure. Despite the downward trend, newspapers remain a traditional tool of religious advertisers, perhaps because of the relatively low cost, and because other religious marketers seem to use the media. Newspaper advertising has the following features of interest to religious advertisers:

1. *Flexibility.* Ad placement, change, or cancellation can be done at relatively short notice. Also, for a small charge newspapers allow the organization to select the page or section where the ad will run. The church or synagogue should make these decisions based on its target market; if the organization is trying to reach the unchurched, it should not run the ad in the religious section.

2. *Timeliness.* The speed with which ads can be placed and the frequency of ad exposure combine to make newspaper ads a good option. However, a newspaper's "short life" (one day or one weekend) can be a disadvantage.

3. *Production simplicity.* This can be both an advantage to the novice who needs the newspaper's production department to aid in the development of the ad and a disadvantage to the advertiser needing a sharp reproduction of a graphic.

4. *Good coverage.* The broad distribution of many local newspapers means that generally a high percentage of large population segments will be exposed to the ad.

> When the ministry team at Salem First Nazarene launched their new ministry programs for singles, divorced persons, and children of single-parent households, they initially had very little response. After three disappointing months they asked themselves three questions: Did we misread the community and its needs (poor situation analysis)? Did we plan poor programs (poor product planning)? Are we failing to get our message to the right people (poor targeting)? They decided that they had indeed listened to the community and that their programs were responsive to the needs. They decided they must have not been getting the message to the target audience.
>
> At that time the congregation was utilizing three modes of communicating with the community: the religious TV channel, its own radio programs, and the religion section of the newspaper. The decision was made not to advertise over the TV channel, nor to announce the programs on their own radio programs, nor to continue advertising in the religion section of the newspaper. Rather, they would run advertisements in the newspaper's sports and entertainment sections. Almost immediately large numbers of persons who were singles by choice, divorced persons, and children of single-parent households began to participate in the programs.

Television. This medium can be very expensive for a small congregation. Television, however, has the ability to reach many people quickly. It combines sight, sound, and motion to generate high sensory appeal. However, it has high absolute cost, high clutter, fleeting exposure, and less audience selectivity as limitations.

Religious organizations contemplating television advertising must consider several factors: channels, costs of spot ads, number of times the ads will be run, and costs and types of creative approaches. We can all cite examples of local ads that were either very effective or bordering on the offensive and infantile.

Using spot ads on local stations or on cable can be a forceful means of getting the message to a target audience, but religious marketers should be aware of the requirements for effective television advertisements before making such an investment.[15]

Radio. Radio stations should be considered on the basis of the audience they reach. Some of the advantages of radio advertising are:

1. *Target marketing.* Radio programming has increasingly segmented the listening audience. For example, where a station may have previously been known as a "rock" station, now there is "alternative rock" for teenagers, "indie" rock for college students, "garage" rock for the over-30 crowd, and "classic" rock for those in their 40s and 50s, Advertisers can "rifle" their message to subsegments of the population more effectively with radio than "shotgunning" with a more mass audience media, such as newspapers.

2. *Flexibility.* Radio ads can be placed or changed on relatively short notice. This could be of value to take advantage of fast-changing market or environmental conditions, such as messages of First Church or inspiration when a local disaster strikes, messages of joy for local good news, and so on.

3. *Urgency and Frequency.* The use of sound can help convey a better sense of urgency to a message. Also, radio messages can reach target audience members more frequently than can some other media.

4. *Cost.* Radio advertising can generate low cost per thousand people reached (CPM).

Direct Mail. Direct mail is a medium that is increasingly being used by nonprofit organizations. Novelli has suggested that direct mail has six important advantages for nonprofit organizations:

1. It tends to be very focused; it can achieve maximum impact on a specific target market.

2. It can be private and confidential, a major advantage for religious organizations, whose spiritual messages are often perceived as very personal matters.

3. Cost per contact and cost per response can often be very low, which is an important appeal to religious organizations with very low budgets.

4. Results are quite often clearly measurable, and this can help make marketing programs more accountable. First Church can learn very specifically the effectiveness of a direct-mail piece that offers

free literature to those who send in a response card, or by counting the number of families who visit the church as a result of the direct mailing.

5. Small-scale tests of proposed strategies are very feasible with direct mail. In fact, direct mail is an ideal field-test vehicle. A number of marketing factors can be varied over several mailings and the results compared to baseline measures. In tests of other media it is often difficult to link a specific surge in response to, say, a flight of radio advertisements. By contrast, if more literature requests come in from those who receive a mailing with a message about "how to achieve peace of mind" than from those who are offered literature on "what happens when you die," it is easy to conclude that a "peace of mind" message works best.

6. The effectiveness of direct mail can be assessed directly in terms of *behavior* (for example, requests and inquiries), whereas other media assessments usually require attitude and awareness indicators, which, as discussed earlier, are fraught with measurement problems.[16]

There are several steps in establishing a strategically effective direct-mail campaign.

1. *Determine the objectives of direct mail programs in advance.* Is the program to generate behavior, create awareness, change attitudes, or make contacts to be followed up through other media? In some cases a phased strategy is appropriate, in which earlier mailers are used to develop awareness and later mailers to generate action.

2. *Determine the target audience.* Some groups are more responsive to direct mail than are others. Refer to one of the direct-mail books listed in the Resource Guide for examples of response rate differences by population groups.

3. *Develop mail lists.* Outside services can be the source of highly tailored prospect lists defined by schooling; occupation area; socioeconomic status of the neighborhood; patronage of particular products, services, or outlets; and so on. Whenever time permits, new rented lists should be tested with small mailings to see if they are productive before a modest budget is committed to an unknown target list. The best lists, however, are always those containing the addresses of people with whom the organization already has some form of

contact. Thus the best prospects are those who have responded to past mailings, who have made inquiries in some other fashion, or who have visited the church or synagogue on some occasion. The geodemographic firms listed in chapter 7 can provide mailing lists for selected geodemographic segments.

4. *Develop effective copy.* Investment in effective graphics and compelling messages is seldom wasted. Direct-mail pieces are meeting more and more competition every day in the "mailbox arena." The religious organization needs powerful messages and compelling visual images to stand out. Attention must be paid to envelope design (to get the message exposed), the cover letter (to get it read), and motivational themes (to get it acted on). Many mailings fail because they are not consciously designed to stimulate responses.

5. *Pretest each mailer.* This can be done inexpensively and, if sample target audience members are used, can both indicate probable successes and point out potential problems.

6. *Schedule mailings carefully.* Some mailings have predetermined timings (i.e., for particular events). In those cases the mailings should arrive just as the evaluation stage of consumer decision-making is taking place. Thus mailings for church events are best when sent six to eight weeks before the event. They are seldom effective in the last week unless they are targeted to an impulse-based audience. When the timing of mailings is discretionary, the marketer should carefully test different patterns, for example, with mailings bunched together in *flights* (a grouping of mailings, released at one time) or spread out over time.

7. *Use responses as feedback.* The savvy direct mailer learns from each mailing what works or doesn't work in the mailing design itself. If a systematic program of experimentation is used over the years, much can be learned about effective tactics for particular audiences. Mail responses can also tell something about the responder.

As Tom McCabe of International Marketing Group notes: "You know exactly who responds and why. . . . Every time someone responds to a mailing, you learn something about that person. Direct marketing is very efficient because eventually you will be able to know what kind of return to expect on every marketing dollar you spend."[17]

437

Telemarketing. Telemarketing is employed to start new congregations and new Sunday school classes, to invite persons to attend existing programs, to announce a new program, and so on.

Under the leadership of the Reverend Bruce R. Ough, the Reverend Nancy Allen, and the Reverend Wesley Daniel, the United Methodist Church of Iowa launched a series of highly creative and effective telemarketing campaigns in small and large congregations. Bruce Ough, at that time, was program council director for the Iowa United Methodist Church. Nancy Allen and Wesley Daniel are program consultants. They call their telemarketing program "teleinviting," and they use the program for church planting and growth. One comprehensive example is that of the Christ Community Church (United Methodist) of Cedar Rapids.

The Reverend Ron Blix was a member of the Congregational Development Committee, which decided to launch a new congregation in the northeast part of Cedar Rapids. He was appointed the founding pastor and was given a parsonage, a budget, and a copy of *The Phone's for You!* by Norman W. Whan, on telemarketing for churches.[18] More than 130 volunteer callers made 53,000 calls in a six-mile radius of the new church location. The volunteers made calls over a period of four evenings. The volunteers received a 15-minute training session. They were given call sheets (script), work tracks (phone numbers) and cards to record names and addresses. They practiced making calls in pairs, using the provided script. The Church Information and Development Services guided which programs and ministries were emphasized in the calls. The average call lasted 60 seconds.

Sixty percent of the people called were at home. Sixty-five percent already belonged to a church. The remaining 35 percent went on the prospect list. This effort yielded a mailing list of 14,300 names. Blix sees the purpose of teleinviting to be the development of a qualified mailing list. Each person on the list would receive 5 items:

(1) a greeting letter from Blix.

(2) a letter from Blix describing his theology and approach to ministry.

(3) a postcard describing the church.

(4) a statement of 10 ways the church could meet needs.

(5) an invitation to attend the first service.

A callback campaign reached 95 percent of the persons on the mailing list, who were invited to attend the church's opening. The church spent $1,000 on newspaper, radio, and TV ads.

More than 440 people attended the first worship service. Some attending had not been phoned, but were invited by friends who had received a call. The service took place in a movie complex that had five theaters (screens). One was used for worship, one as a nursery, and three for Sunday school. The large lobby housed two classes. New attendees kept coming over the next year at a rate of two or three new persons each Sunday, as a response to the call they had initially received. One family did not attend until 14 months after they had been called. Within two years the average attendance settled at 223. An information stub at the bottom of the Sunday bulletin continues to yield new prospect names. The new congregation recently used teleinviting to plant a daughter church after making 25,000 phone calls. The daughter church now has 60 members.

Here is another example of the use of telemarketing.

The Reverend Gene Koth of the Walnut Hill United Methodist Church, west of Des Moines, launched the new congregation by dialing 25,000 phone numbers, yielding 2,600 names. He invested $200 in ads in the suburban paper. To support the effort, 180 lay and clergy volunteers were recruited from other congregations in the Des Moines area. The volunteers received training in a 15-minute session. The group used the phones of a local insurance company, which loaned their facilities and equipment.

Three hundred twelve people attended the first service. Attendance settled at 233. The original 2,600 names were also called to invite them to the congregation's first Easter and Christmas services. Today the congregation has 600 active members and constituents—50 percent brought in by friends, 40 percent by phone calls, and 10 percent from newspaper ads. Each year 7,000 calls are made to new residents.

The ministries and services are directed toward baby boomers. Continual feedback is garnered from survey stubs on the Sunday bulletin. As a result of the feedback, the church uses little printed material. The worship service is simple: there are no congregational readings, and the sermons deal with practical concerns. Ministries are designed for specific small groups (singles, couples, etc.).

Telemarketing carried on within a congregation has a beneficial effect on the volunteers. Most persons in the congregation never had the experience of recruiting a new member. Telemarketing offers them a sense of excitement in seeing how persons respond to their calls, and a sense of gratification in helping their congregation grow.

Online Advertising. Many congregations have discovered that on-line advertising can be a very cost effective means of reaching people with an interest in their organization. There are three primary means of advertising online: Search Engine Marketing, contextual advertising, and e-mail advertising.

Search Engine Marketing. Unlike the other media listed above, where you incur costs whether or not you get any response, with search engine marketing or pay per click (PPC) advertising you pay for only those occasions someone clicks on your ad and is immediately sent to your Web site via the search engine link. PPC is a search engine marketing technique offered by *Google AdWords, Yahoo! Search Marketing* (formerly *Overture)*, and *MSN AdCenter.* These companies help novice Internet advertisers set up their advertising accounts based on their ad budget so that you won't find yourself spending beyond your means. Google, for example, has a tutorial in their learning center called "AdWords Starter Edition" that explains how keyword advertising works, and helps you set up an advertising program on Google, including building a Web site if you don't already have one.

The basic idea of keyword advertising is to direct someone to your Web site who is in the process of conducting a keyword search on a search engine like Google, Yahoo, or MSN, using a keyword or phrase that you believe is relevant to your organization. For example, if someone entered the keywords "Carmel," "Indiana," and "Church" in a Google search pane, there is a possibility that they are interested in seeing what churches are located in that area. Perhaps they are planning to move to Carmel, just moved there, or have

---

Exhibit 10.8   Sponsored Links

Discovery Church
a life-changing, multicultural,
balanced, "spirit-filled" ministry
www.discoveryci.org

Life Church
We're redefining church for
a new generation!
www.lifechurchindy.com

New Church in Carmel, Indiana
great kids' ministry
small groups
contemporary music
relevant talks
www.northparkwired.com

---

lived in Carmel for a while, but the birth of a first child has prompted them to consider joining a church. If they also included the search term "Presbyterian," they might be particularly interested in learning of First Presbyterian Church and their ministries. So, if First Church had entered these keywords in their Google AdWords account, the ad they had developed for their church, including a link to their Web site, would appear in the window with the results of the Google search using those keywords. Entering "Carmel," "Indiana," and "church" in a search conducted in the summer of 2009 generated 131,000 "hits," a Google map with church locations and links, and the ads shown in Exhibit 10.8.

Why pay for such an ad, when these search terms generate your Web site as one of the results (i.e., on the left side of the results page) at no cost to you? Because you have no control over where you appear in the results (however, an understanding of search engine optimization [SEO] can improve your odds of being listed early in the results page), but you can be sure that you'll appear on the first page of the results when you pay for the ad.

In August 2007 an article in the *Wall Street Journal*[19] reported that Facebook would begin an ad system that would let advertisers target ads to Facebook members based on the member's and his/her friend's favorite activities and preferred music. This is described as "demand generation" ad placement, where ads are for products or services in which the person might be interested, based upon that the person's activities or interests. *AdWords*, and other keyword advertising, is referred to as "demand fulfillment" advertising, because it is based upon active search initiated by the individual. The "demand generation" approach to ad placement could be a powerful new way of placing ads on the Internet.

While the strategy and budgeting for search engine, or keyword, advertising is beyond the scope of our discussion here (see sources in the Resource Guide for more on Internet advertising), these quotes from a blog on keyword advertising will provide some perspective on the topic:[20]

• We've used Google *Adwords* for the past year, and we have people that come to Revolution all the time simply because of our Web sites. Our click-throughs aren't that high—54 last month. Very cost-effective marketing!

• We have been using Google *Adwords* since March and have been getting good click through rates. I recently changed the landing page, to see if we can get the people who click to come to be with us.) One tip: Google allows you to rotate ads (split tests), so you can test one ad against another. You should take advantage of it and test one headline versus another, one element versus another, until you figure out the best ad!

• The Rock at Church Ranch in Westminster, Colorado, has tried keyword advertising, and it's working for them. Ryan Dickinson, the church's outreach coordinator and a partner at the Denver area Harper Design, shared that in less than a month they increased visits to their Web site from five per day to 45 per day. They've had little competition for the keywords, so they pay around 10 cents per click. Last month they spent a whopping $32.42 on keyword marketing, drawing 291 click-throughs. They've averaged 28 visitors per month, or about two new families every week. They haven't had a Sunday yet without at least one visitor who came to the church thanks to their Web site. So far this summer their attendance has hit a high of 147, compared to 115 last summer. Some advice from Ryan Dickinson: "Make sure your Web site is geared for visitors, including directions, basic info, and frequent updates. The goal isn't just to get Web surfers to visit your site—it's to get them to visit your church. That requires an effective Web site. Take the time to research and understand what people are searching for. Both Yahoo and Google make this easy. Write effective ads. Both Yahoo and Google will bold the search terms in your ad, so be sure to include those words in your copy. You don't have to bid for the top spot on every keyword. The Rock at Church Ranch averages 3.2 in the ranking of ads. It's not the top spot, but it still works." A bonus of keyword marketing that Dickinson didn't mention is the ability to put a cap on your spending. You can bid on keywords up to whatever dollar amount you specify, which makes it easy to stay on budget.

Contextual Advertising. In this type of advertising ads appear that are related to the content of a Web page being viewed, either in an automated or semiautomated manner. If the viewer is examining an article on how to have a meaningful prayer life, the contextual ad system delivers your ad for a free booklet entitled "How to Talk to God." Contextual advertising identifies the specific content of the ad being viewed by examining the url, keywords, and other information on the page. The contextual advertiser's analysis of this information generates the ad, which appears on the page being viewed. This type of advertising has been somewhat controversial, since people may be annoyed by an ad "popping up" on their screen when they are merely browsing through a page.[21]

E-mail Advertising. Another use of the Internet for promotion is e-mail marketing, in which the receiver gets an e-mail message that includes a promotion for your organization. You probably "subscribe" to several companies that send you e-mail promotions. Of course, you also probably get a lot more that never make it through your spam trap, but most people do open and read, and perhaps respond to, e-mails from some organizations in a typical day. Permission-based e-mails are opened an average of 78 percent of the time.[22] E-mail advertising is typically much cheaper than other forms of online advertising on a per-customer-reached basis. It is also easy to test which types of e-mails are most effective in generating response from your target audience. Research has shown that 73 percent of those interviewed reported making a purchase as a result of e-mail. Interested readers should refer to a source describing the guidelines for operating a successful e-mail advertising process.[23]

Brand Building Online. "The best brand building on the Internet will fuse the attention-getting power of the Web's interactive environment with the targeted relationship techniques of information-driven direct marketing. It will be tightly integrated with offline brand development activities."[24] If you are attempting to build a brand around your congregation or one of its ministries, you will want to use your presence on the Internet to reinforce the brand elements (see chapter 9). The Internet's characteristics of interactivity, immediacy, and involvement can be harnessed to help build the brand's image and support the brand-building activities you are doing offline. Roberts suggests several powerful tools are available for supporting your brand on the Internet:

1. Personalization tools. Registered visitors to your Web site can be greeted by name when they log on, and responses to requests (for example, sending the latest copy of an e-mail newsletter) can be customized based on the database of the visitor's behavior, demographics, etc.

2. Purchase-process streamlining tools. If you begin offering items for purchase on your site, as have some mega congregations, you can provide shopping carts that can be saved for future completion of the purchase, retain customer information (such as shipping address, credit card information, etc.), and attend to other details that facilitate the transaction.

3. Self-service tools. Web sites can be structured to allow the visitor to be entirely self-sufficient in obtaining what they want from your site, or to get phone support or engage in a live online chat if desired.

4. Customization tools. This is the process of generating a product, service, or communication to fit the specifications of the Web site visitor. The most obvious example of this would be a specific prayer request, but there might be other possible customization opportunities for your brand.

5. Creating community. Brand communities can be supported on the Web by providing discussion forums at your site for people

to engage in community building around your brand(s). Brand building can also make use of podcasts, blogs, your Web site, and community bulletin boards (see more on brand building and the use of these tools in chapter 9).[25]

Deciding on Media Timing

The other major decision in media selection is *timing*. Timing the advertising breaks down into a *macro* problem and a *micro* problem.

The macro problem is that of *seasonal timing*. During religious holidays, audience size and interest are higher than at any other time. Some churches and synagogues have concentrated their ads during religious holidays to remind people of the year-round benefits of attending church. The micro problem is that of the *short-run timing* of advertising. How should advertising be spaced during a short period of, say, one week? Consider three possible patterns. The first is called *burst advertising* and consists of concentrating all the exposures in a very short period of time, such as all in 1 day. Presumably this will attract maximum attention and interest, and if recall is good, the effect will last for a while.

The second pattern is *continuous advertising*, in which the exposures appear evenly throughout the period. This may be most effective when the audience needs to be continuously reminded.

The third pattern is *intermittent advertising*, in which intermittent small bursts of advertising appear with no advertising in between. This pattern is able to create a little more attention than continuous advertising, but it has some of the reminder advantage of continuous advertising.

Timing decisions should take three factors into consideration. *Audience turnover* is the rate at which the target audience changes between two periods. The greater the turnover, the more continuous the advertising should be.

Behavior frequency is the number of times the target audience takes the action one is trying to influence (for example, some social behaviors such as smoking or giving blood). The more frequent the behavior, the more the advertising should be continuous.

The *forgetting rate* is the rate at which a given message will be forgotten or a given behavior change relinquished. Again, the faster the forgetting, the more continuous the advertising should be.

Evaluating the Advertising

The final step in the effective use of advertising is *advertising evaluation*. The most important components are copy-testing, ad posttesting, and expenditure-level testing.

Copy Testing. Copy testing can occur before an ad is put into actual media (copy pretesting) and after it has been printed or broadcast (copy posttesting). The purpose of *ad pretesting* is to make improvements in the advertising copy to the fullest extent possible prior to its release. There are several methods of ad pretesting.

1. Comprehension testing. A critical prerequisite for any advertisement is that it be comprehensible. This can be a major problem when dealing with less-educated or even illiterate audiences. When words are used in the advertisement, one or more readability formulas can be applied to predict comprehension. These formulas measure the length of sentences and the number of polysyllabic words.

2. Direct mailings. Here a panel of target audience members examines alternative ads and fills out rating questionnaires. Sometimes a single question is raised, such as "Which of these ads do you think would influence you most to [request literature, attend worship services, etc.]?"

A more elaborate form consisting of several rating scales may be used, such as the one shown in Exhibit 10.9. Here the person evaluates the ad's attention strength, read-through strength, cognitive strength, affective strength, and behavioral strength, assigning a number of points (up to a maximum) in each case. The underlying theory is that an ad must score high on all of these properties if it is ultimately to stimulate action.

At the same time, direct rating methods are judgmental and less reliable than harder evidence of an ad's actual impact on target audience members. Direct rating scales help primarily to screen out poor ads, those that are deficient in attention-getting or comprehension-creating abilities, rather than to identify great ads.

Exhibit 10.9   Rating Sheet for Ads

	(Possible PTS)
Attention:	
How well does the ad catch the reader's attention?	_____(20)
Read-through strength:	
How well does the ad catch the reader to read further?	_____(20)
Cognitive strength:	
How clear is the central message or benefit?	_____(20)
Affective strength:	
How effective is the particular appeal?	_____(20)
Behavioral strength:	
How well does the ad suggest follow-through action?	_____(20)

|_____|_____|_____|_____|_____|_____| _____TOTAL

0	20	40	60	80	100
Poor ad	Mediocre ad	Average ad	Good ad	Great ad	

3. Focus-group interviews. Since advertisements are often viewed in a group setting, pretests with groups can often indicate both how a message is perceived and how it might be passed along. The focus group technique has the following advantages:

• Its synergism can generate more reactions than a one-on-one session.

• It is more efficient in that it gathers data from five to nine people at once.

• It can yield data relatively quickly.[26]

4. Self-administered questionnaires. This approach can be valuable in reaching hard-to-get-at target audiences. Since response rates can be a problem with this technique, follow-up calls are necessary to yield a representative sample.

Ad Posttesting Methods

There are three popular **ad posttesting methods** to assess whether the desired impact is achieved, or what the possible ad weaknesses are.

1. Recall tests. These involve finding persons who are regular users of the media vehicle and asking them to recall advertisers and ministries contained in the issue under study. They are asked to recall or play back everything they can remember. The administrator may or may not offer to aid them in their recall. Recall scores are prepared on the basis of their responses and are used to indicate the ad's power to be noted and remembered.

2. Recognition tests. Recognition tests call for sampling the readers of a given issue of the vehicle and asking them to point out what they recognize as having seen or read before.

3. Direct response. The preceding techniques measure *communication outcomes* of advertising. But favorable communication outcomes may not translate into *behavioral* outcomes! However, behavioral responses can be tracked by using a direct-mail approach as follows:

a. Placing mail-back coupons with a code number or post office box in the advertisement that varies by message and medium. For example, if a church advertises a ministry requiring a phone call or mail response in the morning and evening local newspapers, it can direct respondents to ask for offer E (for evening paper ad) or offer M (for morning paper ad). In this way the church can determine whether the morning or evening paper is generating a greater response. The same approach could be used for radio stations, handouts, posters, and so on.

b. Asking target audience members to mention or bring in an advertisement in order to receive special treatment (for example, reserved seats at a religious concert).

c. Setting up a phone number and asking individuals to call for further information (on which occasion they can be asked where they saw the ad, what they remember, etc.).

d. Staggering the placement of ads so that this week's attendance can be attributed to ad A, while next week's can be attributed to ad B. This is also an effective method for assessing alternative expenditure levels.

e. See previous discussion of advertising on the Internet for ways that permit you to measure behavioral outcomes for this advertising medium.

Religious organizations can learn a great deal about the effectiveness of alternative message and media strategies by designing experiments coupled with careful posttest measures.

Expenditure Level Testing

Expenditure level testing involves arranging experiments in which advertising expenditure levels are varied over similar markets (e.g., target audiences or people in different geographic areas) to see

---

Sports and Salvation at Faith Nights at the Stadium

You would be hard pressed to find two more popular topics in the South than sports and religion. That's why it was inevitable that promoters at minor and even major league teams have found ways to marry the two at Faith Nights at the stadium. On Faith Night at a Birmingham Steeldogs minor league football game before kickoff a Christian band entertained the crowd. Promoters gave away thousands of bobblehead dolls depicting such Bible heroes as Daniel, Noah, and Moses. The home team ran onto the field in special jerseys with Bible verses printed on the back. A pastor at a local Baptist church, Donnie Rhodes, brought 47 sixth graders to the game, and said it was a perfect outing. "It was affordable, safe, and spiritual," he said. "And the kids thought it was the coolest thing." Third Coast Sports, a company specializing in event planning and church marketing for sports teams, scheduled 70 Faith Night promotions in 44 cities in 2006, and many teams produce their own Faith Nights. Nor is this just a minor league phenomenon—such promotions have been held by such major league teams as the Atlanta Braves, Arizona Diamondbacks, and Florida Marlins.

Both the teams and fans get something from these events. Churches get discounted tickets to sporting events with a Christian theme, and they, in return, mobilize their congregants to fill the stands. It all appears to be a win-win proposition—for the Nashville Sounds AAA baseball team, attendance at Faith Nights is 59 percent higher than the team's average attendance.[27]

---

the variation in response. A "high spending" test would consist of spending twice as much money in a similar territory as another to see how much more response (attendance at service, requests for literature, and so on) this produces. If the response is only slightly greater in the high spending area, it may be concluded, other things being equal, that the lower budget is adequate.

Viral Marketing and Guerrilla Marketing

Viral marketing is a term used to describe any strategy intended to encourage individuals to pass along a marketing message to other individuals, resulting in an exponential spread of the message, similar to the spread of a contagious virus. Other terms used to describe this phenomenon are buzz, wildfire, avalanche, organic, fission, or ripple marketing. "Buzz" can either be uncodified, where the messages are not controlled by the marketer, or codified, where the organization sponsors the communications. The latter is what we usually think of when using the term viral marketing. Wilson identified six principles of successful viral marketing campaigns:

1. Provides something of value for free to your target audience. This might be a good, service, event, experience, or information that is valued by the people you are trying to engage in a relationship. The fact that you are providing it free is the catalyst for generating buzz among this group.

2. Provides for effortless transfer to others. The medium that is used to transfer the message from recipient to recipient must provide for easy, replicable communication such as e-mail, Web site, or download, if using the Internet. However you do this, the objective is to make it easy to pass along the message without degradation.

3. Scales easily from small to very large. You must be prepared for success on a large scale. How will you handle the number of visitors to your festival if four times as many as predicted show up? The principle of viral marketing is exponential growth, so you must have contingency plans for growth beyond expectations.

4. Exploits common motivations and behaviors. Understanding the common motivators of people's behavior (chapter 5) allows you to generate messages that people will pass along in a viral network.

People love to repeat a "cool" or catchy phrase ("sons of thunder" [Mark 3:17] is just as catchy in the twenty-first century as it was in the first century), and will pass along messages that exploit some common motivation.

5. Utilizes existing communication networks. The widespread use of electronic communication methods has expanded the social networks of many people. Successfully getting the message into a few of these large social networks can greatly accelerate the viral spread. See the discussion of Facebook in the paragraph below.

6. Takes advantage of others' resources. Community bulletin boards, Craigslist.org, affiliate programs where you can place links on other organization Web sites, and other available resources should be used to help spread the viral message.[28]

Now, marketers can use bits of computer code called applications, or *widgets,* to help spread viral marketing campaigns online. These tiny, highlighted lines of text or boxes can be "dropped" onto a Web page, allowing you to embed news, ads, songs, videos, or many other means of commercial or personal applications. They are used on sites such as Facebook or blogs as means of self-expression, and can be passed from site to site (hence the opportunity to be used in viral marketing campaigns). A *Business Week* article on widgets provided the following example of how widgets work:

"William Tinkler . . . spends a couple of hours a week on Facebook. His page boasts five widgets in all, and his friends are alerted each time he puts up a new one. One shows the jackets of books he is reading, another tells friends who visit his page what movies he plans to rent from online movie store Netflix. . . . He also has a world map featuring the places he has visited highlighted in blue. There's a politics meter on his site displaying where he stands on the conservative-liberal spectrum and a space where friends can convey their feelings about him with goofy gestures such as a virtual "high five." . . . It doesn't bother him that the movie widget includes [an ad] urging visitors to sign up for a free Netflix trial.[29]

One of the key attractions of widgets is that they bring information to you, rather than you having to go searching for it. For example, the iLike software firm has a widget on Facebook that lets

451

people share their favorite musicians with one another, automatically notifies your friends when you make plans to attend a concert, suggests other artists your friends like, and, when you click on a link, tells you other Facebook people attending the show. Growth has been "viral": it took six months for iLike to sign up the first million users; the second million took one week. In 2007 Google was testing Gadget Ads, which lets advertisers convert static display ads into a sort of widget by adding videos, animation, and real-time news or marketing data to them. "The e-commerce implications are potentially huge. Instead of simply building a destination site where people come to shop, sellers can use widgets to bring the store to the buyers."[30] Some companies like Amazon and Wal-Mart use widgets to allow users to search their sites while remaining in the social network or Facebook page of the viewer. It remains to be seen how important widgets will become in the world of online promotion, but it is something with considerable potential for a congregation on a limited budget who would like to reach people inexpensively, and stimulate viral marketing messages about its brand or ministries.

Guerrilla Marketing refers to unconventional promotional activities performed on a very low budget. Jay Levinson[31] coined this phrase to describe a wide variety of marketing activities that are used by small organizations on a limited budget to get maximum surprise and word-of-mouth communication among members of the target audience about the organization's program. There have been some spectacularly ill-conceived attempts at guerrilla marketing, such as the promotion of Time Warner's Cartoon Network's show *Aqua Teen Hunger Force* in 2007. Marketers placed little black boards with LED lights in the image of a character in the show near roads, on bridge spans, and in subway stations to be seen by commuters. Fearing these were planted by terrorists, federal and state law-enforcement agencies were called out, commuters were stopped for hours as areas were sealed off, and Time Warner eventually had to pay $2 million to make amends for a guerrilla scheme gone bad. Levinson identifies seven steps for creating successful guerrilla marketing campaigns:

1. Find the inherent drama within your offering.

2. Translate that inherent drama into a meaningful benefit.

3. State your benefits as believably as possible.

4. Get people's attention.

5. Motivate your audience to do something.

6. Be sure to communicate clearly.

7. Measure your finished advertisement, commercial, letter, or brochure against your creative strategy.[32]

Two good Web sites to read about and view the guerrilla marketing strategies being used by congregations are http://www.church marketingsucks.com/ and http://www.churchrelevance.com.

Public Relations

To carry out its mission, the church or synagogue needs the active support of many diverse publics, and at least the tolerance of a number of others. In chapter 6, we noted five basic types of publics: *input publics* (donors, suppliers, judicatory), *internal publics* (trustees, ruling boards, ministers, volunteers, and staff), *intermediary publics* (publishers, facilitators, broadcast media, agents, marketing firms), *consuming publics* (members, other participants, recipients of services), and *external publics* (local residents, activists, the general public, media, competitors).

These publics can be further divided into (1) those that directly, indirectly, or actively are involved in carrying out the religious organization's mission (for example, donors, suppliers, internal and intermediary publics) and (2) those whose goodwill and tolerance are needed for the organization to exist and to carry out its mission as efficiently and effectively as possible. These two groups can be designated as the *active* and *passive* publics, respectively.

The local community, news media, bankers, local politicians, government officials, social action groups—all may take an active, or reactive, interest in the congregation's activities. Of course, the leaders can attempt to influence these publics in the course of carrying out their other duties.

But sooner or later even a congregation recognizes the advantages of consolidating or coordinating these activities through a public relations manager.

In using a public relations manager (usually a qualified volunteer parishioner), the church or synagogue can gain several advantages:

- better anticipation of potential problems
- better handling of these problems
- consistent public-oriented policies and strategies
- more professional written and oral communications

Public relations is the management function that evaluates the attitudes of important publics, identifies the policies and procedures of an individual or an organization with the public interest, and executes a program of action to earn understanding and acceptance by these publics.[33]

In some churches and synagogues, the public relations manager sits in on all meetings involving information and actions that might affect public perceptions of the congregation. The public relations manager not only puts out fires but also counsels the leaders on actions that will avoid starting fires. In other congregations public relations is charged only with getting out publications and handling news and special events. The public relations people are not involved in policy or strategy formulation, only in tactics.

Public relations is often confused with one of its subfunctions, such as press agentry, organizational publications, lobbying, firefighting, and so forth. It is, however, a more inclusive concept. The most frequently quoted definition of PR is the following.

Sometimes a short definition is given, which says that PR stands for *performance* (P) plus *recognition* (R). The organization not only must perform *good deeds* but must also follow them up with *good words*.

Public relations is not coextensive with marketing. Important differences are that (1) public relations is primarily a communication tool, whereas marketing also includes needs assessment, product development, pricing, and distribution; (2) public relations seeks to influence attitudes, whereas marketing tries to influence specific behaviors, such as joining, giving, and so on; (3) public relations does not define the goals of the organization, whereas marketing is intimately involved in defining the organization's target group(s) and products.

Becoming "Doers"
The Publicity-savvy Administrator

Religious organizational administrators can benefit from free publicity by following some general guidelines for submitting public service announcements (PSAs) and getting other free publicity for your organization:

• Make a point of getting to know the editor of the local newspaper. Many local editors reflect the attitudes and opinions of the local populace and may share similar values with you. Establishing a social relationship with the editor can improve the odds of getting favorable publicity.

• If there is a religion editor, it is of course valuable to get to know that individual as well. Addressing publicity news releases to this person instead of to the "church news department" is good advice.

• Make sure that what you supply to these editors constitutes "news"—special and seasonable programs, concerts, outreach events affecting the broader community, etc.—and reflects an understanding of the editors' needs in providing a newspaper valued by the community.

• This means your news releases should read like news items, beginning with the "lead," which provides the reader with the key bits of information: who, what, where, when, why, and how. Check all facts including the spelling of names, correct phone numbers, etc. Make sure the release is typed, not handwritten (e-mail it as an attachment if that is the preferred form by the editors).

• Follow standard writing formats for publicity news releases including:
1. Submit the announcement early—at least 10 days before the event.
2. Include all facts—the who, what, when, where, and how.
3. Don't be too creative—avoid superlatives and acronyms.
4. Include a pronunciation guide.
5. Provide directions on how to get there.
6. Double-space the copy.
7. Use church letterhead.
8. Include contact information, including Web site url.

Continued on next page

Continued from previous page

If you are making a prerecorded PSA:
1. Use professional equipment.
2. Use professional voices (a local DJ might do the work cheaply).
3. Use appropriate background music.
4. Timing is important—do not run over the time limit by even one second.
5. Include a written script.
6. Contact individual PSA directors at radio or TV stations for specific guidelines.

For news releases:
1. Make it easy to read—double-space, use 8½" x 11" paper, clear font, etc.
2. Use letterhead
3. Provide current contact information.
4. Keep it short and simple.
5. Include a pronunciation guide.
6. Make sure it is addressed to the proper person.[34]

A checklist of activities for the public relations manager for a church or synagogue would include the following.

1. The physical plant

a. Does the appearance of the grounds, buildings, and parking lot tend to enhance the desired image?

b. Is the building properly lighted at night (outside, inside, behind the stained-glass windows, etc.)?

c. If the building is situated near a busy highway or major intersection, is this fact being taken advantage of? Is a display sign properly established, edited, and kept up to date with provocative messages? Is it lighted at night?

d. Are church bells or carillons utilized to remind the community of the church's existence?

e. Are signs posted on main roads leading to the facility, pointing the way?

2. Media and publicity work

a. Have local professional religious editors and other media people been contacted to learn their needs and interests? Are thank-you notes sent when good news coverage is achieved?

b. Are all members periodically reminded (perhaps via a sermon) that PR is everybody's business? Are they aware of channels and procedures for submitting news?

c. Are ideas for major features (for religious monthlies or Sunday editions of the local papers) farmed out from time to time by the PR manager or the editor of the congregation's newsletter?

d. Has a basic publicity brochure been prepared for distribution to new members and prospective members? This would summarize the congregation's purposes, services, staff, facilities, benefits, and so on.

e. Are a series of bulletin boards kept up to date, attractive, and newsworthy? Is a clearly designated editor in charge, and do the members know this? Are the bulletin boards in high-traffic areas? Are they well lighted?

f. Is the newsletter editor being supplied with a steady flow of items from the designated "reporters" and others? Is the layout reasonably professional? Is the newsletter being mailed at the cheapest postal rate? Is it being sent to absent members (away at college, in the armed services, shut-ins, etc.)? Is a copy sent to local church editors? Are copies exchanged with other local churches? (This can lead to a number of new ideas.) Is the newsletter available online?

g. When interesting people drop by (like missionaries back from overseas), are arrangements made for possible radio or TV interviews?

h. Is the church or synagogue part of a regional plan for the occasional broadcasting of services on radio or TV or as a podcast?

i. Are special events dramatized for possible photo or TV

coverage? For example, a routine ground-breaking ceremony might be enlivened by the use of a team of oxen pulling an ancient plow.

j. Is an appropriate ad announcing services placed on the newspaper's church page each Saturday?

3. Miscellaneous

a. Are the staff members (including janitors) trained to answer the phone effectively? Are the yellow pages phone listing and Web site attractive and up to date?

b. Are ushers and other greeters trained with PR in mind?

c. Have cooperative efforts with other local congregations been considered for fund raising (billboards, bumper stickers, signs in buses, radio and TV spots, etc.)?

d. Does the PR committee have a list of members who are in key positions in local clubs and organizations and who can make announcements or appeals?

e. Is there an annual critique of the overall PR effort, and is it coordinated with periodic surveys and audience analysis efforts?

f. Do the members of the PR committee occasionally read books on journalism or PR work? Do they attempt to interview experts in the field, or even take PR courses at local colleges? [35]

In short, the church or synagogue is an institution with a "product" to deliver and an image to maintain. There is nothing wrong with its effort to be well organized and professional. Its adversaries are hardly amateurs. As Augustine phrased it about 1,600 years ago: "Truth must not go unarmed into the arena."

One good example of the church developing well-organized and professional PR materials is "Mission 90," prepared by the Evangelical Lutheran Church in America. Mission 90 comprised a six-videotape series, in which Bishop Herbert W. Chilstrom hosted a discussion series entitled "What Does It Mean to Be a Christian?"[36] The Commission of Communication funded by the Lutheran Brotherhood produced the videotapes. The videotapes are entitled: *Grace; Faith and Sin; Word, Sacrament, and Worship; Life in Family and Community; Personal Stewardship;* and *Creation.*

New Light
Effectiveness of Communication Methods

A survey of pastors on the effectiveness of different communication methods for recruiting or retaining members revealed the following hierarchy:

Recruiting New Members

Most effective
  Personal referrals

Not effective
  television ads

Moderately effective
  radio ads
  brochure
  yellow page ads and listings
  direct mail
  monthly or weekly newsletter
  church bulletin
  telemarketing
  newspaper ads
  door-to-door canvassing
  cable access TV programs

Retaining Members

Most effective
  personal referrals
  church bulletins
  direct mail
  monthly newsletter

Not effective
  yellow page ads or listings
  television ads
  newspaper ads
  door-to-door canvassing
  cable access TV programs

Moderately effective
  radio ads
  brochures
  weekly newsletters
  telemarketing

These results are based on the perceptions of pastors, not on controlled experiments, but do reflect what pastors do believe is working or not in their use of communication tools to retain or attract members.

Adapted from W. Benoy and Marion S. Webb, "Marketing Your Church with Advertising and Promotion Strategies That Work," *Journal of Ministry Marketing and Management* 6, vol. 1 (2000): 19-33.

Individual churches and synagogues minister under tight budget constraints. Most congregations simply cannot afford to hire professional PR firms. Their only chance for excellence lies in the voluntary part-time help of PR professionals who also happen to be churchpersons, or with laypersons who are willing to apply themselves to learning how to do effective PR. To the credit of Christian and Jewish professional PR and marketing persons, we have yet to meet such persons who are not willing to volunteer their skills to their places of worship.

Do's and Don'ts for Religious Advertisers

Below are some actions that should be taken or avoided by religious marketers on limited budgets.

Do's:

1. Radio stations, newspapers, magazines, and other media specialists will frequently give free, valuable help on advertising strategy, especially for small or nonprofit organizations. Sometimes to sell their own medium, the staffs will help you create dynamic ads. Don't be shy about picking their brains about advertising strategy.

2. Ads placed during off-hours or in unusual print locations are charged cheaper rates. Sometimes you can still reach your market targets in these inexpensive, unorthodox media slots.

3. Most of the time your audience needs more than one exposure to remember your business. Repeat and repeat the same successful ads. You'll also save on production costs instead of having to reinvent the wheel.

4. See if media sellers will give last-minute discounts for unused time or space. Late fill-ins could result in discounts of up to 60 percent!

5. If appropriate, consider providing a convenient toll-free number in your ads to get immediate responses and feedback.

6. Try cheaper classified advertisements to see if their drawing power is comparable to more expensive display ads.

7. Consider bartering products or services donated by members in exchange for the production of ads (e.g., artwork and printing) or for media time or space.

8. Use piggyback advertising material in other mailings, such as in newsletters or special announcements, to save postage and other related costs.

9. Try cooperative advertising with denominational or regional church offices. Some judicatory offices, for example, are receptive to sharing advertising costs with local congregations.

10. Take advantage of any media discounts you're offered by paying cash in advance.

11. Try reducing the physical size of the print ad or the time of a broadcasting spot. A full-page ad or 60-second commercial, for example, is not always twice as effective as a half-page or 30-second ad. Sometimes frequency (number of times an ad appears) is more essential than the size or time of an ad.

12. Develop tight production controls to minimize the need to reject finished ads. Don't get carried away with the artistic endeavors in which production concerns outweigh your original advertising objectives.

13. Carefully aim your ads at the prospects or consumers who are most receptive to the ad's message.

14. See if you can sponsor a community or civic event. Sometimes the sponsor is mentioned somewhere in the community ad. Although your congregation's name is not prominently mentioned, the ad is repeated often, which gives favorable and frequent recognition.

15. You can't afford saturation advertising. Instead, work on carefully matching the particular medium—radio, newspaper, or whatever—with the market targets you want to go after. Poor target marketing causes advertising dollars to be wasted. Challenge the media representatives to identify their viewers, listeners, or readers clearly.

16. Fully exploit the advantages of the various types of media; otherwise, you're needlessly paying for the higher costs or rates of certain media. Local cable television ads, for example, give you the opportunity to demonstrate your offerings and allow visual impact. If your ads merely "talk" through the time slot, you might as well opt for the cheaper time slots of radio, billboard, or some other alternative.

17. Saturation and blitz advertising is very costly; therefore, care-

fully coordinate all forms of communication to develop a consistent, systematic, and effective image. With judicious integration of public relations, one-on-one communications, telemarketing, and advertising, you'll develop a total, powerful synergistic impact on the marketplace—and you will better maximize your precious ad dollars.

18. Experiment with an editorial-style format. "There is no need for advertisements to look like advertisements," says David Ogilvy. "If you make them look like editorial pages, you will attract 50 percent more readers." You could provide informative suggestions, written in editorial style, which positions you as an expert in the reader's mind. This strategy could overcome advertising clutter and give better readership for your small budget.

19. Develop copy that appeals to your market while still being different from the big-budget marketers. You can't match them dollar for dollar. Experiment with unusual approaches, such as color, music, slogans, humor, or in media selection to attract the viewers' attention and interest.

20. Consider the use of such alternative media as the yellow pages, billboards, leaflets, community bulletin boards, church signs, booths at fairs, and other methods that are consistent with the target audience media habits, the image you wish to portray, the particular religious product being advertised, the message you're sending, and the advertising budget.

21. Keep close tabs on how well certain ads and different types of media are doing. You cannot afford to spend hard-earned dollars on advertising that is not getting the job done.

Don'ts:

Here are a few common mistakes made by advertisers on low budgets, such as religious organizations have.

1. *Trying to do too much with too few advertising dollars.* You cannot afford to be something to everyone. Too often you may try to say too much, hit many different media, or have a huge, one-time flashy ad to get "your money's worth." It could be a costly blunder. You might need a better focus, a clear niche, or just one powerful message for dealing with competitive advertising clutter.

2. *Choosing a medium based on its low rate rather than on its cost per 1,000 readers, listeners, or viewers.* You should compare audience size, image, and the response results for other religious organizations that have advertised in various media. Don't just look at the ad rates of a medium.

3. *Not advertising frequently enough.* You may need to run an ad several times to increase the awareness and recall of your message.

4. *Making an advertisement bigger than it need be.* Don't sacrifice quality and repetition just for size. Sometimes attention is increased at a diminishing rate as the ad is made bigger.

5. *Expecting too much from creativity in copy and art.* A flashy and innovative ad will not overcome weaknesses in a religious organization's product.

6. *Imitating instead of analyzing.* A frugal religious marketer cannot financially compete with big-bucks religious organization marketers. Avoid 'me-too-ism' advertising.

7. *Not concentrating the advertising on the reader, listener,* or *viewer.* This reinforces our marketing vs. product or sales orientation.

8. *Failing to utilize the unique advantages of the medium, especially television, fully.* For example, if you decide on TV, then demonstrate the virtues of your ministries. Avoid just talking through a TV script without product demonstrations. If you use billboards, avoid copy with a number of words or statements. Passersby will not have time to read them.

9. *Failing to capitalize on the inherent nature of the product, service, or organization.* Carefully match your market's preferences with the strengths of your offerings and congregation.

10. *Having no objective measure of the advertising effectiveness.* Carefully watch and evaluate your ads and the resulting campaigns to see if they're getting the job done.

11. *Believing advertising is more powerful than it really is.* Discover what it takes for advertising to succeed. Advertising cannot overcome a structural organization weakness, nor is it an automatic solution to all of your problems. For example, Dan Danford recounts the lament of a minister who could not find a volunteer to direct Bible school after placing an ad in the church newsletter three weeks in a

row. Danford's observation was that volunteer recruitment is a one-on-one activity, not a job for the impersonal media.[37]

---

[1] Michael Prewitt, "The True Worldliness of Advertising: *Apologia pro Vita Mea*," *Theology Today* 60 (2003): 384-396.

[2] For more on event marketing, see *Event Marketing: A Management Guide*, available at http://www.ana.net/bookstore, or Allison Saget, *The Event Marketing Handbook* (Chicago: Dearborn Trade Publishing, 2006).

[3] See "How Pope John Paul II and Other Religious Leaders View Advertising," *Madison Avenue* 27, no. 9 (September 1985): 18-28, 106.

[4] See "Admen for Heaven," *Christianity Today*, Sept. 18, 1987, pp. 12, 13. Note: The ads refered to in this article are now available at http://www.church ads.com.

[5] As quoted in Martin E. Marty, "Sunday Mass and the Media," *Across the Board,* May 1987, pp. 55-57.

[6] See "Advertising Your Church," *Christianity Today*, Nov. 18, 1977, pp. 30, 31.

[7] See Chaim M. Ehrman, "Can Advertising Be Justified From a Talmudist's Point of View?" Some New Insights," *1987 AMA Winter Educators' Conference Proceedings* (Chicago: American Marketing Association, 1987), pp. 78-80.

[8] Marty, p. 56.

[9] See Stephen W. McDaniel, "Marketing Communication Techniques in a Church Setting: Views on Appropriateness," *Journal of Professional Services Marketing* 27, no. 9 (Summer 1986): 39-54.

[10] There are several models of consumer readiness states. See, for example, Robert J. Lavidge and Gary A. Steiner, "A Model for Predictive Measurements of Advertising Effectiveness," *Journal of Marketing,* October 1961, pp. 59-62. For another approach, see Geraldine Fennell, "Persuasion as Behavioral Science in Business and Nonbusiness Contexts," in Russell W. Belk, ed., *Advances in Nonprofit Marketing*, (Greenwich, Conn.: JAI Press, 1985), vol. 1, pp. 95-160. James Engel's well-known "Complete Spiritual Decision Process Model" is described on p. 83 of his book *Contemporary Christian Communication* (Nashville: Thomas Nelson, 1979).

[11] See Russell H. Colley, *Defining Advertising Goals for Measuring Advertising Results* (New York: Association of National Advertisers, 1961).

[12] For information on the use of fear appeals in advertising, see M. S. LaTour, R. L. Snipes, and H. J. Rotfeld, " Don't be Afraid to Use Fear Appeals," *Journal of Advertising Research*, March 1996, pp. 6.

[13] See T. W. Cline, M. B. Altsech, and J. J. Kellaris, "When Does Humor Enhance or Inhibit Ad Responses?" *Journal of Advertising*, Fall 2003, pp. 31-45.

[14] Burt Helm, "Which Ads Don't Get Skipped?" *Business Week*, Sept. 3, 2007, p. 24.

[15] For good advice on using television as an ad medium, see William K. Witcher, *How to Solve Your Small Business Advertising Problems* (Aptos, Calif.: Advertising Planners, Inc., 1986).

[16] See William D. Novelli, "Social Issues and Direct Marketing: What's the Connection?" Presentation to the Annual Conference of the Direct Mail/Marketing Association, Los Angeles, California, Mar. 12, 1981.

[17] See Belinda Hulin-Salkin, "Strategies of Charities," *Advertising Age*, Jan. 19, 1981, p. 529.

[18] Norman W. Whan, *The Phones's for You!* (Brea, Calif.: Church Growth Development International); newmovers.org.

[19] Vauhini Vara, "Facebook Gets Personal With Ad Targeting Plan," *Wall Street Journal,* Aug. 23, 2007, p. B1.

[20] http://www.churchmarketingsucks.com/archives/2005/07/keyword_adverti.html.

[21] For more on Contextual Advertising and the other types of online advertising discussed here, see Mary Lou Roberts, *Internet Marketing,* 2nd ed., (Mason, Ohio: Thomson, 2008).

[22] "DoubleClick's 2004 Email Study," http://www.doubleclick.com/us/knowledge_central/documents/RESEARCH/dc_consumer_email_0410.pdf, 2. Debroah Fallows, "Can-SPAM a year later," April 2005; http://www.pewinternet.org/pdfs/PIP_Spam_Ap05.pdf .

[23] See Roberts, pp.186-193.

[24] *Ibid.,* p. 154.

[25] *Ibid.,* p. 156.

[26] For an excellent resource on focus groups, see Andre Delbecq, *Group Techniques for Program Planning* (Middletown, Wis.: Greenbriar Press, 1986).

[27] Warren St. John, "Sports and Salvation on Faith Night at the Stadium," New York *Times,* June 2, 2006 (accessed at nytimes.com).

[28] Ralph F. Wilson, "The Six Simple Principles of Viral Marketing," *Web Marketing Today,* Feb. 1, 2000; http://www.wilsonweb.com/wmt5/viral-principles.htm.

[29] "The Next Small Thing," *Business Week,* July 23, 2007, pp. 58-62.

[30] *Ibid.,* p. 62.

[31] Jay Conrad Levinson, *Guerrilla Marketing,* 4th ed. (Boston: Houghton-Mifflin, 2007). See also Levinson's Web site, gmarketing.com.

[32] http://www.gmarketing.com/articles/read/14/Seven_Steps_for_Creating_Successful_Marketing.html.

[33] *Public Relations News,* Oct. 27, 1947.

[34] Adapted from Randall W. Hines, "Church News Releases: Spreading the Word Economically," *Journal of Ministry Marketing and Management* 2, no. 2 (1996): 47-55, and Tammy Cullers, "Get the Word Out," *Your Church,* March/April 2004 (accessed at www.christianitytoday.com/yc/2004/002/7.52.html).

[35] See Ben Ramsey, "Church Public Relations: A Check-off List," *Public Relations Quarterly,* Winter 1977, pp. 17-21.

[36] To order these tapes, write to Commission of Communications, Evangelical Lutheran Church in America, 8765 West Higgins Road, Chicago, Illinois 60631, or call 1-800-638-3522.

[37] See J. Donald Weinrauch and Nancy Croft Baker, *The Frugal Marketer* (New York: AMACOM, 1989); J. Donald Weinrauch, *The Marketing Problem Solver* (New York: John Wiley, 1987); Alec Benn, *The 27 Most Common Mistakes in Advertising* (New York: AMA-COM, 1978); David Ogilvy, *Confessions of an Advertising Man* (New York: Dell, 1980); and Dan Danford, "Targeting Your Church Advertising," *Ministries Today,* May/June 1988, pp. 50-53.

WORKSHEETS: CHAPTER 10

Marketing Communication Decisions

Targeted Segment

From chapter 8, provide the positioning strategy statement for each segment you will target with an ad message:

Targeted Segment	Positioning Strategy Statement
1._____	_____
2._____	_____
3._____	_____

Consider this positioning strategy as well as your branding strategy when making your marketing communication decisions.

Communication Mix

Select the combination of communication methods you will use to reach your targeted segment to implement your positioning strategy:

Advertising	_____
Incentives	_____
Public Relations/Publicity	_____
Events and Experiences	_____
Direct and Interactive Marketing	_____
Person-to-Person and W-O-M	_____

Be sure to design an Integrated Marketing Communications (IMC) plan that makes the best use of each of the methods and that uses the methods in a combination and sequence that capitalizes on their strengths.

Advertising Strategy

List your advertising objectives. Keep in mind the target market characteristics, the response sought from them from your advertising, and the optimal reach and frequency of the advertising.

_____

_____

_____

Set your advertising budget. Refer to the decisions you made in developing your marketing budget as part of your marketing plan in chapter 8.

_____

_____

_____

How will you allocate the budget among the different advertising media?

_____

_____

_____

What is the message you will be communicating to the target audience? Review your positioning statement above when developing your message.

_____

_____

_____

Describe your message execution strategy:

Tone:_____

Style: _____

Wording: _____

Order: _____

Format: _____

Describe your media strategy, including choice of media and timing.

_____

_____

_____

Describe how you intend to evaluate the effectiveness of the advertising.

Pretests _____

_____

Posttests _____

_____

Viral Marketing Strategy

Describe how you will use viral marketing to achieve your communication goals.

_____

_____

_____

Guerrilla Marketing Strategy

Describe how you will use guerrilla marketing to achieve your communication goals.

_____

_____

_____

Public Relations

Describe your public relations strategy.

_____

_____

_____

Make certain you keep in mind the do's and don'ts of your communication plan.

Do's	Don'ts
_____	_____
_____	_____
_____	_____
_____	_____

CHAPTER 11:

Fund-raising Decisions

"Wherever your treasure is, there your heart and thoughts will also be" (MATTHEW 6:21, NLT).

In this chapter we will address the following questions:

1. What are some differences between fund-raising and stewardship?

2. What are the recent trends in giving to religious organizations?

3. What are some of the myths and facts about donating to religious institutions?

4. What are some current fund-raising methods used by religious organizations?

5. How can a religious organization use a marketing orientation for raising funds?

Saint Andrews Episcopal Church is a beautiful building exuding elegance and stability in the small city on the West Coast where it is located. By most standards the congregation is flourishing. Many of the city's wealthiest families call it home. The church roster of 800 is filled with professionals from all sectors of the local economy.

It has a church budget of several hundred thousand dollars, and is able to pay Stuart Morgan, its rector, a good salary and support a church staff and many church programs. Appearances, however, can be deceiving. In the past 10 years demands on the church's resources have increased dramatically. Increases in membership, primarily young families, have not been matched with increased giving. The physical plant needs renovation and expansion, and the local economy, based on the logging industry, continues to suffer a long-term slump. Declining resources available to public service agencies have shifted the burden on the downtown churches, of which Saint Andrews is the most prominent. Morgan strongly believes that his church should be actively involved in servicing these needs. He remembers the church he attended as a seminary student, when attendees would openly pray about being destitute and needing guidance, and how members would respond immediately ("stay at my house until you get on your feet again"). The rector's goal is to have the Saint Andrews' members live out there faith in a similar way to help the economically disadvantaged in their community. While some have accepted the challenge, the prevailing mood is one of concern about the economic well being of its middle-class members themselves. They worry about being laidoff from work, and whether they will outlive their savings, and middle-age parents worry about their children who are struggling financially in setting up their own households. Morgan thinks people would worry less about their own needs if they saw what it means to be really poor. He wishes members would tithe instead of giving the 1 or 2 percent of their income that they now give. His sermons about letting go of material things sound idealistic and naïve to most members, however. The church appears to be at a financial impasse. The middle class members remain stoical, but more and more seem victims of stress and burnout.[1]

This may be the most difficult of all the chapters in this book to write because the topic is so intermingled with both theological precepts and practical exigency. Adding to the problem of discussion is the difference in the meanings between the terms *stewardship* and *fund-raising* (see Exhibit 11.1 for some distinctions that have been

drawn between the two terms). There are scores of entire books devoted to a discussion of how Scripture can inform stewardship principles. True to our focus for this book, we will confine our
discussion to recent trends in religious organizational fund-raising
from a marketer's perspective, and will not discuss the various positions in the theological debate over tithing that continues to rage in
Christendom. As always, we trust readers will apply their own the-

Exhibit 11.1	Fund-raising Versus Stewardship	
	Fund-raising	**Stewardship**
Purpose	fund the specified activity	worship God
Goal	meet budget; pay bills	serve God with integrity
Realm of activity	financial	spiritual
Source of resources	donors	God
Guiding document	institutional budget	Scripture
Motivation for giving	varies	faithful obedience, trust, loyalty, love
Return on investment	personal satisfaction; tax deduction	joy of giving
Precipitating relationship	cause; institution	God
Primary outcome of donation	achieve goal of cause or institution	fulfill spiritual obligation
Reasons for not donating	competing options	lack of understanding

Source: Adapted from George Barna, *How to Increase Giving in Your Church* (Ventura, Calif.: Regal Books, 1997), p. 24.

ological perspectives in determining whether they will adopt the practices of their peers in this matter.

Trends in Giving to Religious Organizations

On a positive note, the absolute dollar amount given to religious organizations has increased over the past 30 years. However, 80 years ago Americans gave 3.5 percent of their household income to religious organizations, while today that number is around 2.5 percent, where it has been for the past 20 years.[2] It is estimated that Jewish giving is between the Catholic 1.5 percent and the mainline Protestant 2.9 percent. The Muslim standard for giving is 2.5 percent of one's net income for *zakat*, one of the five requirements, or pillars, of Islam.[3] On a per capita basis, Christians gave less in 2005 to churches than they did during the Great Depression.[4] Even among born-again adults, only 6 percent report that they tithed in 2002.[5] Of every dollar given to a U.S Protestant church, the average amount that goes to overseas missions is only two cents.[6]

Religious institutions must also compete with an increasing number of other religious and parachurch organizations for a portion of the donation pool. It is reported that the majority of money donated to religious organizations goes to institutions other than the local congregation or denomination.[7]

Leaders of these local congregations are faced with the daunting task of attracting an increasing share of a dwindling resource, a task for which they are ill-prepared to accomplish. Only 2 to 4 percent of the seminaries in the U.S. teach financial principles in their coursework,[8] and 85 percent of the seminary students receive no training in the theology of stewardship.[9] It is also safe to say that few pastors relish talking to their congregants about giving. One of the members of a roundtable discussion on fund-raising organized by *Leadership* magazine had this to say about his experience in stewardship:

> *When I graduated from seminary, I was 26, and a first-time associate pastor. I received the appointment to three committees—youth, evangelism, and stewardship. I told the stewardship committee, "I'll never preach a stewardship sermon, because I don't believe in that. I don't think what, or if, people give is any of my business."*

Ted, the treasurer of the congregation, confronted me after a board meeting: "You don't tithe?"

"That's right," I said. "I don't believe in it."

"Well, how can you not believe in it when it's so biblical?" he said.

They had never taught me that in seminary. I told Ted that. "It's just not there," I said.

"Let me give you some texts," he replied, "and you and your wife pray about it and see what happens."

We did, and he was absolutely right. Chris and I discovered we were giving about 3 percent a year. And there was a lot of rationalizing. "I give my time, I give my life. I don't need to deal with this."

After prayerfully considering it, I went back to him and said, "Ted, you're right." And my wife and I made a commitment to tithe.[10]

It is no wonder that most congregational leaders are at a loss with how to talk about, much less successfully attract, needed financial resources with their members! In addition to these problems related to fund-raising in congregations, there is a general lack of understanding about the facts of money, ministry, and donors. Here are some common myths and the facts that belie the myths about fund-raising:[11]

Myth: Baby boomers' self-centered nature results in sparse giving habits.

Fact: Boomers were the most generous donors in the U.S. during the latter part of the twentieth century.

Myth: People who are theologically, philosophically, or ideologically conservative do not donate to liberal ministries. Liberals don't donate to conservative ministries.

Fact: A large percentage of those who donate to conservative causes also donate to liberal ones. For example, a substantial number of donors to Focus on the Family also donate to Planned Parenthood. One cannot necessarily predict a person's giving habits based on their ideology—giving motives can be very complex.

Myth: Parents with children under the age of 18 are significant contributors to funding missionary efforts, and international relief agencies.

Fact: Parents of young children give more to local needs than overseas needs.

Myth: Christians are the most generous givers to environmental causes, as a way of being good stewards of God's creation.
Fact: Christians are substantially less likely than non-Christians to fund environmental causes.

Myth: The higher the household income, the greater the rate of monthly giving.
Fact: People in lower- to middle-income households are more likely to be monthly donors to organizations such as churches than are the wealthier households.

Myth: Donors must have a relationship with an organization before they will support it with their financial gifts.
Fact: Only 40 percent of donors believe they must have a relationship with an organization before they become a regular contributor to it. "Relationship" in this sense is a sense of partnership in the organization's mission.

Myth: A well-documented and -conceived budget is sufficient reason to generate interest in funding a plan.
Fact: Donors give to people, not plans. A well-conceived budget is a necessary but insufficient reason for making a substantial donation.

Myth: Donors, deluged with information in this information age, don't want to need to know how their donated money is being used.
Fact: As part of the donation "exchange," donors want to know that their generosity has made a positive difference in the lives of people and causes the money was intended to help.

In this chapter we will share with you some ways that fund-raisers can apply marketing principles to the problem of attracting resources. First, we will describe some of the methods currently being used by religious organizations to raise funds.

Current Religious Fund-raising Methods

Contributing Funds Electronically. Congregations have increasingly used the Internet to increase the convenience to donors who wish to give in support of the organization. One way to use this method for fund-raising is to provide visitors to your Web site several options to make donations. See the examples below for an idea of how some congregations have been doing this on their Web sites.

CONTRIBUTING FUNDS ELECTRONICALLY

EXAMPLE 1: Online Giving at First Baptist Church
Now you can give "online."

In our digital age when people are increasingly paying bills and conducting commerce online, First Baptist Church has chosen to make online giving available to those who are interested. First Baptist Church teaches that living "debt-free" is a worthy goal for all Christians. Online giving does involve the use of credit and debit transactions and makes no distinction between the two. You may also utilize electronic funds transfer (EFT). Every giver should exercise care and concern in using credit cards for giving. We offer this option only as a convenience and not as a way to circumvent sound biblical money management principles or incur debt. You are free to give via the weekly offering in the worship service, by mailing your contribution in to the finance office, or now by the Internet, and we welcome you to give whatever God has called you to, however God has called you to.

Please click here to go to our secure FBC E-give page.

Please click here to discover the many other ways you can give to First Baptist Church, including the transfer of stocks, bonds, and real estate.

Source: http://www.fbcocala.org/e-givingfaq.html.

EXAMPLE 2: A Nondemominational Megachurch

Throughout Scripture we are reminded of the importance of giving back a portion of what God has so generously provided. His Word tells us that giving is an act of worship that should be done with a spirit of thanksgiving. Thousands of years later our consumer-driven culture tells us that acquiring "things" is of paramount importance. But the truth of God's Word hasn't changed — He still calls us to give to others and to the work of His church.

Technology has given us new ways of giving, and many of you have expressed an interest in online giving. We are now able to offer you this tool to assist in your giving. Just click on the link below to reach a secure site where you can process your donation.

We are so grateful for the time, talents, and treasures you give in support of this local church. The manner with which you support God's work here is unlike any I have seen. Thank you for being a congregation that strives to put God first in your lives.

Blessings, Bill

Many people who use the Web regularly have contacted Willow Creek about transferring funds electronically for online giving. For their convenience, and as a cost-saving measure for the church, this option is now available.

The system allows you to make a one-time contribution, designate recurring contributions or a combination of both. Encryption technology is used to ensure that your information is transmitted securely. The information you provide is used solely for the purpose of processing your contribution.

If you have any questions or concerns about online giving, contact mailto:onlinecontributions@willowcreek.org or phone (224) 512-6662.

---

http://www.willowcreek.org/giving/default.asp.

Continued on next page

Continued from previous page

EXAMPLE 3: A Jewish Synagogue
There are many ways to support the synagogue

Our synagogue has a variety of tribute and donation funds available. They include opportunities to dedicate a leaf on the **tree of life**, a **Yahrzeit Memorial Plaque**, a **prayer book**, to support a favorite TIC program, such as the Library, Legacy Series, or one of many others, or to make a contribution to the Rabbis' or Cantor's Discretionary Funds.

Click here to see a list of Tribute and Donation funds and their descriptions.

Members of the congregation can make donations using our Online Giving form. If you are a member, please click here to complete the form. Or you can call Susan Galla at 914-948-2800, ext. 112, for more information about any of these funds.

If you are not a current Temple Israel Center member and wish to make a donation, you can print out the form and mail it with your payment by check, made out to "Temple Israel Center," to 280 Old Mamaroneck Road, White Plains, New York 10605. Thank you.

Our **Capital Campaign** offers many exciting opportunities to contribute to our Building Fund. Please contact Executive Director Josef Raboy for more information.

Planned Giving is a way to contribute to the Synagogue endowment. Please contact Stephen Galowitz for more information.

Fund for the Homeless and Hungry

Tribute and Donation Funds available at Temple Israel Center

Tree of Life

Yahrzeit Memorial Plaques

Planned Giving

Two Terrific Ways to Benefit Your Family and TIC

Memorial Plaques and Tree of Life

Source: http://www.templeisraelcenter.org/giving/donations.php

Another related means of using the Internet as a means of collecting donations is to use a commercial service or software that allows people to contribute online. Here are a few of these services that advertise directly to congregations seeking help in setting up an online donation system (listing is for example purposes only and does not constitute endorsement by the authors):

smartpaymentsolutions.com	etapestry.com
clickandpledge.com	EasyTithe.com
acceptiva.com	vchurches.com
QGiv.com	ETransfer.com
ParishPay.com	Vancoservices.com

These and other marketers of similar services and software emphasize the effectiveness and convenience of this method of electronic donation when describing their services:

• Do your collections fluctuate from week to week? Electronic giving programs can help your church increase your collections, make them more consistent, and reduce the amount of effort you spend each week processing donations. We will provide you everything you need to start your program quickly and easily, including sample announcements, a letter to your members, and an easy payment scheduling program. You will hand your members a simple enrollment form. They will fill it out and hand it back to you with a voided check. It's easy! Your members will enjoy not having to write a check each week. Our church clients have had quick success in getting donors to sign up for automated payments.[12]

• At the click of a button, contributors can log in and manage their giving profile. In less than 30 seconds they could set up a one-time gift, set up an automatic recurring donation, and view their giving history. . . . Many churches can almost predict their future donations simply by what month of the year they are in. Each year, from one church to the next, incoming tithe receipts show peaks and valleys. As attendance fluctuates, the weight of the offering plate does as well. As these tithing peaks and valleys plague the traditional church, those churches utilizing online tithing and donations show a more stable flow of income year-round. Why? The offering plate is in the church, but the Internet is in nearly every home in America. That expanded reach coupled with the ability for users to set up automatic recurring donations can have a tremendous impact on the bottom line.[13]

• Traditional paper methods of donating are on the decline. The generation that grew up on the birth of online payments has graduated from college and settled down to raise families. The next generation of fund-raising will take place online, and if your organization is unable to take payments through your Web site you may see significant declines in fund-raising ability.[14]

• Offer your contributors a convenient way of giving and enjoy a consistent flow of contributions. This highly efficient, low-cost alternative to traditional contribution methods will save you considerable time and money. Once your contributor completes a simple authorization form, their information is entered into our system. Then, on the date specified by your contributor, we automatically debit their bank account, crediting their contribution amount to your account.[15]

A New York *Times* article entitled "Pass the Collection Plate and Charge It" commented: "Those who choose to contribute this way can donate while they are away on vacation, manage their church accounts by computer and earn frequent flier miles. And churches, which draw most of their money from donations, can count on a steady stream of revenue, even when summer vacations or winter snowstorms keep people away."[16]

Another controversial means of donation is the use of credit cards to contribute tithes and offerings. Some congregational leaders think it is merely a natural progression of the use of technology in collecting funds from members, while others believe there is a theological issue of supporting, if not encouraging, debt, which violates many churches' doctrines on stewardship. Park Cities Baptist Church in Dallas, Texas, has come to terms with these conflicting forces by including a message on its Web site, where credit card donations are allowed, that says, "Caution: Please use this only if you fully pay off your credit card bill monthly. PCBC does not condone credit card debt."[17] Other congregations assume a more liberal view

Exhibit 11.2	**Giving Kiosk**

of the use of credit cards to make donations, going so far as to install giving kiosks in their sanctuary vestibule (see Exhibit 11.2).

Serving the interests of member convenience comes at a cost, however. Terry Austin, director of stewardship for the Baptist General Convention of Texas, makes the argument this way:

"I believe that giving is a part of worship, and if you take an offering away from the worship context, then to me you've lost the meaning of giving. You've made it fund-raising for the church." He added, "When I have [an offering] automatically withdrawn from my bank or credit or whatever, I can do it without any thought of worship. To me, that's a serious problem." [18]

Others have commented that giving contributions during a worship service is more meaningful than electronic fund transfers, and sets a good example for children who see their parents putting money or tithe envelopes in the collection plate. Proponents of the practice of using advanced technology for collections propose sending cards that say "I've Contributed Online" to those who use this service, or having members take their receipt from the giving kiosk to drop in the collection plate during the worship service.

These changes in the technology of giving have coincided with Americans' growing interest in managing their own financial assets. New Covenant Funds, a family of mutual funds managed according to Presbyterian principles, has capitalized on both trends by allowing members not only to withdraw tithes automatically and systematically, but also to transfer money from an individual's account to a church's New Covenant mutual fund account.[19]

Tithing Consultants

Paralleling churches' use of consulting services on setting up such electronic giving systems is a new service for donors—tithing consultants. These consultants work with clients to determine how much they should tithe, sometimes using an online survey as a starting point. The consultant may then negotiate with the religious institution to determine how the money will be used (e.g., religious education versus operating expenses, etc.), and to establish benchmarks on how efficiently the donated funds are being spent. Eric Kessler, one such consultant, said of his clients, "It doesn't matter if they are giving $100 or $100 million: People now want to make sure that their money is used well. . . . They are treating tithing to the church in the same way as their financial investments."[20] Churches believe that giving up some of their control over the use of donated funds will increase the amount and number of those donations.

Jewish Giving Methods

The Jewish community has two types of organizations, synagogues and federations, which involve financial giving.[21] About 40 to 45 percent of American Jews belong to synagogues that are of either the Orthodox, Conservative, or Reform traditions. An elected board of directors, who set annual dues for the synagogue members, governs synagogues. In about two thirds of the synagogues there is a set fee for a family. Young and elderly members are usually given a lower rate, and if a member cannot afford the dues they may request abatement from the president or rabbi. In the other third of synagogues there is a "fair share" process for setting annual dues. Here the prospective member sits down with the board of directors, reveals his financial status, and arrives at a settlement with the board regarding the member's fair share.

Synagogues still welcome non-dues payers to worship, but on the high holy days, when attendance is at its peak, nonpayers cannot get in. Nonpayers also cannot have a child enrolled in the Jewish school or have a synagogue wedding or bar mitzvah.

In a typical synagogue, two thirds to three fourths of the operating budget comes from dues, with the remainder being raised by auctions, art shows, testimonial dinners, and other fund-raising activities.

Federations are large committees in each city that coordinate Jewish charitable organizations, resembling United Way coalitions. Typically Jewish families give more to its federation than to their synagogue. The duality of synagogue and federation parallels the duality of Jewish identity as a religion and as a secular cultural/ethnic tradition. Many Jews see themselves as unbelievers and secular by nature, yet fully Jewish and supportive of both federation and synagogue activities. The federation is the charitable arm, while the synagogue is a membership obligation, such as a club membership. There is no counterpart to this arrangement in Christianity. Wealthy Jews have historically also been some of the most generous donors to other community charitable organizations, such as United Way, universities, and civic and arts groups.

Selling Goods and Services

A fund-raising method that is perhaps even more controversial than the electronic methods for giving described above is for congregations to become involved in the selling of goods and services. Some large churches have become retailers of goods that can be purchased online at their Web site, or even at their onsite store. For example, here are some of the "gift departments" at the Crystal Cathedral's online store: Clubs and Offers; Dr. Schuller; Books; Music; Video; Bibles; Gifts; Kids; Audio Books; "Sale"; Robert Schuller Institute

Plus, there are "Search," "Customer Service," View Shopping Cart," "Privacy Policy" and "Product Index" links. Clicking on "Product Index" lists items for sale at the site that cover 24 Web pages. Other large congregations have used similar online stores as profit centers.

Likewise, many of these large congregations have begun to operate institutes that offer a variety of conferences, workshops, and consulting services for smaller churches and parachurch ministries. For example, Granger Community Church in Indiana offers more than 20 workshops for churches in a year, ranging in price from $79 to $239 per person for each workshop.

Fund-raising Suggestions for Smaller Congregations

An article by Sabrina Schiller in *Reconstuctionist* magazine entitled "Synagogue Fund-raising"[22] offered several ideas for smaller congregations looking for fund-raising ideas:

1. *Grocery Script.* The congregation buys $100 of grocery script from a local store for $95, and then sells it to members for $100, making 5 percent on the deal. The author's home congregation of 260 families made $20,000 from this method in the first year it was used. This method can be used for partnering with other local organizations as well.

2. *Brokering Automobiles.* A member who donates a car to the church or synagogue can claim a tax deduction for the vehicle, and the organization can then sell the car to generate a source of funds.

3. *Tribute Cards.* An attractive tribute, memorial, or holiday greeting card can be designed and then sent to someone who is being honored by a member making a donation in their name to one of the congregation's ministries (e.g., to a children's ministry for someone who has had a passion for this service). This could be an attractive substitute for a hard-to-find birthday or holiday gift that would have been gifted anyway, resulting in funds given to the institution without increasing the expense to the donor. On a larger scale, different prices could be attached for specific memorials, such as $3000 for a piano to be named in memory, $5,000 for a stained-glass window, etc.

4. *Events.* Getting an artist to donate their time for a performance at which a small fee for attendance is charged can increase the musician's exposure and generate funds for the congregation.

5. *"Bets."* For those not opposed to this on philosophical grounds, an opportunity to raise funds by having a "betting" pool on an event of common interest could be created. For example, for $5 a member can choose the date that the rabbi's or pastor's wife will have her baby, the winner getting to choose how the pool of money will be used.

6. *Auctions.* Members or local businesses can donate services (e.g., an hour of a lawyer's time for drawing up a will, a piano lesson, an afternoon of sailing, a weekend at a vacation home, etc.) or an item of value that can be auctioned off by the church.

7. *Garage Sale.* Instead of having their own garage sale, members can donate items to the congregation ("gifts in kind"), which can then sell these items in a big garage sale open to the community. Sometimes local businesses will make a (tax-deductible) donation of a hard-to-sell or damaged item that can be sold in a garage sale.

8. *Ad Space.* Congregations may have member directories, calendars, or even worship bulletins that carry advertising from local professionals or businesses that would like relatively inexpensive exposure to members.

Your congregation should also explore other means of raising large donations through endowments, capital funds, wills and bequests, major gifts, life income gifts, life insurance, etc.[23]

Capital Campaigns:
Eight Key Questions to Ask Before You Start Fund-raising

Dale K. Ingersoll, pastor of the Westside Baptist Church in Fort Pierce, Florida, took his church from a 200-member church on half a city block to its relocation on their new 86 acre complex via four capital building campaigns. Commenting on the frequent questions he gets from other pastors, he lists eight issues that you need to understand before starting a capital campaign:

1. Will a capital campaign work in my church?
"The pastor must be certain they have the Lord's leading, and the people who really hold power in the church must support it."

2. Who should lead the campaign?
The primary leaders of the church must be up-front in the campaign, but the pastor must become the spokesperson for the project.

3. Do I really need a fund-raising consultant?
Ingersoll feels that most pastors need to hire a consultant.

4. How do I find the right consultant?
Get advice from pastors who have successfully used a consultant for their campaigns. Interviewing prospective consultants to find a good match with church philosophy is key.

5. How much money can we raise?
"Estimate first how much your congregation will give, then make plans to fit the budget." A general rule of thumb is one and one-half to two times the church's annual undesignated offerings, paid out over a three-year period.

6. If we build it, will they come?
It is better to build when you need the extra room to house the current congregation than to build for a congregational population you think will grow to fit the new facility.

7. How much am I personally going to give?

Pastors need to be prepared to dig deep in their personal giving to demonstrate sacrificial giving to their parishioners.

8. How long will this fund-raising last?

The campaign is usually completed in three to five months, and the pledges are collected in three years.

Dale K. Ingersoll, "Eight Key Questions to Ask Before You Start Fund-raising," Leadership 23, no. 4 (Fall 2002): 56, 57. For more on capital campaign fund-raising, see sources listed in the Resource Guide.

A Marketing-oriented Approach to Fund-raising

Your congregation might adopt one of several different orientations for raising funds:

• *Product Orientation.* Here the prevailing attitude is "People should recognize the need to support their congregation. We are important to their lives."

• *Sales Orientation.* Here the prevailing attitude is "There are a lot of members who might contribute to the institution if we go out and find them and convince them to give."

• *Marketing Orientation.* Here the prevailing attitude is "We must segment the different donor groups, understand the motives for giving or not giving for the groups, and demonstrate value of giving to our institution for each targeted segment."

We are obviously going to suggest that a marketing-oriented approach to fund-raising is the approach that most congregations would benefit from adopting.

Characteristics of Marketing-oriented Fund-raising

A marketing approach to fund-raising will have the following characteristics:

1. It will acknowledge the importance of "outside-in" thinking as opposed to "inside–out" thinking. That is, you will design a strategy for fund-raising by focusing on the "market's" needs,

New Light
Effectiveness of Solicitation Methods

A study was conducted that looked at the effectiveness of eight different solicitation methods in different-sized congregations and metropolitan areas. The eight methods were:

(1) member visitation from the pastor or staff

(2) secret pledging whereby the amount pledged is known only to the contributor

(3) designated giving for specific needs of the church

(4) strong appeals from the pulpit during the regular service

(5) small group meetings that study the meaning of stewardship

(6) mailings to all congregation members describing the needs of the congregation and requesting regular contributions

(7) stewardship material from the denominational office provided to all members

(8) employing professional fund-raisers

Results were sometimes surprising. In metropolitan congregations, utilization of a pledging system actually lowered the rate of contributions. In nonmetropolitan congregations, as expected, the "personal touch" was found to be best—small study/prayer groups and secret pledging were found to be the most effective. Mailings, stewardship material, and professional fund-raisers all decreased the rate of giving. In small congregations the small study/prayer groups discussing the meaning of stewardship were found to be effective, as were appeals from the pulpit. In midsized congregations, professional fund-raising appeals were effective, and in large congregations secret pledging significantly raised contributions. In general, it is safe to conclude that no single approach works best in all conditions. In your congregation this will mean doing some experimentation and noting the results to learn what works best for you.

Adapted from Peter A. Zaleski and Charles E. Zech, "The Effectiveness of Various Solicitation Methods in Raising Member Contributions: Evidence From the Presbyterian Church ("As Ye Sow, So Shall Ye Reap"), *Journal of Ministry Marketing and Management* 1, no. 1 (1995): 97-104.

desires, etc., rather than focusing exclusively on your own (chapters 4, 5, 6).

2. You understand that not everyone will share the same motivation for giving, or the same excuse for not giving, and therefore you think in terms of segmenting your donor market (chapter 7).

3. Drawing an exchange map for each donor group will help you to identify the needs and value that each segment will seek from the exchange with your organization (chapters 6 and 8).

4. You will develop positioning strategy statements for each of the segments that you will target. These statements will describe the benefits that will accrue to each segment's members from giving to your organization. The benefits will be in alignment with your understanding of the segment's needs and sense of value (chapters 7 and 8).

5. The design and implementation of your positioning will be done by carefully attending to the components of your marketing mix (chapters 9 and 10).

Here are a few things to keep in mind when designing your marketing plan for attracting funds from your donor "market":

Motivations for Giving

Several reasons have been given for why people give to charities:

1. Need for self-esteem. These people attempt to build their self-esteem and self-image by giving to feel good about themselves. The opposite of this would be shame or guilt.

2. Need for recognition from others. These people attempt to build their social status or enhance their prestige in the eyes of others. They have a strong need to belong.

3. Fear of missing the blessing that accrues to the giver. This need centers on peoples fear that they or members of there family will miss out on receiving the blessing that comes to those who are "generous to God's work."

4. The habitual giver. These people give out of habit for no real reason other than a desire not to be embarrassed by not contributing to the cause. They give because everybody else does.

5. Nuisance giver. These people give only to get rid of the solicitor.

6. Required to give. Some religious organizations, such as some Jewish congregations, require annual "fees" or "dues" for being able to attend anything beyond the basic worship service.

7. Captive givers. These people feel real sorrow for someone they know who has a problem. They are "other-centered" in that they would earnestly like to aid the victim in some way.

8. People-to-people givers. These people have a real feeling of the "commonness of human beings," a solidarity with other people. This group has internalized the idea of helping others because they want to.

9. Concern for humanity. This segment of givers is concerned about others because they are "God's children." They feel a moral obligation to contribute to the religious organization's work for others. They have accepted the love-for-humanity idea because it is fundamental to their faith.

10. Faithful tithers. These people give a faithful tithe because they believe all they have belongs to God, and as stewards of those gifts from God they are to return a biblically ordained faithful portion to the church.

11. Ministry efficiency. Some donors give because they see the ministry operated by the institution as being the best way to deliver the help to those served by that ministry (i.e., better than other nonprofit competitors).

12. Ministry influence. Baby boomers, in particular, are interested in "giving back" to society and its institutions some of what they feel they have taken on their rise to their current status. They want to give to worthy causes that share the goal of improving the quality of life for those who never got the breaks in life that they did. [24]

Clearly, targeting people with different motivations will need to be done with different marketing strategies. In some cases, the strategy might consist of one-to-one marketing, in which the marketer approaches a potential individual donor with an appeal specifically designed with that donor's motivations or objections in mind. Being "sensitively strategic," as we have described in these pages, is still the best path to achieving mutually beneficial exchange with all potential donors.

[1] Robert Wuthrow, *The Crisis in the Churches: Spiritual Malaise, Fiscal Woe* (New York: Oxford University Press, 1997), pp. 38-42.

[2] John L. Ronsvalle and Sylvia Ronsvalle, *The State of Church Giving Through 2002*, 14th ed. (Champaign, Ill.: Empty Tomb, 2004), p. 36.

[3] Julia Duin, "Giving in Different Denominations: Religious Giving Has Reached All-Time Lows," *Philanthropy*, May 2001.

[4] Gene Edward Veith, "Who Gives Two Cents for Missions? We Do, to Our Shame," *World Magazine*, Oct. 22, 2005.

[5] George Barna, "Tithing Down 62% in the Past Year," news release by Barna Research Group, May 19, 2003.

[6] Veith.

[7] David B. Barrett and Todd M. Johnson, *World Christian Trends A.D. 30-A.D. 2000: Interpreting the Annual Christian Megacensus* (Pasadena, Calif.: William Carey Library, 2001), p. 656.

[8] Christian Stewardship Association, quoted in Holly Hall, "Raising Funds by the Good Book: Churches Use Financial Lessons From the Bible and See Gifts Rise," *Chronicle of Philanthropy*, June 17, 1999.

[9] John Ronsvalle and Sylvia Ronsvalle, *Behind the Stained-Glass Windows: Money Dynamics in the Church* (Grand Rapids: Baker Books, 1996), pp. 156, 157.

[10] "God, Money, and the Pastor," *Leadership* 23, no. 4 (Fall 2002): 26-31.

[11] George Barna, *How to Increase Giving in Your Church* (Ventura, Calif.: Regal Books, 1997), pp. 27-31.

[12] http://www.smartpaymentsolutions.com/ex-churches.html.

[13] http://www.easytithe.com/why.htm.

[14] http://www.qgiv.com/.

[15] http://www.vancoservices.com/vs_nonprofit_egiving_solutions.htm.

[16] Sarah Kershaw, "Pass the Collection Plate and Charge It," New York *Times*, Aug. 11, 2002.

[17] Sam Hodges, "Plastic Replaces Passing the Plate," Dallas *Morning News*, June 30, 2007.

[18] *Ibid.*

[19] Marek Fuchs, "Tithing Evolves as Donors Gain Financial Savvy," San Francisco *Chronicle*, Jan. 7, 2007, p. A-9.

[20] *Ibid.*

[21] The information on Jewish giving is taken from Dean Hoge, Patrick McNamara, and Charles Zech, *Plain Talk About Churches and Money* (The Alban Institute, 1997).

[22] Sabrina Schiller, "Synagogue Fund-raising," *Reconstructionist*, December 1984, pp. 23-26.

[23] See, for example, Wayne C. Barrett, *More Money, New Money, Big Money* (Nashville: Discipleship Resources, 1997).

[24] Philip Kotler and Alan R. Andreasen, *Strategic Marketing for Nonprofit Organizations* (Upper Saddle River, N.J.: Prentice Hall, 1996), p. 253; and Barna, *How to Increase Giving in Your Church*, pp. 58-66.

• •

WORKSHEETS: CHAPTER 11

Fund-raising

A. Target Market

1. Identify the segments that you will target:

Segments Targeted: Describe in detail each targeted segment using insights gained from understanding of their motives for giving, donation patterns, etc.

Target 1: _____

_____

_____

Target 2: _____

_____

_____

Target 3: _____

_____

_____

2. Exchange Maps for Target Markets

Target 1 Map:

Target 2 Map:

Target 3 Map:

B. Marketing Strategy

1. Goals _____

_____

_____

2. Positioning

Describe your positioning strategy statement for each targeted segment.

Targeted Segment	Positioning Strategy Statement
_____	_____
_____	_____
_____	_____

C. Marketing Mix

a. Product (What is the something of value you have to offer to the potential donor? Be sure to see the value through the eyes of the donor segment.)

Segment 1:_____

_____

Segment 2:_____

_____

Segment 3:_____

_____

b. Distribution (use of electronic or others means of obtaining funds)

_____

_____

_____

c. Promotion (message content and media chosen to execute positioning strategy and to fit target segments' characteristics)

_____

_____

_____

d. Price (donation amount being requested)

_____

_____

_____

Part 6:

Connect With Exchange Partners

THE EFFECTIVE MARKETING PROCESS

Adopting a Marketing Philosophy

↓

Develop an Understanding

↓

Plan the Marketing Strategy

↓

Design and Implement the Marketing Tactics

↓

Connect With Exchange Partners
CHAPTER 12: *Fellowship Marketing*
CHAPTER 13: *Evaluating Our Programs*

The reward for having successfully completed the effective marketing process is to make a connection with the other party to the exchange process. By "connection" we mean establishing a long-term mutually beneficial exchange relationship. This was our goal from the beginning. We were not seeking to only make an exchange—we wanted something more lasting, more meaningful, more consonant with the mission of our institution. We sought to make a positive impact on the lives of those we serve within the compass of our mission, and when we successfully achieve that goal we make a connection with them. Consequently, at each step of the process we did not lose sight of our ultimate goal of connecting with our exchange partner. Now we can focus on nurturing the relationship and evaluating the effectiveness of the process that led to this conclusion. The two chapters of this last step of the EMP are devoted to that end. Chapter 12 describes the means by which we can forge stronger bonds with our members and encourage an active engagement with our organization. Chapter 13 provides a description of an assessment program by which we can evaluate our effectiveness in generating these connections. Continuous improvement in our processes is insurance in maintaining these hard-won connections.

CHAPTER 12:

Fellowship Marketing

"Serve one another in love" (GALATIANS 5:13, NIV).

In this chapter we will address the following questions:

1. What are the key concepts for improving member satisfaction?

2. How can we successfully manage "moments of truth"?

3. How can we recover from a failed "moment of truth"?

4. What are the five steps for establishing a service orientation in our organization?

5. How can we successfully recruit and manage volunteers?

M uch discussion to this point has addressed how congregations and other religious organizations can use marketing principles to attract new members and meet the needs of external publics. This chapter will focus on being responsive to the people who make the church or synagogue possible by their attendance, financial contributions, and work. These are the *internal* publics—the members, active constituents, and the workers, both paid and volunteer. It is these internal groups that the leaders often find the most difficult to serve, especially in the areas of communications and public relations. This difficultly occurs because persons in a congregation often relate to the organization in more than one role. At one time a person may be a recipient of a ministry, and at another time be providing a ministry. Each role calls for different communications.

Effective marketing and advertising depend on getting the *right message* to the *right people* at the *right time*. This goal can happen only when the leaders are clear regarding the targeted group, whether leader, worker, active members, or inactive members. This chapter will first consider the problem of creating satisfied members and then the problems of recruiting, managing, and motivating volunteers.

Creating Satisfied Members

Scores of books and articles have been written on how to satisfy customers by delivering great customer service.[1] What does it mean for a congregation to have "satisfied" members? It may mean they are satisfied with the pastor's abilities as a preacher, counselor, administrator, enabler, teacher, leader, nurturer, and so on. It may mean that the member has been made to feel an integral part of the organization's social network. It may mean any of these things or all of them. However, there is one thing it must mean: *The member wants to continue to remain an active participant in the life and ministry of the congregation.*

Pastors and rabbis should see what they do as "value-adding" activities—adding something of value to the lives of members along some dimension that is significant *from the member's perspective* (outside-in thinking). This magnifies the need for a shared frame of reference to exist between pastor and parishioners, between rabbi and congregation. The pastor or rabbi must be able to perceive value in church membership *from the congregant's viewpoint* so that member satisfaction can be truly delivered by building value into the very experience of being a member.

How to Deliver Member Satisfaction

There are many examples from the business world that teach powerful lessons about customer satisfaction and how it is achieved.

498

Perhaps one such example will help you gain insight into satisfaction within your own organization.

Scandinavian Airlines System (SAS) posted an $8 million loss the year before a new president, Jan Carlzon, was appointed. Carlson immediately embarked on a bold plan to turn SAS around. His revolutionary approach focused the entire organization around serving consumer needs! By "turning on" the whole company to the mission of service, he believed consumers would notice and respond to such a difference between SAS and other airlines. Carlzon's belief was that people within SAS, like most organizations, had become so tuned into executing the narrow set of tasks assigned to them that few were putting consumer satisfaction at the top of their list of priorities. Employees were motivated to perform their assigned tasks to a high degree of technical competence but were not seeing what they did from the perspective of how those activities would ultimately contribute to or detract from customer service. "Who," asked Carlzon, "is paying attention to the real needs of the customer?" He set about changing the focus of employees from a process of "producing" airline flights to one of delivering service. In his words: "Our business is not flying airplanes, it's serving the travel needs of our public. If we can do that better than the other companies, we'll get the business. If we can't, we won't get the business, and we don't deserve to."

With the help of key executives, Carlzon began to teach the "gospel of consumer orientation" energetically and persistently throughout SAS, to all 20,000 employees. He and his managers personally shouldered this task of evangelism by traveling from country to country, talking to employees and preaching about service, creativity, and finding a better way. A formal training program was established as well as an internal consulting group, which worked with managers throughout the company to find ways to overcome obstacles and move ahead on various projects. Carlzon also took an aggressive lead in finding ways to serve the consumer. One way was to focus on the business traveler rather than trying to be all things to all people and end up being nothing to everybody. This service for business travelers become SAS's best-known feature and was a big success. Another new program initiated was regular market research studies of consumers to determine their satisfaction levels and to correct little problems in customer service before they became big ones.

The result of these changes? Even with an investment of $30 million to institute the improvements needed to deliver better customer service, SAS went from an $8 million loss to a gross profit of $71 million in a little more than a year. Reflecting on this amazing turnaround, Olle Stiwenus, director of internal SAS management consultants, said, "Jon Carlzon really masterminded the turnabout maneuver. He had a great deal of help from many talented people, but he himself *supplied the vision* to get it going and the energy to see it through."

Albrecht and Zemke, in their book *Service America*, conclude the SAS story with these comments: "Carlzon . . . possessed . . . two key traits that made him the right man for the times: a creative mind and the ability to communicate his expectations [and visions] clearly and dramatically. He managed to get the top management of SAS to rethink the company's destiny and to come up with possibilities that enabled them to see beyond this previous conception of the business."[2]

A passenger review of SAS on epinions.com accessed in September of 2007 had this to say about SAS:

"Feeling like death before I boarded the SAS flight in New Delhi, I seriously wondered how I was going to manage to get my poor body to Copenhagen. I had caught one of those viruses that await one in foreign locations and had to manage to fly with it from Delhi, spending a couple of days in Copenhagen and then on to New York.

"When [feeling like I did on that flight], it's really best to be home, in bed, receiving lots of TLC rather than having to be on a plane for many hours. The sense of smell is severely affected when one doesn't feel well, and the smell of a plane can be torture. Still, I was not contagious and not feverish and needed to get home. My husband was quite concerned for me.

"We got on the plane, and the flight attendant must have noticed how pale I was, because she took me under her care and I was pampered all the way to Copenhagen. Brought me water a million times, pillows, stopped by to see how I was feeling . . . was sweet and attentive.

"The flight was packed, and yet she never passed by me without taking a look to see how I was doing, and made what could have been an uncomfortable ride a very pleasant one for both myself and my husband.

"I have flown SAS other times with similar results. The crew is without exception very professional and courteous and the check-in staff very efficient.

"I would guess that it's a great airline for families because if mothers traveling with young kids get half of the attention that I got with an upset stomach, they are apt to think that SAS is the best airline in the world! And of course, it is under difficult circumstances that one can truly rate the crew. A routine flight without kids, drunk passengers, obnoxious or demanding ones . . . well, anyone can be efficient and attentive when things are well. A crew can certainly show their worth when someone really needs a little care, and SAS did just that for me.[3]

The SAS example suggests an important lesson for congregation leaders. The story points out the crucial difference between internal markets and external markets. The internal markets Jan Carlzon decided to target were SAS's executives and ground crews, flight crews, and sales and reservations personnel. The external markets Carlzon targeted were business travelers and travel agencies.

In addition, the story illustrates a number of key concepts for member and volunteers' satisfaction:

1. *The need for visible, personal leadership in instilling a "service mentality" throughout the organization.* Just as Carlzon made a point of being personally involved in building a service mentality throughout his organization, a pastor or rabbi must do likewise. The clergy should make it clear through their own actions that a philosophy of interpersonal relations will prevail in all interactions the paid and volunteer workers have with the members and all other persons relating to the congregation.

2. *Communicating a vision for the congregation beyond members' pre-*

vious conception of possibilities or destiny. We have talked at several points about "mission" and "vision." Perhaps Jan Carlzon's greatest contribution to SAS's success was to get the people of SAS to "rethink the company's destiny and to come up with possibilities that enabled them to see beyond their previous conception of the business." Such visionary leadership by the clergy can also enable paid and volunteer workers and members alike to envision the congregation's ministry in ways they had not previously seen as possible or necessary.

3. *Understanding what constitutes satisfaction for the target public.* Carlzon decided to focus his company's efforts on satisfying the needs of a specific target market—business travelers—and made a point of knowing what is required to make those customers feel satisfied. Similarly, religious leaders must focus on understanding their targeted "customers" and being in tune with the needs, attitudes, perceptions, values, and motivations of their members.

4. *Having a clear service strategy, instead of assuming that member satisfaction will occur.* When altering SAS's approach to customer service, Jan Carlzon did not simply talk about delivering service; he "walked his talk." To install the service strategy, he:

- Established what was expected of employees by defining what constituted superior service
- Established a service strategy to deliver that service
- Trained employees to implement the strategy
- Measured the performance of employees in delivering service
- Rewarded superior service accomplishments of those employees.

Jan Carlzon did not assume that just because he announced the vision it would be put into action whenever a service encounter occurred. Beyond announcing his vision, he built a structure to make it happen—in measurable terms.

Specifically, an effective service strategy is a nontrivial statement of intent that noticeably differentiates the church or synagogue from others, has value in the members' eyes, and is deliverable by the leaders and workers.[5]

A pastor or rabbi must also develop a service strategy for himself or herself, and for the entire congregation. One thing is almost certain: If the pastor or rabbi does not do this, it simply won't happen. It is not in the character of a congregation for such radical change to happen if the leader is not leading in it.

5. *Researching member attitudes.* SAS and other service-oriented companies are constantly researching and monitoring consumers' attitudes to better understand their wants and needs and the extent to which the organization is delivering satisfaction. Such research is no less important with the internal market of one's own members and participants. When measuring the attitudes of internal markets, two concepts are especially crucial: *satisfaction* and *importance.* By *satisfaction*, we mean the degree to which a member or other participant is satisfied that a program or ministry is meeting one or more of his or her important needs or interests. [4]

By *importance* we mean the degree to which a member or other participant feels a program or ministry is addressing an important need of at least one target group.

So it is possible that a member might be satisfied with what a particular ministry is accomplishing, but he or she may feel that it isn't addressing any important need. On the other hand, a member may feel that a particular ministry is very important and may be highly dissatisfied with its present results. (See, for example, Exhibit 6.11.)

A responsive congregation is one that researches the major needs and interests of individuals and groups within the organization and then works to provide program ministries, with which those persons or groups are fully convinced of their importance and are highly satisfied with their results. This is the muscle and fiber of internal marketing. Soliciting member attitudes not only yields the benefit of knowing the extent to which persons are experiencing satisfaction in their contacts with the church or synagogue, but also involves members in identifying the programs that:

- have outlived their usefulness and should be sloughed off
- are still important, but satisfaction is waning, indicating an overhaul is necessary
- need to be started in order to meet a need not currently being addressed.

Making members a part of the process of building a responsive church or synagogue builds "ownership" of the organization's mission and vision. It also has the side benefit of generating new ideas and suggestions that can result in ministries of importance, delivering even greater satisfaction.

It is important to remember that gathering member importance/satisfaction information, and then not acting on it is worse—far worse—than not gathering the information at all. Importance/satisfaction studies generate high levels of expectation for changed behavior on the part of the congregation's leaders and its workers.

6. Generating commitment throughout the organization. Jan Carlzon made every effort to get his employees to rethink their responsibilities as centered on their customers. His approach was to constantly talk about how to deliver customer service, then he backed up his talk with structures to measure to what extent it was happening. Finally, he built reward systems to reinforce desired behavior.

A pastor or rabbi must get the ruling boards, the paid and volunteer workers, and the program committees to think in terms of their responsibilities in making satisfaction and importance happen. However, Rabbi Harold Schulweis demonstrates that it can be done.

Harold Schulweis describes his Valley Beth Shalom congregation as being "on the cutting edge of religion." Instead of hearing sermons at Saturday services, worshippers at the suburban Los Angeles synagogue are more apt to engage in lively discussions with the rabbi on the meaning of the Torah. In addition, to make the Jewish experience more than a once-a-week event, special programs are held in members' homes or in the temple, which has become a community center between Sabbaths. Some 27 trained laypersons assist Schulweis in his duties. "The laity has to be offered a coequality with the clergy," says Rabbi Schulweis, a nationally recognized leader in Judaism. In 14 years at Valley Beth Shalom, he has changed its country-club image to a model of innovation. Among his ideas is the wider use of the *havurah*, the Hebrew word for "group of friends." Instead of confining the havurah to religious studies, Schulweis has promoted the concept of small groups as a way of counteracting isolation and providing a vehicle for "Jewishness" during the week. Now members can join one of 61 *havurahs*, each of which includes about 10 families. Held in a synagogue member's home, the *havurah* acts as a monthly discussion or special-interest group, or as an extended family. Says Schulweis: "If there is a sickness, nine times out of 10, by the time I get there nine families have already visited." In response to its success, Schulweis has helped many synagogues throughout the United States adapt *havurah* programs. Other activities supported by the $1.5 million annual budget include a counseling center staffed by 40 volunteers, which offers programs ranging from food distribution to childbirth classes, and a Gamblers' Anonymous group. "People come to the temple for everything, and we feel that's the way it should be," says congregation president Sylvia Bernstein. Membership has grown sixfold to 5,000 drawn from a wide area. Says Diane Martin, who joined Valley Beth Shalom after visiting many other congregations: "Sometimes I don't feel like driving so far, but I've tried different places, and I keep coming back."[6]

Successful large congregations are characterized by being "honeycombed" with groups of laypersons that provide for one another's needs. The pastor or rabbi should not—indeed, cannot—take on a member service/nurturing program alone. The SAS example illustrates that successful service programs require the involvement and commitment of everyone throughout the organization. One or two workers who are not committed to serving the needs of the organization's constituents can undo the efforts of all the others—one bad apple can spoil the whole barrel.

7. *Making sure the basics are done well.* Excellent service organizations understand that no amount of extras, special touches, or "fancy packaging" can overcome failure to deliver the core benefits sought from their service by customers. Jan Carlzon understood that on-time flights and comfort in the air for business travelers would make or break SAS. Marriott understands that people are seeking comfort and convenience from a hotel room. McDonald's knows that quality, service, cleanliness, and value are the benchmarks of good fast

food. No amount of frequent traveler points or "win a million" games can make up for failure to deliver on the basics.

Satisfaction with being a member of a particular congregation will not occur unless that experience enhances the sense of community between the person and the congregation.[7] People want to feel a part of something important; something they are willing to sacrifice self-interest to serve as a greater good. Changing the hours of worship to be more convenient, enlarging the parking lot, sending out a church newsletter, and so on will not overcome the limitations of an unfulfilled sense of community and lack of contributing to an important cause.

As the pastor of a church, one of the authors had occasion to work with a highly gifted music director/organist. For several months there was a good deal of amiable discussion, and some tension, as the pastor urged the music director to pay attention to what the congregation seemed to feel and say about various types of music. After a worship service in which a sense of praise and joy was manifest, the music director said, "I now understand what you want me to do. I thought my job was to teach these people music education. Now I see it is to lead them into worship through music."

Successful organizations never lose sight of the basics; they know what they are there to do, and they are obsessive about making sure it's done right. "God is in the details" takes on a new meaning when seen in this light.

Moments of Truth

Another of Jan Carlzon's legacies of value to pastors and rabbis is his concept of "moments of truth."[8] Carlzon said, "We have 50,000 moments of truth out there every day." He defined a moment of truth to be any episode in which the customer comes into contact with any aspect of the organization and gets an impression of the quality of its service.

A *moment of truth* for the church or synagogue may be defined as any episode in which a person comes into contact with any aspect of the congregation and gets an impression of the quality of the membership experience.

A moment of truth can be a phone call to the office to ask a question or obtain someone's address, the response a member gets when making a request for special prayer for a family member in a Sunday school class, the reaction of other members to a dish brought to the potluck dinner, looking in the pastor's eyes and shaking his or her hand at the end of a worship service, hearing (or not hearing) "Thank you for a job well done" when serving on a church committee, and so on. While the church or synagogue may not have as many moments of truth each day as SAS, it is safe to say they are no less important in their contribution to membership satisfaction, and they must be managed just as intentionally—toward creating participant satisfaction.

Positive moments of truth build member satisfaction and loyalty, while negative moments of truth can build a wall separating members from the church or synagogue to which they belong.

Moments of truth do not even have to involve human contact. A friend told one of the authors that she moved to a new town and sought out the local church on Wednesday night for midweek prayer services. Upon arriving at the unlit church parking lot, she saw light coming from an upstairs window, where she expected to find the service being held. Trying several locked doors without success, she returned home without making contact with the worshippers. The following weekend she tried another local church of the same denomination and was made to feel most welcome. Needless to say, she made the second church her new church home.

Moments of truth can occur as people read your congregation's sign, see your ad in the paper, hear the worship service over the radio, visit your church's Web site, or get approval for a group wanting to use a room without prior reservation. Moments of truth occur in "large, bold print" and in "fine print." But they occur, and persons' impressions of the church or synagogue are fixed thereby.

The authors have a friend living in Orange County, California, who decided to seek out a new church home. This was happening at a crucial time in his life, when he was seeking comfort and support. Because he was favorably impressed with Wesleyan theology and the materials published by *The Upper Room* related to spiritual formation, he decided to visit first a church of that tradition.

On his first, and only, visit to the church, he was asked to sign a guest register. This particular Sunday was toward the end of a calendar quarter. In a few days he received a quarterly financial statement from the church, with a note that he had given only one offering to the church that quarter. From then until now he continues to receive quarterly statements, with notes chiding him for not supporting the church. He has also received a letter from the pastor saying the congregation is behind in its mortgage payments and is unable to complete several necessary repairs. Since he had not been giving to the regular fund, would he please make a generous payment to the building fund?

If moments of truth are not managed successfully, the quality of the experience for the member or consumer regresses to mediocrity. This impression of mediocrity will then be transferred to other, unexperienced aspects of the organization—"If the main worship service is this unfulfilling, I can imagine what the Sunday night service must be like." But this works both ways. A well-managed and positive moment of truth can provide a positive lens through which individuals view the organization, while negative moments of truth color a person's entire view of the organization. The scriptural adage is appropriate here: "It's the little foxes that spoil the vineyard."

One way to identify the various moments of truth occasions is to sketch out the "experience cycle" a member goes through when encountering the church in some way.[9] An experience cycle for the main worship service may appear as shown in Exhibit 12.1. Each point of the cycle represents a moment of truth that leaves an impression and that should be successfully managed.

Similar experience cycles can be developed for other occasions during which members and others come into contact with any aspect of the organization. Of course, it is not possible for the pastor or rabbi to be present at each moment of truth to manage its occurrence. Therefore, it is of utmost importance that all personnel (including members themselves) receive "customer service training" so that they see themselves as contributing to positive moments of truth for the entire organization. The paid staff, volunteer workers, ruling boards, program committees, and members must become the managers of their moments of truth—when encountering someone who will form an impression of the organization and its people.

Likewise, because the moments of truth may sometimes not involve a person-to-person contact, the systems and "hardware" of each moment of truth must be devised in such a way as to leave a positive impression. For example, what does your organization's Web site suggest in the eyes of someone seeing it for the first time? What impression would someone have of your church or synagogue when driving by—what message does your lawn and sign commu-

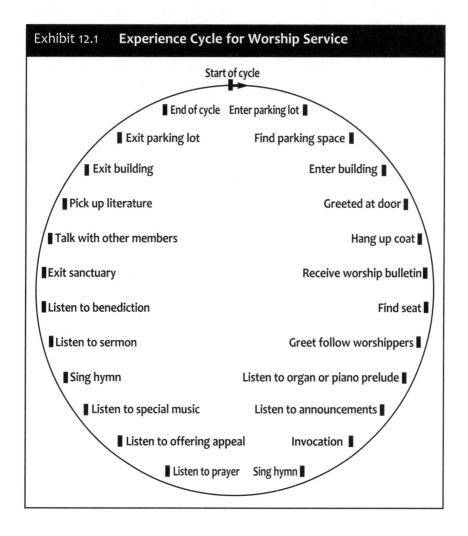

Exhibit 12.1   **Experience Cycle for Worship Service**

nicate? What is the impression left by the moment of truth when someone hears the recorded message on the telephone answering machine at the office or listens to the podcast of your worship service? In all moments of truth, we must be capable of seeing things through the eyes of the beholder.

It is important when considering how to manage the moments of truth to see them as specific occurrences, rather than as traits. That is, the trait of courtesy for greeters at the sanctuary entrance is not the same as a moment of truth for Mr. Doe when *he* enters for worship. If the greeters are generally courteous but are having a bad day when Mr. Doe arrives, a failed moment of truth will occur.

Which of us is comforted with the thought that the airline on which we are traveling has an 88 percent on-time departure and arrival rate when our flight leaves hours late, causing us to miss an important event? Such occurrences are bound to happen. It is the way we recover from such events that determines whether our moment of truth is ultimately a failure or a success.

How to Recover From a Failed Moment of Truth

To err is human. To recover from your error is essential if you are to maintain good relations between paid and volunteer workers, the members, and external publics. A failed moment of truth can either leave a scar or, like a mended broken bone, result in an even stronger bond between the offender and the offended—if the proper recovery method is used.

The term *recovery* originated with Donald Porter of British Airways, based on that firm's efforts to understand customer expectations when they changed from a government-run entity to being privatized.

Recovery was the term we coined to describe a very frequently repeated concern: If something goes wrong, as it often does, will anybody make a special effort to set it right? Will someone go out of his or her way to make amends to the customer? Does anybody make an effort to offset the negative effects of [a mistake]? Does anyone even know where, when, or how to deliver a simple apology?[10]

A sequence of as many as five steps is involved in effective recovery from a failed moment of truth.[11] Whether or not all five are necessary in any particular instance depends on the severity of the failure. We will use as an example a failed moment of truth between an office worker, paid or volunteer, and a member of the congregation.

1. *Apology.* Recovery absolutely demands some acknowledgment of error *immediately following* a failed moment of truth involving a staff member and a congregation member. *Apology is more powerful when delivered in the first person, and as soon after the failure as possible.* An institutional "We're sorry" lacks the sincerity and authenticity of an individual's acknowledging that a mistake has been made.

An apology should contain the following elements: a specific statement of the error to demonstrate that the worker knows what failure has been made, a confession that "I" am the one responsible, an expression of care for any inconvenience or embarrassment, a statement as to what will be done to correct the failure, and an inquiry as to whether this will be sufficient to resolve the matter.

Kenneth Blanchard has invented the creative "one-minute manager."[12] Blanchard teaches us that most apologies need not be long; one minute will do. They must, however, be sincere and genuine. Further, the worker committing the failure should make the apology. The offended person will resent any other person making the apology, even the pastor or rabbi.

If a very serious failure has been committed, the pastor or rabbi, as head of staff, will perhaps follow up with an apology and exploration of necessary corrective steps. But this need should be rare.

If the failure is a systems failure, for which no one person bears sole responsibility, the chairperson of the committee in whose responsibility area the failure has occurred should offer the apology. If the failure is a "total systems error," cutting across several departments, the pastor or rabbi, chair of the ruling board, or some other appropriate person should offer the apology.

2. *Urgent Reinstatement.* The offended member must perceive that the worker is doing the best job possible to make things whole again without delay. If the member believes that the worker (and the church or synagogue) has his or her interest at heart, a great deal of progress

has been made toward restoring goodwill between the offended and the offender.

3. *Empathy.* If a member has felt victimized by the actions of a worker or committee, he or she is likely to desire some demonstration of understanding of why he or she feels victimized *before* steps are taken to redress the grievance. Empathy is the expression of "I understand your hurt—I care about you—I can relate to your pain." In its highest form, the member feels heard, affirmed, and cared about.

Empathy is quite different from expressions of *sympathy.* Sympathy is the sharing of another's pain. Empathy is demonstrating compassion for the person in pain without personally taking on the pain—it's a shoulder to cry on, a source of strength. Sympathy is risky, because the helper enters the same condition as the one needing help or support. Sympathy is making someone weak feel better about his or her condition; empathy is being understanding and helping the person feel strong again.

An apology sends the message to the victim that it matters that there was a breakdown; empathy goes further to say that it matters that the person was hurt in the process. A service expert once said, "When service fails, first treat the person, then the problem."[13]

4. *Symbolic Atonement.* Rather than the proverbial pound of flesh, symbolic atonement is a gesture that says "We want to make it up to you." There are countless ways the worker can go beyond apologizing and empathizing with the mistreated member. Whether placing a phone call on behalf of the offended party, driving out of the way to deliver someone or something, or taking a person to lunch to establish broken connections, the symbolic atonement is communicating the worker's desire to make amends for a failed moment of truth.

The size of the recompense is not as significant as the symbolic impact of acknowledging that the injury has occurred. It is important that the worker demonstrates a sincere desire to atone for his or her role in the injury. Here, actions speak louder than words.

5. *Follow-up.* Depending on the severity of the failed moment of truth, it may be advisable to follow up the symbolic atonement with inquiries to determine whether the relationship with the member

has been redeemed. The pastor or rabbi or some other official representative of the organization should perhaps make this follow-up. Here, a perceived willingness of the organization to "go the extra mile" goes a lot further than earlier efforts to restore the relationship with the aggrieved party.

Research by the Technical Assistance Research Programs Institute of Washington, D.C., found that recovery methods, when done properly, help to build a loyal base of customers.[14] Customers who had complained and had their complaint handled to their satisfaction were even more "brand loyal" than customers who had never complained. However, the same research also showed that a poor or grudging recovery effort might be worse than no effort at all. Doubly dissatisfied customers or members will be less inclined to feel charitable toward an organization that has disappointed them than those who have suffered the first disappointment in silence.

Establishing a Member Service Program

Five steps lead to the establishment of a service orientation in a religious organization.

1. Evaluating the present level of service quality.
2. Clarifying the service strategy.
3. Educating the paid and volunteer workers.
4. Implementing new tactics at the front line.
5. Reinforcing the new orientation and making it permanent.[15]

Step 1: Evaluating the Present Level of Service Quality. The first step in becoming a service-oriented religious organization is to determine the satisfaction level of various served audiences. "Report cards" are needed, which cover the critical components of service delivery. For example:

pastor to members in family counseling

rabbi to couples in premarital counseling

members to visitors at a worship service

members to needy persons in distributing food and clothing

staff to members in committees

nursery attendants to parents, regarding child's needs while under the nursery's care

Marketing research methods, such as focus groups, user groups, in-depth interviews, and surveys (see chapter 4) can help the organization know where it currently stands on delivering satisfaction. If experience cycles have been diagrammed for all those occasions on which persons come into contact with someone in the organization (worship service, soup kitchen, prison ministry, teen counseling, etc.), it is fairly simple to identify the particular moments of truth that are most important to evaluate against the criteria of good performance. To illustrate, if a report card is sought from visitors to the main worship service, and one of the moments of truth to be assessed is the initial greetings, we may include a series of questions such as the following.

When were you greeted? (check all that apply)
- ❏ immediately upon entering the building
- ❏ upon entering the sanctuary
- ❏ after being seated by those around me (us)
- ❏ I (we) were not greeted before service began
- ❏ other; please describe:

_____.

How would you characterize the greeting(s) you received? (check all that apply)
- ❏ very friendly, made me (us) feel very welcome
- ❏ somewhat friendly, I (we) felt welcome
- ❏ neither friendly nor unfriendly
- ❏ I (we) did not feel welcome
- ❏ too pushy, I (we) were embarrassed/prefer to be left alone
- ❏ other; please describe:

_____.

The key for generating useful information on performance begins with *knowing* what it is that the target group desires (outside-in thinking), rather than *assuming* that we know (inside-out thinking). When developing report cards on the pastoral staff, church members will often be reluctant to be perfectly candid. These reservations can usually be overcome if the clergy request their ratings anonymously. Efforts must be directed at obtaining unbiased, candid information.

Step 2: Clarifying the Service Strategy. Developing a sound service strategy may require holding a retreat during which the pastor or rabbi can engage staff and committee leaders in open discussion. There must be recognition that a problem exists ("We are not delivering 'customer' satisfaction as well as we should") and a willingness to be open-minded in considering solutions to the problem. Having report cards showing that a problem exists can provide the impetus for a serious discussion of what the shared vision of service strategy should he. The service strategy can be clarified by addressing the following questions:

• How do our target groups see us at present?

• How well are we delivering on the precepts of our mission regarding service to our members and other participants?

• In what areas are we doing a good job of serving our target groups? What learning can we transfer from these areas to those in which we are not doing as well?

• How do we want to be known with respect to serving the needs of internal and external target groups?

Out of the retreat should come a strategy for delivering satisfaction to the organization's target groups. The following questions need to be asked of the strategy as it is being developed.[16]

• Can it differentiate our church from others? Does it reflect the fundamental values that bind our members together?

• Can people in and out of the church clearly see the benefits of associating with a congregation that serves people that way?

• Can we commit to it? Is it something that the clergy, staff, and members can believe in and work to support?

• Can we make it work?

• Can we communicate it to our target groups in ways they can understand?

• Can we dramatize its value to our members in concrete ways that will mobilize their efforts to make it happen?

• Can we make it real and experiential for our internal and external groups, rather than just an abstract slogan?

A final test of the service strategy is to relate it back to the report cards. Does the strategy zero in on those moments of truth and deliver true, meaningful satisfaction on those dimensions most important to the customer?

Step 3: Educating the Paid and Volunteer Workers. As the SAS experience demonstrates, the leaders, workers, and committees must be trained to implement the service strategy. Since mass training on the scale of SAS is not practical for most congregations, the clergy and lay leaders must take the initiative to demonstrate by their own actions and decisions that they have made this service strategy a guiding principle. It is much easier to communicate the

---

Exhibit 12.2   The Translation of Service Messages— Visitor Relations Mirror Member Relations

Pastor to Member	Member to Visitor
What are your problems and how can I help you?	How can I be of assistance to you?
We want you to know what is happening in the church, so here is what is going on:	I am capable of helping you because I am in the know.
You are part of the corporate body; we all share in the victories of the church.	I take personal responsibility to see that you feel at home here.
We treat each other with respect.	I have respect for you as the individual you are.
We stand behind each other's decisions and support each other.	You can count on me and my church to deliver on our promises.

Adapted from Robert L. Desatnick. *Managing to Keep the Customer* (San Francisco: Jossey-Bass, 1987), p. 20. Adapted by permission of Jossey-Bass, Inc., Publishers.

---

value of such a commitment if people witness the leaders' implementation of the strategy. Here a picture is worth a thousand words. Exhibit 12.2 suggests a pastor's influence on the members' service behavior.

Step 4: Implementing New Tactics at the Front Line. One of the best ways to get commitment is to let those facing the moments of truth define how the strategy should be implemented, rather than telling them how to do it. This does not mean they should be left alone to work it out for themselves, but each person should be fully involved in determining how the moments of truth can be carried out. People tend to support what they have helped to create. This approach generates a tremendous amount of creativity throughout the entire organization.

Many manufacturers have discovered the benefits of "quality circles," comprised of production workers who recommend and then implement ways of improving the quality of their own work. The same principle can deliver great results in your organization. The key is to focus persons' attention on ways to best handle the moments of truth they face, so that the end result is a satisfied member. By this means, the paid and volunteer workers are "lighting their own candles," so to speak.

Step 5: Reinforcing the New Orientation and Making It Permanent. If a congregation is to become transformed into a true service organization, the clergy and lay leaders must find ways to reinforce desired behavior on the part of staff and members. Keeping an eye on the moments of truth these people face and providing immediate, positive reinforcement of well-handled moments is perhaps the best way to ensure continued positive behavior.[17] Virtually every person in the organization wants to know that the pastor or rabbi notices his or her efforts. Further, the program committees owe it to the paid and volunteer pastors to observe and compliment excellence in ministry. Finally, the ruling boards are coequally responsible with the pastor or rabbi for the quality of ministry being offered at every level. All these people need to care enough about the congregation's ministries to know what is going on and to praise the workers who are doing well. Unless commitment to the service strategy and recognition of work well done are carried out at the top leadership level, it simply isn't going to happen.

On the other hand, leaders must also offer immediate and straight feedback to persons who are failing their moments of truth. Having been reminded of the congregation's service strategy, the person must be helped to plan his or her own strategy for correcting the behavior in future moments of truth.

It is sensitive and difficult for clergy to call paid and volunteer workers to accountability regarding the quality and results of their work. In a volunteer organization it is often very difficult to decide who works for whom. Does the pastor work for the members, or do the members, as workers, work for the pastor?

It would be wise, therefore, for lay personnel committees and ruling boards to assume this responsibility. They must recognize that they would be failing *their moments of truth* if they fail to do this. They shouldn't stick their heads in the sand when someone complains that the pastor or rabbi has criticized mediocre performance.

Supervising paid and volunteer workers isn't as difficult as most clergy make it. Peter Drucker is right when he claims that poor performance in religious organizations is perpetuated by the leaders' "temptation to do good"—to protect the mediocre worker. He is also right when he claims this style of personnel management will eventually bring the church or synagogue to regret and ruin.[18] But one should never ask of the staff and volunteer workers what one is unwilling to do oneself. There is no way around it: excellence in ministry and members' satisfaction begins with the pastor or rabbi. If it doesn't begin here, it doesn't begin.

Salaried and volunteer workers alike should know that a significant part of their performance evaluation will be based on their willingness and ability to manage their moments of truth successfully and deliver satisfaction in their contacts with members and other stakeholders.

Showing them the results of the report cards, rewarding excellence in service, and working with them to find innovative ways to deliver service satisfaction will pay dividends to church administrators seeking to lead their church into a new service orientation.

Likewise, seeing church leaders who "walk their talk" and who are personally concerned with their own moments of truth provides a needed role model. Giving people the support systems and tools to deliver satisfaction is also critical. Asking them to "make bricks without straw" is a surefire way to dampen enthusiasm for the service strategy.

Recruiting and Managing Volunteers

One common feature of virtually all churches and synagogues is their use of volunteers to provide a channel for committed people to contribute time to a cause or ministry they believe in, to become more involved with others who share a common spiritual bond, and, finally, to keep down expenses. Religious organizations are the largest volunteer organizations in the world.

The core concept of voluntarism is that individuals participate in spontaneous, private, and freely chosen activities that promote or advance some aspect of the common good, as the persons participating in it perceive it. Religious organizations hold a second, unique, core concept of voluntarism: the conviction that each and every one of God's people are called to use their time, talent, and tithe to further the work of God throughout the world. Each one is called to service.

Volunteers are the first to put their money where their heart is. In recent years, however, the number of volunteers has been declining. Churches and synagogues are having to give increased attention to the problem of attracting more volunteers, providing more volunteer satisfaction and more effectively managing the entire volunteer enterprise. The volunteer problem has been made more difficult because of several important trends in voluntarism.[19]

1. Although people are still volunteering because they feel it's a good thing to do or because they have been taught to do so, new motivations are emerging, such as:

    a. The desire to change society.

    b. The desire to obtain experiences that can eventually be useful on a "regular" paid job.

c. The desire to help a specific cause, such as improving the environment, electing a specific candidate, helping the elderly, removing discrimination, and so on.

d. The desire to improve one's life through meeting others.

e. The desire to engage in a volunteer career upon retirement.

f. The desire to get inside important institutions to see what they are doing and to make sure they are doing the right things.

2. A wider spectrum of people are volunteering. Rather than just the healthy, vigorous middle classes, we now find the "served" (for example, elderly or disabled individuals) and professionals also offering their services.

3. Volunteers are more demanding. They want more input into what they are doing and are no longer willing to be only drones in a larger enterprise.

4. Some groups are challenging the ultimate social desirability of voluntarism. While unions have traditionally worried that voluntarism was taking employment from those who could have been paid, the women's movement has recently challenged voluntarism as perpetuating the notion that what women do (that is, housework or volunteering) is not really valuable because it is unpaid.

The major consequence of these trends is that securing volunteers in the future will be harder than in the past.[20] The pool of those who come forward with little or no encouragement is shrinking. Those who might come forward are more hardheaded about their choices and are likely to be approached by more competitors vying for their volunteer commitment. For example, under the gifted leadership of Frances Hesselbein, the Girl Scouts of America has experienced a renaissance, and now utilizes more than 60,000 volunteers.[21]

For churches and synagogues there is another factor affecting the shortage of volunteers quite apart from societal trends: *the size of the congregation.* Small congregations (fewer than 200 adult members) and large congregations (more than 600 members) tend to experience a perpetual shortage of volunteer workers—and for very different reasons. The small congregation simply does not have enough persons in its volunteer pool to draw upon. Consequently, in small congregations, a few faithful volunteers assume several responsibilities and keep them year after year. The large congregation finds it short of volunteers because by the time the membership reaches 600, the members feel they can hire professional staff.

Medium-sized congregations tend to have a sufficient number of volunteers, or even excess. They have a sufficient volunteer pool, but not a large enough financial base to cause members to think the work can be hired out.[22]

Cynthia Zacher is symbolic of uncounted thousands of deeply committed volunteer workers hidden away in the churches and synagogues of America. Many carry two or more responsibilities because they have a passion for God's work and there aren't enough volunteers to go around. The need for effective strategic marketing aimed at volunteers is becoming ever more apparent. Religious leaders are confronted with two major concerns regarding volunteers: recruiting needed volunteers and managing them.

Recruiting Volunteers

As with any marketing task, a crucial starting point for recruiting

---

Cynthia Zacher lives with her husband, Clayton, and their four children on the family farm, 18 miles out of Elgin, North Dakota. A registered nurse, Cynthia has chosen to work, for less money, as a teacher's aide in the Elgin school system, because she feels her gifts and interests can best be expressed by working with children.

The family belongs to the Evangelical Lutheran Church in America in Elgin, a congregation of 538 baptized members. At the church Cynthia is the organizing force behind all children and youth programming. Presently she serves as Sunday school superintendent, substitute teacher for all classes, teacher of a Sunday school class, and, for the past few years, the director of the daily Vacation Bible School. In addition, she serves on the church council and parish education committee.

Why does she carry so many responsibilities? "Because there just aren't enough people anymore who are willing to work with the kids." And Cynthia has a passion for the kids.

521

is understanding the target audience. Volunteer motivations are as diverse as consumer motivations. One classification of motivations is based on Abraham Maslow's hierarchy of needs (see chapter 5).

Maslow's understanding of changing motivational forces as one ascends or descends the scale of needs suggests important targeting and marketing considerations regarding volunteers. It would seem that a person would develop an interest in volunteering about the time he or she reached the third order of need. Having provided for one's own survival and safety, the individual may now aspire to the relationships and recognition voluntarism might provide.

Motivation for voluntarism might tend to remain high through the

---

New Light
Attracting Volunteers

Research on why and how volunteers are attracted to service in a church has revealed that there are three primary dimensions to volunteering. First, volunteers feel their service is a personal calling from scriptural teachings. Second, they want their work to make a meaningful contribution, to make a "difference." Third, they derive psychological and sociological benefits from their service. For many volunteers, church service allows them to feel needed, useful, and helpful and to interact with like-minded others. Other research has found that promotional efforts to attract volunteers would benefit from either positive framing emphasizing an upbeat message, or negative framing, indicating the negative condition necessitating the need for volunteers. Neutral messages that present facts alone were not as effective in attracting volunteers as were the positive or negative messages.

Adapted from Walter W. Wyner, Jr., "A Qualitative Analysis of Church Volunteerism: Motives for Service, Motives for Retention, and Perceived Benefits/Rewards From Volunteering," *Journal of Ministry Marketing and Management* 5, no. 1 (1999): 51-64; Darin W. White, "Determinants of Altruistic Volunteering: An Empirical Assessment," *Journal of Ministry Marketing and Management* 4, no. 1 (1998): 33-55.

fourth order of need. Persons having reached the fifth order may be altruistic, in that they are no longer concerned about having enough for their own survival or security, they are less concerned about "belonging or status," and they care more about affecting systemic change.

The marketing task in recruiting volunteers is to (1) segment the membership into groups reflecting their own personal concerns, life situations, and motivations; (2) select the target groups or persons to be recruited; (3) prepare and present the recruitment plan to connect with their life situation and to appeal to their unique motivations and interests.

In this manner, it is possible to recruit volunteers from every position on the hierarchy of needs. The content and process of recruiting persons who are experiencing "survival" needs and motivations will, understandably, be different from the marketing approach taken with persons who have achieved self-actualization. This is true not only because they are at a different place economically and psychologically, but also because their spirituality is different—they are experiencing God differently and are asking different things of God.

Schindler-Rainman and Lippitt propose another strategy for targeting groups or persons for volunteer work.[23] They suggest that one might look upon a decision to volunteer as a response to forces pulling toward—and away from—volunteering. They propose that such forces be separated into (1) individual internal forces, (2) external interpersonal forces, and (3) situational forces.

There are still other approaches to identifying and attracting volunteers:

1. *Segmentation studies.* Here the interest is in isolating the demographic, motivational, and lifestyle characteristics that separate *current* volunteers from nonvolunteers. The studies assume that the best prospects for future volunteers will resemble those who have volunteered in the past.

2. *Prospect studies.* Here the interest lies in recruiting volunteers from new segments. The focus is on learning more about clusters of congregation members who might have values or lifestyles to which the congregation can appeal.

3. *Motivational studies.* Leaders of congregations have recognized the relatively superficial nature of using surveys to understand mem-

ber motivation. Thus recent interest has developed in qualitative methodologies, such as focus groups and in-depth personal interviews as efficient, effective ways to reveal more fundamental reasons for volunteering and—just as important—for not volunteering.

4. *Positioning studies.* Leaders who feel they understand motivations typically progress to image studies as a basis for potentially changing their marketing strategies. They recognize that their success or failure as recruiters of particular segments of potential volunteers is tied closely to those segments' perceptions of the church and their perceptions of other organizations that might invite them to volunteer.

With information derived from such studies, the volunteer recruiter can decide whom to focus on, what to say, how to say it, and where to say it.

Retention of Volunteers

Once recruited, volunteers must be retained. Retention has become a very important problem in recent years, as the demand on people's time and energy increases. Two techniques have proven particularly valuable. First, *former* volunteers should be studied to determine who they are and how they differ from volunteers who stayed on, why they ceased their volunteer work, and what steps could be taken to get them to revolunteer.

Second, the church or synagogue should carry out routine formal assessments of *present* volunteers' satisfactions and dissatisfactions. Among the factors that frequently surface are the following:

1. Unreal expectations when volunteering. This is sometimes the recruit's own fault in that he or she has unrealistic fantasies about how rewarding it would be to teach a Sabbath school class, sing in the choir, work in the office. The recruit may also not realize how much time would be involved. But just as often the culprit is the recruiter, who, in his or her zeal to get volunteers, paints an excessively optimistic picture of the volunteer's time commitment, type of work, and probable influence.

2. Lack of appreciative feedback from leaders, paid staff, and coworkers.

3. Lack of appropriate training and supervision.

4. Feelings of second-class status vis-à-vis full-time staff.

> ## Becoming "Doers"
> ### *Increasing Member Commitment*
>
> Commitment to a religious organization consists of a member's willingness to exert effort on behalf of the organization, loyalty to the organization, the degree of goal and value congruency with the organization, and the desire to maintain membership in the organization. Studies or member commitment have shown several positive outcomes to increased levels of commitment: they are more likely to give most of their gifts to the church they attend and be involved in church administration, feel their church looks after its members, perceive they are important to the church and other members, be socially involved with other members, and believe they receive concerned leadership. A scale of 30 items has been developed, and can be found in the source below, for measuring member commitment. Nine strategies for increasing commitment are also described in this reference.
>
> ---
>
> Robert E. Stevens, O. Jeff Harris, J. Gregory Chocehere, "Increasing Member Commitment in a Church Environment," *Journal of Ministry Marketing and Management* 2, no. 2 (1996): 469-479.

5. Excessive demands on time.

6. Lack of a sense of personal accomplishment.

Principles for Managing Volunteers

The use of volunteers is not an unmixed blessing. The mix of volunteers and full-time staff can be a volatile one, with problems arising on both sides.

On the side of the volunteer, many have the attitude that, since they are donating their services and are not being paid, (1) they don't really work for the church and so shouldn't be *told* what to do; rather, they should be *asked* whether they would be willing to do something; (2) they should have a great deal to say about the content and timetable for their assignments; and (3) they deserve continual appreciation for their generosity and commitment.

Further, some persons volunteer, not because they really want to, but because they have been coerced into volunteering by the pastor or peers, or because they wish to be perceived as loyal members doing their part. Just as bad, some volunteer only because they want a built-in group to visit with—a captive audience. Woe to the pastor or office staff when *they* become the captives. Worse yet, some volunteer simply because they want to "straighten things out down there at the church."

A major problem of managing volunteers is the matter of who works for whom.[24] Every pastor or rabbi with a volunteer corps has faced the issue at least once. The issue of who works for whom is unique to those organizations in which the members are the "owner" and the leaders are the "servants." This issue is especially acute in ecclesial bodies with congregational forms of government. The temptation of many pastors is to let volunteers do, or not do, as they wish. However, this is a trap for the organization and the worker alike. For the organization, it results in mediocre ministry, and it deprives the worker of the deep satisfaction that comes when one knows that one has done the job well.

One manager of a large volunteer force has developed what he calls his "rule of thirds." One third of his volunteer force works avidly with very little direction and encouragement. One third will work only with considerable motivation and are effective only under careful supervision. And one third will not work at all under any circumstances and can't be relied upon.

On the side of the organization, there is considerable opportunity for friction to develop if the full-time staff looks on the volunteers as second-class workers. Among the opinions professionals have been known to offer are:

• Volunteers are dilettantes. They are not there for the long haul and, therefore, don't have to live with the consequences of their impulsive or lethargic performance.

• Volunteers never really pay attention to their training and instructions, because they are only part-time, do shoddy work, and weaken the ministry.

• Volunteers often come from occupations in which they boss others and so cannot, or will not, take direction.

The potential for conflict between volunteers and full-time workers is considerable. The situation can be exacerbated if the pastor or rabbi does not take firm control of the situation. Again, it is a matter of *attitude*. If the pastor or rabbi is dominated by feelings of gratitude that individuals have so kindly volunteered, all is lost. Then he or she will be unwilling to "ruffle the feathers" of volunteers. This will only encourage the volunteers' tendencies toward undisciplined performance. At the same time, lay officers will be likely to squelch grumbling among the paid staff for fear that they will upset the volunteers and their friends in the congregation. This will only cause unrest and surreptitious insubordination among the paid staff, with the result that insubordination develops among *both* the full-time and the volunteer staff.

There is a solution, and it is a good one. The organization must develop the understanding that volunteer workers are expected to perform at the same level of excellence as the professional, full-time workers. And having set this standard, it must be enforced. Among other things, this means using the following volunteer standards and managerial practices:

1. Assessing the volunteer's skills and as nearly as possible matching these skills to the tasks to be performed.

2. Setting out job responsibilities clearly and in detail in advance.

3. Setting specific performance goals and benchmarks.

4. Clearly informing the volunteers of these goals and of the fact that they are expected to achieve them.

5. Nurturing and expecting excellence in performance of tasks by volunteers and paid staff alike.

This straightforward, professional style of volunteer management may seem risky to the inexperienced pastor or rabbi. But both volunteer and professional staff responds favorably to it. If they don't, they are the wrong choice.

Most volunteers like to be taken seriously and challenged. They appreciate the opportunity to be well trained and well supervised. Full-time staff appreciates the leader's firmness and the fact that they, too, can treat the volunteer seriously, giving orders as necessary and reprimands as required. Performance standards for both groups improve enormously, and the church's effectiveness, efficiency, and morale rise noticeably. Indeed, the church's volunteer positions can be highly coveted.

The authors are aware of one medium-sized city in the Midwest where the chamber of commerce runs a volunteer program for local nonprofit organizations that requires volunteers to pay a stiff fee and have good references before they can do volunteer work. It is titled the Leadership Program, confers status on those who are accepted, and has a long waiting list of applicants!

Perhaps what is most required is an elevated view of the worth and capabilities of today's volunteer. In almost any congregation there are persons who possess higher educational degrees than the clergy, and members who are more experienced in program planning and management, financial management, personnel supervision, and so on. Yet some clergy harbor low expectations of these volunteer workers, believing volunteers cannot perform "the important ministries," cannot be held accountable for excellence, or cannot be trusted to follow through on important tasks.

Leaders of religious organizations can overcome conflict and obstacles if they follow this brief set of operating principles to help in recruiting and managing volunteer leaders and workers:

1. There is little difference in deploying and managing paid and volunteer leaders and workers. If anything, the volunteer worker should be called to even higher levels of excellence in carrying out the tasks and ministries than the paid worker. Even if a paid worker does a poor job, he or she receives a periodic reward for the time given to the work—in the form of a paycheck. The essence of volunteer ministry, however, is that the worker receives no monetary reward. The only reward a volunteer receives is the satisfaction of knowing he or she performed the task to the best of his or her ability, and the recognition that may be given.

2. A congregation that is fully responsive to its volunteer workers' need for excellence and recognition will see it as the volunteers' right to have a competent supervisor, skilled in attracting good and reliable volunteers and in motivating and rewarding them. A marketing approach means understanding the volunteers' needs and meeting them in a way that draws their support and best effort. The

responsive volunteer manager is likely to sponsor social functions for volunteers, provide experiences designed for their spiritual renewal, confer awards for years of service, and arrange a number of other benefits that will recognize their contribution.

3. Volunteer leaders and workers have a right to know—and the recruitment process should make clear:

a. What they are expected to accomplish, in terms of results, not activities.

b. How these results fit into the overall mission of the church or synagogue and why these results are important to the life and work of the entire congregation and to God's work in this place.

c. What the position will cost them—how many hours will be required each week, what training will be necessary, what administrative meetings they will be expected to attend, etc.

d. What their taking the position will "cost" the pastor or rabbi or the congregation—how much time the pastor or rabbi, or some other leader is willing to commit each week to working with the volunteers, and what resources will be provided to do the job.

e. How they will be evaluated and in what form feedback will be given.

f. How they will be supported in their spiritual life journey.

When these items are built into the recruiting effort and the person to be recruited is carefully selected, fewer than 15 percent will decline to serve; once deployed, they will serve with excellence.

4. Volunteer leaders deserve the courtesy of personal recruitment by the pastor or rabbi or a respected lay leader. In recruiting top-notch volunteers and securing high commitment, nothing will take the place of a hand on the shoulder, of face-to-face recruiting conversation.

5. Effective volunteer ministry requires double duty. Any worthwhile ministry requires hard work—and consumes spiritual and physical energy. The pastor or rabbi should see it as one of his or her major privileges to provide regular spiritual renewal experiences for "workers only"—a monthly meeting for spiritual renewal and fun, an annual retreat, private spiritual direction, and so on.

6. Match volunteer coworkers with care. Since they have different gifts, match them so that they complement one another, thus making one another's weaknesses irrelevant. Some volunteers *love* meetings; others hate meetings. Some are gifted in starting a program from scratch, but have no interest in administering a program once it is up and running. The following taxonomy of abilities will help match coworkers.

• *Idea person*: highly creative at hatching new, innovative ideas, approaches, programs; not good at turning ideas into programs.

• *Planner:* not good at hatching new ideas or envisioning new programs, but very good at planning a program once the idea has arisen.

• *Trigger to action*: highly creative at getting people started on an idea or program once it is ready for action.

• *Administrator:* not good at creating ideas or starting new programs, but gifted in keeping a program going, taking care of all the details after it is up and running.

• *Doer:* not good at ideas, planning, or triggering, but a faithful and effective worker, once the program is ready to go. Action-oriented, wants to be where the "rubber meets the road."

Given these differences in people's abilities and interests, it makes sense to segment the volunteer pool into target groups according to interests and skills. If a "doer" is recruited to an "idea" or "administrator" role, the results will likely be disappointing. The person will either decline the request or, once on the job, will pick out one piece of the program at which he or she can perform adequately, to the total neglect of the details necessary to keep the program running.

7. After they have been on the job 90 days, invite each volunteer leader of a ministry area to rewrite his or her job description. By then, chances are they know more about their job and the ministry requirements than anyone else. Within three or four months as a leader, the person has insights and ideas for making the ministry area more effective. (If the volunteer doesn't, you know you recruited the wrong person.)

Ask the leader to put his or her ideas in writing. Discuss the ideas, being sure that the needs and interests of the target group(s) are addressed and that the ideas support the congregation's mission. Then, together, work the new ideas through with the ministry team or program committee. By this means the leader and the entire ministry team will feel new commitment to their ministry area. People tend to support what they help to create.

---

[1] See Karen Leland and Keith Bailey, *Customer Service for Dummies,* 3rd ed. (Hoboken, N.J.: Wiley Publishing, 2006); Robert Spector and Patrick D. McCarthy, *The Nordstrom Way to Customer Service Excellence: A Handbook For Implementing Great Service in Your Organization* (Hoboken, N.J.: Wiley Publishing, 2005); Ken Blanchard, Jim Ballard, Fred Finch, *Customer Mania! It's Never Too Late to Build a Customer-focused Company* (New York: Free Press, 2004); Dennis Snow and Teri Yanovitch, *Unleashing Excellence: The Complete Guide to Ultimate Customer Service* (Sanford, Fla.: DC Press, 2003); Lisa Ford, David McNair, Bill Perry, *Exceptional Customer Service: Going Beyond Your Good Service to Exceed the Customer's Expectation* (Holbrook, Mass.: Adams Media Corporation, 2001); Ron Zemke and John A. Woods, *Best Practices in Customer Service* (New York: AMACOM, 1998).

[2] The SAS story is taken from Karl Albrecht and Ron Zemke, *Service America!* (Homewood, Ill.: Dow Jones-Irwin, 1985).

[3] http://www.epinions.com/trvl-review-3D9A-14453E30-39CDF287-prod3; http://www.do.yoo.co.uk/airline/sas/95046.

[4] These key concepts were inspired by the SAS story and from several important books on customer service: Albrecht and Zemke, pp. 20-26; Ron Zemke with Dick Schaaf, *The Service Edge* (New York: NAL Books, 1989); Karl Albrecht and Lawrence J. Bradford, *The Service Advantage* (Homewood, Ill.: Dow Jones-Irwin, 1990); Karl Albrecht, *At America's Service* (Homewood, Ill.: Dow Jones-Irwin, 1988).

[5] Zemke and Schaaf, p. 40.

[6] "Spreading God's Work: Five Success Stories," *U.S. News and World Report,* Oct. 22, 1984, p. 71.

[7] See, for example, David Prior, *Creating Community* (Colorado Springs, Colo.: Navpress, 1992).

[8] Jan Carlzon, *Moments of Truth* (Cambridge, Mass.: Ballinger Pub. Co., 1987).

[9] The experience cycle is based on the cycle of service discussed in Albrecht, pp. 32-36.

[10] Zemke and Schaaf, p. 22.

[11] *Ibid.,* pp. 23-26.

[12] The one-minute manager is discussed in a most creative series of six little books on management, which we heartily recommend. In the series Blanchard recommends that compliments and criticisms should be as immediate as possible, specific, and brief—one minute is long enough.

[13] Zemke and Schaff, pp. 23-25.

[14] *Ibid.,* p. 22.

[15] See Albrecht and Zemke, pp. 170-80, and Albrecht, pp. 157-223.

[16] Adapted from Albrecht, p. 178.

[17] One of the best resources for learning to give on-the-spot compliments, or reprimands, is the one-minute-manager series by Kenneth Blanchard.

[18] See Peter F. Drucker, *The Temptation to Do Good* (New York: Harper-Collins, 1984).

[19] See Evan Schindler-Rainman and Ronald Lippitt, *The Volunteer Community: Creative Use of Human Resources*, 2nd ed. (La Jolla, Calif.: University Associates, 1977), pp. 21-45.

[20] See Gordon Mauser and Rosemary H. Cass, *Volunteer at the Crossroads* (New York: Family Service Association of America, 1976); John Vantil, "The Search of Voluntarism," *Volunteer Administration* 12, no. 2 (Summer 1979).

[21] For a taped interview of Frances Hesselbein, see "People and Relationships," *The Nonprofit Drucker*, vol. 4. The interview discusses Mrs. Hesselbein's volunteer and marketing strategies.

[22] Many of the books and papers by Lyle Schaller offer insights into voluntarism in the church.

[23] Schindler-Rainman and Lippitt, pp. 48-50.

[24] For an in-depth discussion of this issue, see Norman Shawchuck, "The Local Church: Who Works for Whom?" *Leadership* 1, no. 1 (1980): 95-100; Alvin Lindren and Norman Shawchuck, *Let My People Go: Empowering Laity for Ministry* (Schaumburg, Ill.: Spiritual Growth Resources).

WORKSHEETS: CHAPTER 12

Developing a
Fellowship Marketing Strategy

Member Satisfaction

Have you done the following key tasks when developing a member-satisfaction plan?

	Yes	No
1. Instilled a visible, personal customer service mentality throughout the organization.	_____	_____
2. Communicated a vision for the congregation beyond members' previous conception of possibilities or destiny.	_____	_____
3. Understood what constitutes satisfaction from the target public's point of view.	_____	_____
4. Developed a clear service strategy instead of just assuming that member satisfaction will occur.	_____	_____
5. Researched member attitudes.	_____	_____
6. Generated commitment throughout the organization.	_____	_____
7. Made certain the basics were done well.	_____	_____

Moments of Truth

Develop an experience cycle for each encounter that members, visitors, publics will have with our organization. Describe how you will build in satisfying experiences for each point on the cycle(s).

_____

_____
_____

Member Service Programs

Have you performed the steps of establishing a service orientation in your organization?

	Yes	No
1. Evaluated present level of service quality	_____	_____
2. Clarified the service strategy	_____	_____
3. Educated the paid and volunteer workers	_____	_____
4. Implemented new tactics at the front line	_____	_____
5. Reinforced the new orientation and made it permanent	_____	_____

CHAPTER 13

Evaluating Our Program

"Test everything; hold fast to what is good"
(1 THESSALONIANS 5:21, NRSV).

In this chapter we will address the following questions:

1. What are some basic evaluations we can do to determine how well we are achieving our goals?

2. Why must we evaluate our ministries?

3. What are the three types of evaluation?

4. What are the four steps of evaluation?

5. What are the basic elements of an evaluation program?

6. How can we employ an evaluation matrix to help us evaluate our programs?

Our goal for this text has been to facilitate your learning regarding how to build strong congregations and to connect better with the people that you desire to serve.

In this chapter you will be introduced to a comprehensive evaluation process (a pattern for doing something) that you can employ to determine how well you have achieved your goal. You may choose not to carry out the evaluation on your own; rather, you may invite a professional in marketing to carry out a full-scale evaluation of your various ministries. This should be done about every three to four years.

Nonetheless, we want you to know what good evaluation entails so that you will be equipped to communicate with your committees and the evaluator.

At a minimum, there are some things you can, and should, do:

1. If you are a pastor or rabbi, you should meet with a small group to evaluate the major worship service(s) *held that day at least twice a month.* The group should comprise those who presented the service and a cross section of the worshippers. Each element of the worship experience should be examined with an eye toward doing it better—the sermon, readings, music, parking, greeting and ushering, printed materials, sound system, etc. The parishioners who are offering the feedback should be about 50 percent of those who have served on the group for at least a year or more, and 50 percent should be new each time. The sooner this evaluation is conducted after the service, the better.

2. Every six months, meet with each major committee and the ministry task force to ask these questions: "What is the mission, and what are the goals, of this ministry?" "What is working well, and why?" (The *why* is at least as important as the *what*.) "What needs doing?" "How will we get it done?"[1]

3. Every three or four years you would do well to conduct a full-scale evaluation of the committees and ministries of your organization, using the evaluation process suggested below.

The following discussion on evaluation could have been appropriately included as the final step of the marketing planning process discussed in chapter 8, "Strategic Marketing Planning," since evaluation is an essential ingredient of marketing control. Instead, we have decided to place evaluation at the end of this book because evaluation should be a part of everything the organization does, not merely its marketing planning. Evaluation speaks to the entire content of this book, not just the chapter on planning.

Evaluation of Ministry

In the Scriptures there is this statement: "Test everything; hold fast to what is good" (1 Thessalonians 5:21). A great deal of work goes into planning and carrying out a program or ministry. Indeed, ministry is costly.

A great deal of time, money, and volunteer energy is spent in any church or synagogue every year. It makes sense, therefore, that the leaders would want to measure the results of their ministries to ascertain whether certain efforts should be continued, or discontinued. It makes sense that leaders and congregations would want to evaluate their programs as a matter of responsiveness to those who have planned, funded, and worked to carry the programs to a fruitful end. And so wisdom says, "Test everything; hold fast to what is good."

Why then is so little formal evaluation conducted by those responsible for the programs and ministries of congregations? The scarcity of evaluation is more a lack of nerve than a lack of skill. The majority of religious leaders know a good deal about how to evaluate, but many avoid it for fear of the consequences—some for good cause. In thousands of congregations across America, evaluation is requested only when the ruling board wants to get rid of the pastor—and so the members carry out something called evaluation, hoping to find something to support their already-decided conclusion. In thousands of congregations laypersons resist evaluation because of the idea that volunteers should not be accountable for their results.

Perhaps evaluation is resisted because no one likes to be given a "grade" for his or her work in which you either pass or you fail! Such evaluation in organizations is almost always counterproductive.

Useful evaluation is never done to grade someone's effort. Evaluation is intended to provide leaders and workers with the information they need to make midcourse program corrections, and to assist in future planning. The purpose of evaluation is to increase program effectiveness and to aid in future planning.

Even though evaluation may be sparse in a congregation, the clergy and lay leaders frequently wish to try new ways of doing things, or they change the way they have been doing something, and now want to know whether the change has made any difference, whether good or ill. Anyone who has defined a problem and constructed a solution for it wants to know whether the solution worked, and if so, how well and at what cost. In all these instances an evaluation will provide a format for determining what difference has been made.

People who raise the following questions often have a need for evaluation:

1. Should we continue the program, and if so, in the same way?
2. Did we use our resources wisely?
3. Should others use this same approach?
4. Is this new program worth the time, money, and effort we are putting into it?
5. Are we meeting our goals? Are these the right goals?
6. Whom are we affecting, and to what degree?

Whenever possible, the evaluation should be begin at the time of planning the event itself. Then the planners or evaluators can gather data as soon as a new program is conceived, or as soon as the leaders decide what they want to learn from the evaluation.

For example, if the planning effort is directed toward improving the quality of religious education in the primary department, the evaluators should immediately begin gathering data to determine the existing quality before any change or event is introduced.

Every evaluation requires an event that is to be evaluated. An event may vary from a single, short-lived incident, such as a one-time advertisement in a newspaper, to a multiyear program, such as one offered for drug abuse by a church or synagogue. Or the event may be in the future; a congregation develops a new ministry outreach program. Whether the event is past, present, or future, an evaluator attempts to determine what has happened as a result of the event.

The leaders, the ruling committees, and the evaluator need to share a common understanding of many concepts, methods, and tasks.[2]

Types of Evaluation

Three types of evaluation are possible: (1) Informal Use of Records, (2) After-the-Event Evaluation, and (3) Before-the-Event Designed Evaluation.

Each has an appropriate role in organizations. Let us consider each of these.

1. Informal Use of Records. Data (bits of information, not yet assimilated) can be gathered from many sources that exist apart from the evaluation procedure. A good journal, diary, logbook, minutes of past meetings, or set of financial records will allow you to partially reconstruct a past event.

Knowing what has happened in the past allows you to evaluate an event in order to make better decisions for the future. This is one good reason that diaries should be kept by the major participants in the event and by the evaluation committee. In addition, correspondence, reports to agencies, or other official papers (covenants, guidelines, etc.) often provide evaluation data.

2. After-the-Event Evaluation. After an event has occurred, a leader or committee may want to ask the following questions: What happened? Why did it succeed or why did it fail? How well did it do? Was it a successful program? Have there been positive or negative *unexpected* effects? Is this project essential to the organization, or is this a benign activity that should be closed out? Answers to questions such as these often provide data for future planning after an event has been completed. The "report cards" idea for evaluating the present level of service quality, mentioned in chapter 12, is an example of this type of evaluation.

3. Before-the-Event Designed Evaluation. This type of evaluation occurs when one plans for the evaluation and starts the data gathering early in the history of the program. An evaluation designed before the event begins allows for evaluation to be made before, during, and after the event. If the event is running parallel to other events, before-the-event designed evaluation allows for comparisons and/or the use of control groups. For example, the evaluation might compare using billboards with telemarketing to see how well each produces the desired results. Measurements of before and after the evaluation can be taken on both to determine what incremental results have occurred. In doing this one may install a new program and compare its performance with an existing one.

Each type of evaluation serves different purposes. If you consider a variety of tasks—such as data gathering, developing procedures and management, devising organizational structures, implementing models, evaluating models, educating users, and measuring impact and the benefits of a system—you may find one approach to evaluation that is more appropriate than the others.

For example, given the interests, resources, and constraints of the organization, a before-the-event designed evaluation may not be feasible. However, keeping historical records, a diary of events and a set of official minutes may allow for an informal use of records evaluation at a later time. Whatever type of evaluation is used, certain basic steps need to be followed. They are described below.

Evaluation Steps

Evaluation has four major steps: (1) defining the mission of the organization, (2) evaluating the goals and objectives, (3) evaluating the program and activities carried out to achieve the goals and objectives, and (4) evaluating the evaluation's impact on the program.

1. What is the mission of the program (or organization)? The program's mission or "guiding principle" becomes the foundation against which evaluative measures will be made. Often the group or organization does not have a clearly defined written mission. The evaluator will then work with the group to define its "assumed" mission. This is done by reviewing the group's major efforts and helping them to decide what core result or condition is the uniting principle of the several programs. The mission, if previously defined, may usually be found in the charter constitution and/or official minutes.

2. Evaluation of goals and objectives. What are the goals and objectives? Collect the documents that contain them (no evaluation can be carried out without a specific statement of goals and objectives). If written objectives do not exist, a set of objectives must be developed by looking at documents, such as minutes, speeches, or constitutions, or interviewing persons to clarify what they are trying to accomplish. It is possible to have more than one set of objectives. In that case, you can evaluate against any set of objectives. Two different groups may want to evaluate the same program against different objectives.

a. Are the objectives and goals stated in measurable terms? Not all aspects of each goal or objective must be measurable, but at least one or more measures must exist in order to have an acceptable objective or goal. Process measures are usable, but outcome measures are preferred. There must be an established time frame for every objective. A measure of a program may be that it relates to attracting 500 unchurched persons a year, or that a boiler must not be down for repair more than three times each winter.

b. Are the goals and objectives consistent with the organization's mission, and primary purpose? You must look at the goals and objectives of the program in terms of the mission or purpose of your organization. The evaluative question is whether the goals and objectives are consistent with the organization's mission. For example, is the goal to achieve 95 percent of attendance at worship consistent with a congregation whose primary purpose or mission is to deepen the spirituality of its constituents? In doing so, the leaders must consistently evaluate the efficacy of the church's ministry.

After you have evaluated your goals and objectives, you should consider the programs and activities that are being carried out in the church; this will help you achieve the goals and objectives of the leaders and the congregants.

3. Evaluation of programs and activities. Is the program consistent with the goals and objectives? You must assess whether the program addresses the established goals and objectives. For example, if the stated goal were to improve the life of homeless persons, a program to increase their scriptural reading would be inconsistent.

a. Is the program effective? To what extent has the program achieved its goals and objectives? Clearly stated, measurable objectives must exist before program effectiveness can be evaluated. Only then can meaningful questions be asked regarding effectiveness.

b. Is the program efficient? What type and amount of resources were expended in the program? Two programs that have the same outcome may score differently when compared in terms of their investment levels.

Another possible approach is to measure against a standard. For example: the cost of teaching Hebrew at a seminary is $10,000 per student. We may want to compare it with a method of teaching Hebrew that costs $50 per student. In one method a full-time tutor is provided, while the other method merely provides each student with a book. The cost of the alternatives must be balanced against how well the students will learn the Hebrew language.

Efficiency involves measuring both the effectiveness of the program and the resources used to achieve it (time, money, people, etc.). One can measure total expenditures and/or cost per output.

4. Side effects or spillover. *Side effects* are unplanned, unanticipated events or conditions that result from the program. *Spillover* is unplanned, unanticipated effects that the program had on other programs. In many instances positive or negative side effects and/or spillover may be more important than the original goal and objectives. For instance, an evaluation may discover that a Weight Watchers program in the church is having little or no effect on the participants' weight goals, but is proving a most popular place for persons to come for short-term crisis counseling or grief support.

A program may have sufficient positive side effects and spillovers to make it worthwhile, even though it is not meeting its stated objectives. On the other hand, it may be causing sufficient negative side effects to warrant its discontinuance even though its objectives are being met.

5. What program changes or new programs should be added to improve goal achievement? The evaluation will often point to the need for program changes or the addition of new programs in order to achieve a goal or objective.

For example, a congregation may design a visitation program to achieve a goal of increasing attendance. The evaluation may reveal that the goal is not being met. In this instance, the visitation program may be changed to include more visitors, or a new advertising program may be added.

Evaluation of the Evaluation

1. Is the evaluation a significant factor in achieving the goals or objectives? Often the evaluation may be more significant in effecting desired change than the program itself. Having members of the congregation keep diaries of their activities may be a more powerful intervention than attending a religious education class that is being evaluated.

2. Apply program evaluation steps regarding effectiveness and/or efficiency to the evaluation procedure. Are the results of the evaluation sufficiently effective and efficient to warrant doing the evaluation? Issues such as data quality, data analysis, inference, and communications must be considered. Are official records legible? Have the right statistics been chosen? Are the computer programs correct? Are the conclusions correct? Is the report clearly written and disseminated?

Basic Evaluation Elements

Certain key elements are basic to all types of evaluation. These must be considered in the design and conduct of all evaluation.

1. Data structures. All evaluation records should include:

(a) Date of writing

(b) Name of writer

(c) Location and time of the event about which data is being recorded

(d) The data itself

(e) Where data will be/is being stored.

Other things to be collected include objectives, measurement techniques, frameworks or models to be used, computer and data processing techniques, file systems and analytic procedures.

2. Measurement techniques. All evaluation involves some type of measurement of the programs and activities against the goals and objectives. Such measurement is often a difficult technical problem involving how one measures achievement, behavior or attitude. This leads us to the question How does one measure the smile in a receptionist's voice? How does one measure the quality of a program, or the level of service? Should one use service per dollar, and volunteer hour, return on investment of time and money, or total budget results?

In this effort, a variety of measurements are generally available to carry out the evaluation process. For example, a telemarketing program may be measured by the number of addresses collected, the number of new attendees, the number of new members, and so on. The measures chosen depend upon the specific evaluation design.

3. Resources and constraints. Any evaluation will require certain resources. Therefore, the evaluation should take into account the system's resources and constraints that impinge upon the evaluation. In all of this the evaluation should be designed to function within the available resources.

4. Environment. The persons doing the evaluation should understand the organization and the environment in which the evaluation will be carried out. For example, is the program unique, or are there many programs just like it? Does the program evaluation encompass the entire organization, or only some part of it?

5. Framework or model. Every evaluation will require an appropriate framework and/or model to measure the event against the goals and objectives and/or to compare it against other events. Should one use verbal, graphic, mathematical, or computer models? How can one measure and analyze the results from the model? How does one determine the extent to which the objectives are being met? How does one discover unexpected events, side effects, or consequences?

6. Data gathering and storage. Who should gather data? When and where should it be gathered? What data should be gathered? How and for how long should it be kept? Should the information be stored in a computer, or should it be in written form for storage in a file cabinet?

Preparing an Evaluation Matrix

One method of designing an evaluation is to create a matrix of data sources versus the evaluation steps (the evaluation data wanted). See Exhibit 13 for an illustration of an evaluation matrix.

You will notice that in the evaluation an X is entered in each matrix cell, which indicates a data source that will be used to gather data for that particular evaluation step. For example, in step 3 one data source will be used, while step 5 will involve seven data sources. Whenever two or more data sources for any step are used, they provide a validity check of the data being gathered.

When two or more data sources for a particular evaluation step exist, the persons doing the evaluation may choose to use only one or two, or it may be desirable to check all sources as a consistency or reliability test. If the same question is answered in each data source but the information being gathered is different, both data sources are important; for example, the information gathered in an interview may answer the same questions as information from a formal written report, but the interview may yield additional or more complete data from that which is contained in the written report.

Constructing the evaluation matrix serves several purposes:

1. It suggests where there are redundant sources of data; i.e., project files and minutes/documents (step 1).

2. It identifies areas for which there is no data (step 9).

3. Once completed, it becomes the basic data collection plan.

After the matrix has been completed, a remaining planning step is to determine who will gather the data from the data sources for each evaluation step. A single person or an evaluation team may be responsible for gathering all of the data; or a single person or subgroup may be assigned to gather data from one or more of the sources. When several people or subgroups gather discrete pieces of data, the evaluator or the evaluation team must collate the data and prepare the final evaluation report.

Additional Evaluation Concerns

The person(s) or organization doing the evaluation may wish to consider other issues in designing and conducting the evaluation.

1. Is the evaluation intended to make a difference in one's performance? For example, if evaluation techniques are being used in a Sabbath school, is it possible that we may eliminate the evaluation and still expect identical performance of teachers and students? The answer is not necessarily yes, because the evaluation procedure itself may influence the behavior of the teachers and the students.

2. Are we conducting a long-term analysis? Do we want to gather data for a current decision, or for a decision a long time hence?

3. Are we being asked to create an ongoing evaluation system, or simply to provide data for decision-making here and now?

Exhibit 13   Evaluation Matrix

EVALUATION STEPS (The evaluation data which is to be gathered)	Project Files and Material	Interventionist's Reports and Diaries	Evaluation Sessions	Evaluation Instruments	Official Minutes and Documents	On-site Observation	Personal Interviews with Leaders	Third-party Reports, Newspapers, etc.	Interviews with Clients
								DATA SOURCES	
1. Do written goals exist?	X(1)				X(1)				
2. Are they measurable?	X				X				
3. Are they coherent with the organization's purpose(s)?					X				
4. Is the program coherent with the goals?	X				X	X	X(5)		
5. Is the program efficient?		X	X	X	X	X(7)	X		X(7)
6. Is the program effective?	X		X		X	X	X		
7. Are there side effects/spillovers?							X	X	X
8. How is the evaluation interacting with the program?	X	X		X		X			
9. Is the evaluation effective/efficient?									

4. Is the present information system adequate to keep leaders up-to-date, or should we install a better information system?

5. Are we to teach people how to make decisions, or merely to give them the data they need?

6. Who is the "client"? Is it the program committee, the leadership team, the ruling board, etc.?

---

[1] Peter F. Drucker first suggested these questions to the authors, in a seminar for pastors and parachurch organization leaders.

[2] Benjamin S. Bloom, J. Thomas Hastings, and George F. Madaus, *Handbook on Formative and Summative Evaluation of Student Learning* (New York: McGraw-Hill, 1971). See also John Van Maanen, *The Process of Program Evaluation* (Washington, D.C.: National Training and Development Service Press, 1973).

Resource Guide:
MARKETING RESOURCES FOR CONGREGATIONAL MARKETERS

We list here resources that are likely to be of value to congregational marketers. While you may be able to access and use all of these sources on your own, it is always wise to make use of the reference librarian at your local public or college library. He or she can help you save considerable time in locating sources of greatest practical use to you.

Note: Inclusion of a Web site, book, or other source in this Resource Guide is for information purposes only, and does not constitute an endorsement by the authors.

Computerized Databases

One of the fastest ways of locating periodical literature addressing topics of interest to you is to use one of the online data retrieval services available at subscribing libraries. Of particular interest to the congregational marketer are the following databases, which can be accessed through a public or university library.

• OCLC First Search. Actually a meta-database that includes dozens of databases, such as Arts and Humanities Search, ArticleFirst, ATLA Religion, Dissertation Abstracts, PsycINFO, Readers Guide Abstracts, Sociological Abstracts, Wilson Business Abstracts, and World Catalog. ATLA Religion covers 1949-present of thousands of periodicals.

• Proquest. Includes ABI Inform and Religious Periodicals. ABI Inform covers 1971-present of thousands of scholarly, professional, and trade periodicals. Religious Periodicals covers 1988-present of hundreds of periodicals.

• Lexis Nexis. Covers 1988-present of a wide range of news, business, legal, and reference information, customer service and biographical information, and industry and market news and trends.

- EBSCO. Covers more than 100 databases in a wide range of fields, with full text records available for many articles.
- Google Scholar. Search across many disciplines and sources from one place—peer-reviewed papers, theses, books, abstracts, and articles; and from academic publishers, professional societies, preprint repositories, universities, and other scholarly organizations. Google Scholar helps you identify the most relevant research across the world of scholarly research.
- JSTOR. Offers researchers the ability to retrieve high-resolution, scanned images of journal issues and pages as they were originally designed, printed, and illustrated. The journals archived in JSTOR span many disciplines.

These databases all allow searches by entering titles, authors, or subjects identified through key words or phrases. As an example of the types of sources available through these databases, a search using the keywords "religion" and "marketing" generated scores of sources, including these:

Newspaper: "Marketing Strategy Splits the Sacred and Secular," New York *Times*, Dec. 27, 2003, p. A1.

Journal: Bruce Wrenn and Phylis Mansfield, "Marketing and Religion: A Review of the Two Literatures," *Journal of Ministry Marketing and Management* 7, no. 1 (2001): 61-80.

Book chapter: Eric Haley and Candace White, "Branding Religion: Christian Consumers' Understandings of Christian Products," *Religion and Popular Culture* (Ames, Iowa: Iowa State University Press, 2001), pp. 268-288.

Internet Search Strategies

This site, NoodleTools' Choose the Best Search for Your Information Needs, helps you choose the search engine best suited to your search goals. Helpful guides aid in the selection with sentences such as, "I need to define my topic," "I need to do research in a specific discipline," "I need facts," "I need opinions and perspectives," etc.

http://www.noodletools.com/

The Religious Marketer's Bookshelf/Internet Bookmarks

Marketing Research. It is hoped that the reader of this book is convinced by now of the wisdom of doing marketing research before making important church marketing decisions. Also, we hope you are convinced that such research can be done, in many cases, at a low cost. Many books are available to help clergy conduct research. Some are specifically written for those with very limited research budgets. Several books that can help clergy do valid, low-cost research are:

- Alan Andreasen, *Marketing, Research That Won't Break the Bank: A Practical Guide to Getting the Information You Need*, 2nd ed. (San Francisco: Jossey-Bass,

2002): http://www.amazon.com/Marketing-Research-That-Wont-Break/dp/
0787964190/ref=sr_1_2?ie=UTF8&s=books&qid=1201234539&sr=1-2

- Robert Stevens, Bruce Wrenn, Morris Ruddick, and Philip Sherwood, *The Marketing Research Guide*, 2nd ed. (New York: Haworth Press, 2006): http://www.amazon.com/ Marketing-Research-Guide-Bruce-Wrenn/dp/ 0789024160/ ref=sr_1_2?ie=UTF8&s=books&qid=1201234759&sr=1-2

- Norman M. Bradburn, Seymour Sudman, and Brian Wansink, *Asking Questions: The Definitive Guide to Questionnaire Design* (San Francisco: Jossey-Bass, 2004): http://www.amazon.com/Asking-Questions-Definitive-Questionnaire-Questionnaires/dp/0787970883/ref=sr_1_7?ie=UTF8&s= books&qid=1201234123&sr=1-7

- Don Dillman, *Mail and Internet Surveys* (New York: John Wiley and Sons, 2007): http://www.amazon.com/Mail-Internet-Surveys-Tailored-Mixed-Mode/dp/047003856X/ref=pd_bbs_sr_1?ie=UTF8&s=books&qid=120123426 9&sr=1-1

- Seymour Sudman, *Applied Sampling* (San Francisco: Academic Press, 1976): http://www.amazon.com/Applied-Sampling-Quantitative-studies-relations/ dp/012675750X/ref=sr_1_8?ie=UTF8&s=books&qid=1201234436&sr=1-8

Online Marketing Research

Full-service Internet research:

- Greenfield Online: http://www.greenfield.com/content/ index.html

Designing questionnaires:

- Vovici: http://www.vovici.com/index.aspx
- Insight Express: http://www.insightexpress.com/index.asp? core=1&pageid=9
- SurveyMonkey: http://www.surveymonkey.com/
- Zoomerang: http://info.zoomerang.com/?CMP=KNC-Gbd1Zoom
- SurveyMethods: http://www.surveymethods.com/
- QuestionPro: http://www.questionpro.com/?utm_id=700001&gclid= COeUv77InJECFQUsPAodjm-jPQ
- My Church Survey: http://www.mychurchsurvey.com/

Distributing questionnaires online and processing data:

- Harris Interactive: http://www.harrisinteractive.com/
- Knowledge Networks: http://www.knowledgenetworks.com/index4.html
- Socratic Technologies: http://www.sotech.com/main2007/eval.asp

Obtaining samples for online research:

- Survey Sampling International: http://www.surveysampling.com/frame_ detail.php?ID=123&current=no&issueID=16&yr=2002

Analyzing data and distributing results:

- SPSS: http://www.spss.com/

Reporting results and additional interactive analysis:
- Burke Digital Dashboard:
  http://www.burke.com/Services/CLRM/services.cfm?id=202

Online panels:
- Lightspeed Research: http://www.lightspeedresearch.com/
- Greenfield Online: http://www.greenfield.com/content/index.html

Consumer Behavior
If you are seeking to better understand why people behave as they do, as explained by behavioral scientists, the following books will be of help.
- Gerald Zaltman, *How Customers Think* (Boston: Harvard Business School Press, 2003): http://www.amazon.com/How-Customers-Think-Essential-Insights/dp/1578518261/ref=pd_bbs_sr_1?ie=UTF8&s=books&qid=1201235006&sr=1-1
- David L Loudon, Bruce Wrenn, Albert Della Bitta, *Consumer Behavior: Putting the Theory Into Practice* (New York: Routledge, forthcoming).

Marketing Planning/Management/Branding
- Robert E. Stevens, David L. Loudon, Bruce Wrenn, and Phylis Mansfield, *Marketing Planning Guide* (Binghamton, N.Y.: Haworth Press, 2006): http://www.amazon.com/Marketing-Planning-Guide-Second-Loudon/dp/0789023377/ref=sr_1_1?ie=UTF8&s=books&qid=1201658131&sr=1-1
- Philip Kotler and Kevin Lane Keller, *Marketing Management*, 12th ed. (Upper Saddle River, N.J.: Pearson Prentice-Hall, 2006): http://www.amazon.com/Marketing-Management-12th/dp/0131457578/ref=pd_bbs_1?ie=UTF8&s=books&qid=1201658625&sr=1-1
- Kevin Lane Keller, *Best Practice Cases in Branding*, 3rd ed. (Upper Saddle River, N.J.: Pearson Prentice-Hall, 2008): http://www.amazon.com/Best-Practice-Cases-Branding-3rd/dp/013188865X/ref=sr_1_4?ie=UTF8&s=books&qid=1201658941&sr=1-4
- Kevin Lane Keller, *Strategic Brand Management*, 3rd ed. (Upper Saddle River, N.J.: Pearson Prentice-Hall, 2008): http://www.amazon.com/Strategic-Brand-Management-Kevin-Keller/dp/0131888595/ref=pd_bbs_sr_1?ie=UTF8&s=books&qid+1206315632&sr=1-1
- AllAboutBranding is an online site devoted to discussion of all things related to branding and brand management: http://www.allaboutbranding.com/
- Jay Conrad Levinson, *Guerrilla Marketing*, 4th ed. (New York: Houghton-Mifflin Co., 2007): http://www.amazon.com/Guerrilla-Marketing-4th-Inexpensive-SmallBusiness/dp/0618785914/ref=pd_bbs_sr_1?ie=UTF8&s=books&qid=1201663957&sr=1-1
- John J. Burnett, *Nonprofit Marketing Best Practices* (Hoboken, N.J.: John Wiley and Sons, 2008): http://www.amazon.com/o/ASIN/047179189X/002-1558476-7119265?SubscriptionId=OPB944ZP1340AE20Z1G2

- Philip Kotler and Nancy Lee, *Social Marketing: Influencing Behaviors for Good* (Thousand Oaks, Calif.: Sage Publications, 2008): http://www.amazon.com/Social-Marketing-Influencing-Behaviors-Good/dp/1412956471/ref=sr_1_78?ie=UTF8&s=books&qid=1206660747&sr=1-78

Demographics and Geodemographics

These sources are useful when working with demographic or geodemographic data.

- Jacob Siegel, *Applied Demography* (Academic Press, 2001): http://www.amazon.com/Applied-Demography-Applications-Business-Government/dp/0126418403/ref=sr_1_1?ie=UTF8&s=books&qid=1201646818&sr=1-1
- Michael J. Weiss, *The Clustered World* (Little Brown, 2000): http://www.amazon.com/Clustered-World-Live-Means-About/dp/0316929204/ref=sr_1_1?ie=UTF8&s=books&qid=1201646879&sr=1-1

The primary source for applied demographics and geodemographic data for churches is the Percept organization: http://www.perceptgroup.com.

Census Data

While many subsites at the U.S. Census Web site might be profitably be explored, we suggest that the best place to obtain basic census data about a city, town, county, or zip code is the American FactFinder site:

http://factfinder.census.gov/home/saff/main.html?_lang=en

Click on "Population Finder" to access the latest profile for the area of interest to you. Numerous commercial organizations have purchased packaged census data and make it conveniently available for a price. Some of the major suppliers are:

- Applied Geographic Solutions: http://www.appliedgeographic.com
- ESRI: http://www.esri.com/data/
- MapInfo: http://www.mapinfo.com
- Claritas: http://www.claritas.com

Promotion

There are many books to help the congregational marketer seeking to know how to design and implement a promotional strategy. The list below is but a sampling.

- Michael Corbett, *The 33 Ruthless Rules of Local Advertising* (Pinnacle Books, 1999): http://www.amazon.com/33-Ruthless-Rules-Local-Advertising/dp/096673839X/ref=sr_1_1?ie=UTF8&s=books&qid=1201646238&sr=1-1
- Thomas C. Egelhoff, *How to Market, Advertise, and Promote Your Business or Service in a Small Town* (smalltownmarketing.com, 1998): http://www.amazon.com/Market-Advertise-Promote-Business-Service/dp/0967105501/ref=sr_1_1?ie=UTF8&s=books&qid=1201646321&sr=1-1
- Moi Ali, *Practical Marketing and Public Relations for the Small Business* (Kogan Page, 2002): http://www.amazon.com/Practical-Marketing-Small-Business-

Enterprise/dp/0749426861/ref=sr_1_1?ie=UTF8&s=books&qid=
1201646429&sr=1-1
- Joe Plummer, Steve Rappaport, Taddy Hall, and Robert Barocci, *The Online Advertising Playbook: Proven Strategies and Tested Tactics From the Advertising Research Foundation* (Hoboken, N.J.: John Wiley and Sons, 2007):
http://www.amazon.com/Online-Advertising-Playbook-Strategies-
Foundation/dp/0470051051/ref=pd_bbs_sr_2?ie=UTF8&s=books&qid=1206
491848&sr=1-2
- Mark Hughes, *Buzzmarketing: Get People to Talk About Your Stuff* (New York: Penguin, 2008): http://www.amazon.com/Buzzmarketing-People-Talk-
About-Stuff/dp/1591842131/ref=sr_1_14?ie=UTF8&s=books&qid=
1206484612&sr=1-14

Public Relations
- Merry Aronson, Don Spetner, and Carol Ames, *The Public Relation Writer's Handbook: The Digital Age* (San Francisco: Jossey-Bass, 2007): http://
www.amazon.com/Public-Relations-Writers-Handbook-Digital/dp/
0787986313/ref=pd_bbs_3?ie=UTF8&s=books&qid=1201235683&sr=1-3

Online Religion
- Morten Hojsgaard, *Religion and Cyberspace* (New York: Routledge, 2005):
http://www.amazon.com/Religion-Cyberspace-M-Hojsgaard/dp/
0415357632/ref=sr_1_1?ie=UTF8&s=books&qid=1201228928&sr=1-1
- Lorne L. Dawson, *Religion Online: Finding Faith on the Internet* (New York: Routledge, 2004): http://www.amazon.com/Religion-Online-Finding-Faith-
Internet/dp/0415970229/ref=sr_1_1?ie=UTF8&s=books&qid=
1201228984&sr=1-1
- Heidi Campbell, *Exploring Religious Community Online* (New York: Peter Lang Publishing, 2005): http://www.amazon.com/Exploring-Religious-
Community-Online-Formations/dp/0820471054/ref=sr_1_1?ie=UTF8&s=
books&qid=1201229165&sr=1-1
- Stewart M. Hoover, *Religion in the Media Age* (New York: Routledge, 2006):
http://www.amazon.com/RELIGION-MEDIA-Religion-Media-Culture/dp/
0415314224/ref=pd_bbs_sr_1?ie=UTF8&s=books&qid=1201229316&sr=1-1

Fund-raising
- Ilona M. Bray, *Effective Fund-raising for NonProfits* (Berkeley, Calif.: Nolo, 2008): http://www.amazon.com/Effective-Fundraising-Nonprofits-Real-
World-Strategies/dp/1413307485/ref=pd_bbs_sr_1?ie=UTF8&s=
books&qid=1201662640&sr=1-1
- Tom Ahern, *How to Write Fund-raising Materials That Raise More Money*, (Medfield, Mass.: Emerson and Church, 2007): http://www.amazon.com/
Write-Fundraising-Materials-Raise-Money/dp/1889102318/ref=
sr_1_2?ie=UTF8&s=books&qid=1201663195&sr=1-2

- Michael D. Reeves, *Extraordinary Money: Understanding the Church Capital Campaign* (Nashville: Discipleship Resources, 2002): http://www.amazon.com/Extraordinary-Money-Understanding-Capital-Campaign/dp/0881773794/ref=sr_1_1?ie=UTF8&s=books&qid=1205111569&sr=1-1
- Christian Stewardship Association, the largest association focusing on educating leaders who raise funds and resources for Christian ministries: http://www.stewardship.org/
- A Web site of the Michigan State University library that has dozens of links to articles, associations, books, nonprofit organizations, etc., devoted to fund-raising for religious organizations: http://www.lib.msu.edu/harris23/grants/4relfund.htm
- Generous Giving: http://www.generousgiving.org/page.asp?sec=4&page=504

Customer Service

- Karen Leland and Keith Bailey, *Customer Service for Dummies,* 3rd ed. (Hoboken, N.J.: Wiley Publishing, 2006): http://www.amazon.com/Customer-Service-Dummies-Business-Personal/dp/0471768693/ref=pd_bbs_sr_1?ie=UTF8&s=books&qid=1201657402&sr=1-1
- Robert Spector and Patrick D. McCarthy, *The Nordstrom Way to Customer Service Excellence: A Handbook for Implementing Great Service in Your Organization* (Hoboken, N.J.: Wiley Publishing, 2005): http://www.amazon.com/Nordstrom-Way-Customer-Service-Excellence/dp/0471702862/ref=si3_rdr_bb_product/104-2980177-0383938
- Ken Blanchard, Jim Ballard, Fred Finch, *Customer Mania! It's Never Too Late to Build a Customer-focused Company* (New York: Free Press, 2004): http://www.amazon.com/Customer-Mania-Never-Customer-Focused-Company/dp/0743270282/ref=si3_rdr_bb_product/104-2980177-0383938
- Dennis Snow and Teri Yanovitch, *Unleashing Excellence: The Complete Guide to Ultimate Customer Service,* (Sanford, Fla.: DC Press, 2003): http://www.amazon.com/Unleashing-Excellence-Complete-Ultimate-Customer/dp/193202106X/ref=si3_rdr_bb_product/104-2980177-0383938
- Lisa Ford, David McNair, Bill Perry, *Exceptional Customer Service: Going Beyond Your Good Service to Exceed the Customer's Expectation* (Holbrook, Mass.: Adams Media Corporation, 2001): http://www.amazon.com/s/ref=nb_ss_b/103-2503038-8703818?url=search-alias%3Dstripbooks&field-keywords=Exceptional+Customer+Service%3A+Going+Beyond+Your+Good+Service+to+Exceed+the+Customer%27s+Expectation+&x=0&y=0
- Ron Zemke, John A. Woods, *Best Practices in Customer Service* (New York: AMACOM, 1998): http://www.amazon.com/Best-Practices-Customer-Service-Zemke/dp/0814470289/ref=pd_bbs_sr_1?ie=UTF8&s=books&qid=1201657720&sr=1-1
- Valarie Zeithaml, Mary Jo Bitner, Dwayne D. Gremler, *Services Marketing,* 7th ed. (New York: McGraw-Hill, 2009): http://www.amazon.com/Services-Marketing-Valarie-Zeithaml/dp/0073380938/ref=pd_bbs_sr_1?ie=UTF8&s=books&qid=1206473984&sr=1-1

Associations and Consulting Services

Congregational leaders who desire professional help in tackling marketing problems may wish to contact an association or marketing consulting organization. In addition to the guides listed below, free or low-cost help may be found by contacting the marketing faculty at your local college, who sometimes look for student project opportunities. Consultants specializing in church-related marketing are:

- ChurchMax.com: http://www.churchmax.com
- Church Community Builder: http://www.churchcommunitybuilder.com
- Center for Church Communication: http://www.cfcclabs.org
- BMC Ferrell: http://www.bmcadvertising.com
- eChurchbusiness.com: http://www.echurchbusiness.com
- Mustard Seed Studio: http://www.mustardseedstudio.com
- Norman Shawchuck: nshawchuck@shawchuck.com
- The Alban Institute: http://www.alban.org/
- American Society for Church Growth: http://www.ascg.org/
- The Barna Group: http://www.barna.org/
- The Center for Church Advancement:
  http://www.healthychurches.org/index.php?ID=92
- Church Growth, Inc.: http://www.churchgrowth.net/
- Church Growth Institute: http://www.churchgrowth.org/
- Church Smart Resources:
  http://www.churchsmart.com/store/dynamicIndex.asp
- Congregational Research Guide:
  http://www.congregationalresources.org/Index.asp

Some Nonprofit Associations That Can Locate Consultants to Help With Church Marketing

- Christian Leadership Alliance: http://www.christianleadershipalliance.com

Web sites for Marketing Services Directories

These Web sites can be used to find marketing service agencies for help with marketing research, promotion, etc.

- Quirks: http://www.quirks.com
- American Marketing Association: http://www.marketingpower.com
- *Green Book* Guide for buyers of marketing research services:
  http://www.greenbook.org/

Web sites for Researching Religion

- Religious Research Association: http://rra.hartsem.edu/
- Society for the Scientific Study of Religion: http://www.sssrweb.org/
- Association for the Sociology of Religion:
  http://www.sociologyofreligion.com/
- Hartford Institute for Religion Research: http://hirr.hartsem.edu/
- The Council of Societies for the Study of Religion: http://www.cssr.org/

555

- The Center for the Study of Religion (Princeton University): http://www.princeton.edu/~csrelig/
- Center for the Study of Religion and Society (University of Notre Dame): http://csrs.nd.edu/
- Center for the Study of Religion and American Culture (Indiana University): http://www.iupui.edu/~raac/
- Center for the Study of Religion and Society (Creighton University): http://puffin.creighton.edu/human/csrs/
- Center for the Study of Religion (UCLA): http://www.humnet.ucla.edu/humnet/religion/home.html
- American Academy of Religion: http://www.aar-site.org/
- Faith Communities Today (FACT): http://fact.hartsem.edu/
- Encyclopedia of Religion and Society: http://hirr.hartsem.edu/ency/index.html
- Denominational Research Resources: http://hirr.hartsem.edu/denom/research.html
- Lilly Endowment (religion): http://www.lillyendowment.org/religion.html

Surveying/Profiling Your Congregation
- Vital Congregation Profile: www.vitalevangelicalleadership.org
- U.S. Congregational Life Survey: www.uscongregations.org/survey.html
- *Revision*: www.perceptgroup.com/Products/ReVision/REVISIONfront.aspx
- Studying Congregations: A New Handbook: http://www.amazon.com/exec/obidos/ASIN/0687006511/hartforsemina-20
- ChurchMetrics: Provides data on attendance, baptisms, giving, etc. Also provides a mobile app so you can access or edit church information on the go: http://www.churchmetrics.com
- Church Check: Sends a team of people to "secretly worship at your church, analyze it in detail, and present you with a report detailing items that are lacking": http://www.thechurchcheck.com

Data Resources on Religion
- Adherents.com (More than 43,000 statistics for more than 4,200 regions): http://www.adherents.com/
- Association of Religion Archives: http://www.thearda.com/
- American Religious Identification Survey: http://www.gc.cuny.edu/faculty/research_briefs/aris/aris_index.htm
- Gallup Research on Religion: http://www.gallup.com/search/default.aspx?q=religion&s=&b=SEARCH
- 2006 National Congregations Study: http://s6.library.arizona.edu/natcong
- North American Jewish Data Bank: http://www.jewishdatabank.org/national.asp
- U.S Congregational Life Survey: http://www.uscongregations.org/

- Database of megachurches in the U.S.: http://hirr.hartsem.edu/megachurch/database.html
- The Pew Forum on Religion on Religion and Public Life: http://pewforum.org/
- Pew Internet: http://www.pewinternet.org/
- Fast Facts about religion in the U.S.: http://hirr.hartsem.edu/research/fastfacts/fast_facts.html
- Summaries of Congregational Research: http://hirr.hartsem.edu/cong/research1.html

Church Marketing Blogs/Forums/Web site Lists
- Church Marketing Sucks: A part of the Center for Church Communication, this nonprofit organization is dedicated to helping the church matter: http://www.churchmarketingsucks.com
- Church Relevance: A free online resource created to help train ministries how to more effectively reach people: http://churchrelevance.com
- *Outreach* magazine's "Top 20 Web Sites for Church Communicators": http://www.christianitytodayoutreachmagazine.com/outreach/articles/top20Web sites.html
- Collide Magazine, "Where Church and the Media Converge:" http://www.collidemagazine.com/index
- Best Church Websites, Part 1, as chosen by Collide online magazine: http://www.collidemagazine.com/article/66/in-search-of-the-best-church-websites-part-1
- Best Church Websites, Part 2, as chosen by Collide online magazine: http://www.collidemagazine.com/article/130/the-best-church-websites-part-two
- Web Marketing Today, a website with links to more than 17,000 resources on Web marketing and e-Commerce: http://www.wilsonweb.com
- Catalyst Catablog: http://www.catalystspace.com/catablog
- Leadership Network's Blog, "using technology to multiply the church's impact:" http://digital.leadnet.org/
- Swerve, "a leadership, technology, and innovation blog for pastors and church leaders:" http://swerve.lifechurch.tv
- Tim Stevens Blog: http://www.leadingsmart.com
- Gospelr, a ministry-microblogging service (like Twitter) for the Christian Community: http://gospelr.com
- Church Marketing Lab, a Flickr group for posting of church ads for comments and suggestions: http://flickr.com/groups/cfcc
- Download and use an entire library of creative materials, absolutely free. Materials include sermon audio, countdowns, promotional design graphics, and opening videos from a wide variety of message series and churches: http://www.openresources.org
- Designed to help churches stream their live services online:

http://www.lightcastmedia.com
- Offers newsy content on many church leadership issues: http://www.mondaymorninginsight.com
- Provides practical advice and tech tips to increase efficiency and productivity: http://www.lifehacker.com
- Kem Meyer's Web site covers many topics of interest to church marketers: http://kemmeyer.typepad.com/less_clutter_noise
- Goal is to help churches work within the standards set by the World Wide Web Consortium. Highlights agencies that are on the cutting edge of Web methodologies: http://godbit.com
- Helps churches to use technology more effectively: http://geeksandgod.com
- Helps improve church Web site design: http://healyourchurchwebsite.com
- A resource for creative ministry and marketing: http://www.outsidetheboxministry.com
- Helps churches use the internet strategically: http://www.strategicdigitaloutreach.com
- Aggregates latest posts from many blogs and Web sites of interest to church marketers, providing links to those sites: http://church.alltop.com